OXFORD STUDIES IN SOCIAL AND LEGAL HISTORY

EDITED BY

PAUL VINOGRADOFF

M.A., D.C.L., LL.D., Dr. Hist., Dr. Jur., F.B.A.

CORPUS PROFESSOR OF JURISPRUDENCE IN THE UNIVERSITY OF OXFORD
HONORARY PROFESSOR OF HISTORY IN THE UNIVERSITY OF MOSCOW

VOL. II

TYPES OF MANORIAL STRUCTURE IN THE NORTHERN
DANELAW

By F. M. STENTON

CUSTOMARY RENTS

By N. NEILSON

OCTAGON BOOKS

A division of Farrar, Straus and Giroux

New York   1974

104243

Originally published in 1910 by the Clarendon Press

Reprinted 1974
by special arrangement with Oxford University Press, Inc.

OCTAGON BOOKS
A DIVISION OF FARRAR, STRAUS & GIROUX, INC.
19 Union Square West
New York, N. Y. 10003

Library of Congress Cataloging in Publication Data

Stenton, Sir Frank Merry, 1880-1967.
Types of manorial structure in the northern Danelaw.

Reprint of the 1910 editions published by Clarendon Press, Oxford, which were issued as v. 2, no. 3-4, of Oxford studies in social and legal history.

Bibliography: p.
1. Manors—Great Britain. 2. Land tenures—Great Britain—History. 3. Feudalism—Great Britain. 4. Rent—Great Britain. I. Neilson, Nellie, 1873-1947. Customary rents. 1974. II. Title. III. Title: Customary rents. IV. Series: Oxford studies in social and legal history, v. 2, no. 3-4.

HC254.3.S73   1974   333.3′22′0942   73-22286
ISBN 0-374-96160-3

Printed in USA by
Thomson-Shore, Inc.
Dexter, Michigan

PREFACE

THE two monographs of the present volume bear on the history of English manorial institutions. Mr. Stenton has examined in detail the evidence as to the different types of manorial structure in the Counties of the Northern Danelaw—York, Derby, Nottingham, Leicester, Lincoln, and Rutland. Domesday book entries form, of course, his principal material, but he has also used for comparison charters of the Anglo-Danish period, as far as they were available, and has supplied some valuable observations based on his study of early twelfth-century documents.

His results enable us to form a more definite view of the contrasts of terminology, of institutional and of economic development between the region colonized by Danes and the South and West of England, which had arrived by the eleventh century to a much more complete and uniform arrangement of society on feudal lines. In this way the phenomena of the 'Growth of the Manor' are presented once more in a strong light.

Miss Neilson has tried to provide students of Mediaeval antiquities with a basis for classifying and comparing the various rents in kind and payments in money which were imposed on the population. It is only through systematic comparison that we are able to understand the meaning of many terms and the incidence of the burdens indicated by them. The labour of taking stock of parallel illustrations and of studying the context in instances which for some reason have been described in a more or less explicit manner is a necessary complement to work based on the intensive study of some isolated groups of evidence. Miss Neilson approaches her task not from the point of view of the philologist, but from that of the student of records, and it can hardly be denied that research should be carried on from both sides in order to solve the many intricate problems arising out of the study of rents and services. Editors and students of cartularies, extents, and courtrolls will, I think, especially appreciate Miss Neilson's contribution. The variety of Mediaeval customs is almost inexhaustible, but it seems the more important to get hold of some guiding threads in the course of their investigation.

PAUL VINOGRADOFF.

III

TYPES OF MANORIAL STRUCTURE IN THE NORTHERN DANELAW

BY

F. M. STENTON, M.A.

FELLOW OF UNIVERSITY COLLEGE, READING; FORMERLY SCHOLAR OF
KEBLE COLLEGE, OXFORD

TYPES OF MANORIAL STRUCTURE IN THE NORTHERN DANELAW

I

THE employment of the term Danelaw as a geographical expression varies considerably in regard to different subjects of historical inquiry. In the history of English law the term covers the whole of that portion of the country in which the specific legal customs resulting from the Scandinavian settlement of the ninth century prevailed; a district, if we may trust our texts, comprising the shires east of and including Yorkshire, Derbyshire, Leicestershire, Northamptonshire, and Buckinghamshire.[1] In political history the term denotes the shires occupied by the various Scandinavian powers which arose in England during the same century—the kingdom of Guthrum,[2] the *heres* of the Midlands, the Five Boroughs, the kingdom of York. But for the student of agrarian organization the term may profitably be used in a more restricted sense, a sense, moreover, for which there exists early authority,[3] covering the modern counties of York, Lincoln, Nottingham, Derby, Leicester, and Rutland. Within this area, distinguished by local names of Scandinavian origin,[4] by the occurrence, within its limits, of a form of local division, the wapentake, otherwise unknown, by its ancient assessment on lines distinct

[1] See Liebermann, Leges Anglorum, 7.
[2] This must be the force of Dena Lagu in Edw. and Guth. The extent of Guthrum's kingdom is uncertain; there is no reason for believing that it included the Five Boroughs.
[3] Edw. Conf. 30. The passage in question presents some difficulty. See Chadwick, Studies on Anglo-Saxon Institutions, 199.
[4] The evidence of local nomenclature proves an extensive displacement of native landholders at the time of the settlement of the ninth century. This displacement is most strongly marked in Lincolnshire and NE. Leicestershire, and is least obvious in Derbyshire.

from those which prevailed elsewhere in England, by the persistence of its political individuality until a late period, a reasonable uniformity of tenurial custom might be expected to prevail, and is in fact expressed with remarkable clearness in the terminology of the Domesday survey. In the following pages the term Danelaw, when used without qualification, will denote the shires enumerated above; with the reservation that the harrying of Yorkshire in 1069 makes it impossible to argue with security from 1086 to the conditions of the Confessor's day, and that the special difficulties peculiar to the survey of Leicestershire to some extent throw the evidence relating to that county out of correspondence with the details recorded for the remainder of this district.

The scheme adopted by the compilers of Domesday in the description of the Danelaw shires recognizes a distinction between three several classes of tenement: the manor, the berewick, and the soke. If the boroughs are excluded from consideration, it is substantially correct to say that every parcel of land in this district is understood to form part of some manor; the berewick and the soke represent the two contrasted types of subsidiary local organization.[1] The questions which arise in connexion with the Domesday *manerium* must for the present be reserved; but of the soke and berewick we may say at once that if the derivation of these terms were an adequate clue to their meaning as employed in Domesday it would present little difficulty. The soke would then be merely a piece of land over whose inhabitants the lord of the chief manor enjoyed justiciary powers; the berewick would become the manorial grange or storehouse, the detached but appurtenant farmstead.[2] Even in 1086 we may find sokes and berewicks to which these simple definitions will apply; but there are also cases, especially as regards the berewick, when the terms have assumed a more special meaning. The latter commonly denotes an outlying member of a larger

---

[1] There is no example in the Danelaw of the employment of the neutral *terra* in contradistinction to *manerium* or *soca*.
[2] Berewick is only one of a series of words compounded with the OE. *wīc*, employed independently in Berkshire to signify a dairy farm.

estate, with holdings dependent in one way or another upon the head manor ; and one aspect of the problem before us is the question of the relation borne by the men of the subsidiary tenements to the central estate and to its lord.

In the first folios of the Lincolnshire Domesday, and with somewhat greater frequency in that of Yorkshire, the term *inland* is occasionally employed in contrast to sokeland, and as equivalent to the more usual berewick.[1] The use of the term under these conditions is noteworthy; for it is clearly quite distinct from any of the meanings which have been deduced for the *inland* of the counties south of Welland and Avon. It is evident that the inland of Lincolnshire and Yorkshire does not correspond to demesne in the normal sense of the word ; we may easily find parcels of inland in this region upon which no demesne has been created.[2] It is no less evident that in these counties inland was in no sense exempt from liability to the geld, for its capacity is invariably expressed in carucates or bovates ad geldum. It would seem, then, that the significance of the term lies in the contrast which it makes with sokeland, and we are driven to inquire in what that contrast consisted ; an inquiry which may be pursued along two distinct lines, neither of which is free from complication. If we proceed by way of the comparison of formulas which seem from their context to be equivalent, it is necessary constantly to bear in mind the instability of the phraseology of Domesday ; a warning peculiarly necessary from the fact that no duplicate entries in this portion of the survey serve to define the meaning of the northern *inland*.[3] If information is sought from external sources, the small number of religious

[1] Thus at Ouseburn, York (fo. 301 b), 'B and S. In Useburne v car. ad geldum. Terra ad v carucas. Inland et soca in Chenaresburg [Knaresborough].' So at Wispington, Lincoln (fo. 340 b), 'S and B. In Wispinctune ii car. terrae ad geldum. Terra ad iiii carucas. Inland et soca in Stratone [Great Sturton] et Cherchebi [Kirkby-on-Bain]. Ibi (sunt) ix sochemanni et vi bordarii cum iii carucis.'

[2] Caenby, Lincoln (fo. 344). 'In Covenebi, inland de Stou [Stow St. Mary] iiii carucatae ad geldum. Terra ad iiii carucas. Ibi xx sochemanni et xv bordarii habent v carucas. Ibi ecclesia et i molendinum iiii solidorum, et xx acrae prati.'

[3] The difficult Yorkshire case of Holne (fos. 299 b and 301) is discussed below.

houses existing within the Danelaw of the eleventh century implies a correspondingly small number of early documents which can be collated with the Domesday text. In the following pages it is intended to employ both these methods, but it is well to define their limitations at the start.

Among the cartularies which relate to the Danelaw, the most famous, and for our purpose the most important, is the Liber Niger of Peterborough Abbey.[1] This document, compiled between the years 1125 and 1128, during which Henry I had taken seisin of the temporalities of the house, was apparently drawn up by some clerk conversant with the formulas of the exchequer, who had derived, from whatever source, information respecting the ownership of certain of the monastic estates at a period as remote as the time of King Edward.[2] The record falls into two parts ;· an extent of the lands of the abbey in the counties of Northampton, Nottingham, Lincoln, and Huntingdon, followed by a section entitled 'Haec est descriptio terrarum Abbatiae de Burch in vicecomitatu Lincolniae'. The attention of students has in the main been concentrated upon the description of the manorial economy contained in the former section ; but for our immediate purpose the brief details given in the Lincolnshire portion of the document are even more important. They are so important, in fact, that it becomes worth while to suggest the distinct possibility, indicated by some of the personal names which occur in the record, that the original of the Lincolnshire sections of the Liber Niger may be referred to a date some twenty-five years earlier than that at which the first portions of the document in question were compiled. We are told that the abbey possessed soke over half a carucate in Walcot near Alkborough, held by Earl Hugh of Chester, who died in

---

[1] Printed as an appendix (pp. 157–83) to the Chronicon Petroburgense, ed. Stapleton (Camden Soc.), 1849.

[2] e. g. p. 182 'Scotter, iii carucatas in dominio et i carucatam socage de terra Aschilli.   Scotter, iii carucatas in dominio et i carucatam socage de terra Alnothi.   Cleatham vii bovatas in dominio de terra Alnothi.' Aschil and 'Alnod' in 1066 were joint owners of Scotter, the latter alone possessed Cleatham.   The evidence of Hugh Candidus shows that₍a record was still preserved at Peterborough in the twelfth century of benefactors to the house a hundred years earlier.

1101. Soke over two bovates in Scawby is assigned in the record to one Osbern, who may safely be identified with Osbern de Arcis, tenant-in-chief in 1086 of a portion of that vill, a baron who was certainly dead before the compilation of the Lindsey survey between 1115 and 1118.[1] Another Domesday tenant-in-chief appearing in the Liber Niger, Godfrey de Cambray, who is credited with the possession of lands in Market Deeping, would appear from the Leicester Survey to have lost his estates by death or forfeiture before the year 1125.[2] It is difficult to explain the occurrence in the record of such names as these otherwise than by supposing that they were transcribed by the compiler of the Liber Niger from a document dating from the very beginning of the twelfth century. This being so, we are at once brought to a date within fifteen years of that of the Domesday survey itself, and may fairly employ the formulas of the Liber Niger in explanation of the local conditions of 1086.

The whole scheme in accordance with which the entries in question are compiled turns on the distinction between demesne and soke; it is assumed that all land must lie either *in dominio* or *in socagio*. ' Hibaldestou : i carucatam in dominio et v bovatas socage. Malmetun: ii carucatas in dominio. Messingham: iii carucatas et dimidiam in dominio et ii carucatas socage'—such entries as these leave no room for any third form of tenement intermediate between the *dominium* and the *socagium*. The latter term is obviously equivalent to the *terra de soca* of Domesday; but it is only by a comparison of the relevant entries that we are enabled to prove that the *dominium* of the Liber Niger and the *inland* of 1086 are identical. The question is settled by the case of Reepham near Lincoln, where the Domesday 'Inland huius manerii (sc. Fiskerton). In Refaim iiii carucatae et vi bovatae ad gel-dum'[3] is represented by the 'Refham. iiii carucatas et vi

---

[1] Ed. Greenstreet, pl. ii, 22. His estate in Scawby was then held by William de Arcis.
[2] V. C. H. Leicester, i. 353. His land in Sproxton had passed to an unknown person described as ' Gilbert's son'.
[3] Folio 345 b.

bovatas in dominio' of the Liber Niger.[1] Like the *inland*
of Domesday, the *dominium* of the Liber Niger clearly includes land in the occupation of the men of the vill as well as
the lord's home farm ; and it would seem, therefore, that the
compilers of the latter record, by dividing the tenements with
which they dealt into demesne land and sokeland, wished to
mark a distinction between land which was considered to be
in the lord's possession and land from which he only received
dues, suit, and service. It does not appear probable that the
fourteen years between 1086 and 1100, the date to which
we may approximately assign the Lincolnshire section of the
Liber Niger, witnessed any material change in the organization
of the Peterborough estates, and we may assume that the
terminology of the later survey in this matter accurately
reflects the distinction marked in the Lincolnshire Domesday
between inland and sokeland.

This distinction between *dominium*, in the extended sense
of the word, and *soca* is indeed to be found, though somewhat
rarely, in the pages of the Lincolnshire Domesday itself. Of
Earl Alan's manor of Brant Broughton, for example, which
represented an 18-carucate vill, we are definitely told that
Ralf the Staller, the earl's predecessor, had there possessed
13 carucates of land *in dominio* and 5 carucates of land *de soca*.[2]
This instance does not stand alone, and it is highly significant.
It is clear that the 13 carucates *in dominio* were distributed
over an area much more extensive than that of the lord's home
farm ; and the whole passage in which the phrase occurs shows

---

[1] Chron. Petroburg. 182.
[2] Fo. 347 b. ' M. In Burtune hundret habuit Radulfus Stalre xiii car.
terrae ad geldum in dominio, et v car. terrae ad geldum de soca. Terra
ad xviii carucas. Ibi habet Alanus comes in dominio iii carucas, et xxxvi
villanos et ix bordarios, et xv sochmannos et alios ix bordarios habentes
xv carucas. . . . De supradicta soca tenet Cadiou vi bovatas terrae, et
habet ibi vi boves arantes.' Compare the Long Bennington entry (fo. 348).
' M. In Beninctun ii hundret habuit Radulfus Stalre xiiii car. terrae ad
geldum in dominio et vii car. et ѵi bov. terrae ad geldum de soca. Ibi
habet Alanus comes in dominio v carucas, et xix villanos, et v bordarios,
et xx sochmannos simul habentes xii carucas. . . . De hac terra tenet
Herveus i car. et iii bov. et habet ibi i carucam.' It will be noted that
while at Brant Broughton the sub-tenancy had arisen on the sokeland, at
Long Bennington it had been created on the *terra*, the land apparently
in dominio. The former tenancy may well have resulted from purchase.

that it is not connected with that distinction between the portions of an estate retained by the lord and those which were sub-let by him to tenants, which is frequently marked in this way in later documents. We may most readily understand the phrase if we take it as including both the domainal messuage of the lord and also the land in the occupation of villeins and bordars, in contrast to the land held within the manor by the sokemen who dwelt there. It must indeed be admitted that as to the exact nature of the rights which are implied by the word *dominium* here and in the Liber Niger we can say little with certainty. We must leave unanswered, for example, the question whether the lord could dispossess at will the men who dwelt within the sphere of his *dominium*. But the mere fact that already in 1086 the term in question could be employed so as to include the land of villeins and bordars as well as the manorial demesne raises wide issues.[1] Such a usage was fully established by the time of Bracton (circ. 1250); it is carefully defined by the author of the Dialogus de Scaccario (circ. 1175); it underlies, as we have seen, the arrangement of the Liber Niger of Peterborough (circ. 1100), but the fact of its employment in Domesday has to a certain extent been overlooked.[2] But the Brant Broughton formula, supported as it is by the terminology of the Liber Niger, suggests two propositions which certainly deserve to be tested in the light of the local information supplied by Domesday. The first is that the land of the local peasantry other than the soke-

[1] The incidental way in which this formula is introduced is clearly brought out in the description of Earl Alan's Lincolnshire fief. Thus, in the entry relating to the large manor of Fulbeck with Leadenham (fo. 347 b) the scribe had originally written ' In Fulebec et Ledeneham habuit Radulfus Stalre xxiiii car. terrae ad geldum *in dominio, et xv car. ad geldum de soca*,' and then, apparently realizing that the twenty-four carucates represented the total assessment of the vill, deleted the words italicized, thus ignoring the distinction between *terra* and *soca* which he had previously marked. So too we were originally told that at Foston (fo. 348), a berewick of Long Bennington, there were 12 carucates *in dominio* and 7 *de soca*; but here also the words from *in dominio* to *soca* have been deleted. This case is important, for the Foston berewick included a population of forty-six sokemen, and the entry in its completed form makes no specific reference to the existence of any sokeland in the vill, a fact which bears very directly upon a considerable number of similar instances.

[2] As by Maitland, Domesday Book and Beyond, pp. 53-4.

men was regarded as the property of the lord ; the second is that the rights which the lord possessed in respect of his soke-land bear a seignorial rather than a proprietary character. It will be our object in what follows to ascertain how far these propositions may reasonably be carried in the interpretation of the Danelaw survey.

It may be well, however, to note in the first place that the distinction which is here suggested is reflected in the termino-logy of later feudal law by the contrast between tenure *in dominio* and *in servitio*.[1] To hold a piece of land *in dominio* meant the power of dealing with it at will, of dealing, more-over, with such portions of it as were in the occupation of unfree cultivators.[2] To be seised *in servitio* merely covered the right to the receipt of profits from the land at issue—rent, it might be, or feudal service. It need hardly be said that this distinction is never explicitly made by the compilers of Domesday Book ; the terminology relating to the various kinds of seisin was only worked out, and that slowly, in the course of the next century, but it was already latent in the contrast, always felt, though rarely definitely expressed, between *dominium* and *soca*.

In the second place, brief reference must be made to another distinction, rarely marked in texts which relate to the Dane-law, but of the highest importance in regard to the shires to the south and west—the familiar distinction between inland and warland. In such a text as the Burton Cartulary,[3] which, it should be noted, includes extents of a small group of estates in south-west Derbyshire,[4] warland bears the double implication of land in the occupation of the dependent peasantry and land rated to the king's geld, to the exclusion of the lords' inland. The inland of the Burton Cartulary clearly represents original demesne ; and its employment in this sense is sharply contrasted with the Lincolnshire and Yorkshire usage which we are considering. And yet, after all,

---

[1] Pollock and Maitland, Hist. Eng. Law, i. 233.
[2] Dialogus, i. 11.
[3] Ed. Wriothesley (Salt Society). Cf. Round, The Burton Abbey Surveys, in E.H.R. xx. 275–89.
[4] Mickleover and its berewicks, Willington, Winshill, Appleby.

the contrast is in part superficial, for the Lincolnshire usage only results from the final extension of a term susceptible, from its very nature, of diverse employment. One extension had already been made in the eleventh century; inland could then cover not merely the lord's home farm, but also plots of land leased to cultivators out of the exempt demesne. It is further to be noted that warland was by no means the inevitable opposition to inland [1]—*utland* and *gesettland* are thus employed. The use which might be made of the term *inland* in any given text might legitimately vary; exemption from the geld was only one among a number of characteristics which might be made the basis of distinction; [2] and in the eastern Danelaw the existence of unusual numbers of free tenants was clearly the fact which led the compilers of Domesday to extend the term inland to cover the whole of that portion of an estate over which the lord had most immediate and direct control, the land of villeins and bordars in contrast to the land of the sokemen. The exceptional conditions of the Danelaw naturally produced a modification of the normal terminology. [3]

With reference now to the Domesday text, it deserves note that the formulas employed in different folios of the Danelaw surveys with the object of marking the distinction between *terra* and *soca* vary considerably, and deserve comparison. The contrast is made in the simplest form by a pair of phrases which appear now and again in the opening folios of the Yorkshire survey, as in the following entry relating to Northallerton, (fo. 299) Alverton: ' Huic manerio appendent xi berewitae. . . .

---

[1] For the inland in general cf. Vinogradoff, Growth of the Manor, 225-7, 283-4; Round, Domesday Studies, i. 93 ff.

[2] It is improbable that the Lincolnshire demesnes were exempt from the geld.

[3] The deplorable condition of the printed text of the Cartulary makes it unsafe to place entire reliance upon its terminology, but there is one passage which suggests very strongly the employment of *dominium* in the Lincolnshire sense. ' In Wilentona [Willington, Derby] nichil Inlandae est. Warlanda se defendit pro iii carucatis. In dominio sunt' (p. 28). A population of 13 *censarii* was seated on this land. In 1086 Willington, which then belonged to Ralf son of Hubert, included no land in demesne, but contained a population of four villeins and two bordars. The cartulary entry reads as if the whole vill was reckoned to be *in dominio*, although no portion of it was exempt from geld nor yet organized as a home farm.

Ad hoc manerium pertinet soca harum terrarum.' The employment of these contrasted phrases makes it very clear that a lord's
rights over his sokeland are rights of superiority, and not of
ownership. The terms berewick and soke do not of themselves
imply this distinction, but an unbroken series of formulas carry
us from these neutral expressions to the *in dominio* phrase on
which comment has just been made. On folio 337 b two successive entries run :—' S et B. In Gunfordebi [Great Gonerby,
Lincoln] sunt vii carucatae terrae ad geldum. Terra ad ix
carucas. Tres carucatae sunt *inland* and iiii soca in Grandham
[Grantham].' ' S et B. In Herlavestune [Harlaxton, Lincoln]
sunt xii carucatae terrae ad geldum. Terra ad xvi carucas.
Novem sunt in soca et iii *in aula Grandham.*' These passages
give us the series of equivalent phrases berewick—inland—*in
aula.* A variant of the latter formula appears on folio 368 b :
' M. In Roscebi [Rauceby, Lincoln] habuit Turvert ix carucatas
terrae ad geldum. ... Ibidem v bov. terrae *pertinentes ad
aulam.* Ibidem habuit Osmund iii carucatas terrae et i bovatam ad geldum. Terra tottidem carucis. Tres bovatae et
dimidia *pertinebat ad aulam eius.* Reliqua erat soca eiusdem
manerii.' Between this formula and the *in dominio* phrase
a link is supplied by the description of the Archbishop of York's
manor of Laneham, Nottinghamshire (fo. 283) : ' In Laneham
cum berewitis his ... viiii carucatae terrae et ii bovatae ad geldum. Terra xxvii carucis. *In dominio aulae* sunt x bovatae de
hac terra. Reliqua est soca.' It is the value of this entry that
it supplies us with the full formula of which the *in dominio*
phrase is probably a condensation. Of the latter, two additional examples may be given: ' M. In Goldesby [Goulceby]
habuit Colegrim iiii bovatas terrae et terciam partem unius
bovatae ad geldum in dominio et tantumdem terrae in soca.
Terra ii carucis'(fo. 370). In this case the fiscal burden incumbent
upon the vill has been divided equally between the demesne and
the soke, but apart from this arrangement, the estate presents
no remarkable features. It is otherwise ·with Robert de Veci's
great manor of Caythorpe in Kesteven, the description of
which deserves to be quoted in part (fo. 363): 'M. In Carltorp
habuit Eilric xix carucatas terrae et ii bovatas in dominio et

xxviii carucatas terrae et vi bovatas de soca ad geldum. Terra totidem carucis, id est xlviii. Huic adiacent iii hundret[1] Fristun [Frieston], Normenton [Normanton], Wilgebi [Willoughby].' The population of this large and compact estate, which extended over the whole of four 12-carucate vills, comprised 113 sokemen, 50 villeins, and 7 bordars; and the interest in its land was divided between Robert de Veci, the tenant-in-chief, with 3 ploughs in demesne; three unnamed men with 4¼ teams; and one Englishman with 1 team. The description of this complex group of tenements in a single entry suggests the handiwork of a hurried scribe, who would not afford the time necessary if the several parcels of inland and sokeland contained within the estate were to be recorded according to their local distribution among the constituent vills of the manor, and considered that he had done his duty when he had indicated the amount of land which fell respectively within the scope of the *dominium* and the soke. The Domesday scribes, as the collection of formulas which has just been given will show, were far from consistent in their choice of terms with which to denote these conceptions; but through it all they are clearly trying to maintain the distinction between the land, the soil of which was vested in the lord, and the land of which the ownership remained with the representatives of the old English free peasantry of the vill.

Here, then, at last, it would seem that we have arrived at a clue to the real meaning of the recurring distinction marked in the Danelaw survey between the berewick and the soke. We have seen that the terms inland and berewick might in a given context be treated as equivalent, and that the inland of 1086 may fairly be interpreted, as in the Liber Niger of Peterborough, as land *in dominio*. This being the case, there results at once a provisional definition of the Domesday berewick. In its relation to the manorial system, the berewick will simply become a detached portion of inland, a holding geographically separate from the chief manor of which it formed part, but owned, as to its soil, by the manorial lord. Conversely, it would seem that we must understand by soke-

---

[1] The 'hundreds' in question were clearly vills of 12 carucates each.

land, land regarded as belonging to the men seated upon it, but carrying a liability to services and dues to be rendered at the manorial centre to which it was appendant. In this distinction lies the real significance of the contrast between the two familiar types of subsidiary tenement, which it may be well to consider in some detail.

It will at once be evident that if we are to maintain this conception of the Danelaw berewick, the ownership of its soil must never be assigned by our text to any man other than the lord of the chief manor. So far as it is possible to speak definitely in regard to a point involving a consideration of so many details this essential condition is satisfied. It is, no doubt, true that the jurors of the West Riding of Yorkshire were in doubt whether Swegn's pre-Conquest manor of Attercliffe with Sheffield had not at some undefined period been inland of Earl Waltheof's manor of Hallam[1]; but we cannot at this distance of time undertake to decide a question which they were compelled to leave open. So, too, when we are told that at Notton near Pontefract, where of six carucates of land two were reckoned inland and four soke of 'Tateshall', Godric had nevertheless possessed a hall,[2] we must see rather an instance of a pre-Conquest manor which has lost its autonomy than any confusion between the rights of Godric and those of the lord of Tateshall. The one passage in the surveys of the midland counties which seems to present a definite obstacle to the theory occurs in the Domesday of Northamptonshire,[3] and may be discussed in this place, for Northamptonshire, of all counties, presents features of tenurial organization the most closely related to those which obtained north of Welland. In 1086 the Count of Mortain possessed an estate in Croughton, freely owned in King Edward's time by one Leofnoth, which, we are told, was formerly a berewick of the adjacent manor of

---

[1] Fo. 320: 'M. In Ateclive et Escafeld Suuen habuit v car. terrae ad geldum. . . . Haec terra dicitur fuisse inland in Hallun.'
[2] Fo. 317: 'M. In Notone sunt vi car. terrae ad geldum. . . . De hac terra sunt iiii carucatae in soca de Tateshalla, et ii carucatae inland. Ibi tamen habuit Godric aulam.' 'Tateshalla' is represented by the modern Pontefract.
[3] V. C. H. Northants, i. 326.

Evenley. Evenley is duly entered as the next manor upon the count's fief; but it is stated that Leofstan had held the manor freely T. R. E., and we are thus faced with the difficulty of explaining how, if Leofstan held the soil of Croughton as a berewick of Evenley, the former vill could appear at the same time in the free possession of another man. Fortunately, the existence of a second Evenley entry in a later folio of the survey enables us to avoid this question, by showing that a Leofnoth, who may safely be identified with the Leofnoth of Croughton, had possessed in 1066 a separate manor in Evenley to which the Croughton berewick had clearly been appurtenant, although by 1086 it had passed to the Count of Mortain, Leofstan's successor, instead of to Walter the Fleming, who took title from Leofnoth.[1] No instance presenting a difficulty of this kind occurs in the Clamores of either Yorkshire or Lincolnshire; and our conception of the relations between manor and berewick clearly need not be affected by the case of Croughton. It is the interest of the latter that it shows an exception of somewhat formidable character brought into conformity with other entries by a consideration of the local relations of the property involved.[2]

It is a more difficult question whether, in addition to inland and sokeland, the Danelaw surveys reveal the existence in this district of a third form of tenement, the thegnland. The general sense of the latter term is well ascertained;[3] it denotes the holding of a thegn, land defended by military service; from which results its frequent employment to cover those portions of the estates of a noble or religious house which had been sublet to persons capable of discharging the military

---

[1] V. C. H. Northants, i. 341 a. Croughton and Evenley are situated in the extreme south of Northamptonshire, in the hundred of Kings Sutton.

[2] A somewhat similar difficulty arising in regard to Claxby, near Normanby, Lincoln, is resolved in the same way. On folio 361 b an entry runs : ' M. In Clachesbi habuit Chetel ii bovatas terrae et Goduin i bovatam terrae inland ad geldum.' The unpleasant necessity of regarding Godwine's inland as dependent on Chetel's manor is removed by another Claxby entry on fo. 350, which shows Godwine himself in possession of a manor of 10 bovates in that vill and in Normanby adjacent to it.

[3] See the discussion of the relations of thegnland and sokeland by Round, Feudal England, 28–35.

obligations which lay upon the fief. Of this term there are only two examples in the Danelaw surveys :—

 fo. 274 b. In Hatune [Hatton, Derby] vi bov. terrae et dim. de soca et i bov. et dim. de Tainland. Haec pertinet ad Scrotune [Scropton, Derby].

 fo. 299 b. Praeter hoc sunt ii carucatas in Holne et altera Holne et Alstanesleie et Thoac. Hanc terram potest i caruca arare. Wasta est . . . Hanc alii dicunt esse tainland, alii socam in Wachefeld [Wakefield, York].

These entries would probably be held conclusive were it not that on folio 301 a duplicate entry is made of the second estate, which raises serious doubts :—

 In Holne Dunstan ii car. ad geldum. Terra ad i carucam. Hanc terram alii dicunt inland, alii socam in Wachefeld.

It is clear that a scribal error has been made in one of these entries, and the question is raised whether we should not read ' inland ' instead of 'tainland' in the first. If we wish to prefer the more difficult reading, we should note that a scribe, familiar with the term inland as employed in the southern counties, would naturally question the propriety of its use in such a context as the entries transcribed above. The contrast between thegnland and soke, on the other hand, would be familiar to him, and he may well have modified the formula before him in accordance with what he believed to be the true reading of the original return.[1] Apart from this consideration, it certainly seems more probable that the contrast between soke and inland, of which more than a score of instances occur in succeeding folios of the survey, should be intended than that we should be confronted with a distinction between soke and thegnland, never marked elsewhere in this part of England.[2]

---

[1] If the original ran, as suggested by the duplicate entry, 'alii dicunt inland,' the change would be facilitated by confusion between the final t of ' dicunt ' and the initial t of ' tainland '.

[2] For the thegnland see Feudal England, 28–9; English Society in the Eleventh Century, 370–2. Essentially, thegnland is a portion of an estate granted out to secure the performance of military service by the grantee, and inalienable without the consent of his lord. In Cambridgeshire it is this last characteristic which mainly distinguishes thegnland from sokeland, but in the Danelaw surveys these tenurial distinctions are commonly ignored, and it is not probable that sporadic reference should be made to them in a couple of isolated entries. *Tainlande* on fo. 287b is the estate of a king's thegn.

If to this it is added that in the south and east thegnland is rarely, if ever, entered as above with explicit reference to a manorial centre other than the vill within which it lay, the probability that a pair of scribal errors are responsible for these sporadic references to a Danelaw thegnland will distinctly be increased. The question cannot wholly be settled on the existing evidence, but it may at least be recognized that these isolated appearances of the formulas in question should be regarded with grave suspicion.

The simplest form assumed by a group of sokeland tenements consists of a vill, or definite portion of a vill, regarded as appurtenant to some manor, but inhabited exclusively by sokemen. This kind of holding presents no difficulty, though it admits of infinite variety of local detail ; and examples may be derived from each of the Danelaw counties. But, although we may perhaps regard these examples as representing the normal type of sokeland, it is more commonly the case that sokemen are found settled on sokeland in company with members of other social classes—villeins or bordars. This is so, even in Lincolnshire, where the sokemen outnumber the combined villeins and bordars; it becomes increasingly the case as we pass across the Danelaw from east to west, and in both Nottinghamshire and Derbyshire it is easy to find parcels of sokeland upon which, to all appearance, no sokeman dwelt. If we are to maintain our definition in face of these facts we must, it would seem, assume the existence of one or other of three conditions :—

1. A depression of the peasantry. The villeins on sokeland were originally sokemen or the descendants of sokemen, who had become implicated in a more embarrassing nexus of service since the Conquest, but had not ceased to own the land on which they were settled. In this connexion, it is very important to remember that the Domesday Survey tells us nothing as to the composition of the rural population of the Danelaw in King Edward's day. In those counties in regard to which we possess the necessary information we can trace a tendency towards a relative depression of the higher

social classes[1]; and we may infer that a corresponding movement in this direction has taken place here, although its progress is concealed from us. It may be added that Yorkshire and Derbyshire, certainly, and Leicestershire in all probability, had undergone devastation at some period between 1066 and 1086.

2. The villani on sokeland, while maintaining their pre-Conquest condition, are referred to a social class lower than that of the recognized sokemen because they are inferior to the latter in wealth, or because they are burdened with heavier customary services.[2]   It is to be noted that while the local distribution of sokeland tenements, as they are entered in Domesday, had been fixed before the Conquest, the social divisions with which we meet in the Survey represent in the main the work of Norman lawyers, and turn much more upon diversities of economic condition than upon strictly legal distinctions between class and class.[3]   The problem would, indeed, be greatly simplified if we might identify the sokemen of the east with the class of six hynd men described in certain Anglo-Norman texts[4] as intermediate between the ceorls with a 200 shilling wergild and the thegn with one of 1,200 shillings.   This, however, we may not do, for the existence of a separate class of six hynd men as late as the date of Domesday is itself very doubtful, and our knowledge of the wealth and local position of the sokemen is sufficient to show their general affinity to the great body of the two-hynd ceorls.

[1] The most detailed evidence comes from Essex, in which county the bordarii exhibit a notable increase at the expense of the villani and the slaves. See Maitland, Dom. Bk. and Beyond, 363; Round in V. C. H. Essex, i. 359–63.

[2] In general, on the Peterborough estates, the sokeman is exempt from week-work.

[3] Cf. Vinogradoff, Growth of the Manor, 341.

[4] In the Leges Henrici Primi, 76, § 2, we are told that the wer of some freemen is 200 (shillings) ; of others, 600; of others, 1,200. Elsewhere, the compiler states that in Wessex wers are of two sorts : two hundred and twelve hundred, applying respectively to villani and thegns. The compiler is evidently contrasting the custom of Wessex with the ' law ' of the Mercians and the Danes. It would seem, then, that the *syx hynd* man of the twelfth century must be sought north of Thames ; we may perhaps find him in the radknight of the west. The fact that the Leges Edwardi Conf. assign the same *manbote* of 12 orae to the villein and sokeman of the Danelaw is against a differentiation of their *wers*.

It is more probable that large numbers of the villani of Domesday have been the victims of an arbitrary classification; that without the agency of any of the forces which made for depression, some slight relative economic inferiority has sufficed to relegate to the villein class many a man who nevertheless continued to own the land which he cultivated, whose status in strict law was identical with that of his more favoured neighbours who secured recognition as *socmanni*. Such a man would inevitably be attracted towards the lower of the two social orders between which he fell, and there would be an end of him.

3. The men of inferior rank may have held their tenements under the sokemen. The influence of dependent tenure in this connexion has to some extent been neglected, but in the surveys of the Danelaw counties there arise at least four clear cases in point. At Long Eaton (Derbyshire) (fo. 273) we are told that 22 sokemen and 10 bordars *sub ipsis* had 9 carucates of land, and the entry relating to Gilbert de Gand's Lincolnshire manor of Baumber (fo. 354 b) includes the passage ' Ibi habet Gilbertus et carucas vt xxi villanos et vi bordarios *et xx sochmannos et xvi bordarios eorum*'. It is significant that the lower stage in both these groups should be composed of bordars ; for where the population of the same piece of sokeland is drawn from two social orders, the members of the second, in a large majority of instances, will be *bordarii*. But the entry relating to the Yorkshire manor of ' Bochetone ' (fo. 314 b) shows us villeins as well as bordars dependent upon sokemen—' In hac villa est soca de xii carucatis et vi bovatis ad geldum. Ibi sunt nunc vii sochemanni *habentes xii villanos et vii bordarios* cum ix carucis'—and the accuracy of the text is confirmed by the record of a similar tenurial arrangement in a Lincolnshire vill (fo. 345 b)—' Soca huius manerii (sc. Scotton in Lindsey) In Torp. [Northorpe] i carucata terrae ad geldum. Terra ad i carucam et dimidiam. *Ibi iiii sochmanni habent ii villanos et i bordarium* cum i caruca.' Explicit statements of this kind are rare ; in most cases where sokemen, villeins, and bordars occur together no clue to their mutual relationship is supplied by Domesday, but there is nothing in the

record to contradict the possible dependence of the bordars, or even of the villeins, upon the sokemen in an indefinite number of such instances. It has been remarked[1] that the coexistence upon the same estate of large and small holdings, such as those respectively of sokemen and bordars, is a natural result of an agrarian system such as that which obtained in the Danelaw. Even without the agency of seignorial pressure, the growth of population called forth a system of small tenancies, subordinate, perhaps, to the larger shares held by the sokemen, but like them anterior in point of origin to any manorial organization; and it seems highly probable that the frequent appearance in our record of bordarii seated upon sokeland may find at least a partial explanation in forces of this kind.

In supplement to these possible cases we should certainly note that, as has been remarked, Domesday will occasionally tell us of the combination of inland and sokeland within the limits of the same subsidiary holding. We certainly cannot trust the terminology of the Survey so far as to assume that it has consistently differentiated inland from sokeland in all cases of the kind. On many estates the land must already by 1086 have acquired parcels of inland which are not distinguished by Domesday from the adjacent sokeland.[2] Scribal error, indifference to the minute details of local organization, and the possibility of confusion in the replies originally

---

[1] Rhamm, Die Grosshufen der Nordgermanen, 140 f.; Vinogradoff in E. H. R. xxi. 355–6.

[2] The existence of demesne teams upon discrete parcels of sokeland is very significant in this connexion, and the figures relating to the soke of Bolingbroke are peculiarly suggestive. This soke contained seventeen members; and in eleven cases the teams possessed by the men of the respective vills are equal both to the carucates of assessment and to the recorded teamlands. On the other hand, in four out of these eleven entries there appears a demesne team in excess of the estimated number: Halton Holgate, 9 C − 9 Tl − 9 + 1 T; Sibsey, 6 C − 6 Tl − 6 + 1 T; East Keal, 4½ C − 4½ Tl − 4½ + 1 T; East Kirkby with Revesby, 12 C − 12 Tl − 12 + 1 T (fos. 351–351 b). In these cases it is clear that the demesne teams are superimposed upon an existing agrarian organization, framed without reference to them, nor is this affected by the fact that the odd demesne team at East Keal seems to descend from a pre-Conquest manerium incorporated in the soke.

given by the jurors, must all fully be allowed for in this connexion.

The exact nature of the ties which united manor and sokeland in 1086 must have varied indefinitely between different
individual cases, but a rough classification of them will be in
place here:—

1. By derivation, the essential feature of sokeland consists
in its subjection to the justiciary power of its lord; and we
may fairly infer that suit of court was demanded from most
sokemen already in 1086. It is a more difficult question how
far beyond the Conquest these judicial powers may reasonably
be carried, and what considerations of rank or wealth entitled
a man to claim them. The earliest quotation for the employment of the term soke in a geographical sense to denote
a group of vills is probably to be obtained from the will of
Wulfric Spot, 1002, in which we read of 'Mortun [Morton,
Derby] and eal seo socna ðe ðærto hæreð and ðæt land ðiderinn
æt Wyllesleage and Oggodestun [Ogston] and Winnefeld
[Wingfield] and Snodeswic into Mortune'.¹ But Wulfric
Spot was a powerful and wealthy thegn, and we may not
lightly argue from him to his less important fellows of equal
rank. There is evidence, as we shall see, which shows us groups
of vills united by common subordination to jurisdictional
powers exercised at a central estate as early as the middle of
the tenth century; and it would seem certain that juridical
dependence was a determining factor in the original differentiation of sokeland from other free tenements; our difficulty is
that in King Edward's time much sokeland was appurtenant

¹ Earle, Land Charters, 220. Kemble, 1280. The Wyllesleage of this
document is, I learn from Mr. W. H. Stevenson, a printer's error for
Pyllesleage, and relates to Nether Pilsley, two miles from Morton. In
1066 this vill (D. B. *Pinneslei*) was itself the *caput* of a manor, but
belonged to the same owner, Swegn 'cild', as Morton and Ogston, and
possessed 2 bovates of sokeland in North Wingfield. The only Willesley
in the county is situated in the extreme south (D. B. *Wivlesleie*), and is
clearly a compound of the OE. personal name Wifel. 'Snodeswic' has
not been identified, it appears in Domesday as an independent manerium
under the form 'Esnotrewic', and probably lay somewhere near South
Normanton. Morton is some two miles from Ogston and four from
(South) Wingfield. The estate had evidently been re-organized between
1002 and 1066.

to manors held by men of small consequence, men whom it is not easy to endow with the right to hold a seignorial court. But in regard to this matter it is necessary to remember not only that we are in virtually complete ignorance as to the social position occupied by the smaller thegns of King Edward's day, but also that we can trace all the more extensive groups of sokeland in the Danelaw back into the possession of men to whom extended franchises are known to have belonged. The famous entry at the beginning of the description of Nottinghamshire, which gives us the names of those who had formerly possessed 'sake and soke, toll and team and the king's custom of the two pennies' over their lands in this county and in Derbyshire is highly significant, but it does not entitle us to assert that no one in this district can have held a court save those magnates whose names are included in the list which follows. When in the Nottinghamshire vill of Clarborough we see an Englishman of 1066 holding with sake and soke a single manor, rated at half a bovate, and valued at sixteen pence,[1] we must admit that very humble people might exercise justiciary powers, whatever their nature or extent may have been.

2. If it is probable that as a rule manor and soke formed a jurisdictional unit, it is certain that in numberless cases they formed an agrarian unit, cemented by the labour services which were rendered by the men of the dependent holding. This agrarian bond must have been at its weakest in the case of large and scattered sokes, and at its strongest where the sokeland was contiguous to the manorial centre. It so happens that we possess a contemporary definition of the services demanded in 1086 from a parcel of sokeland of the latter kind, which has hardly yet received the attention that it deserves. In 1086 the Nottinghamshire vill of Blyth was entered in Domesday as sokeland of the adjacent manor of Hodsock, and as inhabited by four villeins and four bordars (fo. 285). In 1088

---

[1] 'Ibidem habuit Ulchil dimidiam bovatam terrae ad geldum cum saca et soca. Terra ii bobus. Idem ipse Ulchil tenet de Rogero (de Busli) et habet ibi ii bordarios cum ii bobus, et i acra prati.... T. R. E. et modo valet xvi denarios' (fo. 287). The occurrence of the full formula 'sake and soke' places its jurisdictional force beyond doubt.

Roger de Busli, the lord of Blyth, founded a priory of Cluniac monks there ; and in his foundation charter he was careful to define in general terms the nature of the services which the men of that vill had rendered to him, and were to render to the monks, his successors.[1] If the text of the charter may be trusted, which there is no reason to doubt, the men of Blyth were accustomed to plough, do carrying service, reap, mow, make hay, pay merchet, and keep up the dam of the local mill-pool. This instance should not be pressed unduly, for we can hardly suppose that the sokemen of unmanorialized Lincolnshire were normally subjected to the severe burdens which lay upon the villeins and bordars of Blyth ; but it undoubtedly shows that the services which united manor and sokeland were capable of extension so as to include participation on the part of the inhabitants of the latter in all the various kinds of agricultural work which centred upon the manorial demesne.

But the charter has a further value from its bearing upon the general status of the Danelaw peasantry. It is somewhat surprising, for example, to find, barely more than twenty years after the Conquest, and in a remote part of a Danelaw shire, the distinctively servile payment of merchet occurring under the Norman name, but evidently regarded as an accepted custom. One is tempted to suggest a depression of the peasantry ; but in view of the later records which show us even sokemen sub-

---

[1] Our knowledge of this charter, a copy of which is given below, is derived from two independent sources, a cartulary once in the possession of William Sanderson of Blyth, now apparently lost, and the Harleian MS. 3759. The two copies vary in some important respects ; the version in Dugdale's Monasticon begins with the invocation ' In nomine sanctae et individuae Trinitatis ', and omits the witnesses, but both texts contain the clause describing the services of the men of Blyth. In the absence of the original it is, no doubt, possible to regard the clause in question as a late gloss ; but its occurrence in two distinct copies of the instrument makes this supposition highly improbable. The authenticity of the document as a whole is fully established by the names of the witnesses recorded in the Harleian copy (see V. C. H. Notts., i. 225) ; and so few baronial charters of the eleventh century have been preserved in an original form that we are certainly not entitled to regard the statement of services as a suspicious feature. The employment of the West-Frankish invocation formula is paralleled in the almost contemporary Tutbury foundation charter ; and the insertion of a year date is also found in the original Monk's Kirby charter of 1077.

jected to this exaction, it is very doubtful whether this simple explanation would really be true. The Norman merchet has affinities with the Old English *legerwite*, no less than with the Celtic *amobyr* ; its appearance at Blyth in 1088 merely reinforces the probability, which might be argued on other grounds, that some such payment was already made by free men to the thegns of King Edward's day.[1] Apart from the merchet, there is really little in this brief custumal to which a parallel cannot be found in the services of the Peterborough sokemen, forty years later. Carrying service, and the specific field-work here indicated, were incumbent in the twelfth century on sokeman and villein alike ; and even if the men of Blyth were subject to a demand for week-work, improbable, perhaps, but left open by our text, they were no worse off in this respect than the Lincolnshire sokemen of Scotter in 1125.[2] Heavy as these services may seem, there is nothing to suggest that they are in any sense the innovations of a Norman lord ; and we need not hesitate to believe that the little community of humble men at Blyth had substantially maintained the condition that was their lot in the days of King Edward under Wulfsige, then lord of Hodsock and its sokeland.

The Blyth foundation charter is contemporaneous with the Domesday text, but it gives no information as to the amount of the services, of which it indicates the general character. Some exceptionally early evidence relating to this matter, perhaps also, next to the Blyth document, the very earliest extant statement of services due from peasants to a lay lord, arises out of the case of the men of Revesby (co. Lincoln), a vill which in 1086 formed part of the great soke of Bolingbroke. At Revesby, in or about 1142, William de Roumara, Earl of Lincoln, successor to Ivo Taillebois, the Domesday lord of Bolingbroke, established a house of Cistercian monks. His

---

[1] For the payment of *merchet* by free men see Vinogradoff, Villeinage in England, 154-6, 202-4 ; Maitland, Northumbrian Tenures, E. H. R. v. 629, &c.

[2] Chron. Petroburg. 164 : 'Et ibi sunt xxix sochemanni, et operantur i die in ebdomada per totum annum, et in Augusto ii diebus.' Elsewhere on the Peterborough estates the sokemen appear to be exempt from week-work.

foundation charter[1] is very instructive, for he tells us that as the land at issue was not *in proprio dominio* he felt it necessary to compensate the immediate holders. Exchanges of land were accordingly made with three knightly tenants, and with the priest of Thoresby, a neighbouring vill, now lost, and the succeeding portion of the text runs thus :—

Rusticis autem in Scitthesbia (also lost) et Thoresbia et Revesbia manentibus omnibus terram accipere volentibus dedi escambium ad placitum eorum ; quibusdam eorum libertatem cum omnibus suis eundi et manendi ubi vellent absque calumnia. Magis eligentibus et petentibus, sicut eligerunt et petierunt et benigne voluerunt, liberos cum domibus et omnibus bonis suis dimisi.

Haec sunt nomina eorum qui remanentes terram de me acceperunt.

De Revesbia.

(1) Alffernus recepit in escambium duas bovatas in Cherchebia [East Kirkby] per servicium viii solidorum per annum et nihil amplius, et primo anno quietas.

(2*) Normanus recepit in escambium unam bovatam in Hagnebia [Hagnaby] per servicium duorum solidorum per annum *et operationem unius diei in hebdomada* et primo anno quietam.

(3) Edricus recepit unum toftum in Hagnebia et duas acras terrae per servicium viii solidorum per annum, et operationem viii dierum in Augusto et primo anno quietum.

(4*) Godric recepit in escambium unam bovatam in Sticcenaria [Stickney] per servicium duorum solidorum per annum, et unum escheppe bracei ordei[2] contra nativitatem Domini, et operationes iii dierum in hebdomada in Augusto, *et aliis hebdomadis per annum operationem duorum dierum*, et primo anno quietam.

(5*) Ricardus de Revesbia recepit unam bovetam in Sticcefordia [Stickford] *per idem servicium per annum* excepto quod escheppa bracei quam debet dare erit de avena.

---

[1] Mon. Ang. v. 434. Dugdale derived this charter from an original in the possession of Sir Henry Spelman, now apparently lost.

[2] For the (e)*scheppa brasei* compare Chron. Petroburg, 160 [Easton, Northants.] : ' Et isti (sc. xxi villani) debent facere lxiii sceppas de brasio de blado domini.' Clearly, each villein had to produce three ' sceppae '. The term skep is still used to signify a large basket in the NE. Midlands.

(6) Paie Blancherd recepit unum toftum per servicium sex denariorum per annum et nihil amplius, et primo anno quietum.

Unfortunately for our purpose, the greater part of the peasantry chose to take advantage of their lord's licence to depart ; and the document ends with a list of their names : a unique enumeration of the population of a Danelaw vill at the middle of the twelfth century.[1] But on the existing evidence, although all the men of Revesby appear indifferently as *adscripti glebae*—they cannot leave their land without the sanction of their lord—we can trace clearly enough two classes of peasant distinguished from each other by the question of week-work ; and in the light of the conditions which prevailed on the Peterborough estates at this time, we may fairly identify the men whose service consisted only of rent and boon-days with the representatives of the sokemen of 1086. It may be of some significance that already at the latter date a portion of demesne had been created on the soke of East Kirkby and Revesby, which, to all appearance, had not existed there before the Conquest ; [2] a fact which would certainly tend to increase the stringency of the labour services exacted from the local peasantry. To this should be added the probability that the services required for the future from the men who agreed to an exchange of land were lighter than those which had previously been demanded from them while in possession of their original tenements.[3] It is a complicated situation with which we have to deal ; much had happened at Revesby between King Edward's death and the migration of 1142 ; it remains true that the circumstances of the latter event serve to throw a faint light upon a matter in general utterly obscure— the local economy of the Danelaw villages under the Anglo-Norman kings. And although in such a case as this there is always

---

[1] The personal names in the list are too corrupt to be worth reproduction here. They illustrate, however, the adoption of Norman personal names by the native peasantry.

[2] 'In Cherchebi et Resvesbi xii car. terrae ad geldum. Terra xii carucis. Ibi liiii sochmanni et xiiii villani habent xii carucas. Ibi habet Ivo (Taillebois) i carucam et ii ecclesias et clxxx acras prati' (fo. 351 b).

[3] This is the case in regard to the tenants of knightly rank.

a temptation to read more into our texts than is really implied in them, we should note the possibility that the mere fact of an exchange being offered to the expropriated peasants may be due to the lord's recognition that even their small tenements, situated as they were upon ancient sokeland, lay outside his *proprium dominium.*

At a later time the juridical and agricultural aspects of the manor are intimately connected through the communal presentation of offences against the agricultural practice of the township in the manorial court.   By-laws were made within its precincts, and their observance was secured by its sanction. No detail of agricultural life was too insignificant to become the subject of presentment by the jurors of the court leet—the keeping of unringed swine, trespass with oxen in the harvest field, the neglect to scour ditches, breach of the common pinfold, fences out of repair, are visited with amercements imposed by the same authority which punishes assault and the breach of the assizes of bread and ale.   But before we may argue from later practice to the eleventh century, there remain two important questions to be answered ; the questions whether the court of a discrete manor took cognizance of the agricultural routine of its constituent members, and whether the whole procedure by presentment was not an innovation due to the enterprise of Henry II or of the lawyers of his court.[1] As to the presentment of criminals before the sheriff in his tourn, this last point would seem to have been finally demonstrated ; but it is not so clear whether, under this aspect, Henry's work was not the employment for purposes of government of a procedure already operating within the sphere of the manor.   We cannot for a moment doubt the earlier existence of some machinery for securing general compliance with the traditional agricultural practice ; and it is hard to see how an offending rustic could have been brought under the control of the village community without a general agreement that his misdeeds might be brought by any person interested before the notice of the township as a whole.   The creation of manorial courts must

[1] Select Pleas in Manorial Courts (Selden Soc.), Introduction, P. and M. i. 589.

have regulated procedure, and made the decisions of the community more effective; and we may reasonably be confident that the regulation of agricultural routine formed a part, none the less vital because its details are unknown, of the work done by the courts which had arisen by the date of Domesday.

As regards the first question, we are thrown back entirely upon the recorded practice of later times. In the seventeenth century the court of a manor may well exercise jurisdiction in regard to the agrarian life of hamlets whose inhabitants do suit and service there, and if the interval is vast between the time of King Charles and the time of King William, we shall at least do well to remember the intense conservatism of English rural life. The very inconvenience of the arrangement is itself a good argument that the arrangement is no innovation. We should not expect the internal economy of the individual vills incorporated in the wide sokes of Lincolnshire to be regulated by the central court of the soke; and yet, in Elizabeth's time, the soke of Grantham issues general by-laws evidently binding upon all its members. Practice in this respect no doubt varied between different manors; but it would at least be agreed that the performance of labour service was a proper subject for the justice of the lord in his court, and from this to the reception of complaints respecting breaches of agricultural order in the several vills of the soke is an easy step. And we shall probably be justified in concluding that the court of the head manor was in innumerable cases the means through which the whole agrarian organization of the soke was regulated and maintained.

3. It is very probable that in addition to their association with the agricultural routine of the chief manor the inhabitants of sokeland were accustomed upon occasion to assist the manorial population in the performance of the military service demanded from the estate by the king. The passages in the Danelaw Domesday which bear directly upon this point are few but suggestive[1] :—

[1] To these passages the following may be added for the sake of comparison : 'Radulf Pagenel clamat socam et socam (sic) super terram Aluric quam Wido de Credun habet in Osbernebi [Osbournby, Lincoln]. Dicit wapentac quia iste Radulfus debet habere de hac terra unum equum

(1) fo. 368. S. In Summerdebi [Somerby, near Grantham] Adelid vi bovatas terrae ad geldum. Terra vi bobus. Haec soca talis fuit quod nichil reddebat, sed adiuvabat in exercitu regis in terra et in mari. (2) fo. 357 b. In eadem villa [sc. Swaton, Lincoln] habuerunt Alsi et Adestan i carucatam terrae ad geldum. Terra x boum. Aluric frater eorum habebat socam super illos in Hazebi [Haceby, eight miles west of Swaton] solummodo in servitio regis. (3) fo. 366. In Wivelesford [Wilsford, Lincoln] habuit Siward ix carucatas terrae ad geldum. Terra xii carucis. De hac terra habuit Azor frater ejus vi bovatas, et i molendinum, quietum (*sic*) ab omni servitio praeter exercitum.

Now it may be admitted that none of these entries relate to normal examples of sokeland. The two latter examples are clearly connected with the arrangements frequently made between tenants in parage by which one co-parcener defended the whole estate as against the king and received assistance from his fellows to this end. The first case is more difficult, for the 'Adelid' of the Domesday entry seems to represent the OE. female personal name Aethelgyth. The manor to which this lady's estate in Somerby had been annexed in 1066—Keisby, six miles to the south-east—had been held by a thegn named 'Offram' at the latter date, and the nature of his relations with Aethelgyth is obscure. But the main fact, that among the rights implied in the possession of soke could be included the power of exacting military service from those who held under the soke, is clear, and it is enough for our present purpose. The traces, in later records,[1] of the performance of military service by sokemen are few, but they are definite, and the entries given above reinforce the antecedent probability that the freemen of King Edward's time were

in expeditione quando vadit' (fo. 377 b). Ralf's predecessor was Marleswegen, Sheriff of Lincoln, and it may well be that the claim in question was founded on rights which the latter had exercised in his official capacity when calling out the fyrd. He certainly possessed no land in or near Osbournby.

[1] In a rental of Staunton, Notts., *temp.* Henry VI, there is mention of tenants bound by customary service to ride with their lord to Scotland. The marginal entry *Haec est consuetudo* shows that this custom does not result from any feoffment within memory, and it may well be a survival of the military duties of the local peasantry.

bound, if need arose, to take the field at the bidding of their lord. In 1125 the twelve sokemen of Great Easton in Leicestershire were expected to do such service as was incumbent on them of right with the knights of Peterborough; we may be sure that a similar burden lay upon the nine sokemen who dwelt within the vill in 1086,[1] and that their predecessors, seated there under Earl Ralf of Hereford, were expected upon occasion to follow him to war. The sokeman's tenure in 1086 had not the unmilitary characteristics which distinguished the socage of the thirteenth century.

The terminology of Old English law placed beside the *inwara*, which represented the service of dependants to their lord, an *utwara* to be rendered to the king[2]; and the survival of these terms in the Danelaw to a period much later than is commonly supposed may have some bearing upon the present question. Between 1100 and 1200 the texts printed in Dugdale's Monasticon furnish grants of land 'ad utware' relating to eight distinct vills in Yorkshire, Lincolnshire, and Nottinghamshire[3]; and the term in question is found repeated in confirmations of title in a manner implying that the condition of service which it involved continued to be a matter of practical importance. The *inwara* is much rarer; it is contrasted with the *utwara* in the foundation charter of Worksop Priory,[4] of which the original has recently been printed, and

---

[1] Chron. Petroburg. 172, cf. V. C. H. Leicester, i. 310.

[2] For the *utwara* cf. Vinogradoff, Growth of the Manor, 239, 284; English Society in the Eleventh Century, 193-4.

[3] See Athenæum, June 24, 1905, and July 13, 1907, for Nottinghamshire and Yorkshire examples of the Utwara in twelfth century charters, and for a Nottinghamshire reference to the Inwara. The authenticity of the latter is proved by its appearance in the contemporary foundation charter of Worksop Priory. To these may be added the following Lincolnshire instances :—Mon. Ang. vii. 865 (Foundation Charter of Newsham Abbey, circ. 1146) 'sexta parte de ecclesia de Brochelesbi [Brocklesby] et una bovata ad utwar. . . . Ecclesiam quoque de Haburch [Habrough] cum bovata terrae ad utwar.' So also Mon. Ang. vi. 327 (Confirmation Charter of Richard I to Thornton Abbey): 'Ex dono Herberti de Sancto quintino vi bovatas terrae ad upware (*sic*) in Stainton. . . . Ex dono Radulfi de Alt ii bovatas terrae et dimidiam ad Utware et sextam partem molendini in Brunna [Burnham in Areholme] . . . de abbacia beatae Mariae Eborem in Brunn [Burnham] et Thorn dimidiam carucatam terrae cum pertinenciis ad Utware.'

[4] Mon. Ang. vi. 118.

it occurs in an isolated passage in the Liber Niger of Peterborough. There is no need to insist on the military implica-
tions of the utwara, the *forinse servicium* of Bracton ; but the
term also connoted burdens very distinct from service in war.
There is good reason to suppose that it implied responsibility
for the geld, in contrast to the *inwara*, covering land reserved
for the exclusive profit of the lord. Such at least is the
conclusion suggested by the employment of the latter term
in the Liber Niger, where the phrase ' In Estone sunt iii hidae
ad in waram' at the beginning of the entry relating to Easton
in Northamptonshire is contrasted with the note ' Haec villa
adquietat se erga regem pro dimidia hida' in a way which
suggests the traditional balance of inwara and utwara.[1] That
we read nothing of the utwara in the Danelaw surveys may
be explained by the fact that the Domesday commissioners
were incurious about the local apportionment of forensic service
when the title to land was not affected thereby ; it is no
objection to the belief that in 1086 the lord's ancient duty of
compelling his men to seek the fyrd was still one of the forces
which made for the subordination of scattered freeholders to
the control of a central *manerium*.

4. But of much greater importance in this respect, because
of universal extension, are the financial relations which united
manor and soke ; relations expressed in the various payments
in money or in kind which were being derived by the lords of
the eleventh century from their men seated on appurtenant
sokeland. That the compilers of Domesday recognized the
financial unity of manor and soke is proved by a fact which
seriously hinders the investigation of the local statistics of the
Danelaw, the fact that in all but a few exceptional cases the
value or render of the soke is incorporated in the value
assigned to the chief manor of which it formed part. It is
obvious that in the actual working of the manorial economy
the revenues of the soke must have been kept distinct from
the proceeds of the central manor ; in the twelfth century
a baron could endow a grantee with a portion of the exits of

---

[1] Chron. Petroburg. 159, 160. The estate is not made the subject of
a separate entry in Domesday. Cf. Villeinage in England, 342.

a soke,[1] just as the king could charge the farm of a borough
with an annual payment to any given individual; but it is
unusual for the distinction to be marked in Domesday. Now
in so far as this fact merely implies that the Domesday scribes,
working against time, wished to spare their labour, it is of no
particular interest; but an examination of the values assigned
for King Edward's time to those manors which were the
centres of the widest sokes suggests a more significant reason.
A few of these pre-Conquest values may be set out here. In
Nottinghamshire, Dunham produced £30 and six sestars of
honey, Orston £30 by tale, Newark £50, Southwell was
worth £40. In Derbyshire, Repton was worth £15 to the
king, Mickleover £25 to the abbey of Burton. In Lincolnshire, Folkingham was estimated at £50; Greetham at £40;
Caythorpe, Caistor, Drayton, Bolingbroke at £30; Ruskington at £25; Waltham le Wold, Doddington, Sleaford,
Horncastle at £20; Gayton le Wold, Westborough at £15;
Edenham at £10. In Yorkshire, Wakefield was worth £60;
Howden, Aldborough, Driffield, and Warter were worth £40
each; Wilton was worth £20; Otley £10. Figures of this
type, it is clear, do not result from the addition of a number
of casual payments,[2] nor shall we readily believe that they
represent chance estimates of manorial value on the part of
the local jurors.[3] Manors of the type of Drayton, Greetham,
Folkingham, drawing revenue from vills a score of miles away,
stand in a different category from the ordinary rural estate,

[1] Mon. Ang. vi. 97 : 'Dedi et concessi . . . quadraginta solidos in soca
de Staplefordia [Stapleford, Leicester].' Charter of Robert Earl of Nottingham (i. e. Derby) to Breedon Priory, Leicester. Cf. V. C. H. Leicester, i. 319.

[2] There is a remarkable contrast between these figures and those
assigned to the royal sokes of Rothley and Great Bowden, Leicestershire.
The value of Rothley in 1086 represented £3 2s. from the central manor
and £31 8s. 1d. from its members ; at Great Bowden the demesne of the
vill brought in 40 shillings yearly, the men of the vill rendered 40 shillings,
the soke, £7 11s. 6d. It is clear that these manors, unlike the rest of the
royal demesne of Leicestershire, had not been farmed ; but the fact that
the values given here obviously represent actual renders made to the lord
suggests very strongly that the same is true of the neater valets and
valuits of Lincolnshire.

[3] The entry which gives the value of Grantham, Lincoln, is especially
suggestive. 'T. R. E. tota Granham fuit soca ad lii libras, modo reddit
c libras ad pondum. Ecclesia fuit tunc ad viii libras, modo est ad x libras,
sed non valet nisi c solidos' (fo. 337 b). The Northamptonshire evidence
points in the same direction.

of which the value, a matter of plough-teams, woods, meadows, and mills, lay fairly enough within the knowledge of the local peasant. These figures are unintelligible unless we regard them as farms, the sums for which the bailiff of each manor was required to render account to his lord; exactly parallel to the payments which the men of the midland boroughs were making at this time to their lord, the king. And in estimating the forces which at the time of the Survey were holding together the sokemen of the Danelaw in the manorial groups with which that record makes us familiar, the fact of their joint contributions to the common farm of the estate to which they belonged should fairly be assigned high importance.[1]

As, then, the nature of the values recorded for the greater manors of the Danelaw raises issues of some significance, it may be well to examine some of the figures which do not of themselves suggest the existence of any system in the background. In Nottinghamshire, for example, Clifton in Rushcliffe wapentake is valued T. R. E. at £16; Bothamsall and Sutton-with-Scrooby at £8; Arnold at £4. In Derbyshire, Scropton, Eggington, Ilkeston, Weston-on-Trent, and Sawley stand at £8. Markeaton, Morton, and Nether Pilsley at £4. In Lincolnshire, Nettleham and Kirton Lindsey were valued at £24; Stow and Barrow-on-Humber at £32; Claxby and Well at £8; Kirkby Laythorpe at £4; Waddington at £96. In Yorkshire, Loftus and Acklom stand for £48 each; Bridlington, Clayton, Easingwold, Ripon for £32; Laughton en le Morthen for £24; Kippash for £16. Now the unit of £8, to which it is evident that these figures may be referred, was familiar enough to the men of the Danelaw in the eleventh century. It was the sum paid as relief to the king by the Nottinghamshire thegn who possessed more than six manors; it denoted the fine laid upon the local hundreds for certain specified breaches of the king's peace. Its appearance in such associations as these no doubt results from the fact that it included just 120, a round hundred, of those *orae*

---

[1] The regulations in the Leges Henrici Primi for the settlement of disputes between a lord and his *firmarius* prove a common practice of farming estates.

of sixteen pence, current generally in England in the eleventh century. The existence of this eight-pound unit as a basis for computations of manorial value clearly accounts in part for the frequent occurrence, in Yorkshire, of extensive estates estimated at the curious sum of £56 each.[1] The recurrence of this value in relation to estates diverse both in their agricultural capacity and in their assessment to the geld shows at once that an arbitrary estimate has been made in each case ; a fact more consistent with the conception of the 'valuit' as a *firma* pre-determined by the lord than with the assumption that it represents an approximate calculation of potential revenue on the part of the local jurors. In any case, the values based upon the unit of eight pounds clearly fall into line with the normal decimal estimates which have been quoted above as evidence of the conventional character of the pre-Conquest values assigned to the greater manors of the Danelaw.

As to the origin of the payments rendered by sokemen to their lord, little can be said with any confidence. When at last, in such a document as the Rothley custumal,[2] we obtain detailed information as to the internal economy of an extensive soke, the render received by the lord in respect of the several tenements appears in a form indistinguishable from rent in the modern sense of the word.[3] At Rothley there is a marked tendency for tenements of equal size to render to the lord an equal sum of money,[4] a tendency which would not be likely to prevail if the payments in question merely represented the traditional dues exacted in ancient times from the free men of

[1] Thus, on the estate of Drogo de Beurere in Holderness, Hornsea, Kilnsea, Mapleton, Withernsea, Burstwick are severally valued at this sum (see Maitland, Dom. Bk. and Beyond, 473). In every case except the last Earl Morcar is returned as the pre-Conquest owner, and Burstwick is assigned to Earl Tostig, Morcar's predecessor in the Northumbrian earldom. Morcar's manor of Pickering was valued at £88 ; Whitby, which belonged to Earl Siward, at £112. The lands of Tostig and Morcar at ' Walesgrif ' and Pocklington were likewise valued at £56 each, as also was Edwin's manor of Gilling.   [2] Archaeologia, xlvii. 89-130.
[3] Compare Burton Cartulary, 29 : ' Item Ricardus filius Godefredi habet similiter de terra sochemannorum v bovatas et dim. ; iii scilicet et dim. pro xd et dim. sicut sochemannus, et duas quietas sicut Racchenstus.'
[4] This sum, with local variations, approximates to a rent of 2s. 2d. for the bovate, which would give a value of 13 *orae* to the carucate. Very frequently, however, the rents cover a toft in the village in addition to the arable holding.

the soke. On the other hand, if any general remark can in safety be made about these scattered estates of which Rothley is a type, it is that the right of the sokeman to his tenement is independent of, and older than, the manorial organization to which, when we discover him, he is found annexed. And not only is this the case, but, as will appear hereafter, there is no real reason why the original dependence of the sokeman upon his lord should have resulted, in the first place, from the act of either party to the relationship. The action of the Old English kings in granting soke over freemen to thegns, earls, or religious houses undoubtedly played a part, as important as it is obscure, in creating the discrete manors of the Danelaw. And yet, in the relationship thus created, it may well be that payment or services were involved, which, under the different circumstances arising in the eleventh century, might harden into conditions of tenure resembling a modern rent. If the free man, in the days of his independence had, according to custom, contributed money or provisions to the *feorm* of king or earl, we may be sure that this burden was not remitted by the new lord ; we may infer a local regulation of its incidence similar to that which obtained in the case of the geld, and from this point onwards we may accept the desire to co-ordinate the render made by each man with the extent of his holding in the open fields as sufficient to produce the general conformity between render and tenement visible in the thirteenth century. In regard to all this matter, we are arguing in the dark ; but if we are to maintain the original freedom of the normal sokeman it becomes necessary to assume that some process of the kind indicated here lies behind the facts of his condition as they appear when we first obtain knowledge of them.

Among the financial burdens incumbent on sokeland, a prominent place is taken by those payments which are commonly comprised under the generic name of *consuetudines*. This term, which occurs less frequently in the surveys of the Danelaw shires than in those of the counties to the south and east, is sufficiently vague to cover different payments of very diverse natures ; while at the same time it points unmistakably to the fact that the exactions which it covers are being levied as a matter of customary practice.[1] That in some cases the *consuetudines* covered the whole value of the soke to its lord is made probable by the description of the Nottinghamshire soke of Oswardbeck (fo. 281 b); for in two successive entries the 'hi sochmanni reddebant xx solidos de consuetudine' of the first evidently gives the information supplied by the 'haec soca valet x solidos' of the second. But the origin of these payments remains obscure, and indeed it is probable that their incidence was determined by no consistent principle.[2] At times it is clear that the sokeman's payments to his lord represent a commutation of rents in money or in kind; and it is to be noted that actual food-rents must surely have still been exacted in some of those cases where sokeland was dependent upon a manor which included no demesne, and of which the lord held no land in other vills. Then, too, full allowance must be made for payments in respect of suit to the manorial mill,[3] or in connexion with that fold-soke of

[1] Among the payments of diverse origin which have gone to produce the consuetudines rendered by the inhabitants of sokeland an important place should be assigned to the *gafol*, the *gablum* of early texts. Gafol was certainly paid to the king in pre-Conquest times by men who were not seated upon the king's own land (English Society, 210-11).

[2] The Burton Cartulary (page 29) shows that at Winshill (Derbyshire) the lord received the sokeman's heriot, amounting on that manor to 16 shillings (= 12 *orae*). No doubt similar payments were exacted elsewhere.

[3] Little is said in the Danelaw surveys about mill-soke, and that little is confusing. One thing is clear, that it was possible for the soke of a mill to be reserved to some one other than the lord of the manor in which it lay. The case of the mills of Barkston is definite on this point. In 1086 a portion of Barkston formed a berewick of the neighbouring vill of Belton, and contained two mills 'unde iacet soca in Grantham' (fo. 370 b). The greater part of Barkston was itself sokeland of Grantham, and there also were two mills 'which Thurferth the son of Wulfred had—their soke in Grantham' (fo. 338). This must in some obscure way be connected with an enigmatical entry in the Kesteven *Clamores* to the effect that 'Robert de Stafford and Colswegen likewise claim two mills which are in Barkston. The wapentake says that they lie in Marston, and their soke in Grantham' (fo. 377 b). Neither Robert nor Colswegen held land in Barkston, but the former possessed a manor in Rauceby, eight miles to the NE., formerly the property of one Thurferth, probably Thurferth the son of Wulfred. The reference to Marston remains inexplicable. If the analogy of 'fold-soke' is worth anything, mill-soke should imply the lord's power of compelling his men to grind their corn at the manorial mill. It is therefore somewhat strange to find the soke of a mill reserved to a person other than the lord of the manor in which it was locally situated; but this was clearly a possible thing. We may conjecture that in such cases the soke

which we read so much in the East Anglian survey.[1] Probably, also, not a little of what was rendered by the sokeman of the eleventh century was given by way of an acknowledgement of the lord's superiority over his sokeland; a payment which, it may be noted, a Norman baron would find both convenient and easy to confound with the arbitrary tallages which he was beginning to exact. But even after we have enumerated the more obvious sources of the revenue derived from this quarter, there will still remain a residue to which no occasion can readily be assigned, and of which the origin probably lies far back in the unwritten history of the Danelaw vills.

In the previous passage a casual reference has been made to the possibility that food-rents may originally have formed one element in the scheme of payments and services which united the sokeman to his lord. Traces of rents in kind are discernable at a later date than Domesday[2] in the Danelaw; but we read little of this form of render in our texts, and the probability is strong that in most cases food-rents had already been commuted into money payments by the time of the Conquest. A fortunate chance has, nevertheless, preserved a copy or translation of a document coming from the reign of Æthelred II in which the constituent parts of an annual *feorm* are set out with clearness and accuracy.[3] In this text a landowner bearing the name of Ærnketel, a name arguing Scandinavian descent or relationship, and his wife Wulfrun tell King Æthelred that they have granted to Ramsey abbey their land of 'Hikelinge et ... Kinildetun' *cum firma et servitio sicut habetur in dominio nostro*. The lands which formed the subject of the grant cannot with accuracy be identified in Domesday, but they certainly lay in the adjacent vills of

of a mill was represented to the external lord by a fixed and customary payment, the lord of the manor retaining the surplus dues rendered for the service of the mill by the local peasantry, and presumably the miller's rent. It is further probable that this reservation of the soke of the mill accounts for the somewhat frequent appearance of entries which assign merely the site (*sedes*) of a mill to the lord of the manor. The mill itself, we may believe, was in being, but its profits, or a known and definite share of them, were paid by way of soke to the external lord.

[1] Compare the sixteen shillings 'de consuetudinibus pascuarum quae sunt in Scapewic et Cherchebi' which the men of Navenby, Lincoln, retained by force (fo. 376 b).

[2] As in the Revesby case quoted above, p. 25.   [3] C. D. 971.

Hickling and Kinoulton under the wolds of South Nottinghamshire.[1] The document is drawn up in a somewhat unusual form; but as Ramsey Abbey possessed no land in this
neighbourhood in 1086, and claimed no estate there at any
subsequent date, the deed, even if a forgery, must have been
compiled before the close of King William's reign, and the
details which it contains may fairly be cited in evidence of
eleventh-century conditions. Of these details the most important is a statement of the *firma* which was yearly to be
rendered to the abbey from the vill of Hickling. Each year,
on St. Benet's Day, Wulfrun directs that the abbey should
receive 'x mittas de brasio, et v de grut, et x mittas farinae
triticae, et viii pernas, et xvi caseos, et duas vaccas pingues . . .
in capite vero quadragesimae viii isicios'. This represents
a substantial rent, but it was no onerous burden for the men
of a prosperous Danelaw vill,[2] and there was little room for
the interference of the bailiffs of thegn or abbot in the matter
of its incidence or collection. No doubt, in process of time,
the store-house of an absent lord might develop into a hall
with adjacent demesne, and labour upon the latter might
be substituted, at first, perhaps, in times of scarcity, for the
yearly gift of hams and cheeses; but it is at least evident
that this development has not yet occurred in the one Danelaw
vill of which something of the internal economy, in the period
before the Conquest, is known to us.[3] Nor need we hesitate
to argue from the *feorm* of Hickling to the rents paid in

---

[1] The authenticity of the grant is supported by a passage in the Ramsey
Cartulary (Rolls Series, iii. 167), which tells us that Ærnketel and Wulfrun,
parents of Æthelwine, fourth Abbot of Ramsey, were buried there in 1019.
This is clearly derived from independent tradition, and the passage adds
that 'terrram de Hikkeling et de Kuldeton' were given by these persons
to the abbey. The editor identifies 'Kuldeton' with Kilvington, Notts.;
Kemble identifies the 'Hikeling' of C. D. 971 with Hickling, Norfolk.
But the local proximity of Hickling and Kinoulton is conclusive, and the
latter name may well descend from an OE. *Cynehilde tun*, to which the
Kinildetune of the text is an approximation.

[2] In Domesday, part of Hickling was a berewick of Cropwell Bishop,
held T. R. E. by St. Mary of Southwell; two carucates there were sokeland of Granby; and an estate of 3½ carucates was held as two manors by
Turchil and Godwine. It is most probable that this last property represents the land of C. D. 971, but this cannot be considered certain.

[3] Hickling affords a fair field for the processes of manorialization
described by Maitland, Dom. Bk. and Beyond, 319–20.

King Edward's day by the men of other manors of whose burdens we must perforce be content to remain in ignorance.

Between the discrete manors of the Danelaw and those of which we read in the survey of such a county as Cambridgeshire there exists a superficial resemblance which is no doubt sufficiently striking. In both districts the lord of the chief manor appears as drawing revenue from, and as exercising jurisdiction over, free men settled at a distance from the manorial centre. In either case, the divergence from the type of manor represented in the compact estates of the south is remarkable and definite; but there remains a noteworthy distinction between the form of manorial structure revealed in the Cambridgeshire survey and that which tended to prevail in Lincolnshire. Considered with reference to our texts, this distinction may be expressed in the statement that while in Cambridgeshire the economy of the discrete manor is created by the varying relations of groups of free men to their respective lords, in Lincolnshire it arises from the administrative dependence of scattered tenements upon the manorial centre. In part, no doubt, it may be true that these different conceptions represent very similar types of local organization; it is certainly the case that the formulas in which they find expression in the survey are far from identical. Those formulas, so common in the rest of England, which tell us whether this man or that held his land freely, whether he could dispose of it without his lord's licence,[1] will rarely be found in the surveys of the Danelaw shires other than Leicester; and in Leicestershire the distinction of tenements as manors, sokes, and berewicks does not occur. Whatever the reason, the compilers of the Danelaw Domesday seem little interested in questions of tenurial status, either as affecting the relations of peasants to their lord, or in connexion with

---

[1] In the entry relating to Shipley, Derbyshire, the accident of a disputed claim has brought out into the text a statement of the kind. Shipley was held T. R. E. by Brun and Odincar, but had passed by 1086 to Gilbert de Gand, whose usual predecessor in these parts was Ulf 'fenisc'. Accordingly there is appended to the description of the manor the statement ' Hanc terram dicunt homines qui juraverunt non pertinuisse ad Ulf fenisc T. R. E., sed ipsi ii taini (sc. Brun and Odincar) ita tenuerunt ut potuissent dare et vendere cui voluissent ' (fo. 277 b).

the dependence of our pre-Conquest lord upon another in the matter of soke or commendation. The Clamores of Yorkshire and Lincolnshire reveal to us somewhat of the tangled relations which existed among the northern thegns of King Edward's day, but these relations, in so far as they are known to us, cannot be correlated with the formulas which underlie the text of the local surveys. With regard alike to peasant and lord the status and liberties of the holders of lands before the Conquest, elsewhere noted as a matter of rule, are held considerations of little account in the Danelaw.

It is not impossible, however, that a casual recognition of the importance of these matters may lurk behind the occasional appearance in the Lincolnshire survey of an enigmatical formula, unknown elsewhere in Domesday, the *frige soca*.[1] Of this formula there are eight clear examples, and, to all seeming, no more.

fo. 340.

(1) In Schillintune [Skillington, Beltisloe wapentake] habuit Morcar comes iii carucatas terrae ad geldum et Friguist et Bridmer (*rectius* Brictmer < OE. Beorhtmœr) i car: terrae ad geldum . . . Frigesoca in Schillintune.

fo. 346.

(2) M. In Turolvebi [Thurlby, Ness wapentake] habuit Elnod i car: et dim. ad geldum . . . Frigesoca sub Aslac.

fo. 357 b.

(3) S. In Westbi [Westby, Beltisloe wapentake] x bov: terrae ad geldum . . . Frisoca in Heidure [Haydor].

fo. 366.

(4) M. In Bercheham [Barholme, Ness wapentake] habuit Aschil i car: terrae ad geldum . . . Ibi habuit ii homines Godefredi [de Cambrai] dimidiam carucam etv soch' de tercia parte hujus terrae frisocam.

fo. 368 b.

(5) M₂. In Carlebi [Carlby, Beltisloe wapentake] habuerunt Dane et Carle i car: terrae et bis quintam partem unius bovatae ad geldum. . . . Terra Carle fuit frig soca sub Dane.

Ibid.

(6) M₃. In Breseburg [Braceborough, Ness wapentake] et Barnetorp habuerunt Dane et Carle et Ledflet (< OE. fem. p. n.* Leodflaed) xx bovatas terrae ad geldum. . . . Terra duorum ex his fuit frig soca sub Dane.

Ibid.

(7) M₂. In Cretune [Creaton, Beltisloe wapentake] habuerunt Fredgist et Brictmar xii bov: terrae et ii partes ii bova-

---

[1] See Maitland, Dom. Bk. and Beyond, 93 ; Vinogradoff, English Society in the Eleventh Century, 124. It is best to consider the question of the frige soca apart from the marginal notes fꝺ, f, which occur at times in the Lincolnshire survey. The meaning of the latter remains doubtful.

tarum ad geldum. . . . Terra Brictmar fuit frig soca sub
Fredgist.
  (8) M_1. In Rosbi [Rauceby, Flaxwell wapentake] habuit Ibid.
Vlsi iii car: terrae et dim: bov: ad geldum. M_2 et Osmund,
— iii bov: et dim:, et Siward—i car—habuerunt xi bov: terrae
et dim: ad geldum. . . . Terra Siward frig soca sub Osmundo.

Now, we should certainly note that all these entries relate
to vills situated within a moderate distance of each other.
Seven out of the eight properties involved lay within the two
south-western wapentakes of Kesteven ; and Rauceby in Flaxwell wapentake is a bare dozen miles from Westby in
Beltisloe. This is significant, for it suggests that the casual
appearance of the *frige soca* in the Lincolnshire survey is due
to its omission from the local returns sent in from the greatest
number of the Lincolnshire wapentakes. It can hardly be
the result of chance that no example of the term can be
obtained from Lindsey or Holland, to say nothing of Nottinghamshire or Derbyshire. But the interpretation of the term
itself is a more serious matter. If, in accordance with the
analogy of such a compound as *frigman*, we render *frige
soca* by ' free soke ', we still have to discover the sense in
which these particular instances of soke were peculiarly free.
Despite the inherent probability of the suggestion, we cannot
well take *frige soca* to mean soke over free men,[1] for at
Thurlby, Carlby, and Braceborough the highest rank of the
recorded peasantry consisted of villeins. An examination of
the entries themselves may perhaps help us to a different
solution. It is surely suggestive that six out of the eight
entries refer to estates which before the Conquest had been
divided among two or more owners, of whom one had possessed the *frige soca* of his fellows. That one thegn should
possess soke over another, dwelling in the same vill, was no
remarkable circumstance ; but may we not infer that the
essential freedom of the soke in the cases which have been
quoted lay in the fact that it could be withdrawn at will by
the inferior party? If we see in the Elnod of Thurlby, the
Brictmar of Creaton, the five sokemen of Barholme, men who

---

[1] English Society in the Eleventh Century, 124.

could go with their land and soke whither they would, we shall obtain a useful point of contact between the tenurial order of Lincolnshire and that which obtained in East Anglia. How far liberties of this kind were common in the Danelaw shires is a question to which no positive answer is forthcoming. When we are told that in the Lindsey vill of Cammeringham Siward had a manor of half a carucate, and Elnod likewise half a carucate sokeland of the former manor, we may suspect that the jurors of Beltisloe wapentake would have qualified the latter's holding as a free soke, but we can prove nothing. If the form of tenure which we have ventured to infer from the *frige soca* formula was at all widespread in the Danelaw, the compilers of the local surveys have chosen to tell us little about it.

fo. 365.

The result is that the manorial organization of the Danelaw appears in Domesday as far more permanent and stable than the agrarian system of such a county as Cambridge. In the former case, we obtain definite information as to the local distribution of different types of tenement at the time of King Edward's death, with the obvious implication that little change in regard to this matter has occurred between this date and the taking of the Domesday Inquest ; in the latter case, we are shown groups of men, dependent, indeed, upon a lord, and rendering him dues and service, but connected with him rather by personal ties than by their occupation of lands appurtenant, by prescription, to his several estates. The sokeman who could give or sell his land where he would is an unknown character in such counties as Lincoln or Nottingham. It would be highly rash to assume that the silence of Domesday respecting him proves his non-existence ; but it would be no less unsafe to see merely a terminological difference between the sokes or berewicks of the Danelaw and the scattered members of the manors of Cambridgeshire. The whole structure of these rural groups varies in the two districts in question. Instead of the small holdings of isolated free men, interspersed among shots and furlongs rendering soke or custom to many different lands, which distinguished the typical village of Cambridgeshire, the Danelaw surveys reveal the existence of compact blocks of land, very frequently of entire

vills, in subordination to a common manorial centre.   As a
typical Danelaw estate, we may consider for a moment Geoffrey
Alselin's Lincolnshire manor of Ruskington, formerly the property
of the wealthy thegn Tochi, the son of Outi.   To this manor
were appurtenant as sokeland the entire twelve-carucate vills fo. 369 b.
of Donington, Digby, and Rowston, half Dunsby and Leasing-
ham, more than three parts of Brauncewell, and great part of
Rauceby and Roxholm ; Anwick, a vill of six carucates, was a
berewick of the manor.   We shall not lightly assume that an
estate of this kind results from the chance agreement in commendation to a single lord of the 196 sokemen who, apart
from villeins and bordars, inhabited the chief manor with its
dependent members ;[1] we may seriously doubt whether any one
of these men possessed the right of withdrawing his land and
service from the manorial group without his lord's consent.
If we insist on the identity of vill and manor as the characteristic feature of the perfected manorial system, the Danelaw, of
all England, will perhaps appear most remote, in local organization, from the manorial idea ; but it may seem more than
doubtful whether the system developed in estates of the type
just described is not nearer to this end than are the unstable
groups of free men revealed in the shires to the south and east.

In a future section of this essay evidence will be brought
forward to show that the type of manor comprising a central
estate with appurtenant property distributed among scattered
vills already existed in the Danelaw shires as early as the
middle of the tenth century.   Direct evidence of this kind is,
however, rarely to be obtained ; and in general we are
dependent upon conjecture in our attempt to trace the origin
of the greater sokes of the Danelaw.   The one circumstance
which affords a clue, although a faint one, in regard to this

---

[1] Contrast the description of William Peverel's Northamptonshire
manor of Coton-under-Guilsborough (V. C. H. Northants, i. 339 a).   The
members of this estate lay in Thornby—1 hide, 1 team, no recorded
inhabitant : Winwick—3 virgates, 1 team, 1 sokeman : West Haddon—
1½ virgates, ½ team, 1 sokeman : Cold Ashby—½ virgate, ½ team, 1 sokeman : Nortoft—½ hide, 1 team, 1 sokeman : Hollowell—1 virgate, ½ team,
1 sokeman.   It is difficult to resist the conclusion that these five sokemen,
distributed over as many vills, had severally commended themselves to
William Peverel or his unnamed predecessor at Coton-under-Guilsborough.

matter is the curious relation which evidently existed in the eleventh century between the geographical area of the greater sokes and the boundaries of the respective wapentakes within which, in name, they lay.   It is unusual for an important soke to extend beyond the borders of a single wapentake or group of adjacent wapentakes;[1] it is highly exceptional for any wapentake to include more than a single soke of wide extent. For some cases illustrative of this principle a simple explanation lies to hand ; the sokes of Bolingbroke, of Horncastle, of Newark, clearly result from the grant to their owners of the courts of the several wapentakes to which those places gave name ; the Conqueror's grant of Well wapentake to St. Mary of Stow[2] was, in effect, a transfer to that house of the rights which the Countess Godgifu had exercised in King Edward's time.   But this explanation, though attractive, must not be carried too far; for in many cases the courts of soke and wapentake co-existed independently for centuries. The great soke of Rothley in 1086 comprised twenty-one distinct members all lying within the Leicestershire wapentake of Gosecote, yet nothing in the Rothley documents warrants us in assuming that the court of Rothley had ever been regarded as the court of Gosecote wapentake.   Cases of this kind admit, in part at least, of another explanation, suggested by what we read of the Nottinghamshire wapentake of Oswardbeck, the district in the extreme north-east of the county.   Excluding certain small properties, this wapentake, as described in Domesday, fell into three divisions : a group of thirteen manors, to two of which small parcels of sokeland were appur-

[1] Thus in Lincolnshire the soke of Waltham-le-Wold lay entirely in the wapentake of Haverstoe, that of Belchford in Gartree, that of Wragby in Wraggoe, Gayton in Louth Eske, Grantham in Aswardburn, Caistor in Yarborough.   On the other hand, Greetham, the widest soke in the Danelaw, extending over thirty-five vills, is distributed among the wapentakes of Hill, Calceworth, and Candleshoe ; Kirton in Lindsey, between Manley and Corringham.   In Leicestershire the soke of Great Bowden is confined to Gartree wapentake, that of Melton Mowbray to Framland ; Gosecote includes the entire sokes of Rothley and Barrow-on-Soar.   In Nottinghamshire the soke of Clifton was distributed over eleven members all lying in Rushcliffe wapentake ; the royal sokes of Dunham and Orston respectively are confined to Bassetlaw and Bingham.   Such trustworthy evidence as is available supports the tendency indicated in the text.
[2] Eynsham Cartulary (Oxford Hist. Soc.), i. 48–50. Cf. Domesday, fo. 376.

tenant, which had descended from various owners to Roger de Busli, the lord of Blyth ; thirteen distinct pieces of sokeland annexed to the king's distant manor of Mansfield, fifteen miles away upon the further side of Sherwood Forest ; and a number of scattered tenements forming sokes or berewicks of the ancient estates of Sutton and Laneham, in the possession of the Archbishop of York. It is the peculiar value of this instance that it reveals the king with unmistakable clearness as the immediate lord of all those men who are not involved in subjection to other lords[1] ; and that it suggests the probability that some, at least, of the wider sokes of the Danelaw have resulted from a royal grant to thegn or earl of the king's rights over all the unattached free men dwelling within a given wapentake. Such a grant, it will be obvious, would have consequences quite distinct from the effects of a direct bestowal of the wapentake itself ; the independence of the ancient assembly would in no way be affected by the withdrawal of the king's free men from its sessions.

But there can be little doubt that in many cases the king's grant of soke merely gave sanction to an organization which had already come into being[2] through the voluntary submission of its members, or through the aggression of some local magnate. In such cases, the tendency towards the inclusion of the soke as a whole within the wapentake in which the chief manor lay must be sought at a time before men had learned to conceive of a local court distinct from the traditional assembly of the district. If, as seems probable, the court of the immunist was anciently held at the same time and place as the meeting of the wapentake or hundred, we can the better understand the origin of a confusion which persisted

---

[1] A somewhat similar case is presented by the sokeland of Melbourne, Derby. Within a short distance of Melbourne, but on the other side of the Trent, lay six vills, portions of which were surveyed collectively under the heading ' Haec Soca pertinet ad Mileburne in Scarvesdele [Scarsdale] wapentac ' (fo. 272 b). The Domesday scribe has probably got the name of the wapentake wrong ; but the king appears with sufficient clearness as the residual lord of the free men of the district.

[2] We cannot ignore the possibility that in some cases the sokes of 1066 may represent local arrangements formed at the time of the Scandinavian settlement of the ninth century.

after the assembly of the sokemen had normally come to be held within the precincts of the central manor. In any case, it is to this quarter that we must look for the cause of one of the frequent local anomalies presented by the Danelaw surveys —the division of single vills between two distinct wapentakes. The Nottinghamshire vill of Staunton lies within the wapentake of Newark, except that a small portion is annexed to the parish of Orston in the adjacent wapentake of Bingham [1]; and we shall not be wrong in identifying this disassociated tract with the seven bovates, three acres, which in 1066 were sokeland of King Edward's manor of Orston. In Lincolnshire, by the date of the Lindsey Survey, divided allegiance to the manors of Waltham and Tetney had split the vill of Waithe between the wapentakes of Hamfordshoe and Bradley. In Leicestershire, the fact that the vills of Caldwell and Wycomb, in Gosecote wapentake, form to this day an outlier in the wapentake of Framland, may safely be attributed to their ancient inclusion in the soke of Rothley. In such cases as these, it is clear that the force of seignorial control has proved stronger than the force of customary association in determining the boundaries of soke and wapentake; [2] but the fact only points the more definitely to the origin of the manorial group in a segregation of tenements within the borders of the more ancient local division.

Thus far, we have mainly been occupied with the condition of sokeland geographically separate from the head manor to which it belonged. It must now be added that Domesday will often show us sokeland within the manorial area itself. 'In Bulcote, Swegn had 2 carucates of land and 2 bovates of land (assessed) to the geld, and in the same place (there are) 15 bovates of land to the geld, sokeland of this manor' (fo. 288 b) is a Nottinghamshire entry of a type which has many Lincolnshire parallels. In a few valuable cases, as we have seen, the Lincolnshire Domesday inserts the phrase *in dominio* to dis-

---

[1] Thoroton, History of Nottinghamshire (ed. Throsby, 1790), i. 303–5.
[2] Probably the meeting of the immunist's men was held apart from, but contiguously to, the session of the wapentake court. In such cases isolated groups of men over whom the immunist acquired soke would naturally be required to join the meetings of their fellow dependants.

tinguish the manorial portion of the vill from the adjacent sokeland. Elsewhere in the record the distinction is less clearly marked ; and in a very large number of entries the presence of what we may call inter-manorial sokeland is expressed by a peculiar formula which deserves quotation : ' In Eakring Ingolf had 6 bovates of land (assessed) to the geld. There is land for two ploughs. There William, Gilbert's man, has 1 plough, and 3 sokemen on 3 bovates of this land, and 2 villeins and 3 bordars having 2 ploughs' (fo. 290 b). Entries of this type are virtually confined to the surveys of Lincolnshire and Nottinghamshire ; but within these limits there are more than two hundred cases in which the extent of the tenements belonging to the manorial sokemen is defined. Just as, at one time, the compilers of the survey will explicitly mark off the *dominium* from the soke, at another they will content themselves with indicating the amount of land in the occupation of the sokemen ; it was immaterial that one entry should run ' In Merestune [Marston] habuit Alsi i car terrae ad geldum in dominio et x bovatas terrae in soca ',[1] and another ' In Wellebrune [Welbourne] habuit Goduine xii carucatas terrae ad geldum ... Ibi habet Robert Malet ... xxxv sochemanni de vii carucatis hujus terrae' (fo. 368).[2] It is clear that for some purpose it was important to preserve a record of the amount of land held within each vill by the local sokemen.

The nature of this purpose is suggested by the fact that to all appearance the extent of the holdings in question was always expressed in fiscal terms. At times the tenements of the sokemen form a definite proportion, an exact half, it may be, of the total rateable area of the vill. We may particularly

---

[1] fo. 357. Cf. fo. 358 b. The correspondence of sokemen with sokeland is further illustrated by two entries on folio 349 b. (1) ' In Staintune [Market Stainton] habuit Godric ii carucatas terrae ad geldum. ... Dimidia carucata sochmannorum. (2) In Tadewelle habet comes Harold v carucatas terrae ad geldum ... Duae carucatae in soca.' The latter formula is most frequently employed in folios 349–351 b.

[2] Compare the following Yorkshire entry (fo. 314) : ' In Daltone ad geldum xv carucatae et ii bovatae. Ibi est soca pertinens ad ipsum manerium vi car. et vi bov. ad geldum. Ibi est nunc i sochmannus.' Occasionally, but very rarely, a special entry is made of the sokemen's teams. Fo. 304 b [Welton] : ' In dominio vi carucae, et xxxiiii villani, et iii bordarii habentes ix carucas, et x sochmanni cum vi carucis.' Cf. fo. 286 [Tollerton, Notts.].

note three almost consecutive entries on folio 362 b. At Burton, near Lincoln, of 10 carucates, 6 bovates, representing the assessment of the estate, twenty-nine sokemen held 5 carucates, 3 bovates; at Dunholme four sokemen held 1 carucate out of 2 carucates laid on the vill; in the case of Roxby, we are informed by an interlineation that twenty-four sokemen held 21 bovates out of an estate rated altogether at 5 carucates, 2 bovates. Elsewhere in the record the relevant figures, it must be admitted, are less convincing; but there remains a fact which no less definitely emphasizes the fiscal aspect of the sokeman's tenement. If we consider separately the entries relating to Nottinghamshire, Lindsey, and Kesteven, the prevalent ratio between the carucates of assessment and the estimated teamlands is very different in each of these three districts.[1] In Kesteven the teamlands are commonly exactly equal in number to the carucates of assessment, save that in the rich country on the Nottinghamshire border the carucates are not infrequently in excess. In Lindsey, save in some exceptional cases, the teamlands outnumber the carucates, and in Nottinghamshire the excess becomes so great as to suggest the probability that the teamland of this county is really a conventional quantity, the survival of an obsolete assessment.[2] After this, it is surely significant that the average holding of the sokeman is at its highest in Kesteven, declines rapidly in Lindsey, and reaches its lowest point in Nottinghamshire;[3]

[1] The varying relations of carucate and teamland in Lindsey and Kesteven will be discussed in V. C. H. Lincoln, i. Some idea of the facts may be gathered from Eng. Soc. in Eleventh Cent., Appendix ix. Table I, A includes the analysis of 121 entries in which the gelding carucates exceed the recorded teamlands. Of these entries 77 relate to Kesteven, 21 to Holland, and only 23 to Lindsey, the largest division of the three.

[2] V. C. H. Nottingham, i. 211–13.

[3] These facts may be expressed in tabular form :—

In Kesteven 525 sokemen were seated upon 944⅛ bovates.
In Lindsey 917 „ „ „ 779⅓ „
In Notts. 336 „ „ „ 211⅔ „

That is, upon an average, 10 sokemen in Kesteven would possess almost exactly 18 bovates; in Lindsey, rather more than 8½; in Nottinghamshire, rather more than 6¼. The only Holland examples available relate to Frampton, where 2 sokemen had 4 bovates, and to Butterwick, where 36 sokemen had 9 carucates. Out of 56 Lincolnshire entries in which the average sokeman's tenement amounts to less than one bovate, 4 only relate to Kesteven. One Derbyshire entry may be quoted : at Ilkeston 10 sokemen had 2 carucates.

that the typical sokeman's tenement varies in close correspondence with the fluctuations of the prevailing villar assessments. Unless the figures in question represent fiscal terms, it is hard to see why the four sokemen of Barnby-in-the-Willows, on the extreme edge of Nottinghamshire (f. 284), should possess an average holding of but half a bovate, while the twenty-seven sokemen cultivating soil of identical texture and quality in the adjacent fields of Stapleford, across the Lincolnshire border, should hold among themselves no less than 6 carucates and 6 bovates of land (fo. 366 b). It is, in fact, clear that local differences of rating underlie the variations, of which the cases of Barnby and Stapleford are only examples chosen almost at random; but the fact is sufficient to establish the conclusion that the sokeman in 1086 was still held responsible for the geld laid upon the land which he cultivated. Whether this explicit definition of the tenements of the manorial sokemen may be taken to imply that the land of villeins and bordars was being acquitted of geld by their lord raises questions to which it is hardly possible to supply an answer at present; the antecedent probability which is thus created must be considered in connexion with the existing evidence respecting the dealings of the collectors of the geld with the local village communities, and this evidence is inconclusive. For our immediate purpose it is more important to remark upon the fact that, even within the precincts of the manor, the sokemen were regarded as in some sense external to its organization; that the tenements which they occupied were their own property, subject to seignorial exploitation, but co-ordinate with, rather than subordinate to, the lord's demesne. Their position under such circumstances was, no doubt, sufficiently precarious; but the later history shows that on manor after manor the sokemen of 1086 handed on their essential freedom to their successors, and in their lands we may with reason recognize a main source of the ancient freeholds enclosed within the manors of the Danelaw shires.[1]

[1] Compare Massingberd, E. H. R. xx. 699. The determination of the extent and situation of ancient freeholds would be an interesting subject for local investigation.

In all that has hitherto been said, we have been arguing for the general rule that underneath the terminology of the Dane-law Domesday there lies an implied division of all tenements into two great classes, distinguished by the nature of the lord's interest in the land described. Should the land in question be regarded as belonging to the lord, it will be reckoned his inland, and if it formed a subordinate portion of some greater estate, it will normally be entered as a berewick of the latter. Should the lord merely appear in relation to the land as the recipient of dues and service from its inhabitants, it will be returned in our record as sokeland. In face of much diversity of local custom, the compilers of Domesday seem to be trying to maintain this distinction; and if the result of their labours seem to lack somewhat of the symmetry of an ordered manorial system, we shall do well to remember with what a mass of heterogeneous local custom they had to deal. It may be proper at this point to indicate some of the more serious complications which tend to make the distinction before us less definite than might at first sight appear.

If we restrict ourselves for the time to the standpoint of the manorial lord, we shall see that it was possible for an estate to be burdened in many ways, determined by the varying relations in which it stood with regard to other estates. A lord might well have a manor of which the soke lay in another manor external to his fief.[1] This presents no serious difficulty; but it was equally possible for a lord to hold *de soca* a parcel of land the soke of which was yet reserved to some other lord.[2] Such cases compel us to recognize that jurisdiction, dues, and

---

[1] Fo. 363: 'M. In Hermodestune [Harmston, Lincoln] habuit Copsi iii carucatas terrae et dimidiam ad geldum. . . . Ibi habet Radulfus [de Mortimer] i carucam in dominio. . . . Super hanc terram habet Hugo comes socam in Wadintone [Waddington].' Fo. 349 b: Earl Hugh possessed a large manor in Waddington, formerly the property of Earl Harold, to which 20 carucates in Harmston belonged as sokeland. Compare fo. 309: 'In Dirneshala habuit Elsi i manerium de iii carucatis. . . Soca hujus manerii pertinet ad Alverton [Northallerton].'

[2] So, for example, in that part of Hagworthingham, Lincoln, which is entered among the sokeland of Gilbert de Gand's manor of 'Torp'. Fo. 355: 'In Haberdingham vi bovatae terrae ad geldum. Terra x boum. Soca in Greetham.' On folio 349 Earl Hugh is assigned a parcel of land in Hagworthingham as sokeland of Greetham.

service were separable things, that there was no necessity for
a man who rendered service to a lord to be that lord's justici-
able, and that the agrarian and juridical ties between manor
and sokeland were not bound in practice to coincide. But it
is an added complication that by private arrangement the soke
of an estate was partible between individuals. When, for
example, we are told that two brothers had equally divided
among themselves the soke which had belonged to their father,
we may see here the result of a family treaty by which half
the dues received from the estate, half the profits of the
manorial court, and half the services rendered at the manorial
demesne had separately been assigned to each of the contract-
ing parties.[1] Some personal arrangement of this kind presumably underlies the surprising appearance of a half sokeman on
Robert de Stafford's Lincolnshire manor of Scredington and
Robert Dispensator's sokeland of Roughton.[2] Then, too, it
was possible in King Edward's day for one lord to give
soke to another in the witness of the wapentake, a fact
which rendered possible a variety of contested claims to land
and jurisdiction.[3] On all grounds, it is impossible for us to
conceive of the manors of the Danelaw as constituting a series
of mutually exclusive groups: the burdens which determined
the organization of the individual manor were so different in
character and so diverse in origin that here and there, inevitably, some overlapping was bound to result.

It is further to be noted that the systematic employment in
regard to this district of an unvarying terminology serves to
conceal the fact that the local organization, which that terminology was intended to represent, was at this particular
time in a peculiarly unstable condition. The whole scheme
according to which the Danelaw Domesday is drawn together
implies the assumption of an absolute continuity between the
conditions which obtained in King Edward's day and those
of the twentieth year of King William. That this assumption covers a remarkably transparent fiction is sufficiently
obvious; but it is not so easy to make the necessary allowance

---

[1] Fo. 375. The division gave rise to a dispute between the Bishop of
Durham and Eudo son of Spirewic. Compare fo. 340 b with fo. 359 b.
[2] Fo. 368 b, 363 b. Cf. the Torrington entries on fo. 358.   [3] Fo. 376 b.

for it when we argue back from the recorded facts of 1086 to the agrarian organization of 1066. We might illustrate the resulting uncertainty in many ways. There is, of course, a marked general tendency towards the conversion of pre-Conquest sokeland into manorialized estates; and yet there exist definite cases in which the reverse process has happened. If a thegn of 1066, holding a manor of which the soke belonged to some great estate, forfeited his land, it might well be that the land in question should appear in Domesday merely as sokeland of the larger manor to which it was jurisdictionally subject.[1] So too with reference to the difficult questions presented by the appearance of villeins or bordars upon sokeland, we may recognize that these men may very possibly represent native peasant proprietors of humble rank, and yet suspect that the new lord, by purchase, exchange, violation of local custom, assumption of fiscal responsibility, or succession to escheated tenements, has become possessed of land *in dominio* which our record is not careful to distinguish as such. Already in 1086 the great estates of the Danelaw with their satellitic dependencies were beginning to break up into independent *maneria*, and new forms of local association were coming into being; Chesterfield, which is entered in Domesday as a berewick of the royal manor of Newbold (fo. 272), appears in 1093 as a separate manor with berewicks of its own.[2] Vill and manor were as yet far from coincident; in the Danelaw this equation was never to become the rule;[3] but the disintegration of the greater estates was combining with the general amalgamation of the smaller maneria to produce an intermediate type of estate; an estate forming an independent agrarian unit, in which the features characteristic of the later manorial economy might find room for development. The Domesday Inquest was taken while this process was still in an early stage; but the tenurial conditions of the Danelaw were each year

---

[1] Fo. 351. East Keal, Lincoln. In 1086 4½ carucates were held here by Ivo Taillebois as sokeland of Bolingbroke, but at the end of the entry we are told 'Ibi habuit Summerled manerium, et valebat xx solidos T. R. E.—modo simile'. So fo. 303 b : 'Warnesfeld,' York. 'Ad Osboldewic [Osbaldwick] pertinet, scilicet tamen manerium fuit.'
[2] Mon. Ang. viii. 1271.   [3] See below, pp. 64-9.

passing more and more out of correspondence with the facts on which the terminology of the Survey was based.

And lastly, this terminology itself implies a cross division between the different kinds of tenements and the different classes of persons familiar to its authors. On the one hand, we are given the manor, the berewick, and the soke, as the three recognized forms of rural organization; on the other hand, the villeins, bordars, and sokemen, who constitute the rural population, are separated from each other by distinctions which have only a secondary reference to the position occupied by the members of each class in respect of their agrarian environment. On this we have already remarked; but it must be reiterated that we remain in virtual ignorance as to the status enjoyed by the predecessors of these men in King Edward's day.[1] The classical text descriptive of the organization of society in late Anglo-Saxon times, the *Rectitudines Singularum Personarum*, supplies information totally at variance with such evidence as we possess respecting the social classes revealed in the Danelaw Domesday. In part, no doubt, this discrepancy is due to the purpose which inspires the earlier record. The compiler of the *Rectitudines* had no intention of undertaking an analysis of the different orders of society; he wished to describe the services which were due from the several ranks of the manorial peasantry. But it is further probable that the *Rectitudines* relate to conditions which obtained in the south or south-west of England; and an argument from Dorset under King Æthelred to Lincolnshire under King William demands certain preliminary assumptions which we should be very unwilling to make, for the author of the latter tract explicitly tells us that services are many and various, and that he only writes of what he knows. It is at least certain that any attempt to identify in the Danelaw of 1086 the social ranks which are described in the *Rectitudines* breaks down in each instance at some critical point. If, following the terminology of the Glastonbury Inquisition,[2] we

---

[1] The Wantage code of Æthelred II, which from its terminology relates exclusively to the district of the Five Boroughs, contains little directly bearing upon the mutual relations of different social ranks.

[2] (Roxburgh Soc.) e.g. p. 26. Cf. Villainage in England, 144.

would see in the *geneat* of the *Rectitudines* the representative
of the Domesday *villanus*, we shall be compelled to ascribe
to the latter a degree of economic independence which is
scarcely warranted by the Danelaw texts, and to ignore the
many points of similarity between the *geneates riht* of the
Rectitudines and the services of the radknights of the western
shires. Even more improbable is the equation which has
been suggested between the *villanus* and the *gebur* ; for it is
a distinguishing mark of the latter's condition that he be
provided with stock by his lord, and the ubiquitous class of
villani is recorded on many a Danelaw manor whose former
owner, to all seeming, was himself but little wealthier than were
the peasants around him, nor can it be ignored that elsewhere
in England the *gebur* is represented by the *burus* of Domesday.[1] It cannot be doubted that the villein class was recruited
in part from both geneats and geburs, but the uniform terminology of Domesday has made it impossible to estimate
the relative proportions of these classes and to recover the
details of their pre-Conquest status. The correspondence
seems closer between the *cotsetle* and the *bordarius,* and yet
here too the *bordarii* as a whole seem considerably wealthier
than the oxless cottagers of the *Rectitudines* ; nor may we
fairly deny to the bordar of 1086 his share in the common
fields of his vill. Most plausible of all, it may be, is the
equation of the *geneat* with the *sokeman* of Domesday ; and
in this case we obtain for once an explicit documentary con-
tradiction of the suggested identification. In view of the writ,
entered in that most respectable of all English cartularies,
the *Textus Roffensis*,[2] by which the Conqueror grants to
Archbishop Lanfranc Freckenham in Cambridgeshire as Thur-
beorn and Goti held it of Harold in regard to ʽ lands, and

---

[1] This must not be pressed too far, for the burus appears so rarely in
Domesday that it is certain that no systematic record is made of his
existence.
[2] Wharton, Anglia Sacra, i. 336. The date of the writ is approximately
determined by the fact that Lanfranc gave the manor to Bishop Gundulf
of Rochester (app. 1077), and that before his fall in 1082 Odo of Bayeux
presided over a plea relating to the appurtenances of the manor, then in
Gundulf's possession.

meadows, and pasture, and wood, and geneats, and sokemen',
the geneat of Cambridgeshire was clearly a different type of
person from the sokeman of that shire.[1] Further than this
we need hardly go, for the whole tenor of the *Rectitudines*
suggests that in it we are reading the description of some
fully manorialized estate, in which by specialization of function
all the local peasantry have been brought into some definite
relation with an elaborate and highly developed organization
of labour service.[2] We shall travel widely over the Danelaw
shires before we find a manor of this sort ; and unless or until
some other record comes to light we must, it may be feared,
be content to take our sokemen, villeins, and bordars very
much as we find them in Domesday.

[1] The relevant Domesday entry occurs at fo. 190 b, under the name of
Gisleham [Isleham], to which Freckenham was appurtenant (Anglia Sacra,
i. 339). In 1066 twelve sokemen, all of whom could give and sell their
lands, held one hide under ' Turbert '. There was also a popular group
of eleven *villani*. Cf. Freeman, Norman Conquest, iv. 371.

[2] If, as is suggested, the *Rectitudines* comes from the south of England,
it would not be expected that the sokeman should be included within its
scope. Unlike the villein and the bordar, the sokeman bears a name of
English origin, and the writ quoted above carries back the name in
question to the time of King Edward.

IN a former section of this essay it was attempted to indicate the main distinctions between the two recognized types of subordinate tenement, known respectively as the berewick and the soke. It may be well at this point to consider some of the various forms assumed in the Danelaw by the manorial organization as a whole; and in particular to inquire how far it may be possible to trace these forms as already in being in the Old English period.

It is unfortunate that at the very outset of this inquiry we are faced by a problem which seems at present likely to remain insoluble in detail: the question as to the exact meaning which the term *manerium* itself bore to the Domesday scribes. The brilliant section which the late Professor Maitland devoted to the manor in his Domesday Book and Beyond [1] showed the impossibility of a retrospective application of the definitions recognized by the lawyers of the sixteenth century; and it enunciated a new theory upon the subject, of complete originality, which, if valid, would have supplied a clue to many difficult points arising from the terminology of the Survey. But the theory that the manor was the ultimate unit in the collection of the geld has, one must sorrowfully admit, not stood the test of detailed criticism; and the tendency of scholars at the present time is to deny that the word *manerium* was in any sense a technical term to the men of 1086. And so the inquiry has come to assume somewhat of a different form; and instead of seeking for definitions which shall be of general application we are rather compelled to investigate the various characteristic features assumed by the manorial group in different parts of England, and in particular to ask in what manner these features may have been relevant to the general purpose of the Domesday Survey.

In the shires with which we are here concerned we are at

[1] Pp. 107-28.

once impressed with the care taken by the Domesday scribes to record the name of the native owner of every tenement to which the *manerium* formula is applied.[1] We remember that in the famous Ely writ the commissioners were required to ask who held the *mansio* in King Edward's time, as well as the name of the contemporary owner ; and in regard to the Danelaw shires, other than Leicester, the answers to the former question are recorded with unusual consistency. Now this fact seems to argue a general correspondence between the *manerium* of Domesday and the *heafod botl* of late pre-Conquest documents, the *capitale messuagium* of the thirteenth century. Whatever may have been the native word which was represented by the Domesday *manerium*, and there is some evidence to suggest that the Old English *tūn* was employed in this sense in the eleventh century, if not earlier,[2] it must sometimes have connoted the lord's dwelling. Direct evidence in this matter is somewhat to seek ; but it is supplied in a measure by certain Yorkshire entries which suggest that the recognition of a given tenement as a *manerium* depended on the former existence of a ' hall ' on the property. On folio 317 occur the following pair of entries :—

> M. et B. In Cevet [Chevet] sunt ad geldum iiii carucatae terrae . . . Duae car: et dim: sunt in soca de Tateshalla et i car: et dim: inlant. Ibi tamen habuit Norman aulam.

---

[1] Frequent instances in which the name is deliberately interlined or corrected show the importance which the scribes attached to this matter. The formula ' A tenuit B *pro manerio* ' is only used when through exigencies of space the entry relating to a manor was not, according to custom, made in column, where the symbol M could be applied to it.

[2] Such a conclusion is made probable, for instance, by the application of the name ' Esegarestun ' to a Berkshire estate held in 1066 by ' Esegar ' the Staller, an estate in which all the normal features of the manorial economy were already present. Other evidence bearing upon this point is cited in my essay on the Place-names of Berkshire (University College, Reading), pp. 26, 28. It is probable that beside the common employment of OE. *tūn* to denote a village or village community there persisted a distinct usage, going back to the original meaning of the word—' an enclosure '—a usage by which the word came to describe the dwelling or homestead of the lord apart from the neighbouring village. The OE. word most nearly approximating to the Norman *manerium* would seem to be *hām*, an equation not affected by the failure of the suggested correspondence of *hām* and *villa*. (Seebohm, English Village Community, 287.)

S. et B. In Hindeleia [Hiendley] sunt iiii carucatae terrae ad geldum ... Tres car: sunt in soca de Tatesĥalla et i inland.

The distinction of the first of these estates as a manor is clearly occasioned by the existence there, in 1066, of North-man's hall, notwithstanding the fact that by the date of the Survey his holding had been incorporated in the great manor of Tateshall-Pontefract. The possible identification of manor and hall is further suggested by two entries which come earlier in the Yorkshire Survey:—

fo. 309. In Langeton ix car: ad geldum ... Ibi habuerunt Torfin (iii et dim:) et Finegal (ii car:) ii haulas, Torfin cum saca et soca ; et tercius, nomine Tor, reliquam terram cum saca et soca, scilicet non haula.

fo. 309 b. In Stradford ad geldum vi car: ... Ibi fuerunt Tor et Torfin ; iste habuit manerium, alius non.

It is evident that these entries are really expressing a similar distinction in different phraseology : the *aula* of the first is clearly represented by the *manerium* of the second. Very suggestive also are the following entries from the Nottingham-shire Survey :—

fo. 286 b M$_3$. In Fentone [Fenton] habuerunt Ulfac et Leuric et Grim i bovatam terrae et iii^{ciam} partem i bovatae ad geldum ... Wasta est praeter unum bordarium. ...

Ibidem habuit Speravoc ii bovatas terrae et ii partes unius bovatae ad geldum. Terra i car cum saca et soca sine aula.—

for the absence of a hall on Sperhavoc's property is plainly the reason why it is not distinguished as a manor by the marginal symbol M.[1] Finally, the description of Normanton-on-Trent on the previous folio of the survey—' M$_5$. In Normentune habuerunt v taini, Justan, Durand, Elward, Ulmar, Aseloc quisque aulam suam et unusquisque i bovatam terrae et v partem i bovatae ad geldum '—shows not only that the normal manor would contain its hall, but that these halls might well be humble structures, the dwellings of men of little wealth ; the combined estates of these five thegns had been worth but ten shillings in King Edward's time, and none

---

[1] Compare folio 306 [Yorkshire]: ' In Mitune [Myton] habuit Ligulf i M de iiii carucatis et dim. ... In Bratfortune [Brafferton] habuit Haltor i carucatam sine halla.'

of them can be identified with certainty elsewhere in the shire.

From the standpoint which we have now reached, therefore, it seems legitimate to say that the typical Danelaw manor of 1066 comprised a thegn's residence, situate upon an estate to which services were rendered, and at which dues were paid. From this type, indeed, there are many and wide divergences, but this hardly affects the general correspondence of an overwhelming majority of actual instances. It may, in fact, be suggested that the search for manorial definitions in the past has caused somewhat undue importance to be assigned to those manors which do not conform to the general type. The type itself is susceptible of great variation in detail ; but geographical considerations, private arrangements made by individual landowners, incidents in the unrecorded family history of the lesser thegns of the Danelaw, must all fully be allowed for in this connexion. Perhaps, after all, the wonder is rather that there should be such substantial uniformity, in all significant features, among estates so diverse in history, and scattered over so wide an area.

Now, in this connexion, it is well to remember that by making an accurate record of the names of all pre-Conquest holders of manorial tenements the compilers of the Danelaw Domesday were taking a step which was necessary if the main purpose of the Inquest were adequately to be fulfilled. The possession of an estate carried with it a liability to the payment of geld ; very possibly, as we have seen, it implied the responsibility for the geld due from all those portions of the estate which constituted the lord's inland ; and it is at least clear that the latter's title rested upon his succession in the holding in question to some Englishman who in the regard of the law was among his recognized *antecessores*. It therefore seems distinctly probable that in the desire to provide for the settlement of disputed claims to the ownership of land we have the reason underlying some of the more prominent features of the Danelaw Surveys : the systematic definition of given estates as *maneria*, the care taken in such cases to record the name of the pre-Conquest owner, and the attribution of each parcel of inland or sokeland to its own proper manorial centre. It will be seen that the very complexity of the local organization of the Danelaw made it peculiarly necessary to restore, so far as might be, in the terminology of the Survey, the *status quo ante Conquestum*, and it is at least probable that the accurate registration of all pre-Conquest *maneria* represents one aspect of the process. It would be straining a slender thread of evidence to assert that the Danelaw manerium always denoted an estate passed by a single title; but with the Clamores of Yorkshire and Lincolnshire before us we cannot doubt that the majority of disputed claims would involve, at some stage or other, an inquiry into the extent or ownership of some pre-Conquest *manerium*, and the Domesday scribes seem to be trying to supply the information which was necessary if the manors of King Edward's day were to be brought into legal connexion with the estates which represented them in 1086.

It would appear, then, in relation to the manor, soke, and berewick of the Danelaw that the two latter only are contrasted types of tenement. The manor is the lord's residence, the *capitale messuagium*, the tenement of which the possession carries a title to all the land assigned to the estate, either as inland or sokeland, by local repute. The word *manerium*, it would seem, bore no necessary relation to the facts of agrarian or fiscal organization, it was sufficiently vague to cover the most diverse forms of internal arrangement, it was no technical term of law. We may suspect, indeed, that the smallest manors of the Danelaw may, after all, be distinguished in a somewhat arbitrary fashion from the tenements of the independent sokemen who inhabited the unmanorialized vills of the north and east; one manor, we know, might well render soke to another manor, and questions of personal rank, which we can never hope to solve, may at times have influenced the compilers of Domesday when they assigned a manor to one vanished Englishman by name, and consigned his fellow to the undifferentiated class of *sochemanni*.[1]   On all grounds it is

---

[1] There is one, and apparently only one, Lincolnshire entry in which sokemen appear as holding manors before the Conquest. Fo. 366: 'East Deeping. Ibidem habuit S. Peter de Burg v soch(emannos) super

well to be indefinite in regard to this matter ; for concerning the smallest manors of the Danelaw we have no pre-Conquest evidence at all, while already in 1086 these anomalous estates were rapidly being amalgamated into larger agrarian units. But at least we shall have one complication the less if we disengage the *manerium* from its unnecessary contrast with the inland and sokeland recorded for us in relation to subsidiary holdings.

From all this, it will appear that any classification of the maneria of the Danelaw must recognize the essential distinction between the seignorial bond which united manor and sokeland and the proprietary bond which united manor and berewick. This distinction cannot, indeed, be applied with rigour in relation to individual estates ; the seignorial and proprietary forces combine to produce the discrete maneria of the Danelaw ; but it is the peculiar value of the formulas which we are considering that they enable us to trace the local application of these forces with a precision unattainable when, as in the case of Leicestershire, the formulas fail us.   And, on the whole, we may fairly relegate to one great class all those estates in which a central messuage carries a right to the receipt of dues, and the exaction of service and suit of court from tenements which are geographically separated and outside the immediate ownership of the lord ; making always the reservation that it is generally impossible to say whether the economic force represented in the payment of rent and consuetudines, the jurisdictional force represented in subjection to sake and soke, or the tenurial bond created by the act of commendation, is the more powerful in maintaining the organization of the group.   We certainly may not affirm that the very large number of *maneria* which will be referred to this class

v maneria de ii car. terrae et vi bovatis ad geldum.' Here the sokemen were to all appearance tenants of the abbey, differing, probably, in little except rank from those thegnly holders of abbey lands, of whom Hereward was the most famous. The formulas employed in this entry are unique and remarkable, and a scribal error might be suspected were it not that sokemen appear as holding manors in a number of Huntingdonshire and Northamptonshire entries. We may question, in passing, whether the Domesday commissioners would have thought it proper to describe the normal sokeman's toft as a ' hall '.

do more than correspond to one general type; we have seen that since the Conquest lords have steadily been bringing fragments of discrete sokeland within the sphere of their *dominium*, and we may not press the terminology of the survey too far; but if any classification of estates is to be attempted at all, then the manor with dependent sokeland must be regarded as one distinct form of local organization.[1]

If, now, we pass to those estates which may be understood as resting upon a proprietary basis, the work of classification seems naturally to turn upon the varying relation borne by the tenurial unit, the manor, to the agrarian unit, the vill. Everywhere in England manorial development was making for the coincidence of these units; but the process had gone but a little way in the Danelaw at the time of the Norman settlement. For the purpose of our present classification we may relegate to a separate division those manors which are conterminous with the vills which give them name, which have no dependent berewick or sokeland, and in which the common fields of the vill form the sole economic basis of the estate; but, at least in regard to Nottinghamshire and Lincolnshire, an extended study of the local surveys is necessary before a manor which has already assumed this form in 1066 may be discovered.[2] The distribution of landed property in the Danelaw at the close of the Old English period, so far as our evidence goes, had by the process of time been thrown out of all relation to the ancient and natural agrarian divisions of the country, the vills. And it is just here that the work of the new Norman lords, as revealed by Domesday, is on the whole most obvious and most beneficial. In restoring, if not in creating, a general correspondence between the unit of agrarian life and the unit of seignorial organization, they had begun, twenty years after the Conquest, a process which was to arrange

---

[1] The significance of the type is not affected by the fact that parcels of land in neighbouring vills will frequently be annexed as berewicks to the chief manor, as at Mickleover, Derby, Newark and Dunham, Nottingham.

[2] The Nottinghamshire Survey makes entry of some 270 vills. Out of this number it would be difficult to cite more than twenty cases in which there was exact identity between vill and manor in 1066. Most of these exceptions are places of little importance, and some of them have disappeared since 1086.

the manorial geography of England on the lines most con-
ducive to agricultural efficiency; a process which in an un-
conquered England could never have been attempted. We
may admit that their work was followed by a depression of
the peasantry subject to their rule, though there is little direct
evidence to suggest that this frequently happened in the Danelaw shires; but it is well to remember that the imposition
of a heavier burden of service was accompanied by changes in
the direction of administrative economy which made the
incidence of that burden less severe; in particular, cases where
the labourer had to tramp across country to his lord's remote
demesne would now rarely occur.[1]

One obvious aspect of these changes is presented by the
deliberate amalgamation of small estates into single manors,
coincident with the vills from which their names were derived.
Before the Conquest the lands which comprised the Nottinghamshire fief of Roger de Busli (fos. 284 b–287) had been
divided into 183 distinct *maneria*; as recorded in Domesday,
the number had been reduced to ninety. The organization, in
1066, of these small *maneria* is utterly obscure; but we may
with perfect confidence infer a considerable degree of inter-
dependence in the matter of their agricultural life. In Nottinghamshire, at Weston-on-Trent (fo. 285 b), where there were
once six manors, at Eaton (fo. 284 b), where there were ten, at
Carlton-in-Lindrick, comprising six (fo. 285), at Hawton,
comprising five (fo. 289 b), we certainly cannot endow each
manor with a distinct set of common fields, even although we
cannot now recover the details of the arrangements which
must have obtained in regard to the practices of coaration, the
use and apportionment of common pasture, and all the multi-
farious activity of the village community. In such cases as
Killingholme-in-Lindsey, where in 1086 a population of eleven
villeins was working an estate, divided, twenty years earlier,
into six manors (fo. 347), the latter term cannot in any intel-

---

[1] It is to be noted that the whole question of the labour service performed in King Edward's time by the men of outlying *membra* has to be
considered without direct evidence. In most cases it is probable that the
men of the central manor were sufficient for the performance of the work
required by the home farm.

ligible sense have an agricultural signification; the thegn's hall, though not recorded in this particular entry, is clearly the feature which has constituted the *manerium*. And in a number of cases, not now to be determined, we may suspect with reason that the division of a small estate into many maneria results not from the fortuitous association of a body of small landowners, but from the partition of an inhabited holding among a group of kinsmen. Those five thegns of Normanton-on-Trent, each of whom had his hall, bore each an equal share, a bovate and its fifth part, of the assessment laid upon the whole property; and we are reminded of the four thegns of Candleshoe wapentake of whom it is said that in King Edward's time they had divided their father's land among themselves *equaliter et pariliter*.[1] The Survey will at times explicitly indicate the relationship existing between the holders of a divided manor; and in those cases in which a whole group of small estates has been given outright to some Norman lord, we may readily believe that the original unity of the property lay well within the memory of the people of the country-side assembled in the wapentake court.

But this does not always happen; in many villages the little manors of 1066 have been given severally to as many different lords,[2] and in subsequent history have followed quite independent lines of devolution. A remarkable illustration of this development is afforded by the Lincolnshire village of Keelby in Yarburgh wapentake, in regard to which our evidence is unusually consistent. The situation in 1066 is best explained by a table, which incidentally displays the combination of many fractional assessments into a neat 'duodecimal' total of six carucates, and thus gives assurance that the whole of the vill is under review :—

[1] Fo. 375 b.
[2] It may, of course, happen that even when a group of manors within one vill has been given outright to a new lord the individual manors were unequal, at least as regards assessment. Thus at Rothwell, York (fo. 317 b), Harold had 14 carucates; Bared, $7\frac{1}{2}$; Alric, $10\frac{1}{2}$ bovates; Stainulf, the same.

	Assessment Car. Bov.	Teamlands	Teams Demesne	Teams Mens.	Sokemen	Villeins	Bordars	
Soke of Caistor .	1	7 (not given)	—	2	13	—	3	fo. 338 b
Manor, Elaf .	$4\frac{1}{2}$	$1\frac{1}{2}$	$\frac{1}{2}$	—	2	—	2	fo. 339 b
„ Sigar .	$4\frac{1}{2}$	$1\frac{1}{2}$	1	$\frac{1}{4}$	3	2	—	fo. 342 b
„ Aldene.	$5\frac{2}{3}$	$1\frac{3}{8}$	1	$\frac{1}{4}$	—	4	1	fo. 344 b
„ Alwine.	2	$\frac{1}{2}$	$\frac{1}{2}$	$\frac{1}{8}$	—	2	1	fo. 350 b
„ Rolf .	1 0	3	1	2	—	10	1	fo. 360 [1]
„ Grimchel	$5\frac{1}{3}$	$1\frac{3}{16}$	1	$\frac{1}{4}$	—	4	2	fo. 361 b
„ Eiric .	$3\frac{1}{3}$	$1\frac{13}{16}$	$\frac{1}{8}$	—	1	—	2	fo. 365 b
	6 0	$(9\frac{1}{8})$	$5\frac{1}{8}$	$4\frac{7}{8}$	19	22	12	

These figures are instructive in many ways. The proportion of sokemen to villeins and bordars is lower than the average for the county as a whole; a fact probably resulting from the subdivision of the vill into small estates; for sokemen are found in greatest numbers either on unmanorialized sokeland, or else within the bounds of the larger manors of the district.[2] There was little room for the independent freeholder upon the two bovates which Alwine possessed in Keelby. It may also be noted, in passing, that on each manor the carucates and bovates of assessment approximate to half the number of teamlands assigned to the estate; it is just in this quarter, on the north-eastern edge of the Lincoln Wolds, that the Lincolnshire teamlands reach their greatest point of excess over the figures which relate to the geld. But for our immediate purpose the most important feature of the vill is the complete independence, in regard to tenure, of the individual manors into which it was divided. Nearly one-third of the vill, in 1086, belonged to the great royal soke of Caistor, and as such does not concern us here, but Elaf's manor had passed to the Archbishop of York; that of Sigar, to the Bishop of Bayeux; that of Aldene, to the Bishop of Lincoln; that of Alwine, to Ivo Taillebois; Rolf's land, to Dru de Beurere; that of Grimchel, to Norman d'Arcy; that of Eiric, to Waldin

[1] In this entry vel Cotes is interlined above Chelebi, and in the Lindsey Survey this carucate is assigned to Coates. But it is wanted to complete the assessment of Keelby, and the name of this vill is not marked for deletion in fo. 360. Presumably part of the property lay in Coates, and the entry makes mention of a salina, or salt-pan, which we should expect to be found near the coast, a condition which applies to the latter vill.

[2] For example, Robert de Todeni's three-carucate manor of Allington included a population of 14 sokemen, 5 villeins, and as many bordars.

'Ingeniator'. It is evident that at Keelby the identity of vill and manor was as remote in 1086 as in the time of King Edward. And not only is this the case, but the Lindsey Survey, thirty years after Domesday, shows the persistence of these little manors within the vill until at least the middle of the reign of Henry I. Changes of a catastrophic order had placed a new series of lords in possession of the vills of Lindsey; but the seven manors of Keelby maintained their independent existence through all.[1] The successor of the Archbishop of York still held the $4\frac{1}{2}$ bovates which had belonged to Elaf; the Bishop of Bayeux was represented by Manasser Arsic; the Bishop of Lincoln, by his successor; Ivo Taillebois, by Ranulf Mischin; Dru de Beurere, by Stephen of Aumâle; Norman d'Arcy, surviving from a previous generation, remained in possession of his holding; Geoffrey, the son of Payn, had in this case obtained the land of Waldin Ingeniator. The divided lordship of the village of Keelby can thus be established by documents extending over a period of half a century; and this although the figures given by Domesday argue an inevitable co-operation in agricultural work between the men of one manor and the men of another. The ten plough-teams which found employment within the vill in 1086 result only from the combination of the scattered oxen of the men of eight distinct lords with the teams, fractional or entire, working upon their respective demesnes. And so we are reminded again that beneath the superficial distinctions of manor, sokeland, or inland, there lies throughout the ultimate agrarian unit, the vill.[2]

This may be further illustrated in another way. There has been preserved a remarkable series of documents relating to the Nottinghamshire vills of Staunton, Alverton, and Kilvington, which strikingly reveal both the survival to a late period

---

[1] As the soke of Caistor was royal demesne, it is excluded from the scope of the Lindsey Survey.

[2] The intermixture of different estates in the open fields of a village is sometimes illustrated in a striking way by the distribution of the village tithes. The tithes of Flawborough, Notts, for example, were divided between three different churches in a manner which clearly reproduces the ancient division of the village between its various lords. From a detailed survey of 1637 it is evident that three adjacent strips in the fields might well tithe to as many distinct parishes.

of estates formed already before the Conquest, and also the intermixture of these estates in the open fields of the respective villages.   Details could not well be given here without a consideration of minute points of local topography, but it may at least be said that the evidence supplies a useful warning against an exaggeration of the completeness with which the work of manorialization was effected after 1086.   The village of Alverton became united at last in the hands of one lord ; but it was in the reign of Queen Elizabeth.   In the thirteenth century the several Domesday estates are still to be traced, though with some difficulty, scattered in many strips over the village furlongs, interspersed among each other in a way which admits of no simple explanation ; and the tenurial geography is complicated by the results of feofments of which no explicit record has been preserved, made by lords whose identity can only be guessed at.   A grantee will speak of his *capitale messuagium* in a context which implies that it lay in line with the tofts and crofts of the village peasantry ; his lands will be scattered indiscriminately over the common fields.   The court of any given manor was far from being a court for all the men of any entire vill ; in the time of Charles II, twice a year and on the same days, two courts were held in Staunton for the two manors into which that vill was divided, and to one of them the men of Alverton and Kilvington did suit, vills which were already sokeland of Staunton in the time of King Edward.   Nowhere in any early document is there a hint that any lord's demesne was drawn into a compact holding round a central farm.   And although there is evidence which suggests a depression of some at least of the inhabitants of Alverton between 1086 and 1190, many of the later freeholders within the village may well be the successors in title of Domesday sokemen.

And just as we are compelled to admit the frequent persistence in this region of the pre-Conquest division of vills, we are also bound to recognize the occasional survival of those anomalous territorial associations, the Danelaw sokes.   The survival of the great Leicestershire soke of Rothley is well known, owing in great part to the preservation of its thirteenth-century custumal, which reveals the internal economy of one of these groups with a clearness unattainable in other cases. But Rothley was only one soke out of many which maintained their substantial integrity into the thirteenth century or later. In Lincolnshire, for example, Queen Edith's soke of Gayton le Wold, held by the King in 1086, had passed entire to the Count of Brittany by 1116 [1]; an original charter of approximately 1154 has been preserved, in which Count Alan grants to the men ' dē Gattunasoca' all the liberties which they enjoyed in the time of Count Stephen his grandfather, and in the thirteenth century the soke was held by Peter of Savoy,[2] successor of the Counts of Brittany in the English earldom of Richmond. The first entry in the Lindsey Survey assigns to the Earl of Chester 34 carucates 2½ bovates 'in Halton et Soca',[3] the exact assessment, in Domesday, of the manor and soke of West Halton, which belonged to Earl Hugh of Chester, and before him to Earl Harold of Wessex. In Derbyshire, in 1204–5, William Briwere was holding the manor of Chesterfield with Brimington, Whittington, and the soke and wapentake of Scarsdale,[4] a fact which suggests that the Domesday soke of Newbold, of which Chesterfield was then a berewick, arose in close connexion with the court of the wapentake in which these places lay. In general, it may be said that the larger the soke the greater was its power of resistance to disintegrating influences; and royal sokes, in particular, were held together by the exaction from the whole body of aids and tallages. In 1177 the sheriff of Nottingham accounted for £13 13s. 4d. as aid of the soke of Oswardbeck,[5] and also for the aids of Orston and Arnold, royal manors with appurtenant sokeland in Domesday. In 1197–8 [6] the tallage of the soke of Mansfield produced £6 13s. ; in the first year of King John the tallage of Dunham soke brought in £3 16s. More important in this respect, nevertheless, was the performance of suit to the court of the soke : in the reign of Henry III a peasant grantor, in

[1] Lindsey Survey.   [2] Ancient Charters, 54–5 and notes.
[3] Such, at least, is my reading of the abraded opening of the MS. Mr. Greenstreet, in his translation, read ' Halton and Scotho', which is impossible; Mr. Chester Waters (Associated Architectural Societies' Reports and Papers, xvi. part 2, 181) ignored the difficulty.
[4] Pipe Roll, 6 John.
[5] Pipe Roll, 23 Henry II.   [6] Pipe Roll, 9 Richard I.

conveying land to his brother, is careful to add that the rents reserved to the lords of the fee are in lieu of suit to their courts, to shire and wapentake, 'et maxime pro secta quae debetur in sochagio de Horstona die Sancti Thomae apostoli ante natale Domini.'[1] In the time of Charles II the great court on St. Thomas' Day was still held for the soke of Orston.[2] In the north of the same county the important soke of Oswardbeck can be traced in successive grants until at least the reign of Henry VII; under James I we are told that John Thorneaughe, knight, was bailiff of the king's liberty of Oswardbeck soke[3]; and in the thirteenth century we obtain a glimpse of the soke from the tenant's point of view when we are told that Petronilla of Woodhouse[4] held lands in la Wodehouse in the soke of Oswardbeck, and a moiety of a mill in Tilne, doing suit at Oswardbeck court.[5] Even at the present time courts are held in North Nottinghamshire which descend directly from the soke of Sutton which the Archbishop of York held in 1066. We cannot, in face of the evidence of which these facts are merely casual illustrations, deny that during the twelfth and thirteenth centuries the soke was still a characteristic feature of the local organization of the Danelaw shires.

Lastly, reference must here be made to the type of manor which extends into many different vills, and over many distinct sets of common fields—the manor with satellitic berewicks. This type attains its fullest development in the royal manors of the Peak of Derbyshire; it is represented in the ancient estate held by the Archbishop of York at Southwell in Nottinghamshire; it is rarely found in Lincolnshire; and in Yorkshire, although the estate of a great man will frequently be the centre of a large number of scattered berewicks, it will commonly receive the soke of an even greater number of independent tenements also.[6] The organization of the individual

---

[1] Original charter in Staunton MSS.

[2] Thoroton, Hist. Nottinghamshire, ed. Throsby, i. 228.

[3] Ibid. iii. 334.   [4] Inquisitiones post mortem, 52 Henry III.

[5] In an Inquisition of uncertain date under Henry III tenants in Leverton, Saundby, North Woodhouse, Clarborough Wiseton, Fenton, 'Sudbeck', and Little Welham are represented as owing talliage, and suit to Oswardbeck court.

[6] A fine example of this type of estate is presented by the royal manor of Northallerton: 'In Alvertune sunt ad geldum xliiii carucatae. . . . Huic

berewick must have varied greatly according as it constituted a vill of itself or merely formed part, perhaps a very insignificant part, of some villar group. We may not even assume that the employment of the term berewick in all cases implies that the holding to which it is applied possessed any agricultural organization distinct from that of the chief manor to which it belonged. Where a manor straggled over the lands of two or more adjacent vills[1] the whole group may very well have been worked as a single agricultural estate, and the introduction of the term berewick into the Survey may in such cases be only intended to emphasize the fact that the lands of the manor extended beyond the limits of the vill in which the chief messuage lay.[2] Also, as we have seen, there is evidence that the term berewick was actually employed to denote a detached piece of inland—a use carrying no agricultural connotation at all. But these qualifications need not prevent our recognizing this as a type distinct from those other forms of manorial association which we have been considering ; and the manor with dependent berewicks is undoubtedly an institution of high antiquity in the Danelaw as elsewhere.[3]

M appendent xi berewitae, Bretebi [Bretby], Smidetune [Smeaton], Sourebi [Sowerby], " Smitune ", Kirkebi [Kirkby], Corkeholme [Cockholme], Landemot [Landmoth], Bergebi [Borrowby], Gristorentun [? Graystone], Romundebi [Romanby], Yaforde [Yafforth]. . . . Ad hoc manerium pertinet soca harum terrarum, Neuhuse [Newsham], Westhuse [   ], Mannebi [Maunby], Werlegesbi [Warlaby], Eindrebi [Ainderby], Yaford [Yafforth], Leisenchi [   ], Digneshale [   ], Runtune [Rounton], Irebi [Irby], Haressare [? Harlsey], Sighestun [Sigston], Colebi [Coleby], Timbelbi [Thimbleby], Leche [Leake], Chenneton [   ], Ravenestorp [Raventhorpe], Torentun [Thornton], Croxebi [Crosby], Otrinctun [Otterington], Romundebi [Romanby], Brunton [Brompton], Chelvintun [Kilvington], Chenevetun [Knayton].'

[1] For example, the common fields of the Nottinghamshire vills of Kilvington and Alverton can be shown to have been adjacent, with at most a headland between them. It is therefore natural that Colegrim's manor on fo. 291 b should simply be described as lying ' in Chelvinctune et Alvreton ', and it is not probable that the Alverton portion of the estate was organized as a separate berewick.

[2] That strict consistency in denoting berewicks as such was not observed by the scribes is shown by the duplicate entries relating to Overton with Stretton, Rutland. In one entry the word Ber(ewica) is interlined above ' Stratone ', in the other this distinction is ignored. See V. C. H. Rutland, i. 130.

[3] The word berewick does not occur in any early land-books relating to the northern Danelaw. Its first appearance would seem to be in the

In the attempt to carry the study of these manorial types into the period which lies behind the Norman Conquest, we are at once confronted by the fewness and the inferior quality of the texts which relate to this part of England. No land-book relating to any part of the true Danelaw has been preserved in an original manuscript; excluding certain obvious fabrications, mostly perpetrated in the interest of the abbeys of Crowland and Peterborough, the earliest charter available for our purpose is only dated 834,[1] and nearly a century passes before we obtain another relevant document. The total number of such documents, it may be admitted, is somewhat greater than might at first sight be supposed; for in three particular cases the faulty identification of the estates conveyed has referred land-books of Derbyshire, Leicestershire, and Yorkshire origin to Staffordshire, Worcestershire, and Durham respectively[2]; but it is at best with but a scanty collection of texts that we have to deal. To this we must add that the sources from which the greater number of these texts are derived are not of such a nature as to inspire confidence. The Liber Albus of York, from which we obtain four important documents, is a late compilation; the English of the boundaries transcribed in it is so corrupt as to be almost unintelligible[3]; and the charters themselves present grave difficulties of chronology and style. The latter become still more serious with reference to the Hengwrt manuscript, a cartulary compiled in the thirteenth century and apparently in the interest of the abbey of Burton-on-Trent, from which nine charters can be

---

Medeshamstede Memoranda (C. S. 1128) 'Medeshamstede & ta berewican þa þar to heren, & Anlafestun & þam berewican þar to' (*sic*). In the spurious memorandum entered in the Laud MS. of the Chronicle under 963 'thorp' is used as equivalent to berewick, 'Medeshamstede ... & ealle þa þorpes þe ðærto lin, þ is Astfeld & Dodesthorp [Dogs thorpe] & Ege [Eye] & Pastun [Paston].'

[1] This document (C. S. 414) is merely a grant of land at Wirksworth, Derbyshire, by Cynewaru, Abbess of Repton, in return for a rent of lead payable to Christ Church, Canterbury. It is derived from the late thirteenth-century Christ Church cartulary, the text of which cannot implicitly be trusted, but the present deed seems genuine.

[2] C. S. 884, 1283, 1113.

[3] Canon Dixon, in his Fasti Eboracenses, 209, note y, remarks that the compiler of the Liber Albus 'confesses his inability to decipher the Saxon charters which he professes to give'.

cited with reference to the Danelaw.[1] Composed in flamboyant and alliterative Latin,[2] these documents form a class apart from most contemporary texts, and their value for our purpose is seriously impaired by the omission of all boundaries from the manuscript.[3] The Hengwrt texts must perforce be used, but we cannot ignore the diplomatic suspicions to which their character gives rise.

Their peculiar value for us consists in the fact that they throw a faint light upon the early history of what is perhaps the most remarkable group of estates in the whole Danelaw— the ancient demesne of the Peak of Derbyshire. The geographical features of this district, the abrupt alternations of hill and dale, the narrow valleys and wide expanses of moor, admirably fitted for pasture, but ill-suited for cultivation as arable, produced a type of estate quite dissimilar from anything found elsewhere in the Danelaw shires. In this quarter, scattered unevenly over the wide district which extends transversely from the Dove at Ashbourne to the Yorkshire border,

[1] These charters were unknown to Kemble; those prior to 975 have been printed by Birch in the Cartularium Saxonicum. But in the Appendix to the Second Report Hist. MSS. Com. (p. 105) a list is given of twelve more documents dating between 984 and 1048, some of which relate to the Danelaw. Land, for instance, is granted in the vills of Ash, Alfreton, Mickleover, and Eggington in Derbyshire. It is to be hoped that these charters will before long be published.

[2] For the unusual nature of the royal style in a number of these charters see Asser, ed. Stevenson, 148, note 2.

[3] The general impossibility of any successful identification of the estates conveyed by charters which contain no boundaries is most remarkably illustrated by the case of C. S. 978, a document from the Hengwrt series. A tenth-century copy of this charter is preserved, including the boundaries, which are omitted in the cartulary text. The document represents a grant by King Eadwig to a certain thegn, his namesake, of eight *mansae* at 'Brantestun', and the known connexion between the Hengwrt MS. and Burton Abbey would seem to afford conclusive proof that 'Brantestun' is identical with the Staffordshire village of Branston, three miles from Burton, which belonged to the abbey in the eleventh century. This identification, however, is finally disproved by a clause in the boundaries which reads 'of þam cumbe on geriht in on limenan, adun andlang streames oð hit cymð on wiliabys' (*sic*). The *Limine* is the Warwickshire river Leam, on which stands the village of Willoughby near Daventry, represented by the 'wiliabys' (< Wiliabyg) of the text, and the land conveyed evidently lay in the adjacent village of Braunston just across the Northamptonshire border. With this example before us we shall hesitate before we identify the Hwituntun of C. S. 642, for instance, with Whittington near Lichfield rather than with Whittington near Chesterfield.

King Edward in 1066 had possessed eight manors, each comprising a group of berewicks varying in number from three to twelve, but including no recorded sokeland. For the purpose of making a yearly render to the king, a render presented in silver, honey, and lead, these manors were divided into two groups ; and it is highly probable that each group was treated as a separate unit in the assessment to the geld. To the first there belonged the five manors of Darley, ' Mestesford ' (Matlock Bridge), Wirksworth, Ashbourne, and Parwich ; bearing with their 25 berewicks an aggregate assessment of 54 carucates, and containing a population of 89 villeins and 56 bordars. The second group extended northwards in continuation of the first, but probably lay in another wapentake[1] ; it comprised three estates, centring in the vills of Bakewell, Ashford, and Hope, rated at 50 carucates, including 27 berewicks, and supporting at the date of the survey 81 villeins and 13 bordars. Each group had sustained some wastage in the years which preceded the holding of the great Inquest ; but when all allowance has been made on this score, the sparseness of the population scattered over this wide area, and the small amount of arable land included within it, clearly result in the first instance from the conformation of the ground.

Now in the case of this highly exceptional estate it is very probable that the word berewick really bore its primary agricultural signification in 1086.[2] The twelve satellitic hamlets annexed to Ashford, for example, seem individually too small for an independent existence ; their names in general, though no doubt compatible with, do not themselves suggest an original settlement on the lines of the normal village com-

[1] The manor of Darley adjoins the manor of Bakewell. The rubrication of the Derbyshire survey is very defective, but Darley is explicitly stated to be in Hammenstan wapentake, and it is probable that Bakewell and the other northern manors lay in the wapentake afterwards known as that of the High Peak, which is not mentioned in Domesday. For the estate as a whole cf. V. C. H. Derby, i. 295–7, 330–33.
[2] It may be noted that at the middle of the twelfth century the OE. *hiorda wic* retained its original meaning in the Peak. In the foundation charter of Bredon Priory (Leicester) the Earl of Nottingham, that is of Nottingham with Derby, grants *unam herdewicam in Hethcote juxta Hertedona* [*Hartington*] *in Pecco* (Mon. Ang. vi. 97).

munity[1]; and they are most naturally understood as a collection of scattered but dependent farmsteads, playing a part accessory to the agricultural activities of the chief manor. The arrangement, in fact, would seem to have resulted in the first instance from the configuration of the ground; and it thus becomes antecedently probable that these manors, as described in Domesday, represent agricultural groups of some considerable antiquity. The evidence of the Hengwrt land-books, which carry the history of these manors back to the very beginning of the tenth century, is very definitely in favour of such a conclusion.

The tale begins with a land-book of 926,[2] the authenticity of which is proved by the recurrence of its formulas in another charter of the same date, derived from the unrelated cartulary of the Berkshire monastery of Abingdon.[3]   In this document Æthelstan confirms to the *fidelis* Uhtred 60 *manentes* at Hope and Ashford, which, we are told, he had bought from the heathen for twenty pounds of gold and silver, at the command of King Edward and ealdorman Æthelred, *cum ceteris comitibus et ministris*. In the parallel Abingdon document Æthelstan's confirmation relates to lands in the extreme west of Bedfordshire, bought by the thegn Ealdred, also 'from the heathen', for ten pounds. These transactions cannot well be later than 910, the most probable date for the death of ealdorman Æthelred,[4] and they are of remarkable importance as showing that Edward the Elder, before attempting the military reduction of the Danelaw, had formed the plan of compelling thegns under his own allegiance to settle in districts still in the occupation of the Northern *here*. The policy indicated by these texts has, it would seem, been ignored

---

[1] The one exception is Taddington (D. B. *Tadintune* < OE. **æt Tadan tūne*). Even here, however, the original *tūn* may very well have been an isolated homestead.

[2] C.S. 658.

[3] Ibid. 659.

[4] It would be a plausible suggestion that the Abingdon grant was made at the time of the treaty of Yttingaford, assigned by the Parker MS. of the Chronicle to the year 906, for the latter place was situated in the immediate neighbourhood of Linslade, Buckinghamshire (C.S. 1189), barely five miles from the land conveyed by the present charter, which lay in the vills of Chalgrave and Tebworth near Watling Street in Bedfordshire.

up to the present; but for our immediate purpose it is the bearing of the Derbyshire charter upon the condition of the estates at Hope and Ashford which most deserves attention. The land of sixty *manentes*, in the wild region drained by the Wye and the Noe, must have covered a great expanse of country, a territory much wider than would belong to any couple of normal vills in this region. Most unfortunately, the omission of the usual statement of boundaries from the existing text of the charters makes it impossible for us to define the limits of the area conveyed; but we may reasonably infer that already before 910 Ashford and Hope were the administrative centres of groups of dependent hamlets, such as are revealed in the Domesday description of those manors.

The ancient association of the three royal manors of the High Peak is definitely made probable by the fact that in 949 Bakewell, the remaining estate, was granted by Eadred, with a wild florescence of unnecessary verbiage, to Uhtred, *miles et dux*.[1] The significance of this grant has hitherto been obscured by the impossible identification of the land conveyed with the Staffordshire hamlets of 'Bucknall cum Bagnall',[2] near Stoke-on-Trent. But the Badecanwelle of the charter undoubtedly represents the Badecan wiellon of the Parker MS. of the Chronicle, the Badequella of Domesday, the modern Bakewell; and in the grantee we may fairly recognize the Uhtred of Ashford and Hope, now raised to the dignity of an ealdorman. We have no means of estimating the period during which Uhtred or his descendants remained in possession of these estates, nor yet can we determine the date at which they passed into the king's hands; but the fact that already before 950 they were together subject to the same lord is itself a matter of some significance.

With regard to the southern portion of the Confessor's great Derbyshire estate — the manors between the Dove and

---

[1] C. S. 884.

[2] Bucknall derives from an OE. *Bucan healh* or *Bucan holt*; Bagnall, from *Bacgan healh* or *Bacgan holt*. See the early forms of these names in Duignan, Staffordshire Place-names, 9 and 27. None of these forms could possibly be derived from the personal name *Badeca*, compounded in the Badecanwelle of the text and in the early forms of Bakewell.

the Derwent—our unique pre-Conquest information is contained in a single land-book, which tells us little. In 966, forty years after the Ashford confirmation, Eadgar granted to the thegn Ælfhelm ten *mansae*, 'in eo loco qui Anglica relacione Peuerwich appellatur.'[1] 'Peuerwich' is unidentified in the Cartularium Saxonicum, but it is clearly identical with the *Pevrewic* of Domesday,[2] the modern village of Parwich in west Derbyshire. In 1066 Parwich was the head of a manor comprising the three berewicks of Alsop-le-Dale, Cold Eaton, and Hanson Grange; but the whole estate was then rated at four carucates only; and we thus obtain a remarkable discrepancy between the number of agrarian units assigned to an estate in the tenth century and the amount of its Domesday assessment. The significance of this and of other similar discrepancies must be reserved for separate discussion[3]; the only immediate importance of the Parwich charter is in the fact that it in no way militates against the belief that in the middle of the tenth century the royal demesne of the Peak was already organized on the lines which obtained in King Edward's day.

The existence of this vast but coherent domain as an ancient possession of the crown is a geographical fact of some historical importance. It has accidentally happened that in a remote part of the Danelaw a royal estate which, as described in Domesday, bears a strong superficial resemblance to the demesne of the Peak[4] has actually come to affect the modern map of England. In the heart of what is now the shire of Rutland, King William in 1086 possessed the three manors of Oakham, Hambledon, and Ridlington; which with their dependent berewicks constituted the separate wapentake of Martinsley. The names of these berewicks are not recorded;[5] but it is clear that taken individually they were much larger, and more nearly autonomous in agricultural

---

[1] C. S. 1175.   [2] fo. 272 b.
[3] See below, pp. 87-9.
[4] The phrase 'dominium de Pecco' was used in the twelfth century to describe the lands in question. V. C. H. Derby, i. 297.
[5] To Oakham five berewicks were appendant; to Hambledon and Ridlington, seven each. There is evidence which suggests that Uppingham, Wardley, and Belton were included among the berewicks of Ridlington. V. C. H. Rutland, i. 133.

matters, than were the dependent hamlets of Bakewell or Wirksworth. Regarded severally, each berewick of Oakham or Hambledon would seem to have been a fully developed vill, of which the land, for the purposes of the Survey, was considered to belong to the king in demesne [1]; while the inhabitants paid their rents and dues at the chief manor, and doubtless performed certain agricultural duties under the direction of its bailiff. We can speculate to but little purpose about the reasons owing to which the king became possessed of so large and compact an estate in so central a part of the country; but here, too, the local arrangement displayed by Domesday is probably of long standing. We know, at least, that Edward the Confessor had bestowed Rutland upon his wife Edith; we are told by a late but respectable authority that the same estate had earlier been given by Æthelred II to his wife Emma; and we may infer from the same source that it had been granted by Edgar to his second wife, Ælfthryth. The practice was continued after the Conquest; and I have elsewhere argued that it was the custom of regarding Rutland as the normal dowry of successive queens which separated the district from the adjacent shires, and thus created the modern county.[2] Had these Derbyshire manors which we have just considered been chosen for the purpose, a modern shire of the Peak, with its county town at Bakewell, might quite conceivably have resulted from the grant.

Among all the five shires comprising the district which is the subject of this essay, there is not one of which the early history is involved in such utter obscurity as that which attends the condition, before the Conquest, of the county of

---

[1] The statement that part of Empingham lay 'in soca regis de Roteland', and later references to 'Rutland Soken' and Oakham Soke, show that these berewicks contained a considerable area of sokeland. They seem, in fact, comparable with the berewicks of Laneham, Notts., in which also much sokeland was included. See above, p. 12.

[2] V. C. H. Rutland, i. 185-6. Gaimar, from whom we obtain the information connecting Emma with Rutland, also asserts that the district had formerly belonged to 'Elstruet', by which name he means Ælfthryth, second wife of King Edgar. (Compare OE. Chron. D text, *sub anno* 965.) As this lady was daughter of Ordgar, Ealdorman of Devon, the Rutland estate cannot well have come to her by inheritance, and it is only a reasonable inference that it was granted to her upon her marriage to the king.

Leicester. It therefore may be well to refer in passing to the solitary land-book which primarily relates to land within this shire[1]; more particularly as the document in question, in itself of no special importance, has been referred by a mistaken identification to the distant county of Worcester. In 966 Eadgar granted to Bishop Æthelwold 13 *cassati* at Breedon in Leicestershire, where, it would seem, there existed, or had recently been created, a religious house which was to enjoy the property in the future. We are then told:—
'est autem predicta tellus hiis locis comperta; iii videlicet cassati æt Æbredone (*sic*), iii æt Wifeles thorpe, iii æt Ætheredesdune, iiii scilicet æt Digtheswyrthe.' The site of Ætheredesdune is no longer known, Wifelesthorpe may be identified with the hamlet of Wilson on the Derbyshire border,[2] Digtheswyrthe is undoubtedly the modern village of Diseworth. It does not appear from the record that these properties were united otherwise than by their common subordination to the uses of the church of Bredon[3]; and the charter is only cited here for its bearing upon the local geography of Leicestershire at a period when that subject is in general impenetrably obscure.

More important, because more definite, evidence as to the early history of the discrete *manerium* is afforded in relation to the great estate which the Archbishop of York possessed in the centre of the county of Nottingham. Immediately to the north of the Trent, and extending for some eight miles in a north-westerly direction, a compact group of a dozen vills constituted in 1066 the archiepiscopal manor of Southwell. At the date in question eleven of these vills, which are not named in Domesday, were organized as berewicks of the

[1] C. S. 1283.

[2] Wilson is represented by Wiveleston in the twelfth century (Mon. Ang. vi. 97).

[3] It is difficult to trace this estate in Domesday, for the only entry which relates to any portion of it merely assigns 3 carucates in Diseworth to William Loveth. The Domesday account of Diseworth is, however, defective, and it is likely that the whole of the land conveyed by the present charter was included within Henry de Ferrer's manor of Tonge, the pre-Conquest owner of which is not named (V. C. H. Leicester, i. 319, 349). Breedon and Wilson certainly belonged to the Ferrers' family in the twelfth century.

chief manor; and the whole group was rated at 22½ carucates, a sum representing exactly 20 of those nine-bovate units upon which there is reason to believe that the assessment of this part of Nottinghamshire was based.[1]   In or about 956 this estate, as 20 *mansae*, had been granted by King Eadwig to Archbishop Oscytel of York; and the relevant land-book is preserved in a corrupt form in the Liber Albus of the latter church.   This document, which certainly seems to be founded upon a tenth-century original, presents certain unusual features, chief among which is the insertion of a paragraph after the statement of boundaries intended to define more exactly the nature of the archbishop's interest in the property.   ' These are the *tuns* that belong to Southwell with sake and soke; Farnsfield, Kirklington, Normanton, Upton, Morton, Fiskerton, Gibsmere, Bleasby, Goverton, Halloughton, Halam.   In Farnsfield two manslots belong to Southwell; in Halam are sixty acres and three manslots; in Normanton, every third acre; in Fiskerton, the two parts (*dales*) and four manslots out of all the land.'   It would not be in place here to comment on the appearance of the manlot in this text,[2] except to remark that the term is such as no twelfth-century forger would have been likely to invent; but this point is itself of importance, for the present document is the first charter of reasonable authenticity that makes an explicit reference to the grantee's possession of soke over the land conveyed.   The importance of this fact

---

[1] C.S. 1029.   For the assessment of 1086 compare V. C. H. Nottingham, i. 209–10.

[2] Compare Vinogradoff, English Society in the Eleventh Century, 281. A contemporary reference to *gedalland* in the west-midland shire occurs in C.S. 1181, by which Bishop Oswald of Worcester leases to his thegn Wihthelm 2 hides at Clifford-Chambers, Gloucestershire, 'oþer healf hid ge dal landes, & healf hid on þære ege.'   The 1½ hides of gedalland were clearly distributed in scattered strips in contrast to the compact half-hide on the island.   Clifford-Chambers lies on the left bank of the Stour. Another Gloucestershire charter, erroneously referred in the Cartularium to Hampshire (C.S. 764), supplies us with an earlier reference to the system of *gedales*.   The document refers to land at Wotton-under-Edge, and the statement of boundaries ends by including within the estate Oslanwyrth [Ozleworth] and all that belongs to it, and the fourth *dæl* at Byrneswell [   ].   The document comes from the fraudulent Codex Wintoniensis, but seems genuine; and the reference to the ge-dales would be still more remarkable if it were founded upon the agrarian arrangements of the mid-twelfth century.

as bearing on the nature of earlier grants which are silent on this point is very considerable, but it should further be noted that at Southwell we seem for once to obtain a clue to the real constitution of these large and ancient estates at a date more than a century behind the Domesday Inquest. The clause which we are considering is most naturally understood as meaning that while the archbishop would possess sake and soke over the whole estate, parts of it lay outside the range of his immediate ownership. The details about the archbishop's land in Farnsfield, Halam, Fiskerton, and Normanton surely imply that the soil of the remainder of these vills had not passed to the new lord; a conclusion which, it may be noted, is well borne out by the evidence of Domesday.[1] It would seem, in fact, that we are reading of an estate which would already, in its main features, answer to the common formulas of the Danelaw Domesday: the central vill, the dependent tenements, some owned outright by the lord, others only connected with the capital messuage by the fact that they carry a responsibility for suit and service to be rendered there. For it can hardly be otherwise than that, in those parts of Halam, Farnsfield, Fiskerton, and Normanton which appear to be excepted from the sphere of the archbishop's ownership, we have a form of tenement which would correspond, at least in origin, to the sokeland of 1086.

If it stood alone the Southwell charter, a late copy of a difficult text, might perhaps be regarded with some suspicion. But it fortunately happens that, in regard to the clause implying the extension of sake and soke over the property, the Southwell evidence is supported by another document of almost contemporary origin, but of quite independent provenance. In 959 [2] Edgar, as king of Mercia, 'necnon et aliarum gentium in circuitu persistentium', granted to the matron Quen two cassates at Howden and 'Ealdredrege'. In the document by which this grant is made a separate set of

---

[1] In 1086 Walter de Aincurt possessed lands in Fiskerton, Morton, and Farnsfield ; Gilbert de Gand, lands in Kirklington and Normanton ; and Ralf fitz Hubert, lands in Gibsmere and Morton, of which the soke belonged to Southwell.

[2] C. S. 1052.

boundaries is assigned to Howden and to 'Ealdredrege'; but between the two there is inserted the clause 'these are the lands which belong to Howden with sake and with soke', followed by a list of seven vills, each of which can be identified in the angle formed by the Yorkshire Ouse and Derwent of which Howden is the natural centre.[1] In 1086[2] all these vills were still appurtenant to the manor of Howden; though it may be that the distinction of tenure which we have noted in the case of Southwell prevailed here also.   In any case, we obtain valuable confirmation of the Southwell evidence proving the possession of jurisdictional powers by the lord of a newly granted estate at a date considerably earlier than the conveyance of any powers of the kind in the operative words of a genuine instrument; and we may note it as significant that in both instances the existence of the lord's justice is revealed to us in the vernacular phrase sake and soke.[3]

King Eadwig's grant of Southwell was only one of a series of similar gifts through which the patrimony of the see of York was recruited in the third quarter of the tenth century after the fall of the Danish kingdom of Northumbria. Between 956 and the death of Archbishop Oswald in 992 the northern archbishopric had become possessed of the important manors of Sutton in Nottinghamshire, Sherburn in Elmet, and Newbold near Pocklington in Yorkshire.[4] It is only in regard to

[1] Cnyllingtún [Knedlington], Beornhyll [Barnhill], Cafeld [Cavil], Thorp [Thorpe], Hythe [Hythe], Eastringatún [Eastrington], Belleby [Belby], Celpene [Kilpin].

[2] Howden is one of those manors, characteristic of Yorkshire, to which much territory belonged both in the form of berewicks and as sokeland.

[3] The references to sake and soke in the Southwell and Howden landbooks make it necessary slightly to modify the argument of Maitland in Dom. Bk. and Beyond, 258–67. It is, no doubt, true that express grants of jurisdiction became steadily more frequent as the writ-form gained popularity at the expense of the ancient diploma; but the land-books which have just been considered show that the jurisdictional formula could be introduced into a solemn charter if need arose.   The explicit reference to sake and soke at Southwell and Howden is apparently called forth by the fact that these estates were each scattered over a wide area : it was clearly felt necessary to explain that the new lord would possess rights of justice over the whole of the respective properties.   It may be added that the existence of these charters of 956–9 makes the authenticity of the Altitonantis diploma of 964 a matter of less importance than before.

[4] C. S. 1044 [958], 1112 [963], 1113 [963].

the second of these estates that we obtain information which is of importance for our present purpose, but the evidence supplied in the case of Sherburn in Elmet well bears out the conclusions suggested by the charters relating to Southwell and Howden. In 1066 Sherburn with its unspecified berewicks was rated at 96 carucates, a sum which at once suggests that, contrary to the usual practice in such cases, the whole estate was regarded as a fiscal unit upon the familiar twelve-carucate basis. In 963 King Edgar gave to a certain Aslac 20 cassates at Sherburn; but the statement of boundaries incorporated in the charter shows that the land in question formed only a portion of the whole estate conveyed. We are first given the boundaries of 20 hides of 'inland' at Sherburn, a term which in this case probably refers exclusively to the central manor; and then there follows a specification of the lands dependent on the latter which deserves quotation[1]:—
'half a hide in "Hibaldestofte", and one hide in Fryston, (and) in Hillam two oxgangs, and in Lumby two oxgangs, and one and a half hides in Milford and in Steeton, and in Micklefield two hides of land, and all "Luttringham" except one hide, and one and a half hides in Church Fenton, and one and a half hides in Cawood.' The text of the charter is corrupt, but the sense of the present passage is sufficiently plain.

Now the chief fact that arrests attention here is the smallness of the several parcels of dependent territory. The berewicks of Sherburn are by no means entire vills, they are

---

[1] The arrangement of the property at Sherburn, and more particularly the meaning in this case of the term *inland*, are well illustrated by the formulas employed in C. S. 208, a charter purporting to have been granted by Offa in 772, and conveying land at Bexhill, Sussex. The statement of boundaries occupies two clauses: the first headed 'This sind þæra viii hida land gemera *þær inlandes* into bæxwarena lande'; the second 'Thonne syndon þa gavolland *þas utlandes* into bexlea, in hiis locis qui appellantur hiis nominibus. On berna hornan iii hida, on wyrtlesham i etc.' This charter (from Lambeth MS. 1212) cannot be cited for the local organization of the eighth century, but it is fair evidence for a later practice by which the terms *inland* and *utland* were employed in contrast; the former to indicate the home portion of the estate, the latter to denote the outlying properties belonging to it. The former no doubt expresses the nature of the Sherburn inland of 963, and the scattered parcels of land which belonged there are clearly equivalent to the Bexhill *utland*.

disconnected hides and oxgangs scattered over an area more than six miles square. There is evidence, as will shortly be seen, which shows that a loss of territory had recently been sustained by the estate; but the recorded details of the loss are quite insufficient to affect the essential character of the Sherburn berewicks. We are, in fact, dealing here with a type of estates different, so far as our knowledge goes, from the types displayed either in the royal manors of the Peak of Derbyshire or in the king's demesne of Rutland; a type, moreover, to which it would not be difficult to cite parallel instances from Domesday. But perhaps the best commentary upon the local arrangements which obtained at Sherburn is afforded by a Cambridgeshire estate which King Edgar in 970 conferred upon the monastery of Ely.[1] The charter by which this grant was made bestows upon St. Æthelthryth 10 cassates 'aet Lintune', a lost vill now represented by Linden End near Aldreth; and instead of boundaries the limits of the estate are defined by the clause 'This sind ða land into Lintune . . . þæt þonne lið hid mælum & æcer mælum on Wilburhtune [Wilburton] & on hædan ham [Haddenham] & on hille [   ] & on Wichamme [Witcham]', a clause explained by the statement in the body of the document that 'ad hanc autem tellurem multa jugera ex diversis circum-jacentibus villis pertinent perpetua insignita libertate'. The berewicks of Sherburn no less clearly lay 'hide-meal and acre-meal' in the adjacent vills, among the strips held by independent landholders; although the subsequent development of the Sherburn and Linden estates proceeded on different lines. It is significant of the more rapid manorialization of the midlands, that in 1086 Wilburton and Witcham were organized as separate maneria, while the Sherburn estate had maintained its integrity, and indeed by the date of Domesday had become one of the largest manors in South Yorkshire. As to its condition in the tenth century, one most important fact, ignored by the compiler of the charter of 963, is happily recorded incidentally in another text; the lord of Sherburn,

[1] C. S. 1268. The 'Lintune' of this charter represents the 'Lindone' of the Cambridgeshire Domesday; it is wrongly identified by Birch with Linton in the extreme south of the county.

whether the king or another, had formerly possessed soke over the estate, although from whatever cause half the soke had recently been withdrawn. It is very clear that we cannot argue from the silence of our tenth-century texts with respect to the existence of jurisdictional franchises at this time; and we may raise the question, in passing, whether the *perpetua insignita libertas* which distinguished the Linden estate does not indicate the existence of that most important of all immunities, the immunity which gave scope for the development of a seignorial court. Nor should we leave the Sherburn charter without a reference to the clear proof which it affords that the hide was still regarded as the agricultural unit in South Yorkshire in the third quarter of the tenth century.

Extensive as was the appendant territory of Sherburn in Elmet in 963, it merely formed part of a larger estate which had centred in that vill in early times. For our knowledge of this fact, and for other valuable information respecting the early local history of Yorkshire, we are indebted to the preservation of a fragmentary memorandum compiled at the instance of that very efficient man of affairs, Archbishop Oswald, and describing the condition of the estates of his see north of the Humber.[1] This document, which has at present hardly received the attention that it merits, falls into two parts, the first, setting out the lands which had been withdrawn from the three great estates of Sherburn, Otley, and Ripon; the second, recording the territorial acquisitions in ' Northumberland ' of Oswald's predecessor, Archbishop Oscytel. The record bears no date, but as it relates that the archbishop had obtained a grant of the lands in question from King Edgar in person, it may probably be placed within a short time of Oswald's accession in 971–2.

From the standpoint of general history this document deserves particular study as affording evidence in relation to a subject where evidence is sorely needed—the position of the northern archbishopric under the rule of the Scandinavian Kings of York. We might in any case infer that the new lords of Northumbria would show scant respect to the boundaries

[1] C. S. 1278–9. The existing text is corrupt.

of the ancient estates of the see ; it is the present document
which alone gives details in regard to this matter. But for
our present purpose the evidence supplied by this document
with relation to the general character of the Northumbrian
estates at issue is more important ; and this evidence is conclusive. The lands which had been taken from Otley covered
part at least of thirteen vills, distributed over an area of ten
miles along Wharfedale, and extending widely over the moors
on each side of the valley.[1] Of the means by which the archbishop, in the first instance, became possessed of Otley, we
know nothing ; but the tenth-century estate of Ripon undoubtedly descends from that 'monasterium triginta fami-
liarum' which Alchfrid of Northumbria gave to Wilfrid in
or about the year 661.[2] The loss sustained at Ripon
amounted to seven distinct properties, of which one, Helperby
on the left bank of the Swale, had been recovered by Archbishop Oscytel in a remarkable manner ; two brothers, we are
told, had possessed one wife, and had therefore forfeited their
land to the archbishop. But the. noteworthy fact which we
learn about Helperby is that at the time of its recovery the
estate had come to include dependent territory in a number
of scattered vills—' into Heolperby hyrð Mytun twa dæl, et
Wibustan socn et þurulfestun et toletun et þorp '. If then,
as we must infer from our text, Helperby, or an earlier village
on the same site, had in ancient times been annexed to Ripon,
we are driven to the conclusion that at some date subsequent
to the Danish conquest of York the site had been occupied
by a settler who had not only withdrawn his land from its
dependence on Ripon, but had also added to it scattered properties distributed somewhat widely over the neighbouring
country, properties which in one case were subject to the
lord's soke. Beyond this we cannot go ; but if our text may
be trusted, we are certainly dealing at Helperby with a discrete estate existing in the days of the independent kingdom
of York, in which the local organization familiar in the Dane-

[1] Addingham in Wharfedale, the first of these estates, was still in the
hands of the archbishop in 867, when Archbishop Wulfhere retired there
at the time of the Danish occupation of York (Simeon of Durham, i. 225).
[2] Bede, H. E. v. 19.

law of 1066—the central messuage, the dependent tenements, the sokeland—had already been developed.

The case of Sherburn in Elmet differs in some respects from the cases of Ripon and Otley. To the compiler of Oswald's memoranda all these estates alike were ancient possessions of the see of York, which had suffered encroachment during recent disorders. To such an explanation the preservation of the Sherburn land-book of 963 presents a superficial difficulty. The estate, without any reference to its past history, is granted *de novo* by King Edgar, not to the archbishop, but to the thegn Aslac. The only solution of this difficulty which presents itself is the supposition that Sherburn had in some way come into the king's hand, and that the king, in restoring it to the see of York, wished to make one of his thegns a partner in the good work; just as in the same year, when selling Newbald [1] to the archbishop, he conveyed the estate in the first instance to the Earl Gunner, with the customary reservation that the land was to be devoted to religious uses. Happily these details of conveyancing practice do not affect the authenticity of the highly important statement in the memorandum which asserts that half the soke that belonged to Sherburn had been withdrawn; nor do they concern the information which the memorandum and the charter together supply with respect to the outlying members of the estate. The essential fact in this connexion, the annexation of fractional parts of scattered vills to a central estate, is clear; and it carries the implication that whether or no the whole property were subject to the lord's soke, the lord was regarded as the owner of the soil. Already in the mid-tenth century the form of local organization which the compilers of Domesday were to describe under the name of the berewick had come into being.[2]

[1] In the Newbald charter (C. S. 1113) Gunner receives the land in question 'pro obsequio ejus devotissimo'. The real nature of the transaction is indicated by the statement in the Memorandum that Oscytel bought the land at Newbold from King Edgar with 120 mancuses 'of red gold'.

[2] The word itself has passed into local nomenclature under the form of Berwick or Barwick. That the connexion was still recognized at the date of the Survey is shown by the entry relating to Kippax, York (fo. 315) ' Huic manerio adjacet terra quae vocatur proprie Berewit [Barwick in Elmet] '.

Among the forces which made for manorial consolidation in the generations preceding the Norman Conquest an important place must assuredly be assigned to the pressure of the geld upon the rural population. The operation of this force in detail is hidden from us ; but there is evidence enough to suggest that the king and his advisers have been from an early date regarding the lord as in the last resort responsible for the geld laid upon tenements within the scope of his local influence. Earlier in this essay it has been suggested that a main feature distinguishing the position of the sokeman within the manor was his responsibility for the geld due from the lands which he held ; and the argument might well be pressed that it was the lord who acquitted the tenements of villeins and bordars, the unfree tenements of later times. It thus becomes important to inquire, so far as any inquiry is possible, into the question of the date at which the assessment of the Danelaw, as revealed in Domesday, takes its origin, and in regard to this matter the evidence of the early texts which have recently been considered is of some peculiar value.

In the west and south of England it is usually easy to demonstrate continuity between the *mansae* and *cassati* conveyed in extant land-books[1] and the hidage of the relevant estates as recorded in Domesday. The assessment of such a county as Berkshire, for example, was clearly a matter of long standing in 1066. But the case is startlingly different when we investigate the figures recorded in the little group of land-books which have been preserved with reference to the shires dependent upon the Five Boroughs. There is no need to produce evidence to show that the men who distributed the assessment of Lincolnshire or Yorkshire among the several vills of these shires ended by imposing upon the normal vill in this region a duodecimal group of carucates bearing geld ; the fact has already been demonstrated to the full. But it is scarcely realized as yet that the land-books which relate to the Danelaw reveal no trace of any such system. From the

---

[1] Thus, to take a Berkshire example, in 942 King Eadmund sold an estate in Brimpton, estimated at 8 *mansae* (C. S. 802). In 1066 the vill was divided into two manors, rated respectively at 3½ and 4½ hides.

period before the year 975 there remain eleven documents
which definitely specify the amount of land conveyed in each,
and the figures are suggestive. The 10 manses granted at
Eaton in Dovedale, the 5 granted at King's Newton, the 10
at Parwich, all in Derbyshire; the 20 manses of Southwell,
the 10 cassates of Sutton in Nottinghamshire, the 20 hides
of Sherburn in Elmet; are not only out of all correspondence
with the Domesday assessments of these places, they rest upon
a decimal basis of computation identical with that which
obtained in Oxfordshire or Worcestershire.[1] Regarded singly,
these figures furnish a *prima facie* case for the belief that the
distribution of fiscal units in the Danelaw is at the least more
recent than the year of King Edgar's death; they may well
incline us to regard with some respect the vast numbers of
hides assigned in the 'Tribal Hidage' to the men of the
Peak, of Lindsey, and of Mercia.

This conclusion is supported in a remarkable manner by
two unrelated facts. The appearance of the hide as the local
agrarian unit at Sherburn in Elmet in 963 is a very positive
objection to any theory which would assign a high antiquity
to the Domesday assessment of the Danelaw. It may well be
that in the oxgang of the Sherburn text we should recognize
the native word represented by the familiar bovate of Domesday; but the carucate, as a legal term, has clearly not yet
obtained currency in the north. Nor is it unimportant that the
persistence of the hide can be shown at a date nearly forty
years after the Sherburn grant in relation to two other of the
Danelaw shires: the will of Wulfric Spot refers incidentally
to hides at Awsworth in west Nottinghamshire and at Sharnford in south Leicestershire. And in the second place, there
is the remarkable fact that in that collection of fiscal statistics
known as the County Hidage—statistics agreeing too closely
with the Domesday assessments of the shires to which they

---

[1] The 60 *maneutes* at Hope and Ashford, the 30 *cassati* of Newbald,
might be explained as pointing indifferently to a decimal or duodecimal
system. Estates of 30 hides, however, were known at an early date in
the south (799–802, original), e. g. in C. S. 201 'terram xxx manentium in
Middil Saexum' . . . terram totidem manentium, id est xxx, in Ciltinne,
in loco ubi dicitur Wichama' [High Wycombe, Bucks.].

refer to be referred to a date much beyond the opening of the eleventh century—the counties of York, Nottingham, Derby, Leicester, and Lincoln, the carucated shires of England, are omitted. Taken singly, these facts might be explained away; together they raise a very definite presumption that at the close of the tenth century the shire of York, the district dependent on the Five Boroughs, had not yet been brought under the operation of the fiscal system of the south and east.

It is impossible, through lack of evidence, to determine the date at which the change was made. The existence of Æthelred's Wantage code suggests that that king was at least more interested in the internal affairs of the Danelaw than were any of his predecessors—sufficiently interested to legislate for the men of the Five Boroughs. But the reign of the redeless king is by no means the period to which we should be inclined to refer so great an administrative measure as the imposition of a uniform system of assessment upon a fourth part of England. And there remains one fact which suggests very strongly that the distribution of fiscal carucates over the Danelaw is at any rate later than the issue of Æthelred's Wantage code. The Domesday assessment of the Danelaw was based upon a very remarkable system by which, where necessary,[1] vills were grouped so as to form what were termed 'hundreds', each bearing a joint assessment of twelve carucates to the geld. That these hundreds were primarily created to provide for the punctual payment and exact local apportionment of the geld is very probable[2]; but it is clear that they served other purposes as well. They were at least sufficiently organized to give a corporate opinion upon questions relating to the disputed ownership of land[3]; they probably, in former times, fulfilled the functions of a local judicial assembly. Now in Æthelred's Wantage code we are given a singular description

---

[1] In Kesteven, where individual vills were larger than elsewhere, a single vill might well constitute a 'hundred' by itself after the manner of Potter Hanworth and Branston (fo. 461), or a double hundred as at Long Bennington (fo. 348).

[2] This is strongly suggested by the uniformity of the assessment.

[3] Fo. 370: 'In Chisebi' [Keisby Lincoln] habuit Offram iiii bovatas terrae ad geldum. . . . Homines de punchedo dicunt socam jacere in Osgotebi [Osgodby].'

of the fines payable for the breach of the king's peace under different circumstances, which is very pertinent to the present question. Peace given in the general assembly (*geþincðu*) of the Five Boroughs is the most severely guarded; then comes the peace given in the wapentake; lastly, the peace given *in ealhuse*; and it is difficult to believe, if a series of ' hundreds', such as are revealed by Domesday, already existed at the date of the Wantage code, that the peace given there should not be regarded as of greater moment than the peace given in the beerhouse. It is true that the date of the Wantage code is itself uncertain, and that the reign of Æthelred II is very long; but the hide was still the agrarian unit in the Danelaw at the beginning of the eleventh century, and if a date for the assessment of the Danelaw may be suggested on grounds of general probability, then no other period so well fits the known circumstances as the accession of the foreign conqueror Cnut.[1] But whatever conclusion may be reached in regard to this matter, it would seem clear that the men of the Danelaw until a late period were exempt from the fiscal burdens which pressed upon their neighbours to south and west[2]; and it may well be that in this fact we should recognize one among the many causes which contributed to the general liberty which they enjoyed in 1066.

In conclusion, a passing reference should perhaps be made here to one grave problem which becomes increasingly pressing as we trace the history of the Danelaw *manerium* backwards through the tenth century; a problem which arises in

[1] The geld of 1018 brought in, according to the Chronicle, £72,000; more than twice the amount obtained from any previous levy. But how far the figures recorded in regard to this matter by the Chronicle represent the truth is very doubtful.

[2] In other words, it is probable the lands of the Danelaw shires were still numbered according to the system which underlay that ancient record the Tribal Hidage, a system devised in order to meet the elementary needs of a seventh or eighth-century king, but quite inappropriate to the severe burdens of taxation or military defence which lay upon the population of Wessex and the southern and western midlands in the tenth century. In the Tribal Hidage the men of Lindsey answer for 15,000 hides; in the eleventh century, upon calculation from the Lindsey Survey supplemented by Domesday, they were assessed at just 2,000 carucates. There is a superficial reduction here; but it is accompanied by the imposition of fiscal burdens of altogether disproportionate severity.

connexion with the local nomenclature of this district.   In
1066 the vills of the Danelaw were free, to an extent perhaps
without parallel elsewhere in England; they were unmanorialized, and in many cases would appear never to have known
any lord of lower rank than king, earl, or bishop.   The presumption is naturally strong that the liberty which they
possessed in 1066 belonged to them from the beginning of
their history; that the bys and thorpes of the Danelaw
resulted from the settlement of groups of free-men ; that the
lord was in all cases an unoriginal element in the life of these
communities ; and that in many cases he had not come into
being at all at the time when the Norman Conquest extended
the manorial system over the unfeudalized east and north.   This
conception agrees well with the evidence supplied by Domesday ; it enables us to co-ordinate the agrarian customs of the
Danelaw with those revealed by the remains of early Scandinavian law, and undoubtedly it contains a large measure
of truth ; but the place-names of the Trent basin raise a silent
protest which has hitherto been too little regarded.   Brooksby
Thorganby, Gamston, Skegby, are names which will not
permit us to deny a primitive superiority, of whatever origin
or extent, to Broc, Thorgrim, Gamel, and Skegg.   We
may minimize the significance of the eponymous lord ; we
may refuse him the ownership of the village lands ; we may
believe that a village of free settlers coexisted from the beginning beside his dominant homestead ; but we cannot explain
him away ; and it is probable that for a long time yet he will
remain to complicate the earliest phase of the local history
of the Danelaw.   Here, at least, no explanation of his presence can be attempted ; but it is well to remember that
there comes a point at last at which the study of agrarian
types touches the study of local nomenclature, and that the
reconciliation of the personal element compounded in count-
less place-names with the general freedom which distinguished
the Danelaw villages of 1066 is a task which must be under-
taken in the future.

APPENDIX

MS. HARL. 3759, Fol. 103.

[Collated with the independent transcript given by Dugdale, Mon. Ang. iv. 623.]

[1] Notum sit omnibus fidelibus Christianis [2] quod ego Rogerus de Buusli et uxor mea Muriel pro stabilitate regis Anglorum Willelmi successorumque ejus [3] nec non et pro anima regine Matildis et pro salute animarum nostrarum [4] consilio amicorum nostrorum dedi et concessi et hac presenti carta mea confirmavi deo et sancte [5] Marie de Blida et monachis ibidem deo servientibus ecclesiam de Blida et totam villam integre cum omnibus appendiciis suis et consuetudinibus sicuti homines ejusdem ville michi [6] faciebant ; scilicet arare, karare [7] (*sic*), falcare, bladum meum [8] secare, fenum meum [8] facere, marchetum dare, stangnum [9] (*sic*) molendini facere. Praeterea dedi et concessi predictis monachis theloneum et passagium de Radeford usque in Thornewad [10] et de Frodestan [11] usque in hidil. [12] Dedi et [13] eis feriam et mercatum [14] in eadem villa absolute et libere absque ullo retenemento. Propterea [15] (*sic*) dedi predictis monachis omnes dignitates quas habebam in eadem villa, scilicet soc et sac tol et them et infang et thief [16] (*sic*) ferrum et fossam et furcas cum aliis libertatibus uti [17] tunc temporis tenebam de rege. Insuper dedi eis Elleton' [Elton, Notts] et quicquid ei pertinet, Bectonam [Beighton, Derby] et quicquid ei pertinet et quicquid habebam in Barnbeia [18] [Barnby, York.]. Dedi etiam eis [19] decimas [20] viginti trium carucarum mei proprii laboris quarum due sunt in Wateleya [21] [North Wheatley, Notts] et in Marneham due et dimid'. In Aplebeia [22] [Appleby, Lincoln.] due partes decime aule in terris et in essartis et in omnibus minutis decimis.

---

[1] Add ' In Nomine Sancte et individuae Trinitatis ' D.
[2] Omit Christianis D.   [3] Et successorum ejus D.
[4] Omit nostrarum D.   [5] beatae D.   [6] Omit michi D.
[7] kariare D.   [8] Omit meum D.   [9] stagnum D.
[10] Thornewat D.   [11] Frodeston D.   [12] Hidds Hill D.
[13] etiam D.   [14] marchatum D.   [15] praeterea D.
[16] infangethefe D.   [17] ut D.   [18] Barnebeya D.
[19] Omit eis D.   [20] decimam D.   [21] Wateleia D.
[22] Appelbeya D.

In Lactona [Laughton en le Morthenn, York.] due partes decime
aule in terris et in essartis et in omnibus minutis decimis. In
Clifford [Clifford, Gloucester.] due partes decime aule et in terris
et in essartis et in omnibus minutis decimis. In Bingeham [1] [Bing-
ham, Notts] due partes decime aule in terris et in essartis et in
decimis minutis. In Saltebeia [2] [Saltby, Leicester.] et in Gerthorp [3]
[Garthorpe, Leicester.] et in Bersalldebea [4] [Bescaby Leicester.] due
partes decime aule in terris et in essartis et in omnibus minutis
decimis. In Brugeford [5] [East Bridgeford, Notts] due partes decime
aule in terris et in essartis et in omnibus minutis decimis. In
Ludeham [6] et Gunnethorp [7] [Lowdham and Gunthorp, Notts] due
partes decime aule in terris et in essartis et in omnibus minutis
decimis, et in Clipestona [8] [Clipston on the Wolds, Notts] decima
unius caruce, et due partes de decima de Crocheston [9] [South
Croxton, Leicester.]. Hec omnia supradicte [10] ecclesie Blide ad
edificationem loci et victum et vestitum monachorum ibidem Deo et
genetrici servientium concedo in perpetuum, excepto quod unoquoque
anno de omnibus hiis ecclesie sancte trinitatis de Monte Rothomagi
dabuntur quadraginta solidi anglice monete. Testimonio virorum
quorum nomina hic sunt.

> [11] Albertus presbiter.
> Ricard presbiter.
> Willelmus presbiter.
> Fulco de Lusoriis.
> Thoraldus frater ejus.
> Ernoldus de Buulli.
> Godefridus dapifer.
> Turold de Cheverchort.
> Claron.
> Radulphus de Novi Fori.
> Pagan Gladicus.
> W. de Drincort.

Hec donatio facta est [12] anno dominicae incarnationis M⁰ octages-
simo octavo. [13]

[1] Omit 'In Bingeham due partes . . . in decimis minutis' D.
[2] Saltebeya D. [3] Garthorp D.
[4] Berchassebeya D. [5] Briggeford D. [6] Ludham D.
[7] Gunthorp D. [8] Clippestona D. [9] Crokestona D.
[10] supradicta D. [11] Witnesses omitted D. [12] fuit D.
[13] octo D.

INDEX

Acklom, York, 33.
Addingham, York, 85.
Ælfthryth, queen, 77.
Aids from sokeland, 68.
Aldborough, York, 32.
Alfreton, Derby, 72.
Allington, Lincoln, 65.
Alverton, Notts., 66–7, 70.
Appleby, Leicester, 10.
Appleby, Lincoln, 92.
Arcis, Osbern de. 7.
Arcis, William de, 7.
Arnold, Notts., 33, 68.
Aschil, a thegn in Lincoln-
shire, 6.
Ash, Derby, 72.
Ashbourne, Derby, 73–5.
Ashford, Derby, 73, 88.
— berewicks of, 73–4.
Assessment of Danelaw,
87–90.
Attercliffe, York, 14.
Aula, 12.
— constituting manor,
57–9.
Awsworth, Notts., hides
at, 88.
Bakewell, Derby, 73,
75–6.
Barholme, Lincoln, 40–1.
Barkston, Lincoln, mills
of, 36.
Barnby-in-the-Willows,
Notts., 49.
Barnby, York, 92.
Barrow-on-Humber, Lin-
coln, 33.
Barrow-on-Soar, Leices-
ter, 44.
Barwick in Elmet, York,
86.
Baumber, Lincoln, 19.
Beighton, Derby, 92.
Belchford, Lincoln, soke
of, 44.
Berewick, derivation of, 4.
— equivalent to inland,
5, 12–14.
— definition of, 13, 50.
— combination of, 69–70.
— early appearances of,
70–1.
Bescaby, Leicester, 93.

Bexhill, Sussex, 82.
Bingham, Notts., 93.
Blyth, Notts., 22–4.
— foundation charter of,
92–3.
' Bochetone,' York, 19.
Bolingbroke, Lincoln, soke
of, 20, 32, 44.
Bordarii, 54.
— upon sokeland, 19–20.
Bothamsall, Notts., soke
of, 33.
Bowden, Great, Leicester,
soke of, 32.
Braceborough, Lincoln,
40–1.
Bracton, 9.
Branston, Lincoln, 89.
Branston, Stafford, 72.
Brant Broughton, Lincoln,
8.
Braunston, Northants, 72.
Breedon, Leicester, 78.
Bridgeford, East, Notts.,
93.
Bridlington, York, 33.
Brimpton, Berks., 87.
Brocklesby, Lincoln, 30.
Brooksby, Leicester, 91.
Bucknall, Stafford, 75.
Bulcote, Notts., 46.
Burnham, Lincoln, 30.
Burstwick, York, 34.
Burton, near Lincoln, 48.
Burton Abbey, 71.
— cartulary of, 10.
Butterwick, Lincoln, 48.
By-laws, 27–8.
Caenby, Lincoln, 5.
Caistor, Lincoln, soke of,
32, 66.
Caldwell, Leicester, 46.
Cambray, Godfrey de, 7.
Cambridgeshire, manorial
type of, 39, 42–3.
Cammeringham, Lincoln,
42.
Carlby, Lincoln, 40–1.
Carlton in Lindrick,
Notts., 63.
Caythorpe, Lincoln, 12–
13, 32.
Chalgrave, Bedford, 74.

Chester, earl Hugh of, 6.
Chesterfield, Derby, 52, 68.
Chevet, York, 57.
Clarborough, Notts., 22.
Claxby, Lincoln, 33.
Claxby, near Normanby,
Lincoln, 15.
Clayton, York, 33.
Cleatham, Lincoln, 6.
Clifford Chambers, Glou-
cester, 79, 93.
Clifton, Notts., 33.
Clipston on the Wolds,
Notts., 93.
Coates, Great, Lincoln, 65.
Commendation, 43.
Consuetudines, 35–7.
County Hidage, 88–9.
Court Leet, 27.
Creaton, Lincoln, 40.
Croughton, Northants,
14–15.
Croxton, South Leicester,
93.
Danelaw, definitions of, 3.
Darley, Derby, 73.
Depression of peasantry,
17–18.
Dialogus de Scaccario, 9.
Diseworth, Leicester, 78.
Doddington, Lincoln, 32.
Dominium and *soca*, 7–
10, 47.
Dominium aulae, 12.
Drayton, Lincoln, 32.
Driffield, York, 32.
Dunham, Notts., 32, 44,
62, 68.
Dunholme, Lincoln, 48.
Eakring, Notts., 47.
Easingwold, York, 33.
East Deeping, 60.
Easton, Great, Leicester,
30.
Easton, Northants, 25, 31.
Eaton in Dovedale, Der-
by, 88.
Eaton, Notts., 63.
Edenham, Lincoln, 32.
Eggington, Derby, 33, 72.
Eight pounds, unit of, 33.
Elton, Notts., 92.
Emma, Queen, 77.

Escheppa brasei, 25.
Evenley, Northants, 15.
Fenton, Notts., 58.
Firma as food-rent, 37–8.
Firmae of manors, 34.
Fiskerton, Lincoln, 7.
Five boroughs, 3, 90.
Flawborough, Notts., 66.
Folkingham, Lincoln, 32.
Foston, Lincoln, 9.
Frampton, Lincoln, 48.
Franchises in Danelaw, 22.
Freckenham, Cambridge, 54.
Frieston, Lincoln, 13.
Frige soca, 40–2.
Frigman, 41.
Fulbeck, Lincoln, 9.
Gafol, 36.
Gamston, Notts., 91.
Garthorpe, Leicester, 93.
Gayton le Wold, Lincoln, 32, 68.
Gebur, 54.
Gedalland, 79.
Geld of 1018, 90.
Geneat, 54.
— distinguished from sokeman, 54.
Gesettland, 11.
Gilling, York, 34.
Gonerby, Great, Lincoln, 12.
Goulceby, Lincoln, 12.
Grantham, Lincoln, 12, 28, 44.
Greetham, Lincoln, 32, 44.
Gunthorpe, Notts., 93.
Guthrum, kingdom of, 3.
Habrough, Lincoln, 30.
Haceby, Lincoln, 29.
Hagnaby, Lincoln, 25.
Hagworthingham, Lincoln, 50.
Hall, as feature of *manerium*, 57–9.
Hallam, York, 14.
Halton Holgate, Lincoln, 20.
Halton, West, Lincoln, soke of, 68.
Hambledon, Rutland, 76–7.
Harlaxton, Lincoln, 12.
Harmston, Lincoln, 50.
Hatton, Derby, 16.
Hawton, Notts., 63.
Helperby, York, 85.
Hengwrt charters, 71–2.
Heriot, sokeman's, 36.

Hibalstow, Lincoln, 7.
Hickling, Notts., food-rent at, 37–8.
Hides in the Danelaw, 88.
Hiendley, York, 58.
Hiorda wic, 73.
Hodsock, Notts., 22.
Holne, York, 5, 16.
Hope, Derby, 73–5, 88.
Horncastle, Lincoln, soke of, 32, 44.
Hornsea, York, 34.
Howden, York, 32, 80–1.
Hundreds in the Danelaw, 13, 89–90.
Ilkeston, Derby, 33, 48.
Inland, in Lincoln and York, 5.
— contrasted with *warland*, 10–11.
Inwara and *utwara*, 30–31.
Ivo Taillebois, 24.
Keal, East, Lincoln, 20, 52.
Keelby, Lincoln, small manors at, 64–6.
Keisby, Lincoln, 29.
Killingholme, Lincoln, 63.
Kilnsea, York, 34.
Kilvington, Notts., 67, 70.
King as residual Lord, 44–5.
King's Newton, Derby, 88.
Kinoulton, Notts., 37.
Kippax, York, 33, 86.
Kirkby on Bain, Lincoln, 5.
Kirkby, East, Lincoln, 20, 25–6.
Kirkby Laythorpe, Lincoln, 33.
Kirton Lindsey, Lincoln, 33, 44.
Knaresborough, York, 5.
Laneham, Notts., 12, 77.
Laughton en le Morthen, York, 33, 93.
Legerwite, 24.
Liber Niger of Peterborough, 6–9.
Linden, Cambridge, 83.
Lindsey, assessment of, 90.
Local nomenclature, 3, 92–3.
Loftus, York, 33.
Long Bennington, Lincoln, 8, 89.
Long Eaton, Derby, 19.
Lowdham, Notts., 93.

Manbote, 18.
Manerium, 4.
— under soke, 50.
— definitions of, 56–60.
— typical form of, 59.
— as affording title to land, 59–60.
Manor of berewick, 61.
Manorialization, 52.
Mansfield, Notts., soke of, 68.
Manton, Lincoln, 7.
Mapleton, York, 34.
Markeaton, Derby, 33.
Market Deeping, Lincoln, 7.
Marnham, Notts., 92.
Matlock Bridge, Derby, 73.
Medeshamstede, 71.
Melton Mowbray, Leicester, 44.
Memoranda, of Medeshamstede, 71.
— of York, 84–6.
Merchet, 23–4.
Messingham, Lincoln, 7.
Mickleover, Derby, 32, 62, 72.
Military service from sokeland, 28–31.
Mill soke, 36–7.
Morton, Derby, 21, 33.
Nettleham, Lincoln, 33.
Newark, Notts., 32, 44, 62.
Newbold, York, 81, 86, 88.
Newbold, Derby, 52.
Normanton on Trent, Notts., 58, 64.
Normanton by Claxby, Lincoln, 13.
Northallerton, York, 11, 50, 69.
Northorpe, Lincoln, 19.
Notton, York, 14.
Oakham, Rutland, 76–7.
— its berewicks, 77.
Ogston, Derby, 21.
Orae of sixteen pence, 34.
Orston, Notts., 32, 44, 46, 68–9.
Osbaldwick, York, 52.
Osbournby, Notts., 28.
Oscytel, archbishop of York, 79, 84–5.
Oswald, archbishop of York, 81, 84.
Oswardbeck, Notts., soke of, 36, 44–5, 68–9.

Otley, York, 32, 85–6.
Ouseburn, York, 5.
Overton,Market,Rutland, 70.
Ozleworth, Gloucester,79.
Parwich, Derby, 73, 76, 88.
Payments by sokemen, 3.
— their origin, 34–5.
Peak, royal demesne of, 72–5.
Pilsley, Nether, Derby, 21, 33.
Pocklington, York, 34.
Potter Hanworth, Lincoln, 89.
Presentment, procedure by, 27.
'Racchenstus,' 34.
Radknight, 54.
Rauceby, Lincoln, 12, 40, 41.
Rectitudines, 53–5.
Reepham, Lincoln, 7.
Repton, Derby, 32.
Revesby, Lincoln, 20.
— abbey, foundation charter of, 24–7.
Ridlington,Rutland,76–7.
Ripon, York, 33, 85–6.
Rothley, Leicester, 32, 44, 46, 67.
Rothwell, York, 64.
Ruskington, Lincoln, 32, 43.
Rutland,demesne of,76–7.
Sake and soke, 21–2.
— at Southwell and Howden, 79–81.
— at Sherburn in Elmet, 83–4.
Saltby, Leicester, 93.
Sawley, Derby, 33.
Scarsdale wapentake, Derby, 45, 68.
Scawby, Lincoln, 7.
Scotter, Lincoln, 6, 24.
Scotton, Lincoln, 19.
Scredington, Lincoln, 51.
Scropton, Derby, 16, 33.
Sharnford,Leicester, hides at, 88.
Sherburn in Elmet, York, 82–4, 86, 88.
— berewicks of, 82–3.
Shipley, Derby, 39.
Sibsey, Lincoln, 20.
Six hynd men, 18.

Skegby, Notts., 91.
Skillington, Lincoln, 40.
Sleaford, Lincoln, 32.
Sokes, origin of, 44–6.
— partition of, 51.
Sokeland, derivation of, 4.
— nature of, 10.
— definition of, 13, 50.
— intermanorial, 46–9.
Sokemen, 18–20.
— their position in the manor, 46–9.
— their services, 22–7.
Somerby, near Grantham, Lincoln, 29.
Southwell, Notts., 32, 69, 78–80, 88.
— its berewicks, 79.
Sproxton, Leicester, 7.
Stainton, Lincoln, 30.
Stapleford, Leicester, 31.
Stapleford, Lincoln, 49.
Staunton, Notts., 29, 46, 66–7.
Stickford, Lincoln, 25.
Stickney, Lincoln, 25.
Stow St. Mary, Lincoln, 5, 33, 44.
Sturton,Great,Lincoln, 5.
Suit of court, 21.
Survivals of small manors, 64–7.
— sokes, 67–9.
— ancient freeholds, 49.
Sutton, Notts., 33, 69, 88.
Swaton, Lincoln, 29.
Taddington, Derby, 74.
Tallages, 37, 68.
'Tateshall,' 14, 57–8.
Tenements of sokemen, 46–9.
Tenure, dependent, 19.
— *in dominio*, 10.
— *in servitio*, 10.
Thegnland, 15–17.
'Thoresbia,' Lincoln, 25.
Thorganby, Lincoln, 91.
Thorn, Lincoln, 30.
Thurlby in Ness wapentake, Lincoln, 40–1.
Tochi, son of Outi, 43.
Tribal Hidage, 90.
Tun and *manerium*, 57.
Uhtred, earl, 74–5.
Utland, 11.
— contrasted with *inland*, 82.

Values, pre-conquest, 32.
Value as *firma*, 34.
Vill and manor,52,62–70.
Villani on sokeland, 17–20, 52.
Waddington, Lincoln, 33, 50.
Waithe, Lincoln, 46.
Wakefield, York, 32.
Walcot, near Alkborough, Lincoln, 6.
Waltham le Wold, Lincoln, 32, 44.
Wantage Code, the, 53, 89–90.
Wapentake, the, 3.
— and soke, 44–6.
Warland, 10–11.
Wartre, York, 32.
Welbourne, Lincoln, 47.
Well, Lincoln, 33.
Well wapentake, Lincoln, 44.
Welton, York, 32, 47.
Wers in Twelfth century, 18.
Westborough,Lincoln,32.
Westby, Lincoln, 40, 41.
Weston on Trent, Derby, 33.
Weston on Trent, Notts., 63.
Wheatley, North, Notts., 92.
Whitby, York, 34.
Willesley, Derby, 21.
Willington, Derby,10,11.
Willoughby, Lincoln, 13.
Willoughby,Warwick,72.
Wilsford, Lincoln, 29.
Wilson, Leicester, 78.
Wingfield, Derby, 21.
Winshill, Derby, 10, 36.
Wirksworth, Derby, 71, 73.
Wispington, Lincoln, 5.
Withernsea, York, 34.
Wotton underEdge,Gloucester, 79.
Wragby,Lincoln, soke of, 44.
Wulfric Spot, his will, 21, 88.
Wycombe, High, Bucks., 88.
York, kingdom of, 3.
York, *Liber Albus* of, 71, Yorkshire, harrying of, 4.

IV

CUSTOMARY RENTS

BY

MISS N. NEILSON, Ph D.

LECTURER IN MOUNT HOLYOKE COLLEGE, MASS. U.S.A.

CONTENTS

		PAGE
Introductory	. . . .	5
Chapter I. Food Rents.	. . . . .	15
Chapter II. Rents commuting Labour Services		48
Chapter III. Rents paid for Pasture and Estover Rights.	. . . . . .	69
Chapter IV. Condition Rents	. . .	86
Chapter V. Miscellaneous Rents	. . .	105
Chapter VI. Royal Rents: Administrative	.	114
Chapter VII. Royal Rents: Judicial	. .	154
Chapter VIII. Church Rents	. . .	188
Rents paid from Geldable Land as they appear in the Hundred Rolls	. . . . .	202
Documents from which the List of Rents has been chiefly compiled	. . . . .	204
Index	. . . .	207

B 2

INTRODUCTORY

THE typical villein of the manorial period fulfilled three sets of obligations : the first, imposed by the custom of the manor and enforced by the manorial court, consisted both of the rendering of services and the payment of rents to the lord of the manor; the second, political in origin, but influenced during the feudal period by manorial custom, consisted chiefly of the payment of rents to the king through his local officers, or to the lord of the manor, who, under the peculiar conditions of feudal society, was usually the holder of regalia obtained by franchise or usurpation ; and the third, in origin non-manorial like the second, consisted of the payment of tithes and rents to the church.[1]

Of obligations of the first kind, those resulting from manorial custom, the services, as distinguished from the rents, had a certain unity, evident to us in spite of the fact that there are several obscure places in their history. Custumals and accounts make it clear that they were, in the main, agricultural in character, and that they were the essential condition upon which the system of exploitation by means of the demesne rested. In customary rents, on the other hand, a like unity cannot be found. They were not necessarily part of one system ; they represent various periods in the development of manorial life, and various aspects of villeinage, of the disabilities and privileges and occupations of the villein. To the understanding of some of them a study of the services to which they were in a measure complementary is indispensable ; of others an explanation must be sought outside of domanial arrangements. Their composite character as exponents of different aspects of manorial conditions and development is

[1] See Vinogradoff, Villainage in England, pp. 288–95, for the fullest discussion of rents.

due also to the fact that those of the second kind, rents originally royal in character, had become, through the frequent interposition of the lord as the immediate or ultimate recipient of them, in a sense manorialized, and the relation of the villein to the king had therefore become inseparable from his relation to the lord of the manor. A similar process is probably visible in the church rents; they too were in part manorialized in cases where the lord of the manor was also a monastery or religious house. Yet although such processes of manorialization of rents had sometimes gone far, they were not complete; a margin of public responsibility and responsibility to the church remained.

The influence of manorial custom upon church and royal rents sometimes blurs the natural lines of division into the larger classes, and within the class of customary rents properly so called subdivisions are sometimes made uncertain and difficult by the disregarding of logical distinctions in manorial documents. It may well have happened that even by the thirteenth and fourteenth centuries a bailiff or surveyor would have found the explanation of the origin and nature of some of the older rents difficult; *minute consuetudines* lingered on, often as mere names, to furnish the excuse for the collection of trifling rents. Yet in spite of uncertainties of definition, several groups of customary rents seem to separate themselves, with more or less distinctness as the case may be, corresponding to the chief phases of the villein's condition and manner of life; and among royal and church rents also lines of division appear, although less clearly. Among customary rents proper may be included all those that had their origin in the relation existing between immediate lord and dependant in domanial days or in the earlier time, and that were regulated by custom and not by contract or special arrangement between the lord and the individual. This definition excludes the rents to which the term *redditus assise* is usually applied, the fixed rents, of whatever kind, agreed upon by the lord and the villein or freeholder for the holding of certain tenements, whether of assart land, demesne land, or land in the fields of the village, rents which, however originating, were regulated not by the custom of the manor but by agreements depending upon the nature of the land and the advantage to the persons concerned. It should be stated, however, that the term *redditus assise* has sometimes a broader application, and in bailiffs' accounts is made to include also some of the variable and fluctuating rents, *redditus mutabiles*, which by the custom of the manor were placed *ad certum*, at a fixed annual sum. The desire for certainty regarding annual income, a certainty difficult to obtain where the sources of revenue were diverse and fluctuating, led to the extension of this practice of 'farming'—the requirement, that is to say, of a fixed annual sum or farm instead of an uncertain and variable sum—far down into the details of manorial economy. Exclusive, then, of rents which were the results of agreement, customary rents divide themselves into the following general classes, whose limits are not always very clearly marked. In one class are the rents best explained as survivals of an early, predomanial system of exploitation, by which the lord was supported directly by food supplies sent him by his dependent villagers, free or unfree in other respects ; a system of purveyance on the part of the lord, which in the manorial period became obscured and in a measure obliterated by the imposition of the manor on earlier arrangements. In a second class are the rents which were chiefly commutations of occasional services, and were hence connected with the domanial system, forming the complement of the labour on the demesne. Thirdly, the rents paid in connexion with pastoral rights and liabilities and the holding of stock, with which may be grouped for convenience the rents paid for other holdings, houses, special bits of land, and privileges, must be considered ; and, fourthly, the condition rents incident to the villein's servile status, or to the tenure of land in villeinage. In a fifth group are placed a number of miscellaneous payments concerning which too little is known to make it possible to classify them. In the rents which were not manorial but royal in origin a division seems apparent between rents paid originally as part of the public imposts and in aid of the necessary expenses of the kingdom in the maintenance of defence and the administration of order, and the rents which were more directly connected with the holding of courts and judicial procedure. The rents to the church fall into still another group.

With regard to the incidence of these rents within the manor, the responsibility, that is to say, of various classes of tenants for their payment, it is clear from the definition of customary rents that the heaviest burden was necessarily borne by those tenants that held by a purely customary tenure, the typical *custumarii, operarii, werkmen, villani, gavolmanni*, or whatever may have been their name in different localities, whether of the more numerous class of virgaters and half virgaters, the greater *operarii*, or the smaller *operarii*, like cottars holding on a labour basis. Questions arise, however, regarding the distribution of manorial rents within even this limited group; some men of the vill were held to the payment of rents from which other men of the same vill, in other respects with similar obligations, were exempt. An evidence of the diversity of custom resulting from conditions not clear to us is found in the appearance within the manor of lands or tenements to which certain rents and services have become attached, so that the name of tenements is taken from the services or rents due from them. Thus, for example, in Kent are found *averlonds*,[1] lands from which a special service of carting was due ; *wallondes*,[2] held by the service of a certain number of *deiwercas* in making a wall against the sea ; *honilonds, cheeselonds, hoplands, saltlands, maltlands*, held by the payment of food rents.[3] In Essex were *serlonds* and *seracras*,[4] held probably by the service of carting manure or paying *sharpenny* ; *lodland*,[5] like *averlond* or perhaps like *wallond* ; and on Ely manors *bindinglond*,[6] land held by some

---

[1] Cott. MSS. Faust. A. i, ff. 54, 60.
[2] Registrum Roffense, 628. Cf. Faust. A. i, ff. 52, 55, 182, 185. For the *wikarii* of Glastonbury living in manors with a sea-wall, see Rent. et Cust. Michaelis de Ambresbury, pp. 39, 44, 48.
[3] See below, under food rents.
[4] Domesday of St. Paul's, pp. lxxvii, 46, 49.
[5] D. S. P., pp. lxxvii, 49.
[6] Cott. MSS. Claud. C. xi, f. 34.

special service of binding grain. The hill lands in Norfolk and elsewhere suggest the presence of groups of villeins living high up on the downs and holding by services and customs on the whole more pastoral in character than the services of ordinary villeins, resembling, perhaps, those of the Welsh dairy farmers.[1] Not only is it difficult to explain such variations in the incidence of rents upon customary tenants, it is also difficult to draw the lines around customary tenure. There were classes of men within the manor, above and below the typical *operarii* in point of general importance, whose obligation was, in the main, the payment of a money rent, corresponding roughly to the week-work of the ordinary villein, but who were bound also to render occasional services and to pay some of the rents usually regarded as customary. The *molmen* of the northern and eastern counties and Kent, for example, held land by the rendering of certain clearly customary services, *werkerthes, graserths, studewerk,* and the like, and paid the ordinary condition rents of the villein, but they did not perform week-work, and their heaviest duty was the payment of a money rent, probably a commutation of the week-work, at four terms in the year.[2] With them may be

---

[1] Claud. C. xi, f. 199: 'De operariis tenentibus terras que vocantur hyllondes.' Cott. MSS. Tiber. B. ii, f. 171. Compare Bleadon Custumal (Royal Archaeol. Instit., Mem. Wilts and Salis., pp. 182–210) for mountain pastures from which herbage was paid; and S. Mich. Ambres. Rent., p. 135: 'quando animalia sua non possunt ire super montes,' and p. 144: 'super montes domini.' For the Welsh dairy farmers see Seebohm, Trib. Sys. in Wales, p. 46.

[2] Eng. Hist. Rev., i. 734, ii. 103, 332; Vill. in Eng., pp. 183 sqq. Such tenants were classed generally among the *consuetudinarii* on Ely manors and in Kent. In Add. MS. 6159, f. 22, they pay bedrips, hens, and *unthield*; in Claud. C. xi, f. 55, they pay heriot, tallage, relief, gersuma. Ibid., f. 233, they serve as reeves, beadles, or foresters; f. 247, their works are called *studewerks*. Yet in Ely they are distinguished in a measure from the ordinary *operarii*, and connected rather with the *censuarii*. In Bishop Hatfield's Survey of Durham, p. 175, they are called *malmen sive firmarii*, and their predecessors appear in Domesday Book as *firmarii*; on p. 187, they perform some labour services, hold 'avirakres', and elsewhere in the Survey, e. g. App. p. 211, they pay a money rent and are not classed with the *bondi* but described separately. They pay *skat*, e.g. App. p. 207: 'de xiii quar. frumenti receptis de li bondis . . . et de ij malmannis . . . pro eorum redditu de skat . . . de quolibet bondo ii buzs. cumulatis, et de quolibet malmanno i buz.' In a late vacancy roll of the bishopric of London, Min. Acc. 1140/20, the distinction is made:

compared the Ely *pocarii*[1] and the Bury *pokearii*,[2] who are distinguished from ordinary *custumarii*, or holders *in lancectagio*. Many *censuarii*, both those that held virgates and also those that held little cots and crofts and bords, seem to have been in the case of the *molmen*, and even to land which had been very recently assarted from the waste, and to tenements of the demesne let for a money rent, tenements which occur very commonly in earlier as well as in later manorial documents, customary rents were sometimes attached.[3] As a general rule, however, it may be said that assart land and demesne tenements were held by agreement, and were not liable to customary dues. Temporary exemption from customary obligations was often, though not always, extended also to tenements of men holding the little desired manorial offices, the reeves, beadles, and the like; and land which had in some way become attached to a manorial office, passing with it, might be permanently immune, for example the *reveland* and *aldremanlond* of the custumals.[4] A further question regarding the incidence of manorial rents arises in connexion with the class of men, clearly visible in some documents, and called by various names, like *anilepimen* or *undersetles*, who had no tenements of their own but were in the

---

' tam libere tenencium quam tenencium custumariorum vocatorum molmen.'

[1] Tiber. B. ii. f. 117 : ' Apud Pidele sunt quidam pocarii quandoque plus quandoque minus de quibus aliquis dat pro terra sua habenda ad faciendum ollas et pro veteribus seckellon' duos solidos.'

[2] Harl. MSS. 3977, f. 38 : ' tam custumarii quam illi qui tenent pokeaver.' Compare Harl. MSS. 1005, f. 69, where they are subject to the ordinary condition rents of the villein.

[3] See especially D. S. P., 3, 14, 23, 38, 39, 59, *pass.* Claud. C. xi. f. 250, *pass.* ; Faust. A. i, ff. 121, 123, and 125, where the *consuetudines de hinlondes* are *precariae*, Romescot, and money rents. The renting of the demesne was very common also at Glastonbury, and is mentioned often in the early survey of 1189. One of the articles of inquiry in this survey is the amount of demesne land occupied, ' positum foras in libertate vel vilenagio,' and the utility to the lord of the land so occupied (p. 21 : ' Et si ita fuerit domino utilius sicut est vel revocatum '). In one case (p. 121), much of the demesne was occupied by tenants and held like half virgates by a servile tenure and ' homines dicunt quod utilius est domino sic tenere quam si dominus teneret '. And see pp. 23, 82, 105. Sometimes demesne land held ' per vilenagium ' may be only customary land escheated through default of services or tenants.

[4] See below, under condition rents.

'mainpast' of important villeins or freemen. It is difficult to tell whether such men were responsible for manorial rents, and if so, whether they paid such rents directly to the bailiff, or through the tenant to whom they were attached.

Royal rents were in the beginning distributed in accordance with no manorial tradition, and the test of customary or non-customary tenure cannot therefore be applied in determining their incidence. They were regulated by extra-manorial conditions—by the relation of the township or the hundred, that is to say, to matters of taxation and defence and the maintenance of order and justice. The nature of the regulations, however, the working of the original principle of assessment within the vill or hundred, is difficult to discover, because, as has been said, the superimposed manor confused the old arrangements of the vill, and by its substitution of the manorial lord for the king's officers brought about a certain assimilation of two kinds of dues quite different in origin. Clearly, nevertheless, the important line of division within the manor determining the incidence of royal dues was not between men of differing status or tenure, but between men that held geldable land (*terra geldabilis, hydata*) and men that held land for one reason or another not geldable. The land most commonly not geldable was the demesne, and its extent is therefore stated usually in the custumals in real acres, and not in fractions of hides, the units of assessment. It enjoyed its exemption, originally, on the theory that it provided ' for the maintenance of knights or clerics who are performing military service or religious functions, of which the king and the public stand in need '.[1] The freedom of the demesne from some or all of the ' forinsec ' burdens to the king was, however, by no means universal in the thirteenth and fourteenth centuries ; the custom of different manors varied with regard to it, and the lord often enforced participation in rents, especially in the case of tenants newly enfeoffed. Notwithstanding, too, the levelling process of the years after the Conquest, indications remain of the different types of manors of the Domesday period, in

---

[1] Vinogradoff, English Society in the Eleventh Century, p. 186. See pp. 186–96 for the discussion of *inland* and *warland*.

which the demesne necessarily played different rôles.[1]   Some
Ely manors, for example, had no demesne,[2] and there were
manors of St. Paul's in which the demesne was largely assart
land, and in which labour services were therefore very light.[3]
Within the *warland*, or land *de ware*, the geldable land, which
was often coincident with the land in service and held at
a money rent, and which might, as at Ramsey and Ely, be
geldable to the manorial lord and not to the king direct, the
assessment of royal dues was also sometimes very irregular.
Occasionally ' beneficial hidation ' on a small scale is evident,
small tenements having been put out of hidation ;[4] more often
parallels to the customary *averlonds* and *serlonds* are found
in the *wardacres* and *suitlands*, and the like, the tenements to
which royal dues had become attached.   The custumals often
record the responsibility of some individuals within the vill
and not of others for royal rents, while an Ely custumal shows
the curious distribution of royal dues among some manors of
a hundred and not others.   Much remains far from clear, however, concerning the distribution and assessment of royal
dues and the relation of townships to royal taxation and
justice.   A similar exemption of the demesne from church
dues occurs sometimes in manors belonging to monasteries
and religious houses.

The best sorts of material for the study of manorial rents
are the custumals of great groups of church manors and the
accounts of manorial officers.   Of these the custumals are
more descriptive in character than the account rolls, and contain sometimes an explanation of the rent, or a clue to its
meaning, and a statement of the classes and individuals upon
whom it was incident.   They make no attempt at classification.   The later custumals often give more rents and more
details than the earlier, either because the services and rents
had actually increased in number or weight, or else because
greater precariousness in the rendering of them to the lord

---

[1] Eng. Soc. in Elev. Cent., pp. 311 et seq.
[2] Claud. C. xi, ff. 82, 86.
[3] D. S. P., pp. 7 et seq., 73 et seq., 99 et seq.
[4] See, for example, Cranfield, in Ramsey Cartulary, ii. 5, 6, 11, 13.

had led to stricter definition. Where the custumals contain two sets of extents for the same manors dating from different periods, or refer to the older and newer assizes, excellent possibilities are afforded for the comparison of the weight of customary obligations at different times, and for the study of the encroachments of the new money system. Ministers' accounts are not descriptive, but record, under irregularly classified headings, the receipts of rents among the other receipts of the bailiff for the given year, and give the total amount of the rent received from the manor without details as to its incidence on individuals. Such rolls are valuable in showing the actual receipt of the rents described in the custumals, and give much interesting information regarding the general financial status of the manor. Very occasionally they record, under the bailiff's yearly expenses, the paying over of a royal rent by the bailiff to a royal officer, but usually they make few distinctions among manorial, royal, and church rents because all were received by the lord in one capacity or another. Perhaps the most generally useful and convenient of the account rolls for the study of rents are the rolls of the king's custodians of churches during vacancies, in which the manors of a church are grouped together according to their bailiwicks, and the receipts from the manors lying within each bailiwick given very briefly. The important restriction of certain rents to certain localities is thus made evident. The Hundred Rolls also, in so far as they are custumals, although omitting the greater number of the rents shown in other documents, are useful in showing this localization of rents, while with the Quo Warranto Rolls they form the best material for the study of the royal dues. Court rolls, of which comparatively few have been examined, contain sometimes interesting fines for the non-payment of rents of various kinds. An attempt has been made in the following study to cover generally the different counties, but the amount of material remaining unexamined in which rents may be found is very great, and until it has been studied more fully anything approaching an exhaustive list, or a correct classification, is impossible. A greater knowledge of local conditions, moreover, would undoubtedly in many cases help to explain the meaning of rents concerning which little has been discovered, and their interesting limitation to certain districts. Traces of diversity and variation seem to increase in number as the material is more closely studied. The present collection of rents, while incomplete and leaving much unexplained, may perhaps serve as a basis for later additions, and indicate some at least of the main divisions of the subject.

CHAPTER I

FOOD RENTS

THE study of customary rents begins best with those that point back for their origin to an ancient system of exploitation which depended, not on agricultural services and the cultivation of part of the village set apart as the lord's, but on the simpler rendering to the lord of stock and dairy products, ale, grain, provender, and other commutation rents of early rights of progress and quartering. In Wales there are unmistakable traces of such a system lingering into historical times. In England the pressure of the manorial organization succeeded in large measure in obliterating earlier arrangements, yet important food rents and certain other rents and services are hardly to be explained otherwise than as parts of a past order of things, and while it is true that the commutation of most food rents for money indicates that the general utility of a system of purveyance was over, yet even in this later period old conditions had not entirely disappeared ; a gift to the lord's larder was by no means unwelcome, and monastic houses depended for their support upon regular requisitions of food supplies from certain of their manors.

In Wales and Scotland there are indications of a double system of food rents, of the purveyance rights of princes and their households and officers, on one hand—the progresses, or *dovraeth* of the Welsh, and *conveth* of the Scotch—and, on the other, of the *gwesta*, or later *tunc pound* of the Welsh, the *can* or *cain* of the Scotch, the tribute sent to important chieftains.[1] Some rude distinction of this kind probably lies

---

[1] See Trib. Sys. in Wales, especially pp. 154 et seq. ; the Denbigh Survey, especially in the *communes consuetudines* enumerated at the end of the description of each commote (ff. 43 et seq., 146 et seq., 200 et seq., 244 et seq., and Skene, Celtic Scotland, iii. 227 et seq.).

at the base of the Saxon system also, but has been obscured past clear recognition by the processes of manorialization which have tended to assimilate rents and duties of various origins. The rents and services of the manorial period to which an origin may be assigned in older systems of purveyance, public or private, are those surviving from the old *feorm*, royal or monastic, those connected with hunting and the requisitions of officers, and the common food rents paid to manorial lords.

The royal *feorm* retained by the king and not granted away to churches belongs in the main to the earlier period, and need not be included in a study of the later rents.[1] It still appears in Domesday Book as the farm of a day or a night, or a number of days or nights, on those among the ancient demesne manors in which no geld was paid,[2] and it lingered on almost to the days of the *Dialogus*,[3] and perhaps, in rare cases, later still.[4] With it may be connected the requisitions of food from counties, which were soon lost in the farm of the county,[5] but perhaps formed sometimes the excuse for the extortionate demands of grain and stock made by bailiffs and royal officers.

The monastic farms, on the other hand, the *firmae* or food rents paid to monasteries by some of their manors, were a very important part of the later manorial economy. In most, perhaps in all, great groups of manors belonging to churches there was a highly elaborated system according to which certain manors sent up in regular rotation once, twice, thrice, even seven times a year, a specified supply of food. Thus at

---

[1] In Birch, Cartularium Saxonicum, No. 273, the well-known Westbury gafol, the king retains the farm in his own hands; elsewhere he grants it to churches, e. g. Nos. 241, 350, 535, 551, 622, 705.

[2] Round, Feudal England, pp. 100-10 ; Vinogradoff, Eng. Soc. in Elev. Cent., pp. 326 et seq.

[3] Dial. Scac. I. vii : ' Toto igitur regis Willelmi primi tempore perseuerauit hec institutio usque ad tempora regis Henrici filii eius, adeo ut viderim ego ipse quosdam qui victualia statutis temporibus de fundis regiis ad curiam deferri viderint.'

[4] Rot. Hund. i. 291, 380. Cf. i. 146: ' Item dicunt quod dicta villata est quoddam amelettum quod vocatur Stopesfeld quod debet ad fultum domini Regis iis. per annum.'

[5] Maitland, Domesday Book and Beyond, p. 169.

Ramsey a fortnightly farm included 12 quarters of ground wheat valued at 20s. for the monks and guests, and 2,000 *vokepanni* or loaves for the servants, 50 measures of barley for ale valued at 32s., 25 measures of malt valued at 24s., 24 measures of fodder, 10 lb. of cheese, 10 lb. of lard, 2 *treiae* of beans, 2 *treiae* of butter, bacon, honey, 10 fressings, 14 lambs, 125 hens, 14 geese, 2,200 eggs, 1,000 herrings. In addition, 5 cartloads of hay were sent from certain manors, and £4 in money from every manor.[1] An arrangement similar in its essential features is described at St. Paul's[2] and at St. Andrew's, Rochester,[3] and is clearly indicated elsewhere. St. Edmund's manors, for example, owed two, three, seven farms a year, as the case might be, and a special farm called the 'farm of St. Edmund'.[4] Certain services of brewing also are described in connexion with the Bury farms.[5] The manors of Ely threshed and carried the 'farm of St. Etheldreda',[6] Glastonbury villeins reaped, mowed, and threshed *ad firmas Glastonie*.[7] On the Worcester manors of Hanbury and Stoke in Gloucestershire a money rent, with a very ancient name, *ferm fultum*, was paid at Hokeday,[8] and

---

[1] Ram. Cart. iii. 160 et seq., 230 et seq.; i. 65. Compare Chron. Ram., pp. 40, 206.

[2] D. S. P., Introduction. [3] Custumale Roffense, pp. 12, 20, 35.

[4] Harl. MSS. 3977, f. 39: (Heringwelle) 'Firme iii ... redd' ad quemlibet firmam xxxvs. xd. et iid. in communi ... Nota quod villa inveniet focale ad quemlibet firmam sed dominus inveniet ad quemlibet firmam ccc. bruer' ad pistrinam et villata totum residuum et ad Sanctum Edmundum cariabit.' Also, ff. 85, 99, 101: '... que vocatur firma Sancti Edmundi.' Harl. MSS. 1005, f. 68: '... ad sextam et septimam firmam xxvjs. viiid.' Also f. 71.

[5] Harl. MSS. 3977, f. 90: 'Item debet semper ad terciam firmam ad bracinum vid. Ita quod in uno anno erit semel in bracino et in alio anno bis, et cum fuerit in bracino erit quietus de duabus operationibus.' f. 98: 'Omnis qui braciat contra Natale debet unum presentum de pane et cervisia et de gallinis non consuetudine sed amore.'

[6] Claud. C. xi, f. 50: (Wilburton) '... et vocatur firma Sancte Etheldrede'; f. 106: Somersham; threshing of 24 garbs 'ad firmam Sancte Etheldrede'. Vacancy Roll of Ely, P. R. O. Min. Acc., 1132/10: (Somersham) 'Et de vis. ob. q. de opere custumariorum ad blada trituranda vocato Audreferme.'

[7] Inquest of 1189, p. 30: 'et solet falcare metere sumagiare flagellare ad firmas Glastonie.' Compare Mich. Ambr. Rent., p. 180.

[8] Worcester Vac. Roll, 1143/18: (Hanbury in Salso Marisco) '... et de xvs. vid. ob. de quadam certa consuetudine que vocatur fermfoltum ad hokeday.' Again at Stoke, ibid.

at Rollesby in Norfolk, belonging to the see of Norwich, a *ferm penes.*[1] On the Ely manor of Hatfield in Hertfordshire a rent of 16*d. fultume* occurs[2], and on St. Edmund's manors both *fermiping* and *fultume*.[3] Such monastic farms were not due from the tenants primarily, but were chargeable on the vill as a whole, and must have been derived in large measure, except for some supplementary rents of poultry and the like, from the demesne, cultivated by the labour of the villeins. The farm system as it appears in later times was then a method of exploitation of the manor and dependent on domanial arrangements, rather than a rent incumbent on customary tenants within the vill, and as such it does not fall within this study. It seems improbable, however, that for this reason it should be severed entirely from preceding conditions. The question of its relation to the older feorm remains, and is difficult to answer.[4] Whether the monastic farms existed in their later elaborate form hidden behind the frequent brief descriptions in Domesday Book of lands *in dominio, de victu monachorum, de vestitu monachorum*,[5] the older *fosterlands, bedlands*, and *scrudlands* of the charters,[6] or whether they were a conscious later adaptation and elaboration of simpler beginnings, or even a new system formed in some measure on the basis of the old food rents, is not clear. A constant and heavy food charge like that of later times would probably have had great

[1] Norwich Vac. Roll, 1141/1 (18-20 Edw. II).
[2] Claud. C. xi, f. 159: 1 virgate of 40 acres ' dat de fultome sexdecim denarios equaliter '. Cf. Rot. Hund. i. 146, and Tiber. B. ii, f. 141.
[3] Harl. MSS. 1005, f. 72: ' De redd' terre cum xvi*s.* de fermiping.' Harl. MSS. 3977, f. 37: (Bertone) ' Redditus mutabiles scilicet fultume scharsilver average '. Harl. MSS. 1005, f. 69: (Bertone) repeated.
[4] For the older feorm see Birch, Cart. Sax., Nos. 501, 566, 678, 812, 1013, and loc. cit. Compare D. B. B., pp. 234 et seq., Vinogradoff, Growth of Manor, pp. 129-30, 223 et seq., and the Rectitudines (Schmid, App. III., p. 37), where it is stated that the geneat must ' feormian ' his lord and give him the gaerswyn ; the gebur must give him food rents, and in certain places feorms must be rendered.
[5] Thus some Ramsey manors owing a fortnightly farm in later times appear in Domesday Book as ' de dominio ' manors (D. B. i. 192). Cf. i. 65 b, *pass.* Rot. Hund. ii. 429, land *ad vesturam.*
[6] For example, Cart. Sax., Nos. 384, 535, 566, 592, 747, 819, 894, 922, 1045, 1159; and compare 706: ' let him that is bishop there do his full fostaer except from the bedlands of his bishop's hams '; and 705, *738, *1267, K. 956. (Those whose authenticity is suspected by Kemble are starred.)

influence in creating the rudiments of the demesne, 'rustic work' for the cultivation of the lord's tribute being in Domesday Book part of the *consuetudines firmae*,[1] and the distinction between land used to produce the lord's food and lord's land being easily lost.

Other survivals of the old purveyance arrangements are the rents and services connected with hunting expeditions, the instances of which in later documents are rare, but point clearly to heavy and important earlier duties allied to the farm.[2] In Wales, in the fourteenth century, such services were still rendered. The Denbigh Survey, for example, describes the rents paid for the support of hunting parties,[3] and the Record of Caernarvon mentions the *Kilgh' Hebogothion*, or food rent for the falconer.[4] The best known references to such services after the Conquest in England are the passages in Boldon Book, often quoted, describing the *magna caza*, or hunting-house, built for the bishop, which was sixty feet long, sixteen feet wide, and the chapel, which was forty feet long and fifteen feet wide.[5] Certain tenants make the 'service of the forest', forty days in Founesson, forty days in Ruith, and 'feed a horse and dog'.[6] The same services are described again in almost the same words in Bishop Hatfield's survey of a much later time.[7] *Stabilitio Venationis* due to

---

[1] D. B. i. 172 b. Compare Eng. Soc. in Elev. Cent., p. 386.

[2] Compare Cart. Sax., Nos. 366, 395, 413, 416, 443, 450, 488, 489, 540, 612, 848, and especially 454 : ' Ab illis causis quas cum feorme et eafor vocitemus tam a pastu ancipitrorum meorum omnium quam etiam venatorum omnium vel a pastu equorum meorum omnium sive ministrorum eorum. Quid plura ab omni illa incommoditate Aefres et cum feorme nisi istis causis quas hic nominamus . . .'

[3] Denbigh Survey, loc. cit. Compare Trib. Sys. in Wales, pp. 154 et seq.

[4] Record of Caernarvon, pp. 39, 49, 213, 214, and 40 : ' et kilgh Hebbogothion videlicet prandium magistro uni' garcioni et uni' falcon' per diem et noctem.' Trib. Sys. in Wales, App. p. 116: 8 westwas are in the commote. ' Dicunt eciam quod quelibet westwa q' solebat pascere dominum cum familia sua quater in anno et weysenteylu venatores cum canibus domini falconarios cum avibus per adventus suos quod quidem servicium vocatur west' et extenditur per annum ad xxi*li*. viii*d*.' See also p. 12.

[5] Boldon Book (D. B. iv), p. 575. See also pp. 566, 576, 577, *pass.*

[6] Ibid. pp. 571, 572, 575, 578, 580, *pass.*

[7] Bish. Hatf. Surv., pp. 10, 30, 69, 158, 172, 185, 190.

the king is mentioned in Domesday Book.[1] Still other excellent references to hunting services occur in the Winchester documents, where, commonly, the bishop's horses and dogs and falconers had to be fed, and sometimes also 'the dogs of the king which come at the feast of St. James',[2] and this compulsory feeding of horses and dogs occurs elsewhere.[3]

In the west, in manors near the Welsh border, hunting services were especially important. At Sutton in Warwickshire whenever the lord hunted the customary tenants used 'fugare waulassum et stabulum' in the chase of wild beasts, according to the quantity of their tenement, a whole virgate owing two days' service.[4] In a charter to Worcester there is reference to the relaxation of a hunting service of two 'seuras' which the lord was accustomed to have from a certain manor, and also to freedom from *douereth* (Welsh *dovraeth*) *servientium*, or purveyance rights of the lord's officers.[5] To such services as these goes back probably the Gloucester rent, the *hunteneselver*, paid at the heavy rate of 8*d.* a half virgate,[6] and possibly, although not at all clearly, the *hyndergeld*[7] of Gloucester and the *unthield* of Kent. With these rents and services should be compared the exactions and extortions of foresters, woodwards, and other royal officers, which are discussed in connexion with the rents making up the profits of counties and hundreds.

The payment of rents in food to the lord of the manor by the customary tenants from their own produce was a common obligation, and on church manors owing a farm occurs in addition to the farm. Of a recent origin for most of such rents there is no evidence; they were either survivals of the

[1] Cf. Eng. Hist. Rev. xx. 286.
[2] Winch. Pipe Rolls, pp. 3, 6, 14, 17, 22, *pass.* Compare Hazlitt's Blount's Tenures, p. 27 n. The burgesses are to find a man 'ter per annum ad stabliamentum, pro venatione capienda, quando episcopus voluerit'.
[3] Econ. Cond. Ram. Man., App. p. 11.
[4] Dugdale, Antiq. Warw. ii. 911 : 'Et quotienscunque Dominus ad venandum venenerit (*sic*) isti custumarii solebant fugare Waulassum et Stabulum in fugatione ferarum bestiarum secundum quantitatem tenurae suae.' Cf. p. 912.
[5] Reg. Worc. Pr., p. 9 b.
[6] Glouc. Cart. iii. 22, 71, 72, 76. See Vill. in Eng. p. 292, n. 1.
[7] See below, under miscellaneous rents.

same ancient system of purveyance as the farm, being in some way supplementary to it, and existing along with it, or else they represented the remains of the old food rent, side by side with which the newer *firmae* had developed. In general they were trifling in amount, and in themselves would not require a very full discussion. The universality of their occurrence among villein tenants, however, the inclusion of poultry and grain rents among customary obligations as a matter of course, gives them an importance apart from their intrinsic value, and justifies the belief in a connexion between them and some ancient, widely prevalent system of purveyance on the part of the lord.

Throughout England there was general similarity in the kind and amount of food rents paid, and a common increase at certain times in the year, especially at Christmas. The most important rents were made in poultry and grain, fish, malt or ale, and salt, or the commutation of these into money. Payment was made in most cases at three 'terms', or seasons ; poultry at Christmas, eggs at Easter, and grain at Martinmas, and the manner of assessment on the villeins was not widely different in different parts of England. The rents may be studied conveniently in the full custumals of church manors. In the west, on manors belonging to the church of Gloucester, most villeins gave hens, valued at a penny each, at Christmas to their lord.[1] The rate of the payment was a hen from each villein, whatever the size of his tenement, and where two villeins together held one tenement, two hens were paid.[2] The rent was then, in a sense, a capitation payment, incumbent on the person, not the tenement. That it was ancient is proven by the fact that it is spoken of as part of the *antiqua tenura* of a manor.[3] *Censuarii* whose labour services had been commuted entirely or in part, and small tenants by a labour or money rent, sometimes still rendered hens to the lord.[4] The Christmas hen at Gloucester, as elsewhere, was often regarded as in some way connected with the receipt of

---

[1] Glouc. Cart. iii. 48, 62, 63, 71, 95, 97, *pass.*
[2] Ibid. iii. 63, 72.   [3] Ibid. iii. 70.
[4] Ibid. iii. 70, 89, *pass.*

wood by the tenant, and was therefore called the woodhen.[1] On manors of Gloucester lying in Hampshire it is difficult to distinguish the Christmas hen from the churchscot payment of hens and eggs and corn, which was especially heavy in this county.[2] In addition to the hen, sometimes in place of it, the ordinary villein paid eggs to his lord at Easter,[3] but there is no evidence at Gloucester of the necessary agreement between the number of eggs and the number of acres held which sometimes appears elsewhere. Gloucester corn rents are rarely mentioned, except occasional rents of oats,[4] and commutation of food rents was evidently unusual.

For the payment of food rents to the church of Worcester there are two excellent sources of information. One of these, the Register of the Priory, dating from the middle of the thirteenth century, shows that the payment of the Christmas hens and Easter eggs was much less common at Worcester than at Gloucester.[5] More frequent rents in kind were oats, paid at the festival of the Purification in the form of seed with which the villein was bound to sow half an acre of the lord's demesne;[6] sheep and lambs paid at Easter, a rent later commuted for money;[7] bread and ale at Christmas,[8] and grain paid for churchscot at Martinmas. It should be noticed, however, that new assizes had been made recently at Worcester, and it seems probable that according to these the older food rents had been superseded by money rents, paid as an annual lump sum, or *firma*, commuting certain services and most rents; an inference which is confirmed by the

---

[1] Glouc. Cart. iii. 95, 96, and especially 71 : ' Et dabit unam gallinam ad Natale Domini pretio unius denarii et propter illam gallinam consueverunt habere de bosco domini Regis unam summam bosci quae vocatur dayesem ' ; and 95 : ' Et dabit unam gallinam quae vocatur Wodehen et valet unum denarium.' For a similar hen, called ' Rushhen ', Mr. Gray has kindly given me the following reference : ' Misc. B. Treas. of Receipt 163, f. 111 : Customs of Aldeburgh, Suff. Cottagers keeping a fire pay a " russhe henne or ells 2*d.* which is for the rushes that thei gather upon the lord's common mer ".'

[2] Ibid. iii. 39, 40, 43 ; and see below, under church rents.
[3] Ibid. iii. 90, 91, 191, *pass*.   [4] Ibid. iii. 170.
[5] Reg. Worc. Pr., pp. 32 b, 33 b, 44 a, 81 b, Introd. lxiv.
[6] Ibid. pp. 10 b, 14 b, 19 a, 33 b, 51 b, 102 a, *pass*.
[7] Ibid. p. 10 b.   [8] Ibid. p. 34 a.

examination of the second and earlier source of information
for Worcester mentioned above, the roll of the manors of the
church during a vacancy in the very beginning of the century.[1]
In this roll there is frequent reference to hens and eggs *de
redditu* which have been sold and have brought in money
returns.　At Abingdon[2] and Barking[3] the Easter eggs were
commuted for *eysilver*, an unusual rent.

In the account rolls of Winchester hens are accounted for
by bailiffs among the receipts of the manor,[4] and still other
hens are entered on the rolls as churchscot hens.[5]　The rolls
mention also the *semen villanorum*, or seed for sowing the
demesne,[6] the *gavelseed* of other localities, and the Bleadon
Custumal mentions *cotsetlescorn* and *veremecorn*.[7]

In all the manors of St. Paul's food rents were collected,
except in Kenesworth, Hertfordshire, Norton, Essex, and
Drayton, Middlesex, which were largely assart lands, and
exploited not by the services of the *antiqua tenura* but by
the rendering of money and boon labour.[8]　All other manors
paid some food rent to the *firmarius*.　In most cases the rent
took the form of hens and eggs, with the occasional addition
of *gavelseed*, the seed for sowing the demesne,[9] fodder corn,
mallards, and capons.[10]　In Adulvesnasa, Essex, there was an
interesting payment of two *dodds* of oats made from every
house of the *hidarii* in the middle of March, and *ad mescingam*
fourteen loaves.[11]　In the introduction to the Domesday of
St. Paul's the editor defines *mescinga* as the same word as
metsung, food or meat, stating also that it occurs in the unprinted extents of 1279 as *messing silver*, evidently a com-

---

[1] Vac. Roll, 1143/18: (30–31 Edw. I) '. . . Et de xv*s*. de D. ovis de
redditu venditis ad pascham. . . . Et de ix*s*. iij*d*. qu. de lxxiiij gallinis et
quarta parte i. galline de redditu ad Nathale venditis.'
[2] Abing. Acc., App. p. 145: 'to the kitchener for eys[ilver] 16*d*.'
See p. 159.
[3] Dugdale's Monasticon Anglicanum, i. 444: 'Sche must pay to
xxxvij ladyes of the covent for their eysylver . . . and then must sche pay
to the priorie . . . xxxij egges or elles ij d. ob. q.'
[4] Winch. Pipe Rolls, pp. 20, 23, 63, 76, 81, *pass.*
[5] Ibid. pp. 23, 62, 81, *pass.*　　　　[6] Ibid. p. 69, *pass.*
[7] Blead. Cust., pp. 191, 196.
[8] D. S. P., pp. 7 et seq., 73 et seq., 99 et seq.　　[9] Ibid. p. 33; cf. p. 6.
[10] Ibid. pp. 6, 47, 83, and Introd. p. lxix.
[11] Ibid. pp. 43, 47.

muted payment, or *metegafol*, the older form of the word in the *Rectitudines*.[1] In most manors the hens and eggs were due from tenements that show some signs of antiquity, from the regular tenements of servile labourers, virgaters, *hydarii*, or smaller *operarii*, or from assart of the demesne or other land held by *antiqua tenura*, and not from the tenements which are often described as assarted and which were held by a purely money tenure. In most cases one hen was rendered from each house at Christmas, but occasionally on some manors two hens. Once it is stated that every house in the vill owes a hen at Christmas.[2] The number of eggs, on the other hand, depended on the size of the tenement, the rate when stated being, with one or two trifling exceptions, one egg to one acre, and the half virgate being considered for this purpose usually as fifteen acres paying fifteen eggs, the virgate as thirty acres paying thirty eggs. Once or twice the number of eggs is not mentioned, but is left 'ad libitum tenentium et ad honorem domini'.[3] It may probably be taken as a general rule that on St. Paul's manors every acre of land, not newly assarted, paid an egg at Easter. As has been seen, this statement is not necessarily true in other great groups of manors.

Good examples of food rents are found also in the manors of the fen district. To the Abbot of Peterborough hens were usually paid at Christmas and eggs at Easter. As in the case of the other rents mentioned in the Black Book, the total number paid by the vill is given and not the number due from each villein;[4] either the compiler of the record added together the sums from the vills for his own convenience in statement, or else it was usual for the *villate* to make certain payments in common. The villagers gave also, in addition to the hens, eggs, measures of oats, and loaves of bread, in

---

[1] D. S. P., Introd., p. lxxvi.
[2] Ibid. p. 143: 'et quelibet domus totius ville debet gallinam ad Nathale et ad Pascha ova.'
[3] Ibid. p. 51. See also p. 48: 'Et ad pascha ova ad honorem domini.'
[4] Chron. Petrob., pp. 157, 158, 159, 160, and 161: 'In Pihtesle . . . omnes villani reddunt xxxij gallinas ad Nativitatem. Et pleni villani reddunt xx ova dimidii x ova et cotsete v ad Pascha.'

return sometimes for dead wood,[1] and sowed the land of the demesne with their own seed.[2] Few records of Thorney have been found, but from the full custumals in the Hundred Rolls it is clear that several hens were commonly paid by a villein at Christmas.[3] The records of Ramsey food rents from approximately the same locality are, on the other hand, numerous and interesting. Hens at Christmas and eggs at Easter were almost universally paid, both in the twelfth and thirteenth centuries. The rate was usually one hen from each villein, and a varying number of eggs;[4] but more than one hen was sometimes paid by a tenant,[5] and the number of eggs and the acreage of the tenement sometimes agreed.[6] A connexion between the Christmas hen and wood received by the tenant is made, as in the case of the Gloucester *wood-hen*, the virgater taking 'thorns' from the abbot's wood in return for a hen, or giving two hens for *wodegonge*.[7] Other Ramsey rents in kind were *benesed*,[8] or seed for sowing the demesne, a ring of oats for fodder corn at Christmas or in Lent,[9] and a corn bote.[10] Ely food rents too were heavy. In the vacancy rolls of Edward I's reign[11] there are usually recorded large receipts from hens belonging to the Christmas rent which have been sold, and from eggs belonging to the Easter rent. A commuted *foddercorn* is very common. An extent roll of 1319[12] shows the virgaters at Swaffham

---

[1] Chron. Petrob., pp. 160, 161, 162, 163, 165, and 159: 'Et omnes isti reddunt per annum xxij sceppas avene pro mortuo bosco et xxij panes.'
[2] Ibid. pp. 160, 161, 165.
[3] Rot. Hund. ii. 642, 643, 644, 645.
[4] Ram. Cart. iii. 243: A virgater gave a hen at Christmas and carried eggs 'sine numero' at Easter. See i. 44, 287, 335, 345, 384; iii. 253, 271, 281, 305, *pass*. For the egg rent see especially i. 489: 'Colligenda sunt ova ad opus domini de domo in domum ad voluntatem dantis ut vituli sui possunt ablactari communiter in blado totius villatae.' The miller also collected eggs: i. 489.
[5] Ibid. i. 356, 369; cottars gave four hens one year, five the next.
[6] Ibid. i. 322.
[7] Ibid. i. 56, 58, 299, 302.
[8] Ibid. i. 287, 394, 399, 461; ii. 24.
[9] Ibid. i. 287, 300, 345, 357, *pass*.
[10] Rot. Hund. ii. 630.   [11] Vac. Roll, 1132/10.
[12] In the muniment room of Ely cathedral, describing eight manors.

and Wratting paying one hen each at Christmas and twenty eggs at Easter, and at Somersham there is mention of a rent in money from a commuted woodhen called *heynwodeselver* or *heggingwoodsilver*.[1] The Hundred Rolls record Ely food rents of hens, eggs, and a *cornbote* at Michaelmas of a sheaf of winter wheat and a sheaf of spring wheat,[2] while in the custumals of the manors of the bishopric the food rents from the manors in the Isle of Ely, and from manors in outlying counties are described still more fully. The usual rate of the poultry rent was a hen or two hens at Christmas and ten eggs at Easter from the *plena terra* of the typical *operarius*,[3] and sometimes half as many eggs were paid as acres contained in the tenement,[4] while sometimes there is no relation between the two numbers.[5] *Molmen, operarii,* and *cottars* all gave the poultry rent, and the hen is called *Woodhen*[6] and connected with the villein's *wodericht de subbosco*.[7] An interesting distinction is drawn in the description of Hecham, Suffolk, between the hens paid by *operarii* in full standing, for which *wodericht* was received, and the hens of the 'newly enfeoffed' and the *undersetli*, who received no *wodericht* in return.[8] Important grain rents, too, are described in the custumals :— the *foddercorn* of six bushels of oats paid at the sowing time, or commuted for a rent of 3*d.* or 6*d.* which was due at Easter time, and if not paid promptly was, in one manor at least, doubled,[9] the *cornbote* or sheaf of the best wheat

[1] Vac. Roll, 1132/10: 'Et de xxvis. xd. ob. de opere de Wodehenes affirmato termino Nativitatis Sancti Iohannis Baptiste vocato Heynwodesilver.'

[2] Rot. Hund. ii. 543, 605.

[3] Claud. C. xi, ff. 283, 290, *pass.*

[4] Ibid. ff. 152, 169.

[5] Ibid. ff. 171, 217, *pass.*

[6] Ibid. f. 69, Tiber. B. ii, f. 98.

[7] Claud. C. xi, f. 169 : 'Et sciendum quod iste et omnes alii custumarii et censuarii qui dant gallinas debent habere Wodericht de subbosco.'

[8] Ibid. f. 290: 'Item sciendum quod unusquisque consuetudinarius et operarius qui dederit gallinam domino de annuo redditu habebit tria fassicula parva de subbosco per visum et liberacionem ballivi quolibet anno contra Natale exceptis omnibus illis de novo feoffatis qui gallinas dederint et capones et exceptis similiter omnibus undersetlis.'

[9] Ibid. f. 285 : 'Fodercorn die Clausi Pasche iiid. et nisi illo die sol ventur tunc in crastino dupplicabuntur.' See also ff. 220, 263, 272, 292, 304, and Tiber. B. ii, ff. 174, 176.

paid to the lord,[1] the *candelcorn*,[2] and the *sedbede*[3] and *metecorn*.[4]

In other manors in East Anglia food rents were common. A vacancy roll of Norwich in Edward II's reign mentions Christmas hens and Easter eggs, *hedercorn*, and other food rents ;[5] *tolkorn* occurs in Essex,[6] and Bury villeins paid a *cornbote* of 5*s.*, which in other cases appears as a carting service of corn performed by free and unfree in possession of beasts of burden, due at Martinmas or at the summons of the bailiff.[7] One curious statement seems to suggest a connexion of some kind between a 'foddercorn of the Abbot of St. Edmund's' and the hundred, as if the foddercorn were an old hundredal rendering of provender which has passed over into the abbot's hands.[8]

In Kent hens and eggs are recorded on the lands of St. Augustine, where the Christmas hen is called the *wodevoel*,[9] and Christ Church, and on the Kentish manor of Wye belonging to Battle, where some interesting details are given concerning the collection of the rent by the *serviens* of the lord. The *serviens* went once at each season to collect three

---

[1] Claud. C. xi, f. 200: 'Dabit unam garbam melioris bladi quam habuerit de cornbote ex consuetudine et illam portabit ad curiam domini die S. Thome Apostoli quolibet anno scilicet quando curia communis erit apud Brunesgreve pro renovatione plegiorum.' Compare Vac. Roll, 1132/10, Tripplehowe.

[2] Vac. Roll, 1132/10: '(Brigham) Cum vi*d.* . . . pro candelcorn, at All Saints.'

[3] Claud. C. xi, f. 176.　　　　[4] Ibid. f. 178.

[5] Vac. Roll, 1141/1. For Essex see Cust. of 1298, Essex Archaeol. Trans. N. S. 109.

[6] Mon. Angl. iv. 37 (Extent, 18 Edw. II) 'vi quart' Tolkorn'.

[7] Harl. MSS. 3977, f. 82: 'Notandum quod omnes liberi et non liberi portabunt quolibet anno in vigilia S. Michaelis qui averia habeant per quendam consuetudinem que vocatur cornbote. Qui autem non habent averia non portabunt.' See ff. 91, 98.

[8] Ibid. f. 44: 'Foddercorn Abbatis S. Edmundi': measures and sum from each hundred are given; also the names of the men paying it, and the amounts in some vills. Compare Harl. MSS. 1005, f. 83.

[9] Faust. A. i, f. 123: 'Et debent unam gallinam tercia die Natalis Domini et serviens domini queret illam quam vocant Wedevole quia debent habere brueram ad focum.' And f. 124: 'solvit . . . ad Natale Domini gallinam quod [*sic*] vocatur Wdehenne quia clamant habere boscum ad ignem suum.' Compare Vac. Roll, 1128/4; Harl. MSS. 1006, f. xiiii ; Add. MSS. 6159, f. 22.

hens at Christmas and twenty eggs at Easter from each yoke of land. If the rent were not forthcoming on these occasions it had to be carried to the *curia* by the tenants within twelve days. If, however, at the end of twelve days it was still unpaid, the tenants made agreement regarding the hens, and were in mercy 21*d*.[1] Large numbers of hens and eggs were paid to Rochester as part of the *Exennium Sancti Andreae*.[2] *Gadercorn* was paid on manors belonging to Christ Church from land in gavelkind.[3] A Rochester *cornbote* was curiously connected with trespass of pasture; if between Martinmas and the feast of St. John the messor impounded any animal taken in the lord's corn, he received a loaf of bread from the owner of the animal. If the animal were impounded between the feast of St. John and Michaelmas, however, a cornbote was given for all damage done.[4]

In the north of England food rents were common, but were very often commuted for money. At Hexham Priory hens were paid at Christmas by *terrae husbond'* and *cotagia*.[5] The Burton Chartulary mentions the payment of two hens at Christmas and twenty eggs at Easter among the 'ancient customs'.[6] On the manors of Durham the rent hens and rent eggs which are mentioned were probably paid as fixed rents (redditus assise) for the holdings.[7] More clearly ancient were other rents of hens occasionally described[8] and the grain rents on which the chief stress of the surveys falls. Bond and molmen both paid the lord *scat* rents of grain of various kinds, or the commutation of the rent called *scat penys, scat*

---

[1] Battle Abbey Custumal, p. 127. Compare p. 118 et seq.
[2] Cust. Roff., pp. 2, 3, 4; Reg. Roff., p. 133. Compare Exennium Archiepiscopi, Add. MSS. 6159, ff. 30, 32, 55, 56, 174.
[3] Add. MSS. 6159, f. 26.
[4] Cust. Roff., p. 11: '... detur cornbote de omnibus dampnis, sicut jurare voluerit secundum consuetudinem. Et si forte animal veniat ad transitum Domini in campo, per visum emendetur.'
[5] Hexham Priory (Sur. Soc.), ii. 4, 10, *pass.*
[6] Burton Chartulary, p. 85.
[7] Durham Halmote Rolls, pp. 184, 217, 219, 221, 224, 225, 241, 243. Compare maltlands, hoplands, cheeselands, and the like. See Rot. Hund. ii. 605, 747; Batt. Abb. Cust., pp. 33, 95, 155; Oxford Studies, i. 161, *n.*
[8] Bold. Book, pp. 566, 567, *pass.*

being used as a general term for tributary rent.[1] The rents most often described in Boldon Book and Bishop Hatfield's Survey are bushels of *scat*, probably *scat frumentum*, of *scat avena*, and of *braseum*, paid by *antiqui bondi*, later put at a *penyferm*.[2] Occasionally a *scat malt* is mentioned, and *maltpenys*, a commutation of it, both of which were included in the *scat penys*,[3] a general name for commuted grain rents.[4] In the Durham Halmote Rolls *Saint gelicorn* and *gellicorn* occur frequently, and also *avermalt, court haver, court otes*, and *scate haver*.[5] With the *court haver* may be compared the *avermalth* of Boldon Book, which was probably malt carried to the hall.[6] The vacancy rolls of Durham record the receipt of eggs at Easter, and of grain rents commuted into money, *dodcorn, scatfarina*, and the like,[7] and in a vacancy roll of York hens ' de consuetudine' at Christmas, or 'de lak ', are frequently mentioned.[8] *Almessecorn* occurs in a late document.[9]

The evidence from other church lands and from lay lands indicates in general poultry and grain rents similar to those already described. In the Hundred Rolls statements regarding the payment of hens and eggs and other rents in kind are fairly common. It should be noticed that in almost all these

---

[1] Feod. Dun. 32 *n* : 'illud antiquum servitium quod antiquitus vocabatur scat.' Bish. Hatf. Surv., 17 : 'red' de frumento, braseo, et avena de scat sicut bondi . . .,' pp. 21, 102, 128, 133, 145, 157.

[2] Ibid. p. 28.

[3] Ibid. pp. 145, 150, 157, 128: 'et pro scatpenys et averpenys . . . et pro scatpeyns vocatos (*sic*) per tenentes maltpenys 15*d*. et ad festum Purificationis B. Mariae 6 buz. avenarum de scat.'

[4] Ibid. pp. 99, 128, 133, 145, 150, 186.

[5] D. H. R., p. 129 : '. . . Pro una thrava avenae vocata Saintgilicorn detenta . . . 12*d*.' See pp. 159, 221, 241, 243.

[6] Bold. Bk., pp. 585, 586.

[7] Vac. Roll, 1144/17 : '. . . et de lixs. viij*d. q.* de xi mill. dccccxlv ovis de redditu ad Pascha venditis ;' and 1148/18 : '. . . et de lxiij*li.* ij*s.* viij*d. q.* de lxxij qu. ij bu. di. frumenti iiij. xvj qu. ordei et cc. v qu. ij bu. avene de quodam redditu ibidem vocato Dodcor[n] ad predictum terminum S. Michaelis . . . et de iiij. vij*li.* vj*s.* iij*d. ob. q.* de consuetudinibus vocatis scatpeny maltpeny scatfarina scat braseo scat avena et operibus diversorum tenencium . . . arrentatis.'

[8] Vac. Roll, 1144/1 : '. . . de gallinis de lak' . . . venditis.'

[9] Mon. Angl. vii. 870.

cases the poultry rents are uncommuted, while the grain rents in the east and north have often taken on a financial form, and also that the customary rent of hens is almost always fixed at one from each villein, whereas the rent of eggs may or may not be determined by the acreage of the tenement.

The Christmas rents to the lord of the manor were sometimes, as has been stated, connected with the villein's *wodericht*, wood and estover rights, but elsewhere they seem to have formed part of a larger rent, of a Christmas gift, *exennium*, *loc*, or *lok*, or *lak*, very commonly made to the lord, which looks like an old custom, possibly a survival of the winterfeorm of the *Rectitudines*. Christmas rents were not confined to England. The Christmas hens appear in Wales,[1] and also in Scotland and the north of England, where they were called *cain fowls* or *reek hens*, one being paid from every house that ' reeked ', and the payment being called *canage* and connected with a feast.[2] Thus in the Lancashire manor of Ashton-under-Lyne, among the services of tenants holding at the lord's will is regularly included a Yole or Yule present to the lord ' for the sake of partaking in the annual feast of the great hall '. The present was paid, ' as it is written and set in the rental,' in fowls, cheese, or oats, which were named cane fowls, cane cheese, or cane oats, the word cane signifying head, 'and the lord shall feed all his said tenants and their wives, upon Yoleday, at the dinner, if they like for to come.' The lord is ' not bounden to feed all that come ', however, but ' only the goodman and the goodwife '.[3] Durham records

---

[1] Denbigh Survey, ff. 204, 282, 283.

[2] Innes, Scotch Legal Antiq., pp. 204-5 : ' You will sometimes find, especially in church grants, as pertinents, *can* and *conveth*. Tithes are granted by some of our ancient kings *de cano meo*, that is, from customs or rents paid *in kind*. We have the word still in *cain* : the cain fowls of a barony are quite well understood. Cain fowls are sometimes called reek hens—one payable from every house that reeked—every fire house... Conveth seems to have been a due collected by a lord from his vassals, perhaps on the occasion of journeys. Malcolm IV granted to the canons of Scone from every plough ... for their conveth at the feast of All Saints,' a cow and two swine, meal, oats, hens, eggs, candles, soap, and cheese. See Denton, England in the Fifteenth Century, p. 231 n. ; Skene, Celtic Scotland, iii. 227 sqq., and above, p. 15.

[3] Hibbert, Cust. of Manor in North of Eng., p. 45 and App. Compare below, Whitsunales.

describe a 'Yulewayting', a rent paid at Christmas, connected either with some service of watching or, more probably, derived from *waytinga*, an old Scotch form of *conveth*.[1] *Geresgive* occurs in the records of Burton manors,[2] and again in the account rolls of Barton Regis near Bristol as a gift made at Circumcision,[3] with which should be compared the *gevesilver* of Worcester,[4] and the *Newyeresgive* of St. Edmund's,[5] and perhaps as a rent paid at Michaelmas, the heavy *Michilmeth* of Boldon Book, which occurs usually with *yolwayting*.[6]

Another form of the same Christmas custom was the rent *ad lok*, or later *loksilver*, common in Huntingdonshire, Cambridgeshire, Lincolnshire, and elsewhere. At Washingley in Huntingdonshire the lord received from his customary tenant at Christmas one cock, five hens, two loaves valued at 4*d*. each, and 'on the day on which the tenant carries this *lok* he shall dine with the lord, he, his wife, and his family'.[7] At Fleet in Lincolnshire the food so received was called *lookmete*.[8] The almost enforced feasting reminds one of the analogous

---

[1] Bish. Hatf. Surv., p. 18: 'Iidem bondi solvunt pro Yollwayting ad festum Nativitatis 6*s*.' See pp. 22, 5*s*. paid for Yholwayting, 28, *et pass.*; Bold. Bk., *pass.*; Skene, Celtic Scotland, iii. 227, et seq.

[2] Burt. Ch., p. 66: '. . . 20*s*. for geresgive on Christmas Day.' Compare Liber Albus, 130; Liber Cust., pp. 32, 249, 266; Madox, Excheq., 1504. Mrs. Green, Town Life, i, pp. 206–7, says that it was taken by the sheriff to remind him to come, and was collected by scotale if money were short. Hampson, Kal. Med. Aevi, gives much curious information regarding Christmas presents and presents on January first (*dies strenarum*), connecting them with the Roman Saturnalia. He describes also the analogous Scotch custom of presenting the 'sweetieskon'.

[3] Min. Acc. 850/9–10 '. . . et de ciiij*s*. ix*d*. de quadam consuetudine vocata geresgive ad festum circumcisionis Domini.'

[4] Worc. Vac. Roll, 1143/18: 'et de lx*s*. xi*d*. de certa consuetudine que vocatur yevesilver ad festum S. Mich.' For the form compare Harl. MSS. 1006, f. lx, 'yevewerkes, scilicet de dono.'

[5] Harl. MSS. 3977, f. 95 : a tenant by ancient enfeoffment '. . . debet dare ad consuetudinem illam que vocatur newyeresgive vij*d*. et *ob*. sed contradicit.' Compare Harl. MSS. 1005, f. 71.

[6] Bold. Bk., pp. 585, 586; Bish. Hatf. Survey, pp. 18, 22, 28.

[7] Rot. Hund. ii. 635. See also ibid., p. 655, where sokam is wrongly put for lokam, and York Vac. Roll, 1144/1, 'de . . . gallinis de lak;' Claud. C. xi, f. 66, 'et de loc ad festum S. Iohannis;' Tiber. B. ii, f. 191 b.; and Reg. Worc. Pr. 66 a, 'portabit lacs.'

[8] Add. MSS. 35169: 'dabit ij gallinas ad looke ad Natale et habebit cibum suum qui vocatur lookmete,' *pass.*; Claud. C. xi, f. 128: a Cambridgeshire tenant of Ely when he guarded the fold received wool, a marking lamb, 'et unam rodam frumenti que vocatur lokrode.'

custom of the scotale.[1] Where the food rent had been commuted into money the payment was called *loksilver*.[2] The
word *lok* is evidently from the Anglo-Saxon *lac*, a gift, and
the Latin form is *presentum* or *exennium*. In the descriptions
of Oxfordshire manors in the Hundred Rolls the custom of
receiving a meal from the lord in return for a 'present' to
him, or giving him a 'present' in return for a meal is very
common, but it is called simply a Christmas *exennium*, or
presentum, or *donum*. Thus a tenant gave an *exennium* at
Christmas of six loaves valued at 3*d*. each, beer, four hens, two
cocks. He came to a meal with the lord in return for the
aforesaid *exennium*.[3] At Rochester a large *exennium St. Andree*
supplemented the farm.[4] An *exennium Archiepiscopi* was paid
at Christ Church,[5] and *le present* was commonly paid on the
lands of the Templars.[6] At Glastonbury the *donum*, which
in the later extent is described as *de dono ad lardarium* or the
rent *ad lardarium*,[7] a payment occurring also on lay manors
in Wiltshire,[8] and in the form *lardresilver* at Lewes,[9] is so
common and so large that it looks as if it might be a general
commutation of most of the food rents. Except the churchscot
hens and grain, and a pasture lamb, there are few food rents
noted at Glastonbury, possibly because they had been commuted there for this large money rent *ad lardarium*, assessed
according to the size of the tenement, just as all Glastonbury
labour services were often commuted for the *gabulum*. The

---

[1] See below, under administrative rents.
[2] Rot. Hund. ii. 642: 'Idem W. dat vii denarios ad loksilver, scilicet
pro ii denar' panis et v gallinis.' See also ibid. pp. 643, 644.
[3] Rot. Hund. ii. 781. Compare ibid. pp. 728, 772, 785, 787, 788, 817.
[4] Reg. Roff., pp. 6, 133, and Cust. Roff., pp. 2, 3, 4, 35.
[5] Add. MSS. 6159, ff. 30, 32, 55, 56, 174.
[6] Mon. Angl. vii. 826. Cf. iv. 9, Lewes, in a twelfth-cent. document;
'et unum present, valens vi*d*.' Compare Reg. Worc. Pr., p. 34 a, and n.
p. lxvi ; Abing. Acc., p. 6 : 'de dono yemali viii*li*.' ; and p. 61, App. pp. 143,
145 ; and Harl. MSS. 3977, f. 39: 'De presento ad Natale quando
dominus ibi non venerit dim. marcam nova consuetudine.'
[7] Mich. Ambres. Rent., pp. 8, 10, 36, 48, 57, 75, *pass.*; Inqu. 1189,
pp. 23, 39, 72, 75, *pass.* and 33 : 'Totum manerium reddit de dono cxxiii*s*.
et iiii*d*. sicut homines ville illud statuunt.'
[8] Hazlitt's Blount's Tenures, p. 33.
[9] Mon. Angl. iv. 32 (Hen. VIII), 'Redd. Cust.: vocata Lardresilver.'
Cf. vi. 306, Hants.

villein of Bleadon and of Glastonbury received a *ghestum* at
Christmas, a word probably derived from the common Welsh
'gwestwa'.[1] A curious custom is recorded in Tynemouth in
Yorkshire, whereby all men of the priory, horses, dogs, and
servants, went to Whitley, near by, and received from the
lord a feast, *conveyes* or *conyeyes*.[2] Another custom paid at
Tynemouth was the *Welcom Abbatis*. At the coming of
a newly installed abbot of St. Albans to Tynemouth, which
was a cell of St. Albans, the fifteen tenants whose services
are recorded paid forty shillings sterling called *Welcom
Abbatis*.[3]

Certain food rents which were more or less uniformly commuted for money may be conveniently grouped together.
The *fishfee, fishsilver, heringsilver*, or *heringlode*, was one of
the most common customary rents, made to the lord of the
manor in commutation of the service of presenting him with
fish for the Lenten fast, or in order that he might buy fish for
this purpose (*ad pisces emendos*). The rent was paid usually
at the beginning of Lent. On the manors of Worcester it
was very common, being paid almost universally by the more
important customary tenants, but not by cottars, especially
under the old assize, and was sometimes retained under the
new assize also as a sort of recognition payment from the
villeins, together with merchet, or more occasionally included
in the lump sum of money rent paid in commutation of many
of the older customs.[4] The usual rate was $3\frac{1}{2}d.$ a virgate. It
is frequently mentioned in the account roll of Worcester
dating from Edward I's reign, where the payment is usually

---

[1] Blead. Cust., p. 208 : 'Bercator . . . habebit gestum Natalis Domini.'
Mich. Ambres. Rent., p. 83 : 'et debet habere ghestum suum ad Natale
in curia domini, ipse et uxor sua, scilicet ij albos panes, et ij fercula carnis,
et cervisiam sufficientem et honorifice et clera (*sic* ed.—*corr.* clare ?). Et
debet portare secum discum et cifum et mappam.' See also pp. 93,
126, *pass.*

[2] Mon. Angl. iii. 318 : 'Modus faciendi le Conveyes apud Whiteleye . . .
servitium quod dicitur le conyeyes.' The word is probably a form of
conveth (Celt.).

[3] Mon. Angl. iii. 319, from a rental : 'Et in adventu primo novi abbatis
S. Albani ad Tynemuth dabunt xv tenentes xl*s.* sterling' vocatos *Welcom
Abbatis.*' Compare the shirreveswelcome and saddlesilver.

[4] Reg. Worc. Pr., pp. 15 b, 19, 25, 43, 61 b, 65 b, 66 b, 69, 102.

recorded on Ash Wednesday.[1] At Thorney the rent was called *fishpene* and was paid on Ash Wednesday or on the first Sunday in Lent, usually at the rate of a penny a virgate.[2] On Ramsey manors it was almost universal, occurring as *fish-silver*, *phishesilver*, *haringsilver*, money *ad allec*, *ad pisces emendos*, and it is one of the few rents recorded in the extents of the middle of the twelfth as well as in those of the middle of the thirteenth century. The rate was usually the same in both series of extents, varying a little from manor to manor, from a halfpenny to two pence.[3] Sometimes the amount due from a whole vill or from the *operarii* of a vill is recorded in a lump sum,[4] but there is no evidence of the incidence of the rent on any class of tenants except the villeins. In Wistowe, a Huntingdonshire manor of Ramsey, a villein's turn to pay came sometimes once in two years, sometimes once in three.[5] The rent was due usually in Lent, once at Easter,[6] once in the form of *harengsilver* at Christmas.[7] In the vacancy rolls and custumals of Ely, *heringlode* and *hering-silver* are recorded on the lands of the church in Norfolk and Suffolk.[8] At Hartest in Suffolk it was paid on St. Andrew's day. It was paid also on St. Edmund's manors.[9] There is one instance of a payment in commutation of a carting of fish on the lands of Burton.[10] It was much less common in the manors of Gloucester, Peterborough, Abingdon, Battle, and St. Paul's, and the Kentish monasteries. A payment

---

[1] Worc. Vac. Roll, 1143/18 (Bybure): 'Et de iiij*s*. x*d*. *ob*. de quadam certa consuetudine que vocatur Fyshfee ad festum S. Iohannis Baptiste ... (Northwyk): Et de xvj*d*. *ob*. de certa consuetudine custumariorum que vocatur fysfe per annum primo die Quadragesime ', *pass*.

[2] Rot. Hund. ii. 642, 643, 647.

[3] Ram. Cart. iii. 250, 254 ; ii. 31 ; i. 287, 309, *pass*.

[4] Ibid. i. 248, 278 ; i. 371.

[5] Ibid. i. 356: 'in quolibet turno ad fyssilver in Quadragesima dat duos denarios. Qui turnus accidit aliquando semel in duobus annis et aliquando in tribus.'

[6] Ibid. i. 487.   [7] Ibid. i. 299.

[8] For example, Vac. Roll. 1132/10: (Bailiwick of Norfolk) '... de xlvj*li*. ij*d*. *ob*. de redditibus assisis et heringsilver '; (Hartest, Suffolk) '... de xv*s*. iiij*d*. *ob*. de redditibus assisis cum heringsilver.'

[9] Harl. MSS., 3977, f. 108.

[10] Burt. Ch., p. 26: 'Et vadit ad summagium pro sale et pro pisce aut reddit ij*d*. pro utroque.'

of eels occurs frequently in documents relating to the fen country.[1]

Maltsilver, Maltyngsilver, Aletol, Alepenny, Brewingsilver, Breweresteresgeld. Food rents of malt or ale to the lord, although evidently of importance, are often less easy to understand than those of fish, grain, or poultry. The confusion arises from the fact that the ale rents were of two kinds: they were both commutations of an old food rent of ale, or of barley or malt for its making, paid to the lord at certain seasons, and they were also tolls paid by the brewers of the village either for the right to brew, like the *furnagium* paid for the right to bake, or for the right to sell the ale when brewed; and these two kinds of rents are often not clearly distinguished in the descriptions of services. It is probable that the word *maltsilver* was used more often for payments of the first kind, and *aletol* and *brewingsilver* more often for payments of the second, but the distinction is hard to keep, especially since the aletol was itself paid in kind and the original food rents might easily come to be considered as a toll for brewing. For convenience, rents of both kinds will be discussed together. The importance of the brewers on the manor and their value to the lord appears very clearly in the Hundred Rolls,[1] and more clearly still in the Placita de Quo Warranto, in the litigation concerning the assize of ale. Offences against the assize which should have been punished by corporal punishment, by means of the *judicialia* of the manor, were almost universally punished by fines up to certain fixed amounts, which evidently, in addition to aletolls, were an important source of revenue to the lord.[3] There are many statements in extents and rolls regarding ale rents and tolls. The brewers seem to have been usually, but not always, customary tenants,[4] and apparently in some cases at least the industry was very common on the manor, and not confined to

---

[1] Compare the Ely bedrepeeles, Claud. C. xi, f. 42.
[2] For example, Rot. Hund. ii. 283, 541, 547, 549, 602, 605, 626, 629, 743, 766, 768, 775.
[3] See below under judicial rents.
[4] For example, Reg. Worc. Pr., p. 32a ; Ram. Cart. i. 474 ; Batt. Abb. Cust., p. 156.

a few men. The nineteen *operarii* holding five acres or ten acres each in St. Paul's manor of Sandun gave *maltsilver*, and also four times in the year 6*d.*, *ad braciandum* ;[1] five other tenants holding half virgates in the same manor brought *vasa et utensilia ter in anno ad braciandum.*[2] Maltsilver was usually paid on St. Paul's lands at Pentecost, or at the time of the rendering of the farms.[3] In Ramsey manors the typical virgater, and sometimes the cottar, made in most cases one or more measures of malt from barley, oats, or *grute*, and carried them to the *curia*, where he satisfied the brewer of the excellence of the material.[4] When he did not pay the rent in kind he sometimes paid it in money at the rate of 6*d.* a virgate,[5] or, in Therfield, of 10*d.*[6] In Shitlingdon, when a virgater or *censuarius* brewed he gave a *tolpot* or a penny, except at the beginning of the year.[7] The payment was made at Christmas,[8] Easter,[9] or whenever the lord willed.[10] In Elton when eggs were collected by the miller the cottar was freed from making 'the ale of St. Mary '.[11] On the whole, the money payment was less frequent on Ramsey manors than the making of the ale, and in most cases was an annual food rent to the lord rather than a toll for brewing.

On Peterborough manors too the villeins made malt for the lord,[12] and on the manors of Ely *maltyngsilver* occurs as a rent which is evidently a commutation of making malt,[13] and also

---

[1] D. S. P., pp. 18, 19.   [2] Ibid. p. 17.
[3] Ibid. pp. 62, 67, 81, *pass.*
[4] Ram. Cart. i. 345, 357, 368, 432; iii. 259, 271, 279. See especially i. 322 : 'Facit etiam unam mutam et dimidiam braesii ; et triturabit et carriabit dimidiam mutam ad domum propriam a curia, pro qua habebit unum fesciculum straminis, ligatum duobus ligaminibus, ad braesium siccandum ; et mittam integram mittet praepositus ad domum suam ; et carriabit apud Rameseiam dictam mutam et dimidiam cum braesium fuerit. Quod si refutetur a braciatore de suo proprio braciatori satisfaciet.'
[5] Ibid. i. 56, 335.   [6] Ibid. i. 46.   [7] Ibid. i. 474.
[8] Ibid. i. 394, 493.   [9] Ibid. i. 493.   [10] Ibid. ii. 37, 43 ; i. 50.
[11] Ibid. i. 489: 'Et ad Pascha, de consuetudine, molendinarius colliget ova de qualibet domo ad voluntatem dantis et ad opus domini, per sic quod sint quieti de theolonio braysiae ad cervisiam Beatae Mariae faciendam.'
[12] Chron. Petrob., pp. 157, 160.
[13] Vac. Roll, 1132/10 : ' Somersham . . . et de xxvj*s.* v*d.* de opere ad braseam faciendam affirmato termino Annunciationis Beatae Mariae

alemol, which is a toll for brewing paid after the first brewing.[1]
A Suffolk manor of Norwich paid a customary aid ' for making
malt and faldage '.[2] In Battle the tenants sent up a jug of
ale to the lord whenever they brewed;[3] and cottars were
sometimes obliged to carry four gallons of ale or wine.[4] On
the lands of Worcester the toll for brewing was common,
being taken sometimes twice. Those that owed suit at the
mill paid a toll when they brewed ale to sell; a freeman
or *forinsecus* following the soke of the mill *de gratia* gave
a penny or four gallons, a villein gave 2*d*. or eight gallons,
that is to say, a penny for the grinding and a penny for toll.[5]
The toll of the brewers is mentioned among the receipts from
manors in the account rolls.[6] At Glastonbury the villein
paid a heavy toll on a brewing, but the lord furnished him with
utensils and fuel.[7] A Hexham brewer, whether ' on land of
bond or cottage land', an interesting distinction, gave a toll
of two gallons when she brewed.[8] In Durham a penny was
paid from a brewing, called in the account rolls the ' maltpenny '.[9] The toll of ale is commonly accounted for in the

vocato maltingsilver.' Compare Extenta Maner., 'et pro malting silver
si non faciet brasium viij*d*. *ob*.'
[1] Claud. C. xi, f. 315 : ' Item si iste vel alius braciaverit in villa cujus-
cunque fuerit homagii in primo braciato erit quietus de alemol versus
bedellum scilicet de una lagena cervisie vel de uno obolo. Et nisi assisam
tenuerit erit in misericordia. Et si iterum braciaverit tunc dabit predictum alemol. Et nisi assisam tenuerit capietur cervisia sua in manu
domini. Et si tercio braciaverit tunc dabit predictum alemol et sic in
omni braciato nisi in primo ut supra. Et si tercio assisam fregerit tunc
sustinebit judicium tumberelli.'
[2] Vac. Roll, 1141/1. Compare Harl. MSS. 3977, f. 38.
[3] Batt. Abb. Cust., p. 36. [4] Ibid. p. 51.
[5] Reg. Worc. Pr., pp. 32a, 66a, 84a, 102 a.
[6] Worc. Vac. Roll, 1143/18 : 'ij*d*. de tolneto duarum bracinarum,' *pass.*
[7] Mich. Ambres. Rent., p. 82 : ' Et si braciaverit cervisiam venalem,
dabit domino de quolibet bracino ix gallones cervisie, et dominus inveniet
unum plumbum in quo possit braciare et i cuvam et unum penfet et i tinam
dum braciat et fualliam de bosco suo vel unde voluerit sufficientem ad
braciandum cervisiam illam.'
[8] Hex. Pr. ii. 72 : 'braciatrix sive super terram bondorum vel cotagiorum.'
Again, p. 76.
[9] Feod. Dun., pp. 73 *n*., 119, 278, 283 ; D. H. R., pp. 231, 237, 241, 243 ;
Vac. Roll, 1144/18 : 'et de iiij. vij*li*. vj*s*. iij*d*. *ob. q.* de consuetudinibus
vocatis scatpeny maltpeny scatfarina scatbraseum et scatavena et operibus
... arrentatis.'

rolls of York,[1] and Durham records mention a *scat malt*, a toll of ale, and maltpennies, and give regulations regarding the sale of ale.[2] An allowance of some kind was often made for the rendering of ale or malt, or money to the lord. In the Domesday of St. Paul's, for example, it is recorded that a man brewed if he did not carry;[3] in Battle Abbey he was free from works or received pasturage for his sheep on certain cliffs, or he received a small loaf;[4] in Ramsey manors he was free from labour service and sometimes received money or grain.[5] Both *maltscot* and *maltgavel* occur in Kentish documents.[6] The manorial *scotales*, or drinking bouts, attendance upon which was enforced by the reeve of the manor, will be discussed under *scotale*.

Mitesilver, a rent occurring on Ramsey manors,[7] was probably another form for maltsilver, derived from *mitta*, a measure.

Galunsilver, a rent, mentioned in the Domesday of St. Paul's,[8] is also probably another form of maltsilver, the name being derived from *galones*, or *lagenae*, gallons. It should be compared with mitesilver. This derivation seems more probable than that from *gallina*, a hen, suggested by the editor of the Domesday.[9]

---

[1] Vac. Roll, 1144/1 : '. . . cum tolneto cervisie,' *pass.*

[2] Bold. Bk., p. 586 ; Bish. Hatf. Surv., pp. 4, 128, 145, 150, 157.

[3] D. S. P., p. 3 : ' Item quelibet virgata debet parare vj quart. brasii vel dare vj*d.* et erit quieta a vj operacione' (*sic*).

[4] Batt. Abb. Cust., p. 51 : 'Cottarii . . . portabunt quilibet eorum iiij galones cervisiae vel vini . . . nec habebunt companagium vel panem, set habebunt V. bidentes supra petram versus mare Achrokepole usque Boctes Wall et cetera animalia sua supra petram sine dampno domini ; et si dominus non venerit, quilibet eorum dabit per annum i*d.* pro predicto servitio.'

[5] Ram. Cart. i. 317, 368, 394, 432, 493 ; ii. 43.   Cf. Rot. Hund. ii. 605.

[6] Add. MSS. 6159, f. 27, 181 ; Cust. Roff., p. 2 : 'Est et alia consuetudo in . . . Sutflete. Scilicet quod quelibet domus que facit tabernam que Anglice vocatur *cheaphale* dabit curie de Suthflete dimidium sextarium cervisie de ipsa taberna ; et ipse vel ipsa cujus taberna fuerit, habebit tres fasciculos de ferragio de . . . curia de Suthflete. Si aliquid autem ex tribus fasciculis ceciderit infra curiam aut infra quarentenam, curia habebit ferragium et cervisiam.'   The *serviens* may demand better ale if he be not satisfied, and the lord may, if he wish, substitute for the three bundles a half-acre of ' stubles' in the autumn.

[7] Rot. Hund. ii. 601, 657 : 'Et pro mitsilver x*d.* vel faciet quinque quarteria brasei sumptibus suis.'

[8] D. S. P., p. 154*.   [9] D. S. P., Introd. cxxiv.

Elsewhere still other names were given to the tolls for brewing ale, all probably derived from the measure used. *Tyne* occurs in the west as a toll collected by the constable of castles ;[1] *tolcester*,[2] *gavelsester, chepsester*,[3] and *langh'sester*[4] occur in the records of Winchester, St. Paul's, Abingdon, Glastonbury, and Battle. A *tolpot* occurs at Ramsey.[5]

Salt rents. Salt rents were very common both in localities where salt was made and also on manors to which it had to be carried from a distant market. At Piddington in Oxfordshire, for example, a rent of a penny a year was paid by the villeins at Martinmas for the commutation of the service of carrying salt from the market where it had been bought to the larder of the lord.[6] Many statements of salt dues are given in Worcester records,[7] and details of still greater interest in a terrier of Fleet in Lincolnshire. Fleet was on the coast, adjacent to the salt marshes in which the making of salt was a main industry. Part of the village was within, part without, the sea dike, and to the regular arable holdings within the

---

[1] Close Rolls, 1230, m. 16, p. 295 ; Ram. Cart. iii. 253, 1. 57, 58.

[2] Batt. Abb. Cust., p. 156 : ' Et sciendum quod unusquisque tenentium predictorum, tam liberorum quam nativorum, quotienscunque braciaverit ad vendendum, mittet ad manerium domini ij galones melioris cervisiae quod vocatur Tolcestr', et pro quolibet Tolcestro dabitur portanti 1 panis pretii oboli : et sic valent Tolcestr' per aestimationem per annum iij*s*.' See Index, p. 166 ; Rot. Hund. ii. 785 : ' Et quotienscunque braciaverit ad vendendum dabit tolcestr' ;' and pp. 787, 788, where, in the last case, the ale for sale is called Chepale ; Abing. Acc., App., pp. 143, 150 ; D. S. P., p. 47, 'colcestre' ; Hazlitt's Blount's Tenures, p. 123.

[3] Blead. Cust., p. 200 : a tollenagium or toll on the sale of a horse or beer. The toll for beer was sometimes called tolsester, gavelsester, chepsester, from a *sextarius* or sester of beer brewed.

[4] Mich. Ambr. Rent., p. 84 : 'Utrum autem debeat dare Langh'sester si habuerit cervisiam venalem necne, omnes vicini sui ignorant sed dicunt quod nunquam viderunt illum dare.' Compare Inqu. 1189, p. 71 : ' Et si braciat dat duo sextarios.'

[5] Ram. Cart. i. 474 : ' Quotienscunque braciaverit in anno dabit unum tolpot, vel unum denarium pro eo, praeterquam principio anni.'

[6] Kennet, Paroch. Antiq. ii. 137 : ' Et quilibet virgatarius dabit domino unum denarium pro saltsilver per annum ad dictum festum S. Martini vel cariabunt salem domini de foro ubi emptus fuerit ad lardare domini.' Rot. Hund. ii. 717 : ' Pidinton : dabit etiam domino suo ad festum S. Martini pro sale querendo i*d*. de consuetudine quod vocatur saltselver.' Compare Winch. Pipe Roll, p. 4 ; Davenport, Norfolk Manor, pp. 47, 60–1, 65–7 ; Norw. Vac. Rolls, 1141/1.

[7] Reg. Worc. Pr., pp. 34 a, 95 b, 110 b.

dike of molland and workland there were appurtenant holdings outside the dike, called *hogae* and *aree*, for which a rent of salt was paid, usually at the approximate rate of one measure for one acre. The total amount so received was eighty-two and a half measures and two pecks. In addition to this regular 'redditus assisa', the bondman, whenever he boiled salt outside the vill, paid a toll to the lord of one measure called *overgongmid'das*; if he boiled within the vill of the boilers, *infra villam bulleatorum*, he paid for every *patella* one measure called *wellerelonedes*. Then, too, the lord took a toll on salt sold: from twenty measures when sold and carried *extra portum* he received a penny, and all bushels of salt from certain adjoining vills were brought once a year to a 'holy' place outside the dike of the sea, called *lemothow*, and there signed with the lord's sign, as an evidence that they contained true measure. Those that brought bad measure were *in misericordia*.[1]

Brakemol, a rent paid on manors in Norfolk belonging to the bishopric of Norwich,[2] was evidently a payment for salt, like the saltsilver—a commutation either of the old service of supplying the lord with salt, or of carrying salt for him.

Besides these more important groups of food rents, there are some minor rents recorded of miscellaneous character and less common occurrence.

Bredsilver was a rent paid in Fleet, Lincolnshire, from workland.[3] It was probably a commutation of the duty of supplying the lord with bread. It should, of course, be clearly distinguished from the *bredwite*, occasionally mentioned, which was probably the fine for breaking the assize of bread[4]—the fine exacted, as the Placita de Quo Warranto frequently show, for an offence which should have received corporal punishment and not monetary. Bread was frequently given

---

[1] Add. MSS. 35,169.
[2] Vac. Roll, 1141/1: (Gaywood) '... et de iiijs. de quadam consuetudine vocata Brakemol . . . cum iiijs. xid. q. de Brakemol.'
[3] Add. MSS. 35,169. A half bovate of 'werklond' gave 4d. for 'bredsillver et stalage.' The 'Werkmen' of Flete gave 2d. 'de pane.'
[4] For example, Kennet, Par. Antiq. i. 156.

to the lord as a rent in kind in the manor,[1] sometimes at Christmas as part of the *loc*.[2]

Honeysilver occurs occasionally in late documents.[3]

Mesyngpeny, *Messingsilver*. *Mesyngpeny* occurs in the Durham Halmote Rolls in the form of sums of money paid by different manors.[4] It may be the same payment as that recorded in the Domesday of St. Paul's, of fourteen loaves of bread *ad mescingam*, a rent called *messingsilver* in the unprinted rolls of 1279, from which the editor takes the form,[5] and identified by the editor with the *metegafol* of the *Rectitudines*, derived from Anglo-Saxon *metsung*, food or meat.

Metride, a curious rent, was paid on the lands of the church of Durham.[6] It was paid at Martinmas in the form of one cow paid by the vill as a whole, or a half cow paid by a half vill, the fractional payment probably denoting commutation. It is mentioned often with *cornage*, and will be discussed in connexion with that rent.[7]

Wallesilver, *willesilver*, was a rent for wool paid by Ramsey customary tenants. In Elton, Huntingdonshire, a virgater *ad opus* paid in the twelfth century a halfpenny *ad lanam* ; his successor in the thirteenth century paid a halfpenny *ad willesilver*, as the word appears in the Chartulary, *ad wallesilver* as it appears in the Hundred Rolls.[8]

Flaxsilver was a rent occurring on the Ely manor of

---

[1] For example, Ram. Cart. i. 57, 58 ; Reg. Worc. Pr., p. 34 a ; Chron. Petrob., pp. 159–65, *pass.* ; Compotus of Ketteringe, by Wise, p. 4.

[2] Rot. Hund. ii. 642, 645.　　　　　[3] Mon. Angl., ii. 46 ; iv. 60.

[4] D. H. R., pp. 13, 131.

[5] D. S. P., p. 43 : 'Quelibet istarum hidarum debet duas doddas avene in medio marcio et ad mescingam xiiij. panes et quemlibet companagium.' Compare p. 47 : 'Et dare xiiij panes cum companagio portatoribus bladi' ; and Introd. p. lxxvi. The *metesilver* is explained by the editors of the Liber Albus as money for food paid to daubers who filled the framework of gables with mud clay. Introd., p. xxxvi.

[6] Bold. Bk., pp. 569, 570, 571, 574, 579, 581, one vill one cow ; 570, two vills one cow ; 580, a half vill, a half cow ; 580, two-thirds of a vill, two-thirds of a cow. Feod. Dun., pp. 19, 66 *n*, 68 *n*, 114 *n*. : 'et pro metreth quantum ad eandem terram pertinet.' It is commuted in Feod. Dun., p. 29, D. H. R., p. 243, and Bold. Bk., p. 571.

[7] See below, under administrative rents.

[8] Ram. Cart. iii. 259 ; i. 487 ; Rot. Hund. ii. 657. Cf. Mon. Angl. iv. 634 : 'Redd' lanarum vocat' custome wolle.'

Barking in Suffolk.[1] There was a payment of *linum* on Ramsey manors also,[2] and on a manor of St. Paul's services were rendered in connexion with raising and collecting it.[3] *Flexlonde* occurs in a Glastonbury record.[4]

Waxsilver. The Suffolk waxsilver[5] should perhaps be connected with the payment *ad luminare, ad candelam,* a church payment. There are interesting regulations in the Denbigh Survey regarding the finding of bees in the woods.[6]

The rents of lambs and sheep paid to Worcester, the Kentish *lamgafol* or *lamselver,* and the Ramsey *wethersilver* have been included among the pastoral rents. The cows *de metride* also probably belong there. The line between payments in food and pasture payments is sometimes hard to draw clearly.

Still another rent which was common in some parts of England in the thirteenth and fourteenth centuries, must, when regarded from the point of view of its origin, as Professor Vinogradoff and Mr. Round have shown,[7] be included among the rents representing very early arrangements. This is the *gafol,* which in Kent occurs as a separate rent, apparently part of the old tribute on the land. On the manors of St. Andrew's and Christ Church it was due from the *gavolland,* held by *gavolmanni,* and inherited by *gavolkind.* It was included among the *servicia de terra,* and was paid at Mid Lent, usually, although not invariably, at the rate of a penny an acre. It was paid in addition to a *mal,* or *firma,* or *census,*

---

[1] Vac. Roll, 1132/10 : 'de lxivs. iiijd. ob. de redditibus assisis fodercorn, hedernewech flaxsilver et wynsilver,' Claud. C. xi, f. 292 : a *plena terra* gives 1d. flexsilver at Annunciation. Tiber. B. ii, f. 230.

[2] Rot. Hund. ii. 657 : (Abbots Ripton.) '1 becham lini de quolibet remello per sic quod molendinum linum conservet sine dampno.' Ram. Cart. i. 370 : 'Quaelibet virgata integra debet duas garbas lini ... et hoc sive linum seminaverit, sive non.' And p. 489.

[3] D. S. P., p. 37 : 'Memorandum quod tota villata debet ... fodere terram ad linum et linum colligere et in aqua mittere et extrahere et ad domum portare.'

[4] Mich. Ambres. Rent., p. 55.

[5] Claud. C. xi, f. 279 : a *plena terra* gives waxselver at the Nativity of St. John Baptist. Again f. 283. Vac. Roll, 1132/10. Tiber. B. ii, f. 117.

[6] Denbigh Survey, ff. 43, 148.

[7] Eng. Hist. Rev. i. 734 ; ii. 103 ; v. 523.

the ordinary commutation of services, due four times a year
and three times as great as the gafol, amounting, that is to say,
to 3*d.* an acre.[1] Some of the land that paid *mal* was not
gavolland.[2]

The compounds in which *gavol* appears also seem to
indicate antiquity. Thus the *gavolerth* and *gavolrep*, or
govelwerkes, whether rendered in service or commuted for
money, seem to be contrasted in Kentish documents, and in
Ely custumals of manors in East Anglia,[3] with two other kinds
of old services, namely, the *ben* or *wine* services, the *thankacres, filsingerthes*, or *winewerks*, on one hand,[4] and the
greserthes, or pastoral services on the other, and are probably
to be identified with *lagerthes*, services *de ritnesse*, ploughings
demanded not as a grace or aid, *de amore*, but as part of the

---

[1] Cust. Roff., p. 2 : Frendsbury. Each of 21 *juga* of 'gavoland unius
servicii et unius redditus' pays 10*s.* at four terms : 'Hoc est mal,' and
in Mid-Lent 40*d.* 'Hoc est gable'. The *jugum* contains 40 acres.
Darente, p. 5 : '1 jugum gives a gafol of 3*s.* 3*d.*, and a *firma* of 21*s.*,
3 juga and 14 acres give gafol, 11*s.* 2*d.* ; 30 acres, 30*d.* ; 7 acres, 7*d.* ;
2 juga, 6*s.* 9*d.*, and the *firma* on this manor is usually 3*d.* an acre.' Compare pp. 3, 4, 5, 6. See also Faust. A. i. f. 118 : (Littlebourne) 'Et debet
de qualibet acra 1*d.* de gabulo' ; f. 121 : among ' servicia de terra '
from every acre of a sulung at Mid-Lent 1*d.* Elsewhere the rate is less
clear and uniform, e. g. f. 15. Add. MSS. 6159, f. 26 : 'Apud Moneketone
sunt xviii swling' de gavelikende sexdecim eorum . . . facientes servicia
per annum. De gablo reddent de qualibet acra i ob. et de mala de quolibet swling' xx*s.* per annum ' ; also ff. 28, 30, 187.

[2] For example, Faust. A. i. ff. 154, 156, 160, lists of tenants paying mal,
with the gafol entered opposite a few names : ff. 166, 203, list of tenants
by name owing gabulum.

[3] Harl. MSS. 1006, f. lix : ploughing ' de gablo ' opposed to ' beni-
herthe ' ; Add. MSS. 6159, ff. 30, 34, 170, 176, 187 ; Harl. MSS. 3977,
ff. 37, 38, 39, 61, and an especially clear distinction in the extent of
Hadleigh, Suffolk (Suff. Instit. of Archaeol. iii. 229, et seq.) p. 249: ' Item
tenentes de . . . xxii terris et dimidio (*sic*) debent arare ad seysonam
frumenti xliiii acras de gablo, scilicet de qualibet terra ii acras. Item
iidem debent arare de beneherthe xi acras et i rodam '—and so with the
reaping. Tiber. B. ii. frequently contrasts very clearly the ' govelas ' and
the ' benes ' or ' banes,' e. g. ff. 122, 147, 151, 174, 176, 223, 227. For ' govelwerkes ' and ' winewerkes ' see ibid. ff. 174, 176. For ' ritnesse ' see ibid.
f. 219.

[4] For an unusually full collection of benes see Claud. C. xi, e. g. f. 286,
' winewerkes ' opposed to ' gavelwerkes,' f. 301, ' morewe metebene,' the
love boon in return for the meat *precaria*, ' shyredaibene,' with which
compare the carting service at Bury, ' Shirefordrode,' ' metelesebene,' ' hal-
mingbene,' and f. 292, ' grasbene.' Cf. Tiber. B. ii, f. 239. The ' thankacres '
occur in Vac. Roll, 1140/20.

custom or 'law' of the village, and probably antedating boon services. Still a fourth kind of ancient service may have arisen in connexion with the church scot rent. *Gavolseeds, gavelcorns, gavelacres*, and *gaveles*, or *goveles*[1] of ploughing or reaping, are common, especially in the documents relating to Kent, East Anglia, and immediately adjoining counties, and may perhaps justify a presumption that the services they represent were paid by the holders of land 'anciently enfeoffed' on the old tenure, like the gavolmen of Kent. Thus the *gavolmerke* of Sussex may perhaps be explained as the setting up of hedges or some other boundaries, performed as part of an old gavol service.[2] Other common Kentish rents are *hunninggabulum, hellgabulum,*[3] *chesgavel,*[4] *hoppgavel,*[5] *gavelbere, gauelote, maltgavel,*[6] *cornegavell,*[7] *lamgafol,*[8] *gavolrafter, gavel timber, gavol bord,*[9] *forgabulum,*[10] and a *medgavol*[11] which may point back to an old haymaking service. *Horsgabulum* occurs in Wiltshire,[12] at Guildford and elsewhere, *bremegavol, fleggavel*, and *tangavel* or *tengavel,*[13] and at York *gavelgeld.*[14] The late *penygavelland* at Thanet[15] is perhaps the old *gavolland* put at a money rent. *Rodgavel, sandgavel, gavelsest, pridgavel* (for lampreys), also occur.[16]

---

[1] For example, D. S. P., p. 33: 'Terra operaria: singuli virgate debent per annum de landgable xv*d.* et debent de gavelsed iij mensuras quarum vij faciunt mensuram de Colcestr'. Note p. lxxiii. In 1279 'from every half virgate one heaped bushel of wheat was due under the denomination of gavelcorn (I. 107).' Norwich Vac. Roll, 1141/1 ; Harl. MSS. 3977, f. 53, 'by reapacres called goveles' ; and ff. 79, 82, 89.

[2] Batt. Abb. Cust., p. 6. Merle: 'Et debet claudere v virgatas (rods) haiae quae vocantur gavolmerke'; the service is valued at a penny. The editor suggests another explanation, that the gavolmerke were the boundaries between the gavolland and the lord's demesne. See Round, Eng. Hist. Rev., ii. 329, on the *virgata.*

[3] Faust. A. i. ff. 52, 131.   [4] Ibid. f. 56.
[5] Ibid. ff. 5, 52.   [6] Add. MSS. 6159, f. 181.
[7] Mon. Angl. i. 149: Redd. ass., voc. Cornegavell.
[8] Faust. A. i. f. 131.   [9] Robinson's Gavelkind, p. 220.
[10] Batt. Abb. Cust., pp. 52, 117.   [11] Ibid., p. 51.
[12] Ibid., pp. 76, 77 : 'Set sciendum quod de horsgabulo non dimittitur pro aliquo opere, nisi quando fiunt averagia.'
[13] P. Q. W., p. 745. Cf. Vict. Co. Hist. Hants. i. 529.
[14] Mon. Angl. viii. 1193: 'et solvunt gevelgeld tallivis.' Again, gavelgeld.
[15] Mon. Angl. i. 149: Redd. ass., voc. Penygavelland.
[16] Hazlitt's Blount's Tenures, pp. 261, 310.

The form *landgafol* is common with *hawgafol* in towns, as a rent on the land, usually on the arable land.[1] It occurs also, however, in rural districts. It is mentioned, for example, on two Ramsey manors : once at Cranfield, where a virgate in pure villeinage gave 7½*d.* at Martinmas,[2] and once at Burwell, where twenty-four acres gave 6*d. ad londgavel*, and fifteen acres gave 4*d.* for the same payment at the feast of St. Peter ad Vincula.[3] It occurred also on Ely manors lying in Suffolk, where a *plena terra* of twenty acres *de wara* gave in Rattlesdene 22*d.*, in Hitcham 21*d.*, in Barking 10*d.*, at Michaelmas.[4] It was paid in the manors of Bury,[5] of Glastonbury,[6] and of St. Paul's, where the rate was as follows: at Cadendon, Hertfordshire, from the typical virgater 7½*d.*, and nothing from smaller tenants, due at Martinmas;[7] at Belchamp, Essex, 15*d.* a virgate, and none from smaller holdings;[8] at Tidwolditon, Essex, 2½*d.* a virgate, due at Michaelmas;[9] and at Nastok, from eight tenants of bondland, 5*d.* each.[10] It was paid, seemingly, in these cases not by all customary tenants, but by the larger holders only. In a Kentish manor a *landchere* of 3*d.* from every acre was paid;[11] in another case a *landselver* of 6*d.*;[12] and at Lalling in Kent *custumarii* were arranged in groups of three or four, each holding fifteen or twenty acres, to make total tenements amounting to sixty acres, from which 10*d. landgafol* was due.[13] Elsewhere *land-*

---

[1] Round, Domesday Studies, p. 136, with review, Eng. Hist. Rev. v. 141, and Mr. Round's reply, v. 523 ; Eng. Soc. in Elev. Cent., p. 143 ; Vill. in Eng., p. 292 ; Maitland, Township and Borough, pp. 85, 180, *pass.* Perhaps the *Hadgovill*, *Hadgouel*, of a late Bury account is a form of *hawgafol*, see Mon. Angl. iii. 172.

[2] Ram. Cart. ii. 17.   [3] Ibid. ii. 28, 32.

[4] Vac. Roll, 1132/10: ' (Berkinge) et de iiij li. xs. vij*d. ob. q.* de redd' ass' Landgafel et whitepund.' Claud. C. xi, ff. 279, 286, 292; Tiber. B. ii, ff. 174, 175, 176, 177 ; Hadleigh Extent, Suff. Instit. Archaeol. iii. p. 229.

[5] Harl. MSS. 3977, f. 94.

[6] Inqu. 1189, pp. 70, 73, *pass.*

[7] D. S. P., pp. 6 and lxix, with reference to I. 119.

[8] D. S. P., p. 33.

[9] Ibid. p. 56.   Cf. I. 89, quoted in Introd.

[10] Ibid. p. 83.   Cf. I. 76.

[11] Add. MSS. 6159, f. 26 : ' De landchere de qualibet acra iij*d*.'

[12] Faust. A. i, f. 125.

[13] Harl. MSS. 1006, f. xxxi.   Cf. f. xlvi. and Add. MSS. 6159, f. 184.

avese,[1] *landmale*,[2] and *langol*[3] occur. *Landcheap*, occurring in Essex, has been defined as 13*d.* paid in every mark of the purchase money of houses or land.[4]

In Winchester account rolls there is commonly mentioned a *gabulum assisum*, identified by the editors with the *landgafol*, but reaching such large sums (£46 odd at Waltham, £48 at Clera) that it seems probable that it may have included all rents from lands *ad censum*, and have been only another name for *redditus assise*.[5]

On the manors of Gloucester a curious and difficult *landgavol* was paid at Hokeday and reserved to the king. It was a rent from which the king did not exempt the land when he granted it other privileges.[6] Arrangements with regard to the incidences of the Hokeday *gafol* were, however, sometimes made by the abbot; certain lands he exempted entirely,[7] and still other land he freed from all other services on condition of paying the gafol alone, which was incumbent on the eleemosinary land and owed to the capital lord of the fee.[8]

The second use of the term *gafol* occurs especially in Glastonbury, but can be traced elsewhere also. According to this, it sometimes seems to be the equivalent of *census*, or the commutation rent paid in place of all or part of the labour services in a given year. Thus at Glastonbury land was either *ad gabulum* (*ad censum*) or *ad opus*,[9] and if it were

[1] Claud. C. xi, f. 159: (Hatfield, Herts) one virgate pays 16*d.* a year at the feast of S. Andrew, 'de landauese . . . et ad hoc habebit woderich per visum et liberacionem ballivi.' Tiber. B. ii, ff. 140, 141.
[2] Feod. Dun., pp. 73, 74. See Hazlitt's Blount's Tenures. *Gloss.*, but the form is probably a compound with the ordinary *mal*, or rent.
[3] Rot. Hund. ii. 546: 'Dabit de langol ij*d.*'
[4] Hazlitt's Blount's Tenures, p. 210.
[5] Winch. Pipe Roll, Gloss. and pp. i, 5. Cf. pp. 50, 13, 74, and Liber Winton., D. B. Add. iv, pp. 531, 538.
[6] Glouc. Cart. i. 187, 318. For a Kentish reference of a similar kind see Reg. Roff. p. 542; the prior claims one-fourth of all the 'exituum pertinencium ad praeposituram predicte ville excepto gablo domini Regis.'
[7] Glouc. Cart. i. 318: 'Et nos acquietabimus ipsam terram de landgabulo duorum denariorum et unius oboli ad hokedai erga regem de cujus feodo est.' (Grant by Abbot and convent.)
[8] Ibid. i. 175: The abbot grants land to a baker for 16*s.* rent: 'Idem vero (the baker) . . . et heredes sui acquietabunt nos de quatuor denariis de londgabulo versus capitalem dominum ipsius feodi.'
[9] Mich. Ambres. Rent., especially, pp. 21, 64; Inqu. 1189, pp. 28, 65, 95, 103, 116, 124.

ad opus it did not as a rule pay any *gabulum*.[1] This use of the word occurs unmistakably both in the Inquest of 1189 and the later inquest. The rent is often paid at four terms like the *mol* of Kent and East Anglia.[2] At Glastonbury, as at Worcester and Gloucester, the common practice, both in earlier and later records, seems to have been to commute all the services, or none of them, in a given year, according as it should prove *utilius domino*. The reeve carried the money so collected to Glastonbury.[3] *Gabulum* at Glastonbury was used also in compound words for rent for special bits of land, sometimes newly assarted ; thus the common *morgabulum* was paid for land on the moors, on which we are once told forty houses had recently been built,[4] *medgavol* for meadow lands,[5] and *brechegavel* for 'breches', sluices.[6] *Landgavel* also was common,[7] usually at the rate of 40*d.* a virgate, but bonus was sometimes given for prompt payment.[8]

The same use of the *gavol* probably occurs elsewhere. Assart land, for example, in Berkshire, is called *gavolland*,[9] and held by villeins, and in Kent certain tenements are said to lie *gavellate, in campis*.[10]

[1] Mich. Ambres. Rent., pp. 64, 154 : 'Nihil reddit de gabulo cum sit operarius.' Inqu. 1189, p. 67 : 'Si est ad opus non dat gabulum.' But see Mich. Ambres. Rent., p. 206, where weekly 'handaynes' of work are owed in addition to *gabulum*, and pp. 35, 151, *pass.*

[2] Mich. Ambres. Rent., pp. 7, 12, 126, *pass.*

[3] Ibid. p. 67 : The reeve 'debet habere totum tolnetum quod accidit in villa et duos solidos pro gabulo portando Glaston' unde x*d.* et *ob.* debent dari de tota villata communicatus, scilicet, dum manerium est ad firmam in manu illorum.'

[4] Mich. Ambres. Rent., pp. 170, 175, 182. Cf. p. 33.

[5] Ibid. p. 54.　　　　　　　　　　　[6] Ibid. p. 55.

[7] Inqu. 1189, pp. 70, 73, *pass.*

[8] Mich. Ambres. Rent., p. 83 : 'Et si dat gabulum suum ante festum B. Michaelis, habebit i diem quietum ab opere, ad gabulum perquirendum.'

[9] Batt. Abb. Cust., p. 63 : 'Isti . . . sunt similiter willani et tenent de assarto per certum redditum, et vocatur gavelland.' There are twenty such tenants paying money rent at four terms, and from them, as from *virgarii* and *cottarii* the lord may choose manorial officers, 'quia omnes sunt villani.'

[10] Min. Acc. 899/11 (30 Edw. III) : 'De cas' redd'. Et in decas' redd' diversorum tenementorum existencium in manu domini prout patet extra per nomina tenencium lvij*s.* Et in decas' redd' tenementorum heredum Walteri Orpehelle jacent' gavellate apud Eastre per annum viij*s.* In decas' redd' tenementorum Margarete atte Snod' jacent' gavellate juxta Pyrye per annum iiij*s.*' Other tenements lying 'gavellate' are deleted in the MS. See also Misc. Bks. Augm. Off., vol. 57, f. 99.

CHAPTER II

RENTS COMMUTING LABOUR SERVICES; CARTING RENTS

IN most custumals and other manorial documents, especially in those of manors in the east of England, certain rents are recorded which were evidently derived from domanial arrangements. These rents are not always easy to distinguish from other classes of manorial rents, but in general they may be taken as money payments made in the place of some of the labour services which were counted among the 'works' of the villein, forming thus part of the regular exploitation of the demesne by the lord, and being substituted for days of week-work, and, although less frequently, boon-work. In proportion to the whole number of rents incumbent on the customary tenant they were not very numerous; they were small in amount, and they are of interest chiefly because of their possible connexion with the general process of commutation of labour services for money. That they may be taken solely as indicative of the beginning or continuation of the change from one system to another is not probable. Although they occur with greater frequency in later than in earlier documents, and are especially common in the custumals of groups of manors in the east, in those belonging to Ely, for example, and are entered again in the late bailiffs' accounts of the same manors, yet there is no indication in the records of their very recent origin. The names given them are English names with a certain ring of antiquity about them, and the fact that their appearance was possibly more frequent in the eastern counties cannot prove that commutation was proceeding more quickly there than in the west, in the face of the special emphasis laid in western custumals like those of Glastonbury, Gloucester, and Worcester, on the possibility

of the substitution in any given year of a *gabulum* or *census*
for the whole service of the vill.[1] The rents commuting
individual services cannot be omitted from any study of the
commutation of labour services as a whole, but they must
always yield precedence to the much more important evidence
of the custumals and account rolls regarding the sale to the
villagers of the whole number of spring, summer, autumn, and
winter works (*opera vendita*), and the substitution for those
works of hired labour which is suggested by the stipends paid
to special labourers 'for their comings' (*ad suos adventus*),
and by the statements in manorial documents of various kinds
regarding the renting of parts of the demesne and the work
of that class of lesser men of the manor, whose economic
status has not yet been very fully studied, the *undersetli*, who
laboured both for the lord and also for the more prosperous
villagers. Such 'selling' of works and hiring of labour are
the more significant lines of change. The occasional, and
perhaps temporary, shift of some special service into a money
rent is to be ascribed as much to the momentary convenience
of the lord, who found that for some service he did not need
the whole working capacity of the manor, as to the impelling
force of any general tendency towards money rents. This
conclusion is strengthened by the kind of service usually
commuted; it is not often part of the regular ploughing of the
demesne, except in occasional cases of members of the villata
residing at a distance, nor of the regular reaping, but rather,
as a rule, of some more special service which did not require
any special skill, such as watching the crops, cutting reeds, or
constructing hedges, for which the labour of a comparatively
small number of men sufficed. The rents arising from the
miscellaneous services thus commuted may be conveniently
divided into rents commuting part of the week-work, rents
commuting boon-works, and rents commuting carting duties
—carting or *averagium* holding in the custumals of some
manors an important position somewhat apart from the

---

[1] For similar substitutions in the east see Harl. MSS. 3977, f. 98:
'Ad festum S. Michaelis ad primum halemot ponet dominus quos rusticos
vult ad censum et quos vult ad operacionem.' Tiber. B. ii. f. 116.

regular week-work. The commutations of week-work may
be arranged, in general, although very roughly, according to
the season in which the service in question usually was due,
and at which the rent was therefore paid. A late general
worksilver is once mentioned [1] with which, it may be, *mol*
should be compared.

(a) Rents commuting part of the week-work: *hedernewech,
edernewech, hethernewech* (OE. *heððern*, granary). The guarding of the crops brought in before Michaelmas, and threshed
and stored in the granaries, was commonly the duty of the
villagers, and is frequently described as one of the manorial
watching duties. The safety of the crops while standing was
the care of the *messor*.[2] The records of Ely show that the
guarding of the stores and granaries was sometimes still performed, but more often commuted for a rent called *hedernewech*. All the customary tenants of a Norfolk manor, for
example, were to watch in turn by night, in summer and
winter, in the *curia*, in order to guard the granaries of the
bishop.[3] In other manors in Norfolk, Suffolk, and Cambridgeshire belonging to Ely,[4] and in the manors in Norfolk
belonging to the see of Norwich,[5] *hedernewech* was commonly
paid by customary tenants, the assessment being made *per
capita* regardless of the size of the tenement. The amount
paid by virgaters, half virgaters, and cottars was often a penny

---

[1] Sheriff's Tourn in Wilts, 1439. Wilts. Archaeol and Nat. Hist.
Mag. 13, p. 111: All Canninges copyholders used to pay worksilver
2s. 2d.
[2] Batt. Abb. Cust., p. 67: ' Messor vero, si sit electus de custumariis,
habebit relaxationem iis. de redditu suo et cibum ter, ut Praepositus,
et in autumpno quia vigilabit noctu circa blada domini.'
[3] Claud. C. xi, f. 195: (Walepole) ' Isti vigilabunt quociens opus fuerit
per noctem in curia domini episcopi pro granario vel grangiis domini
custodiendis tam in hyeme quam in estate secundum turnum vicinorum
suorum sine cibo et opere. Eodem modo vigilabunt omnes operarii et
consuetudinarii tam maiores quam minores.'
[4] Ibid. f. 214: ' Et dat de hedernewech, *id. ob. q.*' See ff. 66, 250,
255, 263, 279, 292. The Ely vacancy roll, 1132/10, exactly confirms the
custumal, mentioning the rent on the same manors, e.g.: ' Et de iis. de
quodam certo redditu quod vocatur hethernewech ad Natalem Domini ;'
Tiber. B. ii, *pass.*
[5] Norwich Vac. Roll, 1141/1: (Thornham) ' Et de lxiijs. vd. ob. de
communi auxilio et quadam consuetudine vocata hodernewech terminis
Omnium Sanctorum et Sancti Martini.'

each, due in different manors at Christmas, the Annunciation, or the feast of St. Andrew.[1] Sometimes the custumal states the total sum due from the vill.[2]

Wood rents: *woodpenny, woodsilver, wodeladepenny, sumere-wodesilver, somerlode, woodhire, woodweye, wodericht, heyn-wodesilver, woodwerksilver, wodefare, woodhew.* In autumn or late summer were due many of the services connected with the care and use of the lord's wood. The most common was the carting of wood to the *curia* for the lord's fuel during the winter, a service which was often commuted for the rent *woodpenny* or *woodsilver.* The Ramsey Cartulary describes very clearly the service for which this rent was paid. Between Michaelmas and All Saints two virgaters went to the wood and each took thence a cartload and load (*summagium*) to the *curia*, where each received food and wood. If the virgater did not perform this service he paid 2*d.* a year for *woodpenny.*[3] On the manors of St. Paul's the service of carrying wood to the *curia* was sometimes commuted in whole or in part, sometimes still performed. A customary tenant with a half virgate might pay as much as 8*d.* for *woodsilver,* while, on the other hand, a tenant with a whole virgate might pay only 4*d.*[4] A *woodpenny* or *woodsilver* occurs frequently in the account rolls also—in those, for example, of the manors of Worcester[5] and Abingdon,[6] in those of Barton Regis in Gloucestershire,[7] and Walsingham Parva, Norfolk.[8] The *somerlode* of the Ely molmen in Norfolk[9] and the Thorney *somer-wodesilver*[10] may probably be explained as rents paid in place

---

[1] Claud. C. xi, f. 221 sqq. [2] Ibid. ff. 220, 233, *pass.*
[3] Ram. Cart. ii. 37, 43 ; Rot. Hund. ii. 629.
[4] D. S. P., pp. 6, 26, 56, 62, 82, 85, 90, 94.
[5] Vac. Roll, 1143/18 : ' Et de v*s.* iiii*d. ob.* de certa consuetudine vocata Wodeselver per annum ad idem festum ' (i. e. S. Mich.).
[6] Abing. Acc., note the prominence of the *lignarius,* and p. 5 : ' Recepcio : De redditu de Wodeselver x*li.* iii*s.* et non plus quia x*s.* Leukenore soluuntur Abbati per composicionem.' See also pp. 143, 145, 150, 159.
[7] Min. Acc. 850/10 : ' Et de viii*s.* ix*d. ob.* de quadam consuetudine vocata wodepeny ad idem festum ' (i. e. S. Mich.).
[8] Min. Acc. 945/2 : (under opera vendita) ' Et de vii*s.* 1*d.* de lyng penye wodepeny et wodelodepeny.'
[9] Claud. C. xi, f. 247 : (Shipdham) ' Sumerlode de molmen.'
[10] Rot. Hund. ii. 642, 643 : ' i*d.* in vigilia Natalis Domini ad Somer-

of collecting wood in the summer time, and as a similar rent
the *summer housesilver* of Kent.[1] The *woodwege* [2] and *woodfare* rents, which occur frequently, probably have the same
general meaning, the going of carts to the wood for loads
of fuel or underwood for the lord. Woodfare rents were
especially common in Ely manors, where they are sometimes
coupled with *sefare* or *sesilver*, probably denoting carriage
by water.[3] *Sefare* occurs also in St. Neot's, Hunts.[4] *Woodwerksilver* is another Ely payment.[5]

Probably most wood rents had to do with this carting of
wood for the lord, for fuel or other purposes. But the villein
too had need of wood, and his *wodericht*, the conditions under
which he could take wood from the woodland of the manor,
had to be carefully defined. To cut wood without permission,
within the forest or without it, was a very serious offence,
included in the Ramsey custumal with theft and bloodshed
as offences not to be compounded for by *fulstingpound*.[6] The
extents of manors often give the regulations regarding the
use of the woods by the lord alone, or in common by
the villagers, stating especially the rights of pannage, and
the allowance of wood at Christmas time by the lord to the
virgater, called *wdetale* at Glastonbury,[7] in return for his

---

wodesilver.' See Batt. Abb. Cust., p. 20 : 'Debet cariare boscum de
bosco domini usque ad manerium per duos dies in aestate cum uno carro
et tribus animalibus propriis, pretium operis ix*d*.'

[1] Robinson, Gavelkind, p. 220 : 'In lieu of providing a house of
planks and boards when the lord visited the dens in the weald to dispose
of their pannages in the summer time.'

[2] Kennet, Par. Antiq., i. 505 : (Banbury) ' wudeway iii*s*. vii*d*.' Cf. p. 566.
Rot. Hund. ii. 772, 'pro wodeweye iiij*d*.' Cf. Faust. A. i. f. 186 ; Exeter
Vac. Roll, 1138/2 : 'Et reddit censar' et cariagium et restingwode ad
festum S. Martini ' ; and Batt. Abb. Cust., p. 153, 'Restwode.'

[3] For wodefare and sefare rents see Ely Vac. Roll, 1132/10, *pass.*
in Norfolk. Claud. C. xi, gives full descriptions of these rents in Norfolk
and Suffolk ; for example, ff. 194, 198, 255, 310. Tiber. B. ii. f. 181.
Compare Ram. Cart. i. 56.

[4] Extent of 18 Edw. II, printed in Dugdale, Mon. Anglic. iii. 478 : '. . .
de certo redditu vocato Seefare x*d*.' from half virgaters, 3*d*. from Tenacre
men.

[5] Vac. Roll, 1132/10 : (Stratham) 'et de ij*s*. de quodam certo redditu
quod vocatur wodewerkesilver.'

[6] Ram. Cart. ii. 22 ; i. 283, 306, 395.

[7] Compare Mich. Ambres. Rent., p. 83 : 'Debet habere husbote ad
aulam suam de bosco domini, et haybote similiter sine vasto per libera-

exennium of a 'wood hen', which has been already mentioned.[1] Probably the *wodelode* and *woodlodepenny* of the rolls of Durham, Coventry and Lichfield, and Canterbury,[2] the *woodhire* and *woodsilver* of Durham,[3] and the *lignagium* and *woodsilver* of the forest pleas,[4] the last made to royal foresters, were payments made by villeins for the use of the wood. It is not clear, however, that the distinction between payments for carting the lord's wood and payments for the villein's *wodericht, housebote,* was always maintained strictly. *Woodsilver,* for example, may sometimes have been used as a general name for any wood rent, and the documents often fail to describe the labour service of which the rent was the equivalent. A money payment is mentioned at Glastonbury 'de consuetudine Wodiarorum',[5] and two other curious wood payments, *wodehac* and *wodewelleschot,* are classed among the royal payments.

Money payments were made for the duty of bringing in other supplies also for the lord, especially in the autumn and early winter when labour in the fields was light. Thus on the Ely manor of Somersham in Huntingdonshire the lord received a rent called *collyngsilver,* a commutation probably of the service of providing the lord with fuel.[6] Other refer-

cionem ballivorum. Et debet habere Wdetale contra Natale, scilicet unum truncum . . . et debet habere Wenbote, scilicet unumquodque plaustrum, unum lignum, et hoc debet recipere quando incipiunt falcare prata' (compare the cartbote of other localities). And ibid. p. 135, 'debet auxiliari ad Wddewaste.'

[1] Vac. Roll, 1132/10 (Ely): (Somersham) 'Et de xxvis. xd. ob. de opere de Wodehenes affirmato termino Nativitatis S. Johannis Baptiste vocato heynwodesilver.' In this case the Christmas carting must have been of underwood rather than of wood for fuel.

[2] D. H. R., p. 24, 'wodladpenys'; Bold. Bk., pp. 566, 568, 570, 582, 584, 585, 'lades and wodilade'; Vac. Roll, 1128/4: 'wodelode'; Add. MSS. 6159, f. 30; Coventry and Lichfield Vac. Roll, 1132/5: 'wodelode'. For an apparent distinction see Min. Acc. 945/2: 'de viis. 1d. de lyngpeny wodepeny et wodelodepeny'. Cf. Ashmol. MSS. 864, Bl. Bk. Coven. f. 5: 'Et cariabit maeremium de bosco usque curiam episcopi Lich' quotiens necesse fuerit pro domibus faciendis et sustinendis.'

[3] D. H. R., p. 94; Bish. Hatf. Surv., p. 10, *pass.*

[4] Abing. Acc. ii. 303, 305, 321, 'de consuetudine lignandi'; Sel. Pl. For., p. xxxv. n.; D. H. R., pp. xc, 2; Rot. Hund. i. 24.

[5] Mich. Ambres. Rent., pp. 72, 74.

[6] Vac. Roll, 1132/10: 'Et de iis. xd. ob. de opere ad carbonem faciendam affirmato . . . quod vocatur Collyngsilver,' Tiber. B. ii. ff. 113, 117.

ences to coal and charcoal occur in rolls of the manors of
York and Durham,[1] and in the Worcester Register[2] and
Glastonbury records.[3]   In many places nuts were collected,
a service commuted on Ramsey manors for *nutsilver*, which
was considered the equivalent of one man's work for one day,
and was valued at about a penny.[4]   In Norfolk, at Walsingham Parva[5] and Thorpe,[6] the rent *lyngmole* or *lyngpeny* was
paid, probably in commutation of cutting or carting ling for
the lord, or possibly in return for the villager's right to cut
his own ling, and at Rollesby in the same shire a similar rent,
turfdole,[7] occurs, which is perhaps the same as the *Turfeld* or
Torefeld (turf yield) of Dengmarsh, Kent, a payment made
insteadof cutting turf.[8]

Here may be included too the *shernsilver* or *sharpenny*, the
commutation of the very common service of carting manure
to the lord's fields and scattering it.[9]   The rent appears under
this name both in the east and west.   It is found, in the
west, on the manor of Littleton belonging to Gloucester, as
a custom valued in ordinary years at 12*d*.[10]; *sharland* occurs
at Rudford,[11] and a *certus redditus* of *sharnselver* of two

---

[1] Vac. Roll, 1144/1 : ' Et de cxxiiii*li*. vj*s*. v*d*. *ob*. de dominicis affirmatis
firma molendini tolneto chiminagio carbonibus marmis fructu gardini et
passagio de Tyne affirmatis.'   Compare Bish. Hatf. Surv., pp. 219, 220 ;
D. H. R., pp. 91, 139, 197 ; Bold. Bk., p. 587.

[2] Reg. Worc. Pr., p. 56 a.

[3] Mich. Ambres. Rent., p. 90 ; Inqu. 1189, p. 17.

[4] Ram. Cart. i. 358.   For the commutation rent, Notesilver, see
Wystowe Min. Acc., Econ. Cond. Ram. Man., p. 71, and App. 76, *pass*.
See also Ashmol. MSS. 864, f. 17 ; D. S. P., pp. 37, 90, *pass*. ; Rot.
Hund. ii. 622 ; Charnock, Man. Cust. of Essex, p. 17.

[5] Min. Acc. 945/2 : ' et de vii*s*. 1*d*. de lyngpeny wodepeny.'

[6] Norwich Vac. Roll, 1141/1 : ' et de xlv*s*. iii*d*. de consuetudine videlicet
cornu et clau' et lyng mole.'   Compare Tiber. B. ii, f. 183, a service of
collecting ling.

[7] Vac. Roll. 1141/1 : ' Et de v*s*. xi*d*. *ob*. de consuetudinibus vocatis turfdole
fermpenes et melderfe.'

[8] Batt. Abb. Cust., pp. 47, 49.

[9] Claud. C. xi, f. 176 : ' spargere fimum ' ;   Norw. Vac. Roll, 1141/1 :
' cariagio fimorum.'   Compare Jacob's Law Dict. : ' Some customary
tenants were obliged to pen up their cattle at night in the pound or yard
of the lord for the benefit of their dung ; or if they did not do so they
paid a small compensation called sharpenny or sharnpenny ' (A.S. *scearn*).
' In the north,' Jacob continues, ' cow dung is still sometimes called
cowshern.'   Probably, however, the rent was also a commutation of
carting and scattering manure.

[10] Glouc. Cart. iii. 37.   [11] Ibid. iii. 109.

shillings a year on Worcester's manor of Hertlebury.[1] At Bleadon men were obliged to go to the *sherntrede*, to help manure the lord's land.[2] In the east it is found on certain Ely manors in Norfolk and Essex. In Pulham, Norfolk,[3] *coterelli* with acre holdings paid a penny, *sharsilver*, if they had cattle of three years' age. For one animal they paid a halfpenny, for two or three a penny, and for every additional three a penny. The total sum cannot be given, the custumal states, because it 'increases and decreases' with the number of cattle. In Littlebury, Essex, an acre owed 12*d. de sarpenni*, and tenants on the same manor paid *scharpani*.[4] The rent occurs among the *redditus mutabiles* of the Bury custumals, usually at the rate of a penny an animal,[5] and in Essex manors belonging to St. Paul's, *seracres* and *sarlond* were probably held by the same service.[6]

Rents paid in commutation of services in the fields in connexion with the growing grain, or of haymaking in the meadows, were very few in number. Ploughing rents, except the commuted *gafolerth* and *graserth*, were rare. A *wedselver*, or commutation of weeding, occurs in a Kentish document.[7] *Repselver* also occurs in Kent, but may refer to the rent from a boon-service rather than a week-work.[8] Perhaps the Norfolk *wrougsheryng* is another harvest rent, but the statement regarding it is not clear.[9] Very occasionally rents were paid in commutation of haymaking. Thus 'meadow-cutting'

[1] Worc. Vac. Roll, 1143/18: 'De certa consuetudine que vocatur sharnselver.'
[2] Blead. Cust., pp. 182–210. [3] Claud. C. xi, ff. 217, 220.
[4] Claud. C. xi, ff. 174, 175 : 'R. tenet unam acram in curia sua pro duodecim denariis de Sarpeni.' *Scarpani* also occurs; and see Vac. Roll, 1132/10: 'Et de vi*d*. quadam consuetudine coterellorum vocata shersilver hoc anno in estate.' Tiber. B. ii. f. 223.
[5] Harl. MSS. 3977, f. 37: 'De sharsilver pro quolibet animali 1 *ob*. et est redditus mutabilis.' Elsewhere 1*d*., e.g. ff. 38, 39, 83.
[6] D. S. P., pp. lxxvii, and 46, 49. The editor explains that 'sexlond' should be 'serlond'.
[7] Add. MSS. 6159, f. 174 : 'De wedselver ij*s*. iij*d*.'
[8] Faust. A. i, f. 120: 'Et de Repselver ij*d. ob*.' Also, ff. 114, 124, 'ripselure' and 'ripselwere'; Harl. MSS. 3977, f. 13, 'repselver' at St. Edmunds Bury. See Ashley, Econ. Hist. i. 115 ; Mrs. Green, Town Life, i. 171 n.
[9] Min. Acc. 945/2, Messor's account : (Walsingham Magna) 'Et de xiii*s*. iiii*d*. de quadam consuetudine messionis xxvi acrarum iij rodarum terre vocat' wroughsheryng.'

on a Rochester manor was paid as a man or a penny from each house, and a *sithpeni* occurring on the same manor is probably another form of the same payment.[1] *Medwesilver* is found in East Anglia.[2] Much more common was some special allowance made at haying-time by the lord to the villeins, apparently in recognition of a service in the nature of a boon—the fork full of hay, the ale or food given in the field, the 40*d.* from the lord's purse, the *medsipe, werthale,* or *manesef,* or the sheep loosed in the meadow. Similar allowances to villeins were made after other precarial services, for example at the *Repegos* and the *forthdrove* at Ramsey.[3]

Wascheyngpene was a late Ramsey commutation of the common service of washing sheep[4].

Heggingsilver, Heyningsilver, Heynwodesilver. The setting of hedges round the growing grain, to keep out cattle, and of hedges round commons or pasture lands, to keep the cattle and other animals in, were services more often commuted. The custumals usually describe a service to be performed by the villagers in the collection of thorns, sticks, twigs, and underwood, *wodecast, restingwode,* for hedge-making. The commutation of the actual setting of the hedge was probably called *heggingsilver,*[5] *heyningsilver,*[6] and the commutation of

---

[1] Cust. Roff., p. 4.   [2] Add. Ch. 37,763.

[3] Reg. Worc. Pr., p. 83 b: 'omnes habebunt in communi ... unum arietem ab antiquo et xii*d.* de novo, pro herbagio quod solebant habere super falces, et unum caseum pretii iiij*d.* vel iiij*d.*' Compare Ram. Cart. i. 298, 307, 324, 460; ii. 39; iii. 65; Rot. Hund. ii. 717: 'Quod omnes custumarii venient in tempore falcationis ad pratum domini falcandum per unum diem et habebunt xl*d.* de consuetudine de bursa domini et vocatur medsipe.' See pp. 720, 721, 818, 866; 'manesef,' 505; 'wambelok,' 817. Ram. Cart. i. 476: 'Ad diem quo falcant pratum domini habebunt unum multonem ... ita scilicet quod ipse multo libere ponetur in prato in medio eorum, et si ipsum comprehendere possunt, habebunt illum, si evadere possit, eo anno perdent illum.' Cf. ibid. i. 493 for 'werthale' or 'wetherale'.

[4] Econ. Cond. Ram. Man., App. p. 95.

[5] Sel. Pleas. For., f. xxxv. n., quoting Inq. P. Mort., 23 H. vi, No. 14: 'A ... died seised of the custody of the forest of Rutland "Cum wynd fallyn wode dere fallyn wode cabliciis wodsylver heggyngsylver attachiamentis forestariorum"'; Rot. Hund. i. 24: for little thorns for keeping up the 'hayas' 8*s.* a year; Gr. of Man., p. 328; compare Hex. Pr. ii. 4 'faciet le hege-yard.'

[6] Claud. C. xi, f. 115 (Ditton, Camb.) : 'Et de heyningsilver ad parcum de Haffeuld obolum ad festum S. Michaelis ad placitum domini.' Cf. 'parcselver'.

the collecting of the wood for it probably *heynwodesilver*.[1] A rent occurring on Ely manors, and paid on the feast of St. John Baptist, *hirdel penny*, by metathesis *hildersilver*, mentioned in Norfolk[2] in connexion with faldage and pasture payments, may have been a similar payment substituted for the duty of setting up hurdles for sheepfolds and the like. In Kent a similar *Watelsilver* occurs.[3] *Hedgebote, heybote,* was the common rent, of a slightly different character, paid by the villein for the right to take '*heynwode*' for his own hedging.[4]

Segsilver, Seggesilver. Some time during the summer or early autumn occurred the cutting of sedge, or reeds for thatching. A *segsilver* commuting this service is common in the fen district. In the Ely manor of Dunham a *plena terra* of fourteen acres gave 4*d.* a year for *seggesilver,* or else cut and bound sixteen cartloads each containing forty sheaves of great rushes.[5] In other Cambridgeshire manors virgaters paid commonly 6*d.* *segsilver,* half virgaters 3*d.,* cottars 2*d.* In manors in Norfolk and Suffolk *segsilver* was paid at the lower rate of a penny, or a fraction of a penny.[6] The cutting of

---

[1] Vac. Roll, 1132/10. Compare Vinogradoff, in Quar. Journ. Econ., 22, pp. 62, sqq.: 'pulling up of hedges or the haining of sheep, cows, and horses out of the commons': 'It is ordered that the sheepfolds shall be hained out of the corn-fields'; and compare Charnock, Man. Cust. Essex, p. 5: Frampole fences were 'such fences as every tenant of this manor (Writtle) had against the lord's demesne; whereby he had the wood growing in the fence and as many trees or poles as he could reach from the top of the ditch with the helve of his axe, towards the repair of his fence.'

[2] Norwich Vac. Roll, 1141/1 (Eccles, Norfolk): 'Et de vij*s.* x*d.* de consuetudinibus custumariorum videlicet faldagio bosagio hildersilver et hussilver.' Min. Acc. 954/2 (Walsingham Parva): 'Et de vii*d.* *ob.* de quadam consuetudine vocata hirdelpeny relaxata per annum termino Inventionis S. Crucis . . . et de xix*d.* *ob.* de hirdelpeny.' Professor Vinogradoff suggested the identity of hildersilver and hirdelpeny.

[3] Add. MSS. 6159, f. 177.

[4] Claud. C. xi, f. 34: 'Et de seggesilver per annum quatuor denarios equaliter vel falcabit et ligabit sexdecim carectatas grossi rosci scilicet quelibet carectata de quadraginta garbis sed non cariabit. Et tunc erit quietus de predicto segselver.'

[5] Claud. C. xi, *pass.* See also Eng. Hist. Rev. ix. 418: 'from a cossetle 2*d.* for sedgesilver.'

[6] Claud. C. xi, ff. 263, 279, 286, 292: at the rate of ½*d.* or 1*d.* See Ely Vac. Roll, 1132/10: (Hecham, Suff.) 'Et de liij*s.* vij*d.* *ob.* de redd'. ass'. de seggesilver de termino Nativititas S. Johannis Baptiste.' And also

rushes was a very common duty of the Ramsey villein also. The rushes were used for thatching, for bedding for stalls, and for other purposes.[1] A similar payment was probably the Ely *roserye*.[2]

Other rents, not to be assigned to any special season, were paid in commutation of the duty of maintenance of parts of the demesne or the *curia*. Thus at Crondal and adjoining manors in Hampshire a *poundpani*, or *pundpani*, at the heavy rate of 3s. 2d. a hide, 9½d. a virgate, was paid probably for the maintenance of the pond.[3] *Poundsilver*, perhaps a different rent, occurs on a Canterbury manor.[4] A pond in the *curia* of Swaffham, Cambridgeshire, was valued at 18d.,[5] and the duty of keeping the mill pond in repair is often mentioned.[6] *Parkselver* was paid at Shelford in Cambridgeshire by customary tenants, probably in commutation of the service of keeping in repair the fence round the park.[7] *Lardersilver*, mentioned in extents of manors belonging to Worcester and St. Paul's, was probably the commutation of some service connected with the salting-house.[8] At Glastonbury, as has been said, the commutation of a large food rent was paid *ad lardarium*.

Winyardsilver, or *wynsilver*, the rent in commutation of

Norw. Vac. Roll, 1141/1 : (Blofield, Norf.) ' Et de xlixs. iijd. de feno arundine segges et agistamento averiorum.'

[1] Claud. C. xi, f. 42 : (Littleport) ' rushes carried from the Thackfen.'

[2] Vac. Roll, 1132/13 : ' Cum quibusdam certis redditibus et consuetudinibus vocatis wodefare Somerelonde seggeselvere coupeny et Roserye.' And Tiber. B. ii, ff. 108, 253.

[3] Crondal Records, p. 51 : 'Reddit compotum de xlvli. vjs. ixd. ob. qu. de toto redditu assisae in manerio de Crundalle cum pundpani.' Cf. pp. 75, 84, 86, 91, 95, 97, 105. Gloss., p. 510, defined as rent for keeping Flete ponds in repair.

[4] Harl. MSS. 1006, xlvj, Hadleigh : custumarii pay poundsilver 10½d.

[5] Ely, Extenta Maner.

[6] Ashmol. MSS. 864, f. 17: ' Et mundabunt stagnum molendini de Heywood et val. ob.' Compare Inqu. 1189, p. 26: ' facere meram in grangia.'

[7] Claud. C. xi, f. 129: A half virgate pays parkselver ½d. at Michaelmas. ' Summa de parkselver per annum de operariis ixd. ob. q.' Tiber. B. ii, f. 217.

[8] D. S. P. Introd., p. lvi ; Worc. Vac. Roll, 1143/18 : (Hanbury in Salso Marisco) ' Et de lixs. de certa consuetudine custumariorum debita ad lardarium ad festum sancti Michaelis.' So at Stoke. Mich. Ambres. Rent., p. 7, *pass.*; Inqu. 1189, *pass.* See above, under food rents.

labour performed in the vineyard, was very frequently paid. Sometimes virgaters or half virgaters furnished either a man for a day's work in the vineyard, or the equivalent of his labour, usually a penny ; sometimes the villeins in common furnished a man to work for a week or more, or paid a lump sum of money.[1] *Yaresilver* was paid in the north for the repair of weirs or dams.[2]

(*b*) *Commutations of boon services.* The rents commuting week-work were comparatively few in number, but rents commuting boon-work were almost unknown. Boon-works, *filsinerthes, winewerkes,* opposed on one hand to *gavelwerkes, lagerthes,* and on the other to *graserthes* and other services of a pastoral nature, while probably later in origin than the *gavelwerkes,* and always regarded as supplementary and in theory *de amore,* or *ex gratia,* not *de consuetudine,* were less unwieldy than the week-work, and the lord was therefore reluctant to surrender them. Boon-work was demanded from tenants owing no other labour services, and was naturally enough the last service to be commuted.[3]

Bedripsilver occurs in a court roll of Addington, Surrey, of Edward II's reign,[4] and again in a Bury St. Edmunds custumal.[5] Some indication of the commutation of the reaping service is found also in a late account roll of Barton Regis in Gloucestershire, a roll which records a number of commuta-

---

[1] Rot. Hund. ij. 543, 603, *pass.* ; Ram. Cart. i. 288 : ' Ad vineam etiam colendam de Rameseia semel in anno per unum diem inveniet unum hominem laborantem, ita quod post solis occasum domi redeat ; vel magistro vineae pro opere illius diei dabit unum denarium, tam pro homine misso in vinea, quam pro denario dato de uno opere.' And i. 302, 325, 356 ; ii. 27, 31, 41, 46, *pass.* ; Claud. C. xi, ff. 38, 115, 121, 171, 263, 276, 299 ; Tiber. B. ii, f. 127, *pass.* ; Reg. Worc. Pr., pp. 47 a, 51 b.

[2] Bish. Hatf. Surv., p. 78 : ' Cariagium cum yaresilver . . . tenentes . . . reddent pro qualibet bovata 2½d. pro yaresilver, ad festum S. Martini tantum.' And pp. 80, 137.

[3] Econ. Cond. Ram. Man., pp. 39–48.

[4] Hone, Manor, p. 152, quoting court roll of Addington : ' Thomas Cubbel is summoned because he has concealed 2½d. of bedripsilver forthcoming of a certain tenement which is called le popeland and has detained the said 2½d. for seven years past and still detains it.'

[5] Harl. MSS. 1005, f. 68 : ' de Bedrepesilver in festo S. Petri ad Vincula xvs.'

tions of labour services,¹ and in Bishop Hatfield's Survey of Durham.²

Bene was probably, like the bedripsilver, a commutation of boon-work. It is found in the same late roll of the manor of King's Barton, Gloucestershire.³ 'Thankeacres' occurs as a rent in a late roll of the manors of the Bishop of London.⁴

Benesed was evidently a commutation of the obligation of furnishing seed for the sowing of an acre or half-acre of the demesne, in addition to the *gavolsed*. It also was paid at King's Barton.⁵ It is tempting to connect the *wiveneweddinge* of the same manor with some weeding boon performed by women, like the *bedewedinge* of Ely, and the *weddis* of Ramsey, but the term seems to mean literally 'wives' wedding' (see p. 113).⁶

(*c*) *Carting Rents.* In some cases time was allowed the villein in his regular week-work for carting services, in others such services were regarded as extra services, like the boons, not counted to him for 'works', and sometimes even paid for in part by the lord with a small sum of money, or food, or drink.⁷ Even in the later extents much carting had still to be rendered by the villeins, and the service was in large measure uncommuted, although there is some evidence in the account rolls of a class of hired carters,⁸ men coming, *de prece*, either from outside or, more probably, from within the manor, from the cottars, crofters, and lesser *censuarii*, who might be

---

¹ Min. Acc. 850/10 (13 H. V): 'et de xxx*s*. vij*d. ob.* de quadam consuetudine vocata Bedripp' ad idem festum' (i. e. S. Mich.).

² Bish. Hatf. Surv., p. 174: *servientes* commute their precariae for 12*d.* a year.

³ Min. Acc. 850/10 (13 H. V): 'et de vij*s*. vij*d. ob.* de quadam consuetudine vocata Bene ad idem festum' (i. e. S. Mich.).

⁴ Vac. Roll, 1140/20: 'Et de xij*s*. vj*d.* de redditu vocato Thankeacres ad Terminum Pasche, videlicet xxxix opera.'

⁵ Min. Acc. 850/10: 'et de xviij*s*. iiij*d.* de quadam consuetudine vocata Benesed ad festum Omnium Sanctorum.'

⁶ See below under miscellaneous rents, and Glouc. Cart. iii. 70, 71 ; Claud. C. xi, f. 64.

⁷ Claud. C. xi, f. 43: a *plena terra* pays 2*s.* for average and carries one day called Beneweynes, three 'navatas bladi cum tota villata per annum de consuetudine usque ad lennam sine opere'. The lord supplies the boat. Compare f. 50: a *lawefother*, probably opposed in meaning to *beneweynes*, one being regular, the other precarial. Compare also Cust. Roff., p. 10: carters have 1*d.* for drink. D. S. P., p. 34: fifteen days credit given for carting.

⁸ Econ. Cond. Ram. Man., App., pp. 36, 46, 48, 63, 95.

sent as paid substitutes by the villagers, or hired outright by the lord, when occasion demanded, the more unwieldy service of the regular *operarii* being in consequence commuted for money. Carting rents might also arise where not all the carting exigible from the manor was required, and the surplus could conveniently be turned into money. For the regular virgaters with fields of their own to till in addition to their labour on the demesne, the distant carriages sometimes described, requiring more than a day and a night, must have been a serious inconvenience, and one from which they would gladly have escaped by means of a money payment.

A distinction is suggested in the Liber Custumarum between *aversilver*, the payment made by tenants in place of furnishing a beast of burden, and *summagium*, the payment made in commutation of the actual carriage of loads.[1] *Averare* is, however, the common verb meaning to cart or carry, and a distinction between carrying and furnishing the means to carry does not seem to be maintained in the documents. Carriages, *averagia*, were usually of two kinds, the manorial carting, and the long or short cartings outside the manor. The carting within the manor consisted of carrying grain to the granaries, of *wodelodes* from the wood to the *curia*, of rushes and hedging material from the marsh and the wood, of manure from the fields.[2] This carting was usually included in the week-work, 'counted to the villein for a work,' and was not often separately commuted. The longer cartings outside the manor, on the other hand, were more in the nature of special services. In a number of cases they were subject to commutation, in whole or in part, and the descriptions in some customaries of them and the rents commuting them are full and detailed. The Ramsey villein in Shitlingdon, for example, had to perform both long and short carriages outside the manor,[3] and long carriages were made from Ramsey

[1] Lib. Cust. gloss.
[2] Econ. Cond. Ram. Man., pp. 37-39. Compare Harl. MSS. 3977, f. 80 : ' si autem averagium illud sit de blado ad vendendum vel braesio vel hiis similibus . . . si autem opus fuerit ad portandum semen ad campos die Sabbati.'
[3] Ram. Cart. i. 462.

manors to places as distant as London, St. Albans, Cambridge, Bury St. Edmunds, Colchester, Ipswich. The long cartings in St. Edmund's manors were called *langerode*, *poperode*, and *schirefore*, the third possibly connected with suit at the county court.[1] An important part of the carting on the manors of St. Paul's was the carriage of the food farms to London, a service which fell on some manors several times a year. The duty of carrying such farms was a villein obligation, assessed 'secundum quantitatem tenementi' on the lands *ad operationes*.[2] In Essex this carriage was made by water, at the cost and risk of the villein, although the *firmarius* of the manor sometimes furnished the boat and its steersman. If the boat were lost and any escaped, the villeins met the expenses.[3] The smaller holders in these manors of St. Paul sometimes helped load the boats ; in other cases they themselves went to London driving the herds of swine.[4] The carriage by land is sometimes commuted under the name *aversilver*,[5] the carriage by water under the name *shepsilver*.[6] Tenants of Ely and Ramsey manors and others in the fen land also had carriage by water to perform whenever grain or other supplies for the farm or other purposes had to be taken to the monks, and the commutations of this carriage appear frequently as *sefare*, *sesilver*, and *seesilver*.[7] The

---

[1] Harl. MSS. 3977, f. 98 : one average a year called langerode, one called poperode, and another called schirefore, 'tertium debent averagium quod vocatur schirefore tunc debent quatuor homines ire ad primum comitatum . . . et ad primum hundredum et sic acquietare villam. Et ad aliud comitatum ibunt alii quatuor.'

[2] D. S. P., p. 34 : 'facit xij averagia firmarum per annum et pro quolibet averagio quietus erit ab una operacione.' And pp. 6, 17, 47, 56, 64, 67, 68, 82. Compare Harl. MSS. 3977, f. 98.

[3] D. S. P. p. 67 : 'et debet portare ad navem cum suis paribus firmam ducendam lond' et cum proprio custo ducere Lond' . . . Set dominus inveniet navem et rectorem navis suo custo set iste operarius erit quietus de operibus suis dum fuerit in itinere illo.' And pp. 47, 57, 64, 68, and Introd. lxxviii.

[4] Ibid. pp. 27, 68.

[5] Ibid. p. 90 : Eight workacres gave 3½d. 'de averselver eo quod non debeant longius averare quam ad granarium S. Pauli.'

[6] Ibid., Introd. lxxviii, quoting I. 89.

[7] Tiber. B. ii, ff. 177, 179, 181 ; Vac. Roll, 1132/10 ; Claud. C. xi, ff. 94, 198, 255, 310.

customars of Newton and Hawkston, for example, provided a man with a boat to take to Ely a bushel of the best corn.[1] Carting services at Ely were sometimes commuted for large payments, amounting to £9 13s. 6d. a year when placed *ad certum* in Somersham in Huntingdonshire.[2] At Littleport and Stratham a 'full land' of twelve acres paid 2s. *de averagio*, and other lesser tenements paid in proportion to their size.[3] A small *waynselver* was paid on the Ely manor of Northwold, Norfolk,[4] and a more important rent, the *londenelode*, or *londenepeny*, was paid, evidently instead of carriage to London, in Thelford and Grantesdon, in Cambridgeshire, at the rate of 12d. from a half virgate of eighteen acres.[5] On the manors of St. Edmund's in Suffolk *lodesilver* appears.[6]

There were two kinds of carting rents at Durham, the payments in place of carrying loads of wood, *wodelades*, and the *averpennies*. Bishop Hatfield's Survey, compiled in 1382 from an ancient feodary, shows clearly the carriage duties. For example, every bovate of a bond land at Derlington carried a cartload of *wodelade*, made *ladas* on the visits or journeys of the bishop, and in addition to these services made three annual cartings of wine, herrings, and salt.[7] The *woodlade* was often commuted for a money rent paid at the feast of the Nativity of St. John Baptist,[8] and in addition a *woodsilver* was paid.[9] The commutation of the other *ladas* or carriages,

---

[1] Extenta Maner. Cf. Ram. Cart. i. 432: 'faciet etiam averagium quater per annum per aquam usque ad Sanctum Ivonem, et Rameseiam ad remotius et habet unum panem competentem; et non computabitur pro opere nisi impediatur per procellam, quod non possit tempestive redire.'
[2] Claud. C. xi, ff. 96, 109.
[3] Ibid. f. 43 *et pass.* for commutation.
[4] Ibid. f. 258: a *plena terra* of 48 acres gives ½d. waynselver.
[5] Ibid. f. 127: 'dat duodecim denarios ad festum S. Andree de Londenelode.' And ff. 129, 130, 149; Tiber. B. ii, ff. 136, 215, 236, 240.
[6] MSS. Gough, Suff. 3 Bodl. (13 H. VI) f. 14: 'et pro lodesilver qr.' And ff. 38 b, 42 b.
[7] Bish. Hatf. Surv., p. 4: 'et unaquaeque bovata unam quadrigatam de wodelade, et facere ladas in itineribus episcopi, et praeterea iij ladas per annum ad vinum, allec et sal ferendum.' And pp. 8, 99, *pass.*
[8] Ibid. pp. 4, 18, 28, 45, 128, 186, 200.
[9] See woodsilver.

occasionally called *outlads*,[1] when made outside the manor, were called *averpennies, daverpennies*, and were a large item of receipt.[2] There is mention frequently of *averacres, avereth*, or *avererth*, which is taken by the editor of the Survey to refer to oats, but seems more probably connected with carriage duties, like *averlond* elsewhere, the land supporting an *affrum*, or carting horse,[3] or owing special carting service. *Wodlade, wodladepenys*, and *averpennies* occur commonly in Boldon Book, and again, with an *avermalt*, in the Durham Halmote Rolls.[4]

Of still greater interest is the information regarding carting in Kent. The Rochester manors that owed a farm to the monks owed also the carriage of the farm, four hundred and forty-four *averes* being necessary for the carriage of the farm of two months, out of a total of five hundred and fifty *averes* mentioned on the manor of Southfleet. When, moreover, the lord wished to send loads to London the *gavelmanni* came with horses and carts and took each three-quarters of a load to Gravesend or Northfleet, putting the loads on the boats in their own sacks. If the sacks were lost, no further carting was done until they had been replaced by the lord.[5] Elsewhere special provisions were made for carting in case of a visit from the archbishop.[6] A very remarkable arrangement is recorded in Wye, the great Kentish manor belonging to Battle.[7] The *juga* of the manor were divided into *juga libera* and *juga servilia vel averagia*. Of the servile or carting *juga* there were thirty, which were

---

[1] Bish. Hatf. Surv., p. 31 : 'Et quaelibet bovata reddit pro outlad ad term' Martini per annum 12*s*. 11*d*.' And p. 200.

[2] Ibid. p. 38 : one bovate pays daverspenys 8*d*. And pp. 45, 78, 99, 128, 173, 186, 190.

[3] Ibid. p. 100 : 'daveripe, daverethe'; p. 95 : 'arare de unaquaque caruca ij acras de avereth.'

[4] D. H. R., pp. 13, 24.

[5] Cust. Roff., p. 2 : 'Summa de averes D et L. Opportet inde expendire ad firmam duorum mensium cccc averes et xliiij.'

[6] Ibid. p. 9 : 'Et de quolibet avero sequenti archiepiscopum habebunt unum panem. Et si archiepiscopus esset in villa, portabunt corredium de proximis foris.' Compare Batt. Abb. Cust., p. 51 : 'Hii vero qui tenent debent facere averagium bis in anno si abbas ibidem adveniret, scilicet invenire xij equos cum custodibus ad portandum panem de Wy.'

[7] Batt. Abb. Cust., pp. 122 sqq., 131. Misc. Bks. Augm. Off., vol. 57, ff. 61 sqq., 99.

grouped into three equal *wendi*, each *wendus* making ten cartings every three weeks ; one *jugum*, that is to say, making one carting, on Saturday, in order to carry half-loads of corn or barley from Wye to Battle. In addition free *juga* owed thirty-three *averagia* in summer. In this case the heavy carting service seems to have been the distinctive mark of subjection. *Wenlonds*[1] and *averlonds*[2] also occur in Kent, and the cartings seem to have been still actually rendered at the time of the compilation of the extents. *Cornlode*, a con-suetudo arentata, appears with *housebote* and *wodelode* in Addington, a manor of Canterbury.[3]

The carriage made by the villeins and more important *operarii* of the manor was usually of food supply, either of the farm for the monks or of the surplus grain and stock of the manor, to 'neighbouring markets', or elsewhere.[4] The large amounts arising from the sale of this surplus produce, and the frequency of the sales as they are recorded in the bailiffs' accounts, deserve study.[5] The statements give an impression of more freedom of intercourse, greater mobility of trade, and less economic self-sufficiency than we are usually disposed to allow the mediaeval village.

Special or occasional cartings are sometimes described of mill-stones, wood, or salt.[6] In Durham ' le courtegere ' (court

[1] Add. MSS. 6159, f. 30. Compare Mich. Ambr. Rent., p. 83: ' Et debet habere i wenday scilicet unum diem ad carrum suum preparandum antequam cariet quietum de omni alio opere.' And p. 136: '2 wensewes,' probably sheaves, received when he carted.

[2] Faust. A. i, f. 57. Cf. f. 63 : 'averlonds,' whence salt or corn should be carted to Canterbury.

[3] Vac. Roll, 1128/4: ' Et de lxxviij*s*. ix*d*. *ob*. de quibusdam consuetu-dinibus que vocantur wodelode cornlode housbote et aliis diversis con-suetudinibus arentatis per annum.'

[4] Harl. MSS. 3977, f. 85: ' Item antecessores sui solebant facere averagium apud Donewyc . . . et alia mercata vicina et provisum est quod dabit pro illo averagio ad festum S. Edmundi ij*d*. *ob*. et allocabitur ei pro uno opere.'

[5] Feod. Dun., pp. 59, 129, 141. Bold. Bk., pp. 583, 584, 585.

[6] Glouc. Cart. iii. 55: ' Omnes debent cariare molas, scilicet petras molares ad molendinum domini vel dabunt in communi tredecim denarios quadrantem.' And pp. 61, 92, 93, 95 ; Exeter Vac. Roll, 1138/2 ; Harl. MSS. 3977, f. 85 ; Batt. Abb. Cust., pp. 29, 39; Mich. Ambr. Rent., p. 144, *et pass.*

gear?) was carried,[1] and in Yorkshire *lades* and *rades* are mentioned.[2] These special cartings were often made by the smaller tenants of the manor, the cottars, and crofters, and small *censuarii*. If they had no horses they usually made the *fotaver*, or carriage *super dorsum*, or its equivalent.[3] In a Cambridgeshire manor the *averagium pedile* was, it is said, for the purpose of carrying 'letters, ducks, eggs, and those sorts of things'.[4] The St. Paul's cottar, as has been shown, drove the swine to London as his share in the carriage of the farm. The *serviens* of the lord could send the St. Edmund's villein on such service as part of his week-work.[5] Sometimes, however, the cottars and lesser holders had horses of their own, and therefore carried horseloads, *horsavers* as they were called in Kent,[6] or else, as on a manor of Battle, paid a rent called *horsgabulum*.[7] The *pokeavers* of Bury St. Edmunds may also be connected with carting services. The *averaker-silver*, which has been taken as ' silver for oats ', *aver* being taken to mean oats, is explained in a passage quoted by Professor Vinogradoff in which every cottar on a Kentish manor is said to have a *horseacre*, from which he supplies a horse to carry grain and the like to Canterbury.[8]

---

[1] Feod. Dun., p. 322.   [2] Mon. Angl. i. 417.
[3] Claud. C. xi, f. 220.
[4] Ibid. f. 125 : ' Et intelligendum est quod averagium pedile est portare breve ballivi aucas ova et huiusmodi.' Compare Batt. Abb. Cust., p. 29.
[5] Harl. MSS. 3977, f. 85 : ' si serviens velit mittere eum apud Sanctum Edmundum cum aucis et gallinis pullis gallinis columbis ovis butiro caseo vel consimilibus quae portare poterit sine caballo allocabitur ei pro uno opere.'
[6] Faust. A. i, f. 134 : ' horsaver sancti Andree.' And f. 31 : ' Item de eisdem sullin' de quolibet sullmanno xvj*d*. de Horsav' pacandos ad equinoc' autumnale.' ff. 11, 97 (16*d*. a sulung).
[7] Batt. Abb. Cust., pp. 72 sqq. Note cartings ' de monte et sub monte '. And pp. 76, 82: ' Omnes qui debent horsgabulum per annum debent averrare in adventu Abbatis cum somoniti fuerint, apud Britholton' vel Sarum vel alibi, ad voluntatem domini usque ad xx leugas, et erunt quieti illo anno de horsgabulo.'
[8] Charnock, Man. Cust. Essex. See Vill. in Eng., p. 286, quoting Add. MSS. 6159, f. 28 : ' De predictis cotariis unusquisque habet unam horsacram et de ista acra debet unusquisque invenire unum equum ad ducendum cum aliis frumentum de firma ad cantuariam, et pisas, et sal, et presencia portare.' Compare Blead. Cust., p. 208 : ' Habet unam acram stipularum . . . ad pascendum affrum suum et vocatur averlonde.'

From this manorial carting should be distinguished the *avera* or carrying services due to the king, which are often mentioned with *inwards* and *outwards* in the earlier documents. The word is frequently found with this meaning in the lists of immunities in charters. The king's wood was still carried in the time of the Hundred Rolls.[1]

---

[1] D. B. B., pp. 130, 138, 169, 240 ; Glouc. Cart. i. 72 ; ii. 127, 131, 220 ; Rot. Hund. i. 183 : 'Dicunt quod W. . . cariare fecit meremium domini Regis per abbates et priores usque Glouc' et preterea cepit xx*m*. in hundredo pro dicto cariagio.' And i. 211.

CHAPTER III

RENTS CONNECTED WITH PASTURE AND ESTOVERS

NUMEROUS rents were paid to the lord of the manor for the pasturing of the villein's cattle, the agistment of his swine, the use of the pasture-lands, wood, and waste of the village. Some of these rents were evidently ancient, going back to times when pasture-rights and the related management of the waste were of very great importance. They are distinguished from other rents based upon stock, for example from the *tonnutum*, which were considered not as payments for privileges, but as in a sense recognitions of villein status. It should be noticed, too, that in many cases rents which had no necessary connexion themselves with pasture or with cattle were assessed upon the number of animals held by the villein. Thus the common method of assessing the lord's tallage on the manor, and in some cases the *wardpenny* also, was either according to the amount of the tenement, or according to the number of the animals held.

Among the most ancient pasture payments were the *gaerswyn* and the *graserthe*. The *gaerswyn* appears in the *Rectitudines*, and in Domesday Book, in the accounts especially of Sussex and Surrey.[1] It was a rent of one out of a certain number of swine belonging to a villein, in Domesday Book the seventh, and was paid for the right to pasture all sorts of animals, resembling strictly therefore herbage rather than pannage. It probably appears in later times in the *garsanese*, *gershenese* rent commonly paid in the manors of St. Paul's[2]

---

[1] For Mr. Round's discussion of these rents see Vict. Count. Hist , Surrey, i. 291, and Sussex, i. 365.

[2] D. S. P., p. 6: 'Reddent eciam singulis annis garsanese scilicet iiij*d.* et *ob.* de qualibet virgata quae averat et quae non averant faciunt fotau-

and of St. Edmund's,[1] and in certain manors in Bedfordshire, Huntingdonshire, and Oxfordshire,[2] as they are described in the Hundred Rolls, usually as a money rent, and sometimes no longer clearly distinguished from pannage or *thac*, the money paid for the agistment of swine only.[3] Thus St. Edmund's customary tenant, if he had ten swine, gave the lord the tenth ; if he had fewer than ten and they were ' in pannage', he gave the lord a penny *gresenese* for yearlings, a halfpenny for half yearlings.[4] At Ramsey and elsewhere, however, the payment of one from a certain number of swine owned by the villein was probably in the beginning a pasture payment.[5] The *gavolswine*, which in origin was a food-rent to the lord unconnected with pasture, was also probably later identified with the common pannage. In Kent it is defined as a rent paid by tenants in the Weald for licence to keep swine and agist the swine of others.[6] It occurs also at Lewes.[7] In spite of a confusion of rents in later times, in early days probably one usual method of securing pasture-rights of all sorts was the render of the *grass swine* to the lord.

Another kind of return for pasture-rights seems to be indicated by the frequent *graserthe* services of the custumals,[8] or the rents commuting such services. Reminiscences often appear in the later documents of the ancient threefold division

ever, et si habuerint porcos dabunt de pannagio . . .' Also p. 51 and Introd. p. lxviii.

[1] Harl. MSS. 3977, f. 94 : ' Si pauciores porcos habeat quam decem et sint in padnagio dabit pro quolibet porco ij*d*. Si autem non sint in padnagio pro quolibet dabit j*d*. quod vocatur gresenese si sit unius anni.'

[2] Rot. Hund. i. 6 ; ij. 613.

[3] Ibid. ii. 785 : ' et dabit pannagium videlicet gershenese . . .'

[4] Harl. MSS. 3977, f. 94.

[5] Ram. Cart. i. 323, 345, 356 ; Burt. Ch., p. 73 ; D. S. P., p. 71 ; Rot. Hund. ii. 872.

[6] Robinson, Gavelkind, p. 220.

[7] Mon. Angl. iv. 9, quoting a twelfth-century document : ' Terra de Breham. xxx et ij de servitio et x carratas de busche et unum present valens vj*d*. . . . et gavelswin.'

[8] For example, Rot. Hund. ii. 768 : ' Item si habeat carucam integram vel cum aliis sociis conjunctim illa caruca arabit domino ij acras terre ad yvernagium et herciabit quantum illa caruca araverit in die et istud servicium appellatur greserthe pro quo servicio ipse Willelmus et omnes alii consuetudinarii habebunt pasturas dominicas ad diem ad Vincula Sancti Petri usque ad festum B. Mariae in Marcio et prata dominica.'

of services into *gavol* or *lage* services, part probably of the
original *consuetudines firmae*; *ben*, or boon, or *filsing*, or *wine*
services, rendered theoretically as a favour to the lord, *de
amore* and not *de consuetudine*, and this third kind, surviving
in the common *graserthe*, or ploughing rendered in return for
pasture privileges.[1]

A passage in the Bury custumal, a custumal full of references to gavol services, or *goveles*, gives an excellent example
of arrangements that look like late elaborations of the *greserthe* principle, although the service is not here called
graserthe. Every tenant of land except the free reaps one
half-acre of grain if he have *averia*, and as many half-acres
as he has cows, unless his cows be in the lord's fold at the
vigil of St. Peter. All the cattle of the tenant except his
milch cows and ploughing oxen lie in the lord's fold. In
addition, a quite separate rent of *thac* is paid for his swine.[2]
The ploughing appears again very clearly at Glastonbury;
' he shall have no ox in the pasture of the lord except those
which he acquits by *grashurde*.'[3] The custumal of Bleadon
explains that two annual *graserthe* ploughings were 'invented'
so that the lord, in consideration of the ploughing, should
make no *winter hage*, winter hedges, on his land to keep out
cattle.[4] A similar explanation is given for the custom at

---

[1] See above under gavol.

[2] Harl. MSS. 3977, f. 82 : ' Omnes qui tenent terram de domino exceptis liberis . . . debent metere pro porcis quilibet eorum dimidiam acram
siliginis. Et omnes homines domini exceptis liberis debent metere pro
vadiis dimidiam acram siliginis si habeant averia. Et omnes isti supra-
dicti metent pro vaccis quot vaccas tot dimidias acras de frumento met'
si autem vacca sit in falda domini in vigilia S. Petri non metet si domum
remaneat (*sic*) metet ut predictum est. Si autem vacca eat in caruca per
annum non metet pro ea. Omnia autem averia istorum exceptis caru-
cariis bobus et vaccis lactantibus . . . iacebunt in falda domini . . . et pro
quibuslibet v. berbiciis metet j rodam avene si unum tamen habeat metet
unam rodam. Si excedat numerum v. metet dimidiam acram et sic
deinceps usque in infinitum.'

[3] Mich. Ambr. Rent., p. 109: ' Item, non habebit aliquem bovem in
pastura domini nisi illos quos aquietabit per garshurde.' And p. 135:
' et debet arurum (*sic*) que dicitur gareshurthe '; p. 84: he ploughs a
' garslod' scil. iiij acras in terra domini '; p. 87 : ' garslond.'

[4] Blead. Cust., p. 201 : the customar makes two graserth ploughings,
one before and one after All Saints : ' Et inventa fuit ista arura ita quod
dominus nullum defensum facere deberet in hieme quod dicitur winter-

Pidington, a manor of St. Frideswide's. All the ploughs come on a day near Michaelmas at the summons of the reeve for the *graserthe* ploughing, 'racione quod dominus hagam nec pasturam separabilem faciet ab hominibus intra campum warectabilem ; tantum hoc diem faciet et non amplius'.[1] At King's Barton, Gloucestershire, the *graserthe* ploughing was commuted for a large rent of 20s. 10d.[2]

In later times, however, the common forms of pasture rents were pannage for the agistment of pigs, herbage for the pasturing of all sorts of animals, and faldage for the folding of sheep and cattle.

Pannage was practically universal, except in case of special exemption, wherever and whenever there were swine to be fed on the demesne or the waste. The payment was made usually by villeins only,[3] freemen having probably some wood-rights of their own, and being therefore independent of the lord's mast. Usually pannage was the return made by the villeins for permission to turn swine out into the wood, but very commonly there are cases where villeins had to pay pannage even when they kept their swine at home. In other cases the lord seems to have required that the villeins should agist their swine on his land whether they wished to do so or not. On manors of Ramsey, for example, the custom varied: sometimes, especially when nuts were plentiful, the villein paid pannage whether he drove his swine into the lord's wood or kept them at home, sometimes he paid it only when his

haye contra averia sua in nullo loco super terram suam propter eandem aruram.'
    [1] Kennet, Par. Antiq. ii. 137.
    [2] Min. Acc. 850/10 : 'Et de xxs. xd. de quadam consuetudine vocata garserthe ad idem festum.'
    [3] Ram. Cart. i. 287, 298, 309, *pass.*, among the obligations of customary tenants. Worc. Vac. Roll, 1143/18 '. . . de pannagio porcorum custumariorum' ; Glouc. Cart. iii. 217 ; D. S. P., pp. 6, 33, 37 ; Rot. Hund. *pass.* ; Min. Acc. 742/17–20, 850/10 ; Durham Vac. Roll, 1144/1 ; Norwich Vac. Roll, 1141/1 ; Coventry and Lichfield Vac. Roll, 1132/5 (*tallagium porcorum*); Crondal Records, pp. 52, 76, 95, and commonly elsewhere. Compare Vinogradoff, Growth of Manor, p. 311 : ' Customary payments of pannage for swine and cattle grazing on the waste, customs of so-called grass earth labour, fines for cutting down trees, and especially hunting and fishing privileges, are among the earliest manifestations of manorial lordship over tracts of waste lands, and, of course, they get more and more elaborate as cultivation and social progress increase.'

swine were *in nemore domini*.¹ Again, the Hundred Rolls describe a Bedfordshire manor where once pannage was paid only when swine were turned into the wood of the lord, but where at the time of survey it was taken *per vim et extorsionem*, even if the swine were kept at home.² In this, as in other cases, unjust encroachments by the lord became in the course of time recognized as his rights and part of the custom of the manor.

For swine fed in the royal forest pannage was paid to the king, and from the obligation to pay it the king often granted immunity. The receipt of the royal pannage was an important part of the duty of the forest officers or agistors at the Martinmas *swainmote*.³

Pannage was paid annually at Martinmas,⁴ according to the number of animals agisted. The ordinary rate was a penny for a pig over a year old, that is to say, a year old on the last Holy Cross day, a halfpenny for a half-yearling or for a pig just separated from its mother. Little pigs and sows were often free.⁵ This rate was usual on the manors of Gloucester,⁶ and in Oxfordshire,⁷ and on the manors of Abingdon,⁸ Lichfield,⁹

¹ Ram. Cart. i. 288 : 'pro porco dat pannagium, si sit de pretio duorum solidorum, ad minus duos denarios, pro porco dimidii anni obolum, pro porcello nihil, pro sue porcellos habente unum denarium ; et sic dat pro porcis suis quolibet anno, licet ad astrum suum eos pascat sive copia glandis fuerit, sive non.' Again, 309 : 'et licet porcos suos domi retinuerit in anno quo copia glandis fuerit, nihilominus pro eis dabit pannagium.' And i. 323, 335, 345 ; Claud. C. xi, f. 121 : 'sive mittat sive non mittat.'
² Rot. Hund. i. 6. Compare Glouc. Cart. iii. 208 : 'De pannagio praestando pro porcis haesitant juratores quia nunquam viderunt ipsum pannagiare porcos suos.'
³ Rot. Hund. ii. 18, 40, 710 ; i. 25, 26, 33, 152. Reg. Worc. Pr., p. 145. Abing. Cart. ii. 22. Burt. Ch., p. 129; cf. Sel. Pl. For. and Manwood's treatise.
⁴ Burt. Ch., p. 129. Ram. Cart. ii. 37, 48. Rot. Hund. i. 25, 26; ii. 18, *pass.*
⁵ Claud. C. xi, ff. 96, 229, and elsewhere for instances of pannage paid or not paid for sows.
⁶ Glouc. Cart. iii. 50, 53, 66, 79, 88, 124, 125, 138, 140, 143, 182, 200, 217.
⁷ Rot. Hund. ii. 758 : 'suemque lactantem cum porcellis quietam habebit,' and 764, 768, 775, 785, *pass.*
⁸ Abing. Ch. ii. 301.
⁹ Ashmol. MSS. 864, quoting Bl. Bk. Coventry, f. 5 : 'et dabit pannagium pro porcis suis scilicet pro quolibet porco unius anni *id.* et pro porco infra annum *ob.* Et si habet decem porcos dabit unum porcum et tunc non dabit argentum pro aliis infra decem sed si excedat decem dabit

Burton,[1] Battle,[2] St. Paul's,[3] Ely,[4] Ramsey,[5] and in Northumberland.[6]   In   Shropshire [7]   and   Wiltshire [8]   the   rate
was higher, 2d. a yearling, a penny a half-yearling ; and in
Ramsey, too, sometimes 2d. was paid for a yearling, a halfpenny for a half-yearling, and a farthing for a little pig of
three months.[9]   Battle Abbey tenants sometimes paid 2d. for
pigs of 'fullest age', while for younger ones the amounts
were graduated.[10]

Other payments occur which were closely connected with
pannage, or were probably the same payment under other
names.   *Retropannagium*, which is especially common in
descriptions of royal forests, was the pannage paid for the
agistment of swine after the termination of the ordinary
season, that is to say, after Martinmas.[11]   *Thac*, which appears
in St. Oswald's letter under the form *tace* or *swinescead*, and
which with *ciric sceott*, *toll*, and the fulfilment of the law of
riding made up the service of the *riding men*,[12] still lingers in
the thirteenth-century register of Worcester, but has become
a mark of villeinage, paid usually by tenants holding under the
old assize, and occasionally by those holding under a newer
arrangement.[13]   When, however, land in villeinage was put at
farm, the *thac*, with the *thol* or payment for selling animals,
was usually compounded for with a money rent, *merchet* and

pannagium pro illis qui excedunt sed dicunt quod consueverunt habere
suem matricem quietam de pannagio de gratia ballivi.' Cf. f. 17 : 'et dabit
grestakes pro porcis suis.'
    [1] Burt. Ch., p. 73.   [2] Batt. Abb. Cust., pp. 61, 79, 89.
    [3] D. S. P., p. 51, cf. p. 67 : 'pro quolibet porco . . . in stipula dabit j
pullum galline.'
    [4] Claud. C. xi, ff. 96, 117, 121, 244.   [5] Ram. Cart. i. 289, *pass.*
    [6] Rot. Hund. ii. 18.   [7] Ibid. ii. 56.
    [8] Batt. Abb. Cust., p. 75.
    [9] Ram. Cart. i. 309, 356.
    [10] Batt. Abb. Cust., p. 149, cf. p. 136.
    [11] Rot. Hund. i. 26 : 'Dicunt quod idem I . . . habet retropannagium
ita scilicet quod quando dominus Rex die S. Martini accipit pannagium
suum omnes illi qui porcos suos habere voluerint ultra illum diem sicut
prius fuerunt in dominicis boscis dabunt pro quolibet porco dicto forestario
i ob.' See Sel. Pl. For., pp. 67, 124, and Rot. Hund. i. 25 ; ii. 56, 115.
    [12] Kemble, Cod. Dip. 1287. Cf. D. B. B., p. 307, tace is 'apparently the
pannage of a later time'. It has degenerated from a payment by the
riding man to a test of servile status.
    [13] Reg. Worc. Pr., pp. 10b, 43b, 51b, 52b, 56a, 61a, 69a, 73a, 75b.

the lord's tallage alone remaining as distinctive marks of status.[1] *Thac* was paid according to the number of pigs held by a villein, and at the usual pannage rate ; a penny for a yearling, a halfpenny for a half-yearling, the money being due at Martinmas, and payment being enforced whether pigs were fed in the lord's wood or not.[2] Once it seems to have been paid in addition to pannage.[3] At Bury it was paid sometimes in the form of the fifth or the tenth pig, like the *garsanese*. A villein's father, we are told, paid *thac* (*thaciabat*) for his swine, 'so that for all his swine he gave one, and he himself chose one, and the lord had the second.'[4] The ' *thac* of Westmore ' is mentioned in the roll of a Somerset manor,[5] and the older form is preserved in the *tak' porcorum* of Northumberland,[6] and the *tak* of Hereford[7] and York,[8] and, in composition, in the Gloucestershire *thisteltake*,[9] the Cambridgeshire *shepestake*, and the Staffordshire *grestakes*.[10] *Thacsilver*, found on the manor of Glatton, Huntingdonshire,[11] may be another form of *thac,* or perhaps, since no connexion is made with the villein's stock, refers to some commutation of the service of thatching. The curious payments of *Danger* and *Leafyield* or *leavesilver* occur in Kent, duties payable by the tenants for leave to plough their land in pannage time, between Michaelmas and Martinmas, when it was thought

---

[1] Ibid., pp. 43ᵇ, 73ᵃ. Cf. p. 59ᵃ, and D. H. R., p. 74 : 'Quod quilibet pascat communem porcum.'

[2] Reg. Worc. Pr., p. 15ᵃ: 'Villani dabunt Thac, scilicet de porco superannato, exceptis matricibus suibus, i denarium, de non superannato obolum, scilicet die sancti Martini.' See pp. 66ᵃ, 104ᵃ, Introd. xli.

[3] Ibid. pp. 14ᵃ, 19ᵃ. [4] Harl. MSS. 3977, f. 94.

[5] Bath and Wells Vac. Roll, 1131/3 : '(Kingsbury, Somerset) . . . et de ixs. de Thac' de Westmor'.'

[6] Mon. Angl. iii. 321: 'Decima Feni cum Tak' Porcorum' (Temp. H. VIII).

[7] Hazlitt's Blount's Tenures, p. 32 : 'Terra Custumaria . . . et debet quasdam consuetudines, videlicet tak et toll et faldfey et sanguinem suum emere.'

[8] Mon. Angl. i. 417 : 'tol, tac, et mercet.'

[9] York Vac. Roll, 1144/1 : ' et de xs. vijd. de operibus custumariorum . . . cum pannagio quod dicitur thisteltake . . .' Scrutton, p. 40, and Hazlitt's Blount's Tenures, p. 123 : 'Thisteltac for killing a swine over a year.'

[10] See below.

[11] Rot. Hund. ii. 657 : 'Item dat obolum de thacsilver.' For thatching services see D. S. P., pp. 55, 62, and *passim* in manorial custumals.

that ploughing might be a danger to the lord's right of pannage.[1]

Herbagium. The payment made for the pasturage of animals other than swine ' horn under horne ' [2] on the demesne of the manor was called herbage. ' Agistment was of two kinds : first, the herbage of the woods and pastures, and secondly of the mast of trees ; the latter was called pannage.' [3] Herbage was, like pannage, an important source of revenue to the lord. Both payments are noted regularly, for example, in the receipts from the manors of Winchester, sometimes one and sometimes the other being the greater.[4] Once in Winchester records the payment seems to have been made in sheep,[5] not money, a survival of a custom resembling the old *gaerswyn.* For animals turned on the common of the vill as well as for those fed on the pasture of the demesne herbage was sometimes paid. Thus at Glastonbury the villata declares that the pasture ought to be divided into two parts, and the lord ought to have the half he chooses for his own uses, and the villata the other half. The lord may have his half in defence from Purification to Midsummer ; the villata should pay a penny to the lord for every animal turned to pasture on its half.[6] Sometimes, on the other hand, a certain number could be turned on the common pasture without payment by

---

[1] See Robinson, Gavelkind, p. 219 : showing pannage in the weald to be a very important privilege and rent. A court was held once a year called *curia legalis*; with which compare the court of the Denes, and Kemble, i. 483. See also Robinson, Gavelkind, p. 214: 'by the custom of Droveden the lord was to retain all great oaks, ash, and beeches, and pannage on land of tenants in gavelkind. The tenants had underwood.' And p. 216. See Faust, A. 1, f. 43 : for drofdenne and donger or danger ; and Misc. Bks. Augm. Off., vol. 57, f. 15 : ' pro Danger et lefield.' Cf. f. 82[b].

[2] Claud. C. xi, f. 235, *et pass.* [3] Burt. Ch., p. 129.

[4] Winch. Pipe Roll, p. 1 : ' Idem reddunt compotum de v. li. ixs. vj*d.* de pannagio. Et de xxj*s.* viij*d.* de herbagio.' And pp. 5, 9, 11, 16, *pass.*

[5] Ibid., p. 22 : 'Et de xlvij ovibus de consuetudine herbagii post partum et ante tonsionem.' See below under Lamselver.

[6] Mich. Ambr. Rent., p. 67 : ' Item villata dicit quod pastura dividi debet in duas partes equales et dominus habebit quam partem eligere voluerit ad opus suum, et villata alteram. Et pro quolibet animali quod in parte sua villata habuerit, habebit dominus j*d.* scilicet super illa medietate quam villata habuerit. Et dominus habebit partem suam in defenso a Purificacione usque ad Vincula. Sed postea communicabit tota villata ubique cum Domino.' Also p. 101.

the villein, while for all in excess of that number he must pay the lord. The rate of payment varied with the custom of the manor. On a manor in Oxfordshire one horse, six oxen, six pigs, fifty sheep might be turned into the common pasture with no payment except the pannage; for more than this number herbage was due.[1] Common on Dartmoor was paid for at the rate of a penny for every work beast, 2*d.* for a horse, but it should have been paid for at the rate of only a halfpenny for an ox and a penny for a horse.[2] In Abingdon there was given at 'faldrove' a penny for every yearling ox or cow, and a halfpenny for one that was younger: a penny for every ten sheep, a halfpenny for every nine sheep.[3] On St. Paul's manors the rate was $3\frac{1}{2}d.$ for every animal in the lord's pasture.[4] A special payment was made to Peterborough for goats,[5] because they injured the herbage.

The common terms for herbage rents in the east of England, especially on Ely and Bury manors, were *coupenny, cupeny, cusilver,* and *busagium, bosing, bosingsilver,* and *bossilver. Bullocksilver* and *oxpeni* also occur. *Cupenny* occurs with great regularity on Norfolk manors, and is sometimes described in detail. Thus in Brigham [6] it was paid from a virgate at the following rate: one ox a penny, one cow a penny, one *bovettus* a penny, one *juvenca* of three years a halfpenny, unless she lie at the lord's fold. In Feltwell the rate was the same.[7] The cattle of the villata pastured *horn under horne,* and a *plena terra* paid for a cow a penny called *cupeny,* for a bullock a penny called *bullockpeny.* Cottars and *anilepimen* paid at the same rate. The *cupeny* is mentioned also in Cambridge-

---

[1] Rot. Hund. ii. 757: 'Tenet viij acras terre cum pertinentiis et habebit j equum vj boves l oves in communi pastura bosci quietos salvo domino pannagio porcorum.'

[2] Rot. Hund. i. 76, 77.

[3] Abing. Acc. ii. 301; and see also Drove, *infra.*

[4] D. S. P., p. 51: 'Omnes ... debent de pastura v ovium in estate dare j*d.* et in hieme pro x j*d.* et de singulis animalibus iij. *ob.* per annum si ad pasturam domini venerint similiter de equis et de singulis porcis j*d.* pro Garsavese.'

[5] Chron. Petrob. App., pp. 157, 164; cf. Burt. Ch., p. 129.

[6] Claud. C. xi, f. 250: 'Summa de cupani per annum innumerabilis est quia quandoque plus quandoque minus.'

[7] Ibid. ff. 254, 255, 257. Cf. f. 258.

shire[1] and in Suffolk.[2] In the Cambridgeshire instance the customary tenant enclosed for every cow one perch length of hedge around the crops, a service somewhat similar to which was performed on the Battle manor of Apuldreham in Sussex, where every cottar possessing a cow reaped and bound one half-acre of oats.[3] On St. Edmund's manors *cusilver*, which is once written *culsilver*, was common, and *oxpeni* also occurred.[4] In Wiltshire *veal money* is mentioned.[5]

Busagium also was a payment connected with the pasturage of cows,[6] but was paid more particularly, on a Ramsey manor at least, for the right on the part of the customary tenant to fold his own cattle.[7] It was paid at the rate of a penny for a full-grown cow. The Ely *bosing*, *bosingsilver*, or *bossilver* seems to have been paid for the pasture of the cart-horse with which carrying service was performed. It occurs at Wisbech, Cambridgeshire,[8] at the rate of a penny from a *plena terra*, and at Leverington [9] at the rate of a halfpenny from those tenants of messuages that had horses and carts. It is possible, however, that *bosingsilver* may refer to some commutation of carting service. *Bossilver* occurs once.[10]

¹ Claud. C. xi, f. 64 : ' De consuetudinibus censuariorum ... et si habeat bovem vel bovetum vel iuvencam dabit de kupeni per annum pro qualibet unum obolum quam cicius aliquem dentem jactaverit et claudet pro qualibet vacca unam perticatam sepis ante segetes domini.' Cf. Ely Vac. Roll, 1132/10. The manors on which it is recorded are the same as those in the custumal.
² Claud. C. xi, f.·310.
³ See above note and compare also Batt. Abb. Cust., p. 56 : ' et quicunque eorum (maiores cottarii) vaccam possideat debet pro vacca metere j acram avenae et ligare.'
⁴ Harl. MSS. 3977, f. 94, for ' oxpeni'.
⁵ Hazlitt's Blount's Tenures, p. 33.
⁶ Min. Acc. 945/2 : (Walsingham Parva, Norfolk) '... et de *id.* de busagio unius vacce.' Cf. Norwich Vac. Roll, 1141/1 ; Eccles: among customary *consuetudines*; Ely Vac. Roll, 1132/10.
⁷ Ram. Cart. i. 402 '... si habuerint vaccas, dant ad busagium unum denarium, et pro juvenca pregnante unum obolum, et pro eo quod non jacebunt in falda domini.' Cf. iii. 266.
⁸ Claud. C. xi, ff. 80, 81 : ' Si unusquisque tenens unam plenam terram dat de bosingsilver unum denarium.' Ely Vac. Roll, 1132/10 : ' redd. voc. bosing, grippure shepestake.'
⁹ Claud. C. xi, f. 85 : ' unusquisque predictorum mesuagia tenencium dabit de bosingsilver unum obolum (S. Mart.) ... si habeat equum et carectam.' Cf. f. 82.
¹⁰ Tiber. B. ii, f. 237.

Other pasture payments for cattle were *splotgabulum*, a Winchester rent on the manor of Walda,[1] and *lesselver*, a rent found commonly on the Battle manor of Brightwalton, Berkshire,[2] paid for every animal of two or more years on the feast of St. John Baptist. *Lactagium* was paid for the pasturage of cows on the manors of Bath and Wells,[3] and *lacsulfer* at Abingdon.[4]

Animals had to be guarded so that they might not injure the crops or wander from the manor, and this duty was performed either by regular herdsmen paid by villein contributions or by the villeins themselves in turn.[5] In Durham manors the guarding was called *hirsill*, and if it were not properly kept a penalty was attached, 6*d.* for a pig in the corn, 2*d.* for a duck astray. After St. Cuthbert's day in March no one might allow his beasts to leave the vill without *hirsill*.[6] If beasts of strangers wandered on the lord's commonable waste in Norfolk *resting geld* was taken by the lord,[7] and in Lanca-

---

[1] Winch. Pipe Roll, 83, under *Purchasia*, with fines from certain tenants for breach of pasture regulations.

[2] From the Anglo-Saxon *laes*, pasture. See Batt. Abb. Cust., p. 60: a *virgarius* should give the lord 'pro quolibet animali aetate duorum annorum vel amplius ... ad festum S. Iohannis Baptistae unum denarium quod vocatur Lesselver.' See Index, p. 165. It occurs also in the account rolls of the manor, e.g. 742/17: 'de lesselver ad festum S. Iohannis hoc anno ijs. viij*d.*' Again, 742/18-19.

[3] Bath and Wells Vac. Roll, 1131/3: 'de lactagiis scilicet de vaccis Episcopi defuncti pro pastura. Idem reddit compotum de lijs. xj*d. ob.* receptis de lactagiis xxxj vaccarum Episcopi defuncti commorantium ibidem in pastura per xlj dies, videlicet de qualibet vacca per diem obolum pro pastura et custode earundem.'

[4] Abing. Acc., p. 37: 'De lacsulfer vijs.'

[5] Burt. Ch., p. 26; D. S. P., p. 105: 'omnes isti ponunt faldam suam singulis annis super terram dominici ab hokedai usque ad advincula et habebunt ibi oves et omnia animalia sua. Et pro custodia cujuslibet averii dant Bercario domini iij *ob.* exceptis ovibus quas ipsimet custodiunt et pascuntur in communi pastura domini a pascha usque ad festum S. Michaelis et si ita non custodiuntur non dabunt argentum.' Rot. Hund. i. 35: land called 'sceperdeslond' held for guarding king's sheep; ii. 745: cottar guards swine and has the 'markinghog'. Cf. *herdershift* and *schepersulver*.

[6] D. H. R., pp. 56, 59, 61, 74, 148, 167; 101: 'Ordinatum est ex communi assensu quod quilibet eorum veniat ad preceptum prepositi ad ponendum freth' hircill et omnibus aliis ordinacionibus ad communem proficuum.'

[7] Scrutton, Commons, p. 40; Blomefield, Norfolk, ix. 294: 'Also he claims liberty of resting geld, of the beasts of any strangers resting one

shire, Cheshire, and Gloucestershire *thistletake* was paid for beasts on the common if 'only as much as a thistle were cropped'.[1] *Escapium* was 'money paid for beasts escaping into forbidden enclosures'.[2] The forest proceedings show large fines given for *escapium*.

Drove was probably the commutation of a service of driving out the cattle of a village into pasture.[3] The commuted service occurs in King's Barton, Gloucestershire, in a late roll, which mentions also under *exitus manerii 5s.* derived from 'drifft' pullanorum'.[4] The 'forth drove' and *forth drovesilver* of Ramsey should be compared with *drove*, the former representing probably the uncommuted form of the service.[5] With *forth drove* should be compared also the *faldrove* of Abingdon.[6] In Kent[7] land was held by the service of driving cattle to market or pasturage, and hence was called *droveland*. The *drofmannus* was in charge of the drove. There was also on

night on the common of the said village, in shack time, or in the time when the lands are enclosed of any tenant ... And he hath also another custom of resting-geld, that of all goods, chattels, things and merchandises coming to land by sea ... resting upon the land one day and one night.'

[1] See above among pannage payments.

[2] Rot. Hund. i. 135 (Yorks) the bailiffs take *escapium* 'videl. de bove iiij*d.* de equo iiij*d.*' Cf. Sel. Pleas. For., p. 64, and Gloss., p. 141, quoting Duchy of Lancaster Forest Proceedings : 'Tota campania infra metas suas est in defenso per totum annum; et similiter Eydal'; ita quod nemo habet communam nec accessum in eadem cum aueriis. Et si aueria vel animalia ibidem uenerint per eschapium, dabitur pro eisdem, videlicet, pro affro ij den' pro boue j den' et pro quinque ouibus j den., etsi hec inveniantur bis infra duo placita attachiamentorum foreste, quod si tercio inueniantur infra duo attachiamenta tunc debent appreciari ad opus regis, uidelicet, affrum prout valet, bos ad sex solidos, vacca ad quinque solidos et reliqui auerii (sic) minoris precii ad quatuor solidos et reliqui auerii infra duos annos ad duos solidos ; et ouis ad xij den' : et porcus superannatus ad xij den'.' (Duchy of Lanc. For. Proc., Bundle 1, No. 5, Roll 15 d.)

[3] Mich. Ambr. Rent., p. 92 : 'Et debet droviare semel in anno versus Glaston.' And p. 44: 'quoddam iter quod vocatur Drofwei.' Compare Tiber. B. ii, f. 154: 'Tenet unam dravam.'

[4] Min. Acc. 850/10 (13 H. V.): 'et de xxx*s.* vj*d. ob.* de quadam consuetudine vocata Drove ad idem festum (S. Michaelis) ... et de v*s.* de drifft' pullanorum hoc anno in Kingswode.'

[5] Econ. Cond. Ram. Man., p. 84, and App., pp. 58, 63, *pass.* : to shepherd, swineherd, &c. 'pro forthdrovesilver ij*s.* ex consuetudine,' a rent to the herdsmen.

[6] Abing. Acc. ii. 301.

[7] Robinson, Gavelkind, p. 215. Cf. Faust. A. 1, f. 43 : 'Inde debetur drofdenne et donger.'

Winchester manors the payment of *innynge* or *innedge* money, an annual rent for turning the cattle into the 'hams' or meadows when other pastures were under water.[1]

Faldagium. The payment made for the folding of sheep, and sometimes of cattle also, outside the lord's fold was usually called *faldagium*. At Abingdon *faldgabul* occurs,[2] with which should be compared the *oxfoldgable* of Southampton.[3] Regulations regarding the folding of sheep, the old *soca faldae*, are often described in detail in the custumals, and large receipts derived from faldage payments are entered in the bailiffs' accounts. The distinction implied in Edward the Confessor's writ still held,[4] and the obligation to have sheep at the lord's fold was considered a mark of villeinage; men that folded their sheep at the lord's fold, that is to say, were usually villeins, although not all villeins were subject to the restriction. From this point of view faldage should be included among the condition payments.

The account in the Ramsey custumals of the faldage requirements is unusually full. If a villein had but one sheep he might keep it at his own fold, if he had many, more than six, he must put them in the lord's fold.[5] The sheep of cottars and strangers,[6] and in St. Ives, of strangers and of those that had no land in the Vicus Pontis, the chief street of the fair, were kept at the lord's fold.[7] In Girton both those that had land, and those that had not,[8] used the lord's fold from Hokeday to Martinmas. The abbot's fold was moved constantly

---

[1] Blead. Cust., pp. 198, 201 : 'et j*d. ob.* de redditu ad hokedaij que dicitur innynge ut possit habere ingressum in pastura in parte australi prati domini.' Compare Mich. Ambr. Rent., p. 159 : ' Memorandum quod omnes villani . . . donant pro qualibet vacca quam habent uno anno pro ingressu libero habendo in Serphan j*d.* et altero anno *ob.*'

[2] Abing. Acc. App., p. 143 : ' Of faldgabul nothing because no fold.'

[3] Mon. Angl. ii. 457 (temp. H. VIII) : ' Redd. Cust. tenenc. voc. oxfoldgable.'

[4] D. B. B., pp. 76, 77 and note, p. 91. Gr. of Manor, pp. 181–2. Eng. Soc. in Elev. Cent., pp. 387, sqq., 424, 435.

[5] Ram. Cart. i. 416 : ' Ponet in falda domini Abbatis omnes bidentes suos, si plures habuerit, et Abbas inveniet custodem ad custum suum,' and ibid. i. 419. Cf. iii. 267.

[6] Ibid. i. 332.   [7] Ibid. i. 284.

[8] Ibid. i. 495.

from place to place, and the maintenance of it was part of the labour service of the villeins.[1]

Interesting faldage regulations regarding cattle as well as sheep are common in Eastern England and Kent. Thus, in a Canterbury manor sheep fed in a common pasture called 'tunmannemers', and in the marsh, were kept at the lord's fold from Hokeday to All Saints, and all oxen and cows were paid for,[2] and in an Ely manor in Norfolk a *plena terra* gave for *faldagium* for every ox a penny, for every sterile cow a penny, for every *juvenca* of two years a halfpenny, and for every five sheep a penny, and by reason of this payment neither sheep nor other animals were required to lie at the lord's fold.[3] The Glastonbury *faldicium* was paid for cattle and for sheep.[4] The *faldagium* payment for cattle seems to be equivalent sometimes, as has been said, to *busagium*.

A few other payments connected with the keeping of sheep appear in the custumals and elsewhere. In Kent a *lamb peni*, *lamselver*, or *lamgabulum*,[5] is fairly frequent. It seems to have

[1] Ram. Cart.. ii. 28: 'Et debet ducere valdam Abbatis de uno loco ad alium locum cum villata.' Cf. Claud. C. xi, ff. 129, 130, and Winch. Pipe Roll, p. 44, the *potfalda*.

[2] Add. MSS. 6159, f. 187: 'Item est ibi pastura communis que vocatur tunmannemers et omnes oves que pascantur in illo marisco . . .' are to lie at the lord's fold from Hokeday to All Saints; and so also all oxen and cows, for which a payment is to be made of 2*d.*, but 1*d.* for a *bovettus*.

[3] Claud. C. xi, f. 225: faldagium is given 'pro bobus boviculis multonibus et hogastris suis et pro qualibet juvenca etatis duorum annorum'; f. 229: faldage is paid 'et ideo nec oves nec alia averia sua jacere debent in falda domini'; and f. 244. Cf. Harl. MSS. 1005, f. 71: 'Nota quod quilibet potest habere faldam de animalibus ita scilicet pro quolibet animali duorum annorum et amplius dabit j*d.* domino vel iacebit in falda domini exceptis animalibus liberorum hominum preter R. . . . qui debet habere in falda domini iiij boves pro omnibus animalibus suis.'

[4] Mich. Ambr. Rent., p. 101 (Damerham, Wilts.): 'debet dare faldicium ad Hockeday, scilicet, pro qualibet vaccá j*d* et pro qualibet juvenca vel boviculo duorum annorum ob. et pro quolibet amullo superannato qu. et pro iiij ovibus j*d.* et habebit j cuillardum quietum de faldicio.' Cf. p. 109: '. . . non habebit aliquem bovem in pastura domini nisi illos quos aquietabit per grashurde.'

[5] Add. MSS. 6159, ff. 30, 60: Lambpeni at Assumption 6*d.*; and f. 26 2 lambs to be paid in summer; Faust. A. 1, f. 120: At Littlebourne a half sulung gives 'ad lamselver vj*d.*'; f. 124: 'lamgabulum'; f. 29: 'De eisdem sull' reddent duos agnos separabiles ad festum Sancti Iohannis et illos solebat dominus colligere per bedellum et pastorem suum apud domos sullmannorum'; cf. f. 16. Cf. Cust. Roff., p. 3: 9 juga of Gavelland give 9 lambs at Easter; *pass.*

been the commutation of a rent in kind of two lambs, which
the lord collected from the houses of the ' sullmen ' on St.
John Baptist's day, or elsewhere of one lamb from a sulung, commuted for sixpence.   At Ramsey a rent was paid *de separacione agnorum*.[1]   Lambs were paid at Norwich and Worcester
also,[2] probably as pasture rents resembling the *gaerswyn*,
although they may be parts of an old food-rent.   Once a similar
rent of sheep *de herbagio* was collected on a manor of Winchester,[3] with which should be compared the rent on Ramsey
manors of *wethersilver*, or the penny *ad arietem*,[4] for supplying
a wether to the flock, a rent occurring again at Kettering,
Northamptonshire,[5] and on Glastonbury manors,[6] where
either a penny or a lamb was given on Hokeday.   A rent
called *shepestake* is found on the Ely manor of Wisbech, in
Cambridgeshire, probably a pasture rent, like *thisteltake*, in the
north.[7]   On the manors of Bury *shepsilver*, or *schepsilver*, was
common at the rate of a penny for six sheep, or, once, for
eight sheep.[8]   In Norfolk it was sometimes the custom to
pay *herdershift* for the maintenance of the shepherd,[9] and in

---

[1] Econ. Cond. Ram. Man., App. p. 4.
[2] Norw. Vac. Roll, 1141/1 : (Thornham) ' Et de xxiij*s. vd. ob.* de vj. qu.
salis, cxiij gallinis de iiij^{xx} ovis j libra cimini et ij agnis de redditu'; and
Reg. Worc. Pr., p. 10^b: ' Quilibet ... dabit in ebdomada Pasche pro
alba ove cum nigro agno v*d.* et thac et thol.'
[3] See above.
[4] Ram. Cart. iii. 272, Wistowe : the *villani* give two *arietes*. i. 357 : ' pro
multone j*d.*,' on St. Benedict's day.   iii. 254, Warboys : ' j*d.* ad arietem.'
i. 309 : ' pro multone j*d.*'   iii. 271, Upwood : ½*d.* on St. Benedict's day ' ad
arietes emendos '.   i. 345 : ' et ad festum S. Benedicti pro Wethersilver
obolum '; cf. i. 314.
[5] Compotus Ketteringe (1292), p. 4 : ' Et de v*s.* de consuetudine de
wethersilver in festo Apos. Petri et Pauli'; p. 45, 1½*d.* a virgate.
[6] Inqu. 1189, p. 65 : ' In die hoccadei xij tenentes Hildrodi debent dare
vnam ovem cum agno.'   And pp. 70, 73 : ' ad hoccadei unum denarium ad
ovem quandam'; p. 125 : ' Preterea de herbagio pro unoquoque averio debet
arare ad seminandum unam acram et ad warettum j acram preterea debet
dare domino decimum agnum.   Et erunt reliqui in custodia domini
a tempore quo ablactantur usque festum S. Iohannis '; cf. p. 138.
[7] Ely Vac. Roll, 1132/10 : ' redd. voc. bosing' grippure shepestake.'
[8] Harl. MSS. 3977, f. 37 : ' De scepsilver pro vj ovibus j*d.*'   Also ff. 37,
38, 39, 83, 94, 99 ; and Harl. MSS. 1005, f. 69 : ' De scepsilver pro vj
ovibus j*d.*'; but f. 72 : ' De cepsiluer v sol. quandoque plus quandoque
minus scilicet pro viij^{to} ovibus i [*d.*] ad voluntatem domini.'
[9] Blomefield, Norfolk, ix. 294, Eccles : ' He also hath other custom,
heweschift, reveshift, hirdeshift, ingeld' felsne, and bedgild.   Herdershift,

Norfolk and Suffolk the lord had sometimes the right to *shack*,[1] or 'the liberty of feeding his sheep at pleasure on his tenants' lands during the six winter months'.

In addition to payments directly connected with pasture, the lord of the manor derived certain other profits from the woodland and waste. The most important of these rents were connected with the estovers taken by the villeins, especially the common *heybote* and *housebote*. *Housebote* was the taking of wood for the repair and building of houses, and is used to denote both the privilege and also the rent paid for the privilege.[2] On the manor of Wye in Kent the appearance of *housebote* among a villein's obligations was regarded as a sign of villeinage. Three juga and a virgate which were free were yet held by the same rent as servile tenements, except that they did not carry, *housebote* (*husbotant*), or brew, 'which seems remarkable,' the extent goes on to say, 'since each pays 7s. 5d. in the manner of those that carry.'[3]

Heybote or *hedgebote* was the villein's privilege of taking hedging material (*heyningwode* and the like) from the demesne and waste, and his payment for the privilege.[4] *Heybote* was especially common in the West of England, and occurs also in Wales.[5] It should be distinguished from *heggingsilver*, and *heynwodesilver*, the commutations of the service of setting hedges and collecting hedging-material for the lord. Occa-

whereby the whole homage ought every year to choose one shepherd for whom they ought to answer,' cf. D. S. P. p. 105, and *schepersulfer*.

[1] Charnock, Man. Cust. Essex, p. 7 : 'In the former county (Norfolk) shack extended to the common for hogs in all men's grounds from harvest to seed time, whence to go a-shack is to feed at large; and in New England shack is still used in a somewhat similar sense for the food of swine, and for feeding at large in the forest.'

[2] Rot. Hund. i. 14, 21 ; ii. 336, 838 ; cf. Dugdale, Antiq. Warw. ii. 911 : Sutton : heybote and housebote are 'secundum quantitatem tenurae per visum forestariorum et woodewardorum temp. Quad. sufficienter pro haiis et domibus emendandis super bondagii tenura'.

[3] Batt. Abb. Cust., p. 131. Cf. p. 133. Index, p. 165.

[4] Rot. Hund. i. 14, 21 ; ii. 336, 838. Kennet, Par. Antiq. i. 295; ii. 137. Canterbury Vac. Roll, 1128/4.

[5] Denbigh Survey, f. 147, and Mich. Ambr. Rent., p. 83: 'Et debet habere husbote ad aulam suam de bosco domini et haybote similiter sine vasto per liberacionem ballivorum et debet habere wdetale contra Natale . . . et debet habere wenbote.'

sionally other *botes* are mentioned, for example the *cartbote* or *wenbote*, the *ploughbote*, and the *firebote*,[1] the taking of wood for the carts, the ploughs, and fuel. Other rents were paid by the villeins for the use of special bits of meadow or other lands. A rent for a meadow 'halew' occurs on the Ramsey manor of Hemingford Abbot's[2]; *medsilver* occurs in Kent,[3] and *medweselver* in East Anglia.[4] *Medgavel* and *brechegavol* were probably similar payments made at Glastonbury for the use of meadow and *breches*, or for haying services.[5] The Ramsey *hangerlondsilver* was probably paid in years when a certain piece of land was sown. The word *hangra* has been taken to mean a wood on a hillside. A passage in a Wistowe account-roll records the omission of the rent in a given year 'because it (the hangerlond) was not sown', and the payment of the rent in years when the land was sown.[6]

Side by side with the rents paid for the pasture of cattle and other animals and for special privileges, may be placed the rent paid on houses, although perhaps it might equally well be considered in connexion with the *landgafol*. The common *hawgafol*, or house rent, of the towns does not occur by name in the rural districts of England, but there is a rent recorded for the Ramsey manors in Huntingdonshire which looks very much like it,[7] the *heuschire* or *heusire* of the

---

[1] Hone, Manor., p. 114; Mon. Angl. iv. 327: 'hedgeboote, fyerboote, plowboote, et carteboote.' Cf. D. S. P., p. 158*.

[2] Rot. Hund. ii. 680. Cf. Glouc. Cart. iii. 50: 'Tota villa de Clifforde dat in communi de annuo redditu pro quadam parva pastura scilicet [in] quadam via sex denarios.' Cf. 171 : All *villani* of village hold 23 acres of meadow called Hay, and pay 23*s*. 3*d*.

[3] Add. MSS. 6159, ff. 174, 182.

[4] Add. Ch. 37,763 : Poss. Elien. in Norfolk, temp. Edw. iij.

[5] Mich. Ambr. Rent., p. 54, a list of those paying medgavol for bits of meadow ; p. 55, Brechegavel paid at Michaelmas when the eastfield was cultivated.

[6] Econ. Cond. Ram. Man., pp. 67, 71, and App. p. 20 (Roll of 1307): '... et de hangerlondsilver iiij*d*. quia seminatur hoc anno'; p. 42 (Roll of 1316), '... et de hangerlondsilver nichil quia non seminatur hoc anno'; p. 74 (1368), ' De j acra dimidia hangylondi quae reddit solutum xij*d*. quando seminatur, hoc anno seminatur.' Cf. pp. 22, 53 ; Ram. Cart. i. 328: 'et tenet unam rodam super Hangrelande pro qua dat unum denarium.' Compare Reg. Worc. Pr., p. 51ᵃ: 'pro longa hanga in mora de dominico'; and Crawford Charters, p. 134.

[7] Econ. Cond. Ram. Man., p. 52.

Ramsey Cartulary and the Hundred Rolls. This was an
ancient rent, mentioned commonly in the earlier as well as
in the later extents,[1] and paid usually at the rate of 12d. or
13d. a virgate,[2] 6d. a cotland,[3] at the terms of the feasts of
St. Andrew and St. Benedict.[4] Occasionally the extents
seem to indicate that the possession of a croft implied
heusire.[5] The assumption that *heusire* is a form of house
rent or 'house hire' is borne out by the *Liber Albus*, where
the actual word *househire* occurs. 'Et issint, d'arrester pur
househir devaunt le jour, si le tenaunt sort futif'; the mayor
or sheriff, that is to say, was accustomed to arrest for *househire* before the day on which it was due if the tenant were
about to abscond.[6] *Hussilver*, common in Norfolk, looks like
the same payment.[7] *Husegabell* occurs at York[8] and *stedegabol* at Wells,[9] and *highgabull* at Huntingdon,[10] perhaps
different forms for the same rents. The termination -*gavol*
seems to have been very common in towns.[11]

[1] Ram. Cart. iii. 244; i. 381; iii. 280; i. 287; iii. 281; i. 298; iii. 253;
i. 309; iii. 271; i. 344; iii. 279; i. 369; *pass.*; Rot. Hund. ii. 600, 631
(henthyre = heuthyre?).

[2] Ram. Cart. espec. iii. 279, 280: 'In Hoctona sunt triginta tres virgatae
ad operationem. Et dant triginta tres solidos ad heusire. Et decem
cotlandae dant quinque solidos. Et tresdecim toftae dant tresdecim
solidos.' Cf. i. 287; iii. 281; i. 298; iii. 253; i. 309; iii. 306, 258: but see
i. 381, &c.

[3] Ibid. iii. 279, 280; i. 296, 302, 369.

[4] Ibid. i. 287, 298, 335, 381, 487: showing slight variations in terms at
which paid.

[5] Ibid. i. 292: 'sed Robertus (a virgater) non dat heusyre sicut
Ricardus, quia non habet croftam pertinentem mesuagio suo.' Cf. i. 478.

[6] Liber Albus, p. 220, Eng. trans. iii. 55. For heushire, eusier, cf.
heusebonde. (R. C. i. 426, 457.)

[7] Norwich Vac. Roll, 1141/1 (Eccles): 'et de xxxiijs. ijd. ob. de quadam
consuetudine vocata hussilver . . . et de vijs. xd. de consuetudinibus custumariorum videlicet faldagio bosagio hildersilver et hussilver.'

[8] York Vac. Roll, 1144/1: 'Et de xlviijs. iijd. de husegabell' et tolneto
nundinarum.'

[9] Bath & Wells Vac. Roll, 1131/3: 'iijs. iiijd. qu. de Stedegabel in
burgo de Welles.'

[10] Mon. Ang. iv. 526.

[11] Rot. Hund. ii. 788. Winch. Pipe Roll, p. 77 and Gloss., 'burgabulum.'
D. B. Add. pp. 535, 536. P. Q. W. p. 745.

CHAPTER IV

CONDITION RENTS

A GROUP of rents of great interest in illustrating the tests in common use to determine a tenant's probable freedom or unfreedom are the condition rents, the liability to which was considered as generally indicative of villeinage, as establishing at least a presumption in favour of villeinage. Professor Vinogradoff has treated these rents very fully, and has shown how they, with other liabilities and obligations of villeinage closely allied with them, are evidence of the 'state of fermentation' of the 'whole law of social distinctions'.[1] Two questions, he says, might be asked in cases where a man's status was to be determined : one regarding the certainty, or uncertainty, of his services to his lord, the other regarding the kind of services he owed. Sometimes one, sometimes the other was asked, and it is in the answers to the second that the most important references to the group of rents in question occur.

The usual disabilities of the villein thus enumerated to prove villein status were : first, his obligation to pay *merchet* or *vedfee*, or *gersuma* when his daughter was married, sometimes also when his son was married, *leirwite* and *childwite*, fines for incontinence on the part of his daughter, and *heriot*, the ancient payment which went back to the surrender of a man's *heregeat* to his lord, and was the payment on the person analogous to the relief on the land paid by military tenants ;[2] secondly, his obligation to pay a tallage to his lord, usually at his lord's will. Less common, but still fre-

---

[1] Vill. in Eng., pp. 153–4, 82, 83.
[2] Bracton, i. 681 : 'There is another kind of payment which is called a heriott, and which has no comparison to a relief, to wit, where the tenant, free or serf, on his death remembers his lord from whom he holds, remembers him with his best beast, or his second-best beast, according to the custom of the country, which gift indeed is rather made of grace than of right, and which does not affect the inheritance' (ed. Twiss, Rolls Series).

quent, was his obligation to pay a toll on the sale of his animals (*tonnutum, thol, stuch*), which was often coupled with merchet. Other tests of status were the obligation to pay the Christmas hen and the Easter eggs, to serve as *messor* or reeve, to fold his sheep at the lord's fold, to grind at the lord's mill,[1] and also his subordination to certain regulations regarding the cutting of trees,[2] the tonsure of his sons,[3] the withdrawal from the *dominium* of his lord,[4] and the succession to land.[5] On Gloucester manors 'consuetudines non taxatae quae ad terram suam pertinent' generally implied villeinage.[6]

While it may be said that the occurrence of such rents, services, and disabilities in the descriptions of a man's position certainly established a strong presumption against his freedom, yet, as Professor Vinogradoff has shown, none of these obligations alone, not even merchet, the most significant, can be taken as a final test, or one of universal application, both because they may fall, in exceptional cases, on freemen holding freely,[7] and also because they occur very irregularly in different localities, varying, for example, in two hundreds of the same county lying side by side. The fullest lists given in the Hundred Rolls are for Huntingdonshire, but frequent references to them occur in the rolls of Cambridgeshire, Norfolk, Suffolk, Lincolnshire, Oxfordshire, and Buckinghamshire, and the church custumals show the tests applied in other places.

Of the three most common condition rents, *heriot, merchet,* and *leirwite, heriot* was probably the least characteristic as a test of villeinage, because it was paid in a fairly large

---

[1] See Ely, Extenta Maner. for good lists of such restrictions.
[2] D. S. P. p. 157*: 'vel arbores in haiciis suis extirpaverint vel succiderint sine licencia.'
[3] For example, Reg. Worc. Pr., pp. 15 a, 83 b; Vill. in Eng., p. 156; Rot. Hund. ii. 722.
[4] Extenta Maner., Ely.
[5] Ibid., and Vill. in Eng., p. 156.
[6] Glouc. Cart. iii. p. 50, *pass.*
[7] The reverse is sometimes true, and villeins pay rents that are generally characteristic of free tenure. Thus customary tenants in some cases pay scutage. See, for example, Rot. Hund. ii. 414, 417, 419, 458, 558, 563, 580, 583, 584, 709, 784, 814, 815, 817, 849, 865.

number of cases by men who were not villeins. It was paid by a freeman,[1] by a tenant who held land by charter,[2] or even by sergeanty.[3] It was often paid by the tenant of land *ad censum*,[4] and it was occasionally paid simultaneously with relief.[5] It consisted sometimes of the payment of a horse, or saddle, or sword, or lance.[6] The ordinary *heriot* from the ordinary villein, however, was the best plough-beast or cart-horse.[7] Sometimes the vicar received the second-best beast when the lord received the best beast.[8] Occasionally the lord did not take the *heriot* at once, but left it to the wife for thirty days after her husband's death, to be rendered to the lord intact at the end of that time.[9] A curious passage in the description of Sutton in Warwickshire shows a confusion of *heriot* with feudal aids. After the death of his customary tenant the lord was to have in the name of heriot his best animal, 'and not more'. ' Neither goods nor chattels, neither during the man's life nor after his death, were to be taken, except only on the marriage of the lord's eldest son or daughter,' on which occasions the lord may have, if he will, the third of the goods of those dead ' before the administration of the executors', and the half of the goods of the living, saving the necessary wainage.[10]

Especially in the later records the heriot was often commuted for money, and there seems to have been a general

---

[1] Reg. Worc. Pr., p. 15 b : together with homage, *curialitas*, and relief ; Glouc. Cart. iii. 46, 49, 56, 149, 150, 170 ; Rot. Hund. ii. 871 ; Claud. C. xi, f. 176, *pass*.

[2] Glouc. Cart. iii. 46, 49.

[3] Ibid. iii. 150.

[4] Batt. Abb. Cust., p. 1 ; Reg. Worc. Pr., p. 58 ; Glouc. Cart. iii. 48, 133, 135, 140.

[5] Batt. Abb. Cust., p. 1, *pass*. ; Reg. Worc. Pr., p. 15 b.

[6] Glouc. Cart. iii. 49, 56, 150, 180 ; Rot. Hund. ii. 768, 871, *pass*. ; Ashmol. MSS. 864, f. 7.

[7] Glouc. Cart. iii. 43, 46, 59, 87, 143, 172, 204, 211 ; Ram. Cart. i. 411, 416, 464 ; Reg. Worc. Pr., p. 15 a ; Claud. C. xi, f. 31 ; Harl. MSS. 3977, f. 83.

[8] Glouc. Cart. iii. 133, 170, 172 ; Reg. Worc. Pr., p. 44 a.

[9] Claud. C. xi, f. 31 : ' et dabit de herieto meliorem bestiam. Ita tamen quod uxor eius habebit dictam bestiam post obitum ipsius ad sustinendum waynagium per triginta dies tantum tamen quod bestia illa non deterioretur' ; Ram. Cart. i. 350.

[10] Dugdale, Antiq. Warw. ii. 911.

tendency to value it at 32*d.* or 2*s.* 6*d.*[1] Occasionally it was heavier.[2] Sometimes a year's rent was paid in place of a fixed sum,[3] an arrangement which seems to connect itself rather with the fine for ingress on the part of the heir than with the original *heriot.* The fine for ingress and for egress is described in cases where a tenant could depart from his land, or take up other land ; thus *onfare* and *offare* were paid at Ely by a free tenant who still paid *heriot.*[4] The provisions regarding the maintenance and remarriage of the widow of the deceased villein are various. They are described in detail in the Ely extent roll.

Merchet was more generally characteristic of villeinage than *heriot,* and yet it, too, was occasionally paid by freemen. Thus the thegn in Northumberland paid it,[5] and also free tenants by military service of Durham.[6] The statements regarding it differ very much in different localities. In the west the phrase ' redimere filios et filias ' is common, and sometimes in the east too the fine was paid on the marriage of sons as well as daughters, or on the withdrawal of sons from the land.[7] In the east *gersuma* usually appears for *merchet.*[8] Different regulations were often in force for marriage inside and outside the lord's liberty. For marriage within the liberty there was usually no fee, but permission from the lord's bailiff was necessary.[9] In Kent, if a tenant

---

[1] Cust. Roff., p. 11 : ' Si aliquis moriatur, Dominus habebit melius catallum quod habuit. Et si non habeat nisi unum equum, equus debet vendi et Dominus debet habere 30 denarios pro heriath, et vidua alios denarios'; Claud. C. xi, f. 35 (32 d); Batt. Abb. Cust., p. 156 ; Ram. Cart. i. 411, 416; Canterbury Vac. Roll, 1128/4; Worcester Vac. Roll, 1143/18.

[2] Ram. Cart. i. 312, 325, 337 : a heriot of 5*s.*; and the widow free from work for 30 days.

[3] Misc. Bks. Augm. Off. vol. 57, f. 21.

[4] Claud. C. xi, f. 315 : ' Et si vendiderit terram suam in totum ita quod nichil retineat nec velit in dominio episcopi remanere tunc dabit pro recessu suo qui dicitur offare triginta duos denarios et ingrediens pro ingressu suo qui dicitur onfare dabit triginta duos denarios.'

[5] Red Bk. Excheq. ii. 564.

[6] Feod. Dun., p. 13, *pass.*

[7] Glouc. Cart. iii. 50 ; Reg. Worc. Pr., p. 15 a : ' et rediment filios, si de terra recesserint, et gersummabunt filias '; Batt. Abb. Cust., p. 67.

[8] For example, Claud. C. xi, ff. 160, 236.

[9] Batt. Abb. Cust., pp. 67, 89; Ashmol. MSS. 864, f. 5.

wished to marry his daughter to any one within the vill he informed the *custos ville*, and asked him to be present. If he wished to marry her to any one outside the vill, or if his daughter were his heir and he wished to marry her to any one whomsoever, he procured the lord's permission.[1]   In Hertfordshire if a tenant married his daughter to a freeman within the vill, merchet was paid.[2]   The fee for marriage between villeins within the vill, when it was exacted, was usually 16*d.* ; for marriage outside the vill it was 32*d.*, or the best arrangement possible with the lord.[3]

The *leirwite* commonly mentioned with the *merchet* fine was sometimes fixed,[4] occasionally left at the will of the lord.[5] In the east, especially in Norfolk and Suffolk, it seems to have been identified with *childwite*.[6]

Tallagium or *auxilium custumariorum.* The tallage or aid of villeins taken at the lord's will, a rent ' on the border-line between personal subjection and political subordination,'[7] was almost as common an indication of villeinage as *merchet*, and was more burdensome.   Liability to be tallaged at the lord's will was not, except in rare cases, consistent with freedom.[8] The tallage was paid annually—as a rule, at Michaelmas.   The usual assessment was made on the land or chattels of the tenant, and the rate was variable and dependent on the lord's

---

[1] Cust. Roff., p. 2 : 'Si quis autem in predicta villa maritare voluerit filiam suam alicui de ipsa villa, tantumodo ostendet illud custodi ville et rogabit eum ut veniat ad nupcias et maritabit eam sic. Si quis vero filiam suam extra villam dare voluerit, non licebit ei hoc facere nisi per licenciam et voluntatem domini sui.   Similiter si quis habuerit filiam heredem vel filias, non poterit eas maritare infra villam nec extra nisi per licenciam et voluntatem domini sui.'
[2] Claud. C. xi, f. 160 : 'Si . . . . filiam suam maritare voluerit alicui consuetudinario domini in ista villa tunc non dabit gersumam pro ea nisi maritaverit illam alicui homini libero sive alicui de alieno feodo.'
[3] Claud. C. xi, f. 176 ; Ram. Cart. i. 472, 384 : ' Dat merchetum pro filia, sicut melius finire poterit, ita tamen quod non excedet summam quinque solidorum, sive maritando fuerit infra villam, sive extra.'
[4] Harl. MSS. 3977, f. 83 ; D. H. R., pp. 61, 62.
[5] Rot. Hund. ii. 768, 770, 771.
[6] Claud. C. xi, ff. 223, 236, 249, 279 ; Harl. MSS. 3977, f. 37 ; Charnock, Man. Cust. Essex, p. 6.
[7] Vill. in Eng., p. 162.
[8] Rot. Hund. ii. 528, 530, 619, 620, 621, 623, 642, 651, 657, 705, 717, 823, 829, 830, 832, 844, *pass.* In Claud. C. xi, f. 127, the free land from which it is due was once *operabilis.*

will. Another method of assessment was probably on the
vill as a whole, an arrangement having been reached whereby
the villata paid a given sum, a mark or a pound, to the lord,
called the *commune tallagium*, the distribution within the vill
being left to the members of the villata. The payment thus
made to the lord is not always easy to distinguish from rents
like the *fulstingpound* or *witepund*, which were of quite
different origin. The *marcselver*, *custumpand*, and the curious
tunnus census of Bury St. Edmunds, for example, may belong
to either class.

On the manors of Gloucester the customary tallage, since
it was paid at Michaelmas, was called sometimes 'the aid of
St. Michael'.[1] The rate was high compared with that of
other customary payments, and the amount derived from
a single manor was sometimes large, as much as £4, or 102s.,
or 8 marks.[2] The assessment was usually based upon the
number of animals held by the villein and the amount of his
land.[3] Thus the virgaters 'paid in common, each according to
his land and the number of his animals', for a horse, an ox, or
a cow a penny, for a yearling ox a halfpenny, and for four
sheep a penny.[4] Again, it is stated that if in the 'taxatio' of
the aid he have concealed an animal, the villein can be forced
to take the oath, and, if convicted on the witness of his
neighbours, he can be punished at the will of the lord.[5]
Sometimes the rate for a virgate is given, the amount being
a penny an acre or less ;[6] sometimes, on the other hand, the
total sum owed by the manor is stated, to which the customary
tenants are said to give 'in communi'.[7] The aid was paid by

[1] Glouc. Cart. iii. 88, 97, 100, 103, 110, 119, 121, 124, 149, 158, 167,
pass.
[2] Ibid. iii. 88, 97, 104, 119, *pass.* The lists of amounts given, iii. 104, may
be compared with those given in the descriptions of the manors.
[3] Ibid. iii. 53 : 'Et dabit auxilium secundum quantitatem terrae et numerum animalium.' Cf. pp. 50, 57, 62, 180, 185, 188, *pass.*
[4] Ibid. iii. 182.
[5] Glouc. Cart. iii. 208 : 'et si impositum fuerit eidem quod in taxatione
auxilii aliquod animal concelaverit, potest cogi ad sacramentum prae-
standum, et se super hoc purgandum, et si per vicinos suos convictus fuerit
super hoc, puniendus est pro voluntate domini.'
[6] Ibid. iii. 100, 101, 110, 121, 129, *pass.*
[7] Ibid. iii. 97, 133, 191, *pass.*

the customary tenants generally, and occasionally by the *censuarius* or tenant of 'penilond ad vitam et ad voluntatem domini'.[1] It was not paid from land that had been bought free,[2] and was sometimes permitted to lapse on account of the poverty of the tenant.[3] The aid from free tenants sometimes mentioned was apparently paid on special occasions, 'quando currit';[4] the customary tenants, on the other hand, were responsible 'quodam servili obsequio quod auxilium abbatis nuncupatur'.[5] It was paid beyond question to the abbot, and was called 'abbot's aid' in order to distinguish it from *auxilium vicecomitis*, which was also common, and which went to the abbot only if the franchise were in his hand.[6]

The evidence regarding the manors of Worcester Priory points also in the same direction of an annual aid collected by the prior from the customary tenants. Here too the time of payment was usually Michaelmas,[7] although an aid paid at other seasons is occasionally mentioned—the aid at the feast of St. Andrew, or at Christmas, or at Purification.[8] The aid when paid at Purification may have been the same as the 'Pukerelleschild'.[9] On Worcester manors too the aid was due almost exclusively from customary tenants, and is often enumerated with *thac* and *thol* 'et hujusmodi' as a sign of villein status.[10] It is interesting to observe that the *auxilium*, like *thac, thol*, or *fisfe*, is common in the older assizes: in the

---

[1] Glouc. Cart. iii. 120, 135, 137, 151, 180.
[2] Ibid. iii. 211.
[3] Ibid. iii. 183, 187.
[4] Ibid. i. 386; ii. 153, 220: 'Cum vero dominus Abbas auxilium suum cum aliis posuerit franchelanis suis'; and p. 267: 'W . . . et heredes sui dabunt nobis rationabile auxilium quotiens caeteri liberi homines nostri auxilium nobis dederint.'
[5] Ibid. ii. 102; cf. iii. 47, 88, 97, 119, 126, 139, 145, 169, 171, *pass.*
[6] Ibid. i. 256, 259, 386; ii. 102; cf. iii. 100, 101, 102, and 51: 'et ibi quaedam collecta annua de tota villata de Clifforde, scilicet quindecim solidi et inde liberantur annuatim hundredo de Theuk[esburia] decem solidi, et quinque remanebunt domino.'
[7] Reg. Worc. Pr., pp. 10 b, 12 a, 93 a, 104 a, 173 b, *pass.*, and Introd. xcviii. n.; compare Rot. Hund. ii. 836, 845, 848, 849.
[8] Rot. Hund. ii. 717, 775, 785.
[9] Ibid. ii. 691: 'pro tallagio ad Purificationem vi*s*. vi*d*.'
[10] Reg. Worc. Pr., pp. 15 a, 43 b, 52 b, 56 a, 59 a, 72 a, *pass*. From cottars, pp. 51 b, 59 b, *pass*. Rendered in threshing service, p. 15 b, Introd. p. xli.

new assize the payment is sometimes commuted in the general rent from the land even in cases where *merchet* remains.[1]   The manner of assessment and the rate are not clearly stated.   It was probably called *auxilium prioris*,[2] and there is no indication that it was not like other payments paid regularly to him.   There is reference also to a special aid which the abbot might have on his installation, and a statement that the abbot might demand an aid when he was heavily indebted to the king,[3] but from the regularity of the incidence there is doubt if the abbot or prior waited for times of special stress for its collection.   In a vacancy roll of the end of Edward I's reign the *auxilium* or *tallagium custumariorum per annum* is entered with great regularity, sometimes under the title *commune tallagium*, which points probably to a payment by the vill as a whole.[4]   The sums range from 9*s.* in Paxford to £4 in Ripple.   It was usually paid at Michaelmas.

The Ramsey evidence agrees in the main with the foregoing.   In the thirteenth-century extents [5] of most manors there is mentioned a tallage, or aid, or geld paid to the abbot.[6]   It is spoken of as the monk's tallage,[7] or annual tallage,[8] or the tallage or aid at the feast of Saint Michael,[9] or on Cambridgeshire manors as *monkgeld*,[10] and was occasionally paid at two seasons, at Easter as well as Michaelmas, *pro voluntate domini*.[11]   A mark given at the feast of

---

[1] Reg. Worc. Pr., pp. 19 a, 61 b, 66 b, 69 a, 71 b, 84 a, 102 a.
[2] Ibid. pp. 43 b, 138 a.
[3] Ibid. p. 138 a.   See note, Introd. p. cxvi, quoting Add. MSS. 14849, f. 138 a : 'Dicunt etiam quod omnes custumarii debent talliari ad dominum suum abbatem in primo adventu suo in sua abbatia auxiliendum secundum quod ratio exigat.   Praeterea si abbas pro aliqua certa causa versus Dominum Regem graviter fuerit indebitatus tunc debent auxiliari dominum suum, si habuerit generale auxilium per Abbatiam suam.'
[4] Min. Acc. 1143/18 : '. . . et de lviij*s.* iiij*d.* de communi talliagio custumariorum ad festum S. Michaelis per annum,' *pass.*
[5] Ram. Cart. i. 281, *et seq.*; ii. 6, *et seq.*
[6] Ibid. i. 59, 286, 287, 296, 298, 302, 309, 424, *et seq.*
[7] Ibid. i. 45.
[8] Ibid. i. 495: 'Omnes praedicti, tam virgatarii, quam tenentes dimidiam virgatam, et cothmanni, et croftmanni participant ad annuale talliagium.'
[9] Ibid. i. 55, 57, 59, 424 ; ii. 37 ; iii. 315.
[10] Rot. Hund. ii. 472, 481, 482.
[11] Ram. Cart. ii. 37, 43, 48.

St. Andrew in addition to tallage is once mentioned.[1] The amount is rarely stated; once it reached £4,[2] on one or two manors the rate seems to have been 13*d.* or 12*d.* a virgate,[3] sometimes it was paid ' ad voluntatem domini'.[4] The manner of assessment, in the two cases where it is stated, was according to the number of animals and chattels, and the amount of land held.[5] Here as elsewhere the tallage was evidently a servile custom, rendered by virgaters,[6] cottars,[7] and crofters,[8] and very rarely by those that held by money rent.[9] The general impression gained from the instances of its occurrence is distinctly that it was paid to the abbot, rightly or wrongly, every year, although the phrase in one or two extents is: 'Whenever they, the customary tenants, are tallaged.'[10] One passage points to its being considered distinctly a grievance,[11] and the fact that it is rarely mentioned in earlier extents may possibly indicate a recent origin, or at least an extension of an ancient privilege. It is mentioned first in the vacancy rolls of the earlier half of the thirteenth century, printed in the chartulary, where it appears among the large regular receipts of the royal custodian of the abbey. In 1211–1212, £88 16*s.* 8*d.* was collected, some manors which were put at farm being excluded;[12] in 1254–1255, £71 16*s.* 'de tallagiis villanorum per maneria.'[13]

On the manors of St. Paul's no payment that can be surely identified as an annual tallage taken by the lord occurs. A manor in Surrey paid every year an *auxilium* of a marc, at

---

[1] Ram. Cart. i. 431.
[2] Ibid. i. 45.
[3] Ibid. i. 344, 489.
[4] Ibid. ii. 37, 43, 48.
[5] Ib. ii. 25: 'Dabit ad tallagium secundum terram et catalla sua, sicut et alii de villa;' compare i. 45, and Rot. Hund., ii. 687: 'dabit ad tallagium viij*d.* et quinque magis sicut animalia sua multiplicant.'
[6] Ram. Cart. i. 59, 356, 456, 472, 495.
[7] Ibid. i. 296, 302, 370, 489, 495; ii. 7.
[8] Ibid. i. 349, 370, 381, 390, 495.
[9] Ibid. i. 364.
[10] Ibid. i. 322: 'cum villanis, quotienscunque ipsi talliantur;' cf. i. 365.
[11] Ibid. i. 344: Two virgates of the *censuarii* used to give a tallage of 12*d.* at Michaelmas and Easter: 'Quod talliagium ob favorem W. prioris . . . huc usque est pretermissum; quod quidem talliagium tota villata, injuste, et ad magnum ipsorum gravamen hucusque persolvit.'
[12] Ibid. iii. 215.
[13] Ibid. iii. 12.

the rate of something less than a penny an acre from the land of *censuarii* as well as demesne land,[1] and this may possibly be the tallage or aid of other localities. It seems more likely, however, that this payment and the *donum* at Sutton in Middlesex[2] are occasional payments like the ' auxilium Regis' and the *census* paid *post festum Sancti Michaelis* by *censuarii* and *operarii* at Horlock and Waleton in Essex.[3] In the later Articles of Visitation of Manors, a document printed near the end of the Domesday of St. Paul's, an inquiry is made as to those that are liable to tallage at the will of the lord.[4]

In Peterborough and Winchester documents also the reference to the customary *auxilium* is doubtful. On Peterborough manors the villein paid ' de consuetudine ' a certain sum of money to the lord, at Pihtesle, 5s. at Christmas, 5s. at Easter, and 32d. at the feast of St. Peter ;[5] at Esctone, 5s. before Christmas and 5s. at Easter.[6] At Collingham £4 was rendered *de gabulo*, and no hens or eggs were paid.[7] In the Winchester Pipe Rolls an *auxilium*, a *tallage*, and a *gabulum* are all mentioned, but without very clear definition of any one of them. The *gabulum* was probably, however, the *land-gabulum* and other fixed rents put at farm,[8] and the tallage was perhaps a royal payment, since its place was once taken by *scutage*.[9] The *auxilium* was possibly the customary aid,[10] but may have been an occasional levy. Clearer references to the tallage occur in the account rolls of other churches. The *juga* of Rochester paid ' scot ' *ad donum domini ville* and for the service of the lord king:[11] at Exeter the *auxilium nati-*

---

[1] D. S. P., p. 107 : ' Bernes. Tota villata dat annuum auxilium unius marce.'

[2] Ibid. p. 95.

[3] Ibid. pp. 46, 48, 51, 73, 74.

[4] Ibid. p. 155*, and n. p. cxxv : ' Item qui possunt talliari ad voluntatem domini et qui non.'

[5] Chron. Petrob., p. 161.

[6] Ibid. p. 162.   [7] Ibid. p. 159; cf. p. 164.

[8] Winch. Pipe Roll ; see Gloss. and pp. 1, 5, 8, 10, 11, 15, 16, 20.

[9] Ibid., Introd. p. xxi, and compare Feod. Dun., pp. 16, 23, 58, 64, 111. Whenever a common aid is placed on the lands of St. Cuthbert, the tenants pay ' quantum ad tantum terram pertinet '.

[10] Winch. Pipe Roll, pp. 24, 45, 46, 80.

[11] Cust. Roff., p. 4 : ' De omnibus decem jugis debent scotare ad donum domini ville et ad servicium domini Regis.'

vorum is mentioned,[1] at Durham the tallage of the *bondi*,[2] at York the tallage of the *bondi* or of the *villani*,[3] and at Norwich the common aid or *auxilium custumariorum*.[4] On Ely manors both regular customary tenants and molmen were 'talliabiles ad voluntatem domini ',[5] and on the manor of Fleet in Lincoln-shire both *molelond* and *werklond* gave *auxilium*.[6] The tallage on ancient demesne manors must of course be distinguished from the ordinary tallage.[7]

Next in importance to the *heriot* and *merchet* payments and the tallage were the tolls paid by villeins on the sale of their live stock or ale. The lord was nearer than other men in the matter of purchase, as the phrase went, and had the right to the refusal of the animal or article to be offered for sale, and sometimes the right to purchase it at a low rate. The villein, perhaps originally in recognition of this right of the lord, often paid a toll for permission to sell. Sometimes the restriction on sale was confined to animals of the villein's own rearing, or malt of his own making, or to the animals with which he actually ploughed or carted.[8] The tax on the

---

[1] Vac. Roll, 1138/2: 'et de x*s*., superoneratis per auditores de auxilio tenencium ibidem pro eo quod tenentes qui auxilium illud facere consueverunt mortui sunt. . . . Cum auxilio nativorum ibidem.'

[2] Vac. Roll, 1144/18: 'et de ccclij*li*. x*s*. iiij*d*. de tallagio bondorum et aliorum episcopatus predicti per idem tempus' (Sept. 23—Dec. 23, 7 Edw. III).

[3] Vac. Roll, 1144/1: 'Beverley . . . et de xxxiij*s*. v*d*. de tallagio bondorum de villis aquaticis . . . Burton . . . et de xx*s*. de tallagio villanorum.'

[4] Vac. Roll, 1141/1: 'Et de lij*s*. ij*d*. ob. de communi auxilio custumariorum ad festum omnium Sanctorum'; *pass*.

[5] Extenta Maner.

[6] Add. MSS. 35169: a half bovate of molelond gives ' auxilium merchet et similia pro voluntate domini'.

[7] Rot. Hund. ii. 6, 844; Kennet, Par. Antiq. i. 565; ii. 137, 411.

[8] Cust. Roff., p. 2: 'Si quis habuerit pullum de proprio jumento, aut vitulum de propria vacca, et pervenerit ad perfectam etatem, non poterit illos vendere nisi prius ostendat domino suo, et sciat utrum illas velit emere sicut alius,' *pass*. Ram. Cart. i. 325: ' Si voluerit equum vel bovem vendere, faciet primo ballivo vel praeposito constare, ita quod dominus, ex ejus insinuatione, propinquior sit ad emendum quam alius;' again, i. 464: ' Bovem vero vel equum proprii nutrimenti vendere non debet absque licentia; et si illis dominus indigeat, leviori foro quatuor denariorum quam alius possidebit; et si absque licentia eos vendiderit, amerciabitur;' and i. 358: ' Non potest suum equum, pullum masculum, vel bovem vendere, quousque quaesierit a ballivo, utrum ad opus domini eos emere voluerit.' Rot. Hund. ii. 463: '. . . si ipse habeat pullum, vel boviculum et tamen laboraverit cum illo non potest vendere sine licentia

sale was called by different names in different localities. At Worcester it was coupled with *thac* and called *thol*, at Gloucester it was called *tonnutum*, at Burton it seems to have been called *stuch* or *stud*. Usually it is called by the general term *theoloneum* or *toll*. The toll most often mentioned is that on animals, but there are many references to the tax on brewers, discussed already under *maltsilver*. A curious passage in the Glastonbury Inquest of 1189 points to a counter privilege on the part of the lord.[1] If he wish to sell his corn the men of the manor must buy it or give the lord 20*s*. In Maldon in Essex a *tolteray*, *totteray*, or *tolltray* was paid by the tenant for every bushel and a half of corn sold.[2]

The Worcester records give a number of details concerning the *thol* payment. It is defined as follows :—' Thol, quod dicitur, Theoloneum est, scilicet, quod habeat libertatem vendendi in terra sua.' [3] It included the selling of beer as well as animals, being, in this case, the same as the *aletol* or alepenny of other localities. The rate is stated several times; at every brewing a penny was given, or four or six gallons, in ancient times twelve gallons ; for a horse sold a penny, for an ox or a horse a penny, for an ox a halfpenny, for pigs one year old a penny, of less age a halfpenny.[4] The payment is more frequently mentioned in the old assize than in the new. In Gloucester the *tonnutum* was paid at a somewhat higher rate—for beer a penny or the equivalent at a brewing, for buying or selling a horse 4*d*.[5] No Ely villein could sell an ox or *stott* without permission.[6] On Ramsey manors the

domini; sed si non laboraverit licitum est ei vendere sine licentia.' Mich. Ambr. Rent., p. 141 : 'et si velit vendere equum masculum vel bovem, dominus erit propinquior omnibus aliis, et si non placeant domino sed vendantur extra manerium dabit de toll' 1*d*. de equo, de bove *ob*., et si infra manerium vendantur nichil dabit.' Claud. C. xi, f. 31.

[1] Inqu. 1189, p. 101: 'Si dominus vult vendere bladum suum homines de manerio debent illud emere vel dare domino xx*s*.'

[2] Charnock, Man. Cust. of Essex, p. 8.

[3] Reg. Worc. Pr., p. 16 a.

[4] Ibid. pp. 15 a, 66 a, 102 a, *pass*.; cf. Worc. Vac. Roll, 1143/18 : 'et de viij*d*. de tolneto viij boum custumariorum venditorum,' *pass*.

[5] Glouc. Cart. iii. 50, 62, 79, 117, 121, 125, 127, 134, 140, 151, 195, 197, 212. [6] Ely, Extenta Maner.

same rule held, but sometimes nothing was paid for the permission ; and, in one case, an ox might be exchanged for
a cow in the same vill, without permission.[1] The payment
depended somewhat on the time of year. Thus, if a pig were
killed or sold before Purification a halfpenny for lost pannage
was paid ; if between Purification and the Gules of August,
nothing was paid.[2] Even the hour of the day at which the
swine were sold sometimes made a difference, especially at
Martinmas.[3]

The *stuch* payment of Burton is not clearly defined ; it
probably refers to status,[4] and was an annual rent, not paid
on occasions.

Other common restrictions on villeins were the obligations
to fold at the lord's fold, which has been discussed under the
pasture rents, to grind at the lord's mill, to bake at the common oven, and to serve as reeve or in some other manorial
office. The *multure* payment made for grinding at the
lord's mill, and the prohibition from grinding elsewhere, were
especially common in the north of England. Whether or not
a tenant could be held for suit at the lord's mill was a fairly
frequent source of litigation,[5] and provisions had to be made

---

[1] Ram. Cart. i. 437 : 'Nullus praedictorum vendere potest bovem suum,
vel equum masculum, sine licentia domini vel ballivi. Nihil tamen dabit
pro licentia habenda. Sed excambiare potest bovem pro vacca sine licentia
domini, infra villam.'

[2] Ibid. ii. 37, 48 ; i. 335 : 'Post festum S. Michaelis porcum suum vendere
non potest sine pannagio prius dato ;' Rot. Hund. i. 629: 'Et si vendat
vel occidat porcum de etate iij quart anni et amplius inter Gulam Augusti
et Purificacionem dabit abbati pro pannagio obolum ;' Harl. MSS. 3977,
f. 98.

[3] Ram. Cart. ii. 43; i. 309 : 'Die autem S. Michaelis, ante nonam, sine
licentia et calumnia domini, de porcis suis pro voluntate sua potest dis-
ponere et post nonam nequaquam.'

[4] Burton Ch. 66 n.: The cause lost in a case relating to status because
the jury found that the defendant owed a yearly rent, sometimes more,
sometimes less, called *stud*. Again, in a similar quarrel a man admits
that he is a nativus, holding at will, and giving *stuch* every year and
merchet, and, on account of ancient customs, poultry rents.

[5] D. H. R., p. 33: 'Injunctum est omnibus tenentibus villae quod
nullus eorum molat bladum extra dominium dum molendinum Domini
Prioris molere possit sub poena 20s. ;' cf. p. 40 ; Newminster Cart. pp. 16,
58, 59 ; Burt. Ch., pp. 55, 72, 76 ; Cockersand Chart. i. 61 ; Hexh. Pr.
ii. 24, 76 ; Guisbor. Ch. i. 12, 13, 114, 235 ; Bold. Bk., p. 572 ; Feod.
Dun., p. 174 ; cf. Dugdale, Antiq. Warw., ii. 912 ; Bennett, History of
Corn-milling.

against the maintenance of millstones by private persons who took toll for grinding the corn of their neighbours.[1] The lord's profit from the mill, excluding the ordinary payment made by villeins to the miller for his services, is called the *multura*, or *moltura*, or *molta*.[2] It was paid as a rule as a percentage of the corn ground, the tenth, thirteenth, six-teenth, or twentieth *vas* being given, or every four-and-twentieth grain, 'according to the custom of the land and the strength of the water-course.'[3] Occasionally the *multura* is stated in money.[4] Sometimes no multure was charged on corn grown on a villein's own land and used for his own con-sumption. In Brawby, a manor of Hexham, for example, the tenants ground at the prior's mill and paid multure, yet they could make the corn and oats growing on their own land into malt without paying the toll called *kyn' multure*. If any one bought any barley or oats for this purpose, how-ever, he paid multure to the twentieth *vas*.[5] In Worcester, too, malt ground and brewed for private use paid no toll.[6] In Shitlingdon, a Ramsey manor, every villein owed suit at his lord's mill. If the mill or mill-pond were broken, or if between the Gules and Michaelmas he took his corn to the mill and could not get it ground, he could grind it where he would. If, however, he were convicted of not making suit when he should, he gave 6*d.* before judgement, 12*d.* after it. He ground his corn thus throughout the year, but he gave a toll for *multura* only at Christmas and Easter.[7] If he

[1] Sel. Pl. in Man. Courts, p. 47. Two tenants of the abbey of Bec 'are convicted by inquest of the court of wrongfully having millstones in their houses and taking toll and multure to the great damage of the lord as regards the suit to his mill. Therefore be they in mercy and it is commanded that the said millstones be seized into the lord's hands.'

[2] Winch. Pipe Rolls, Gloss.; defined as payment for not grinding corn in the lord's mill.

[3] Burt. Ch., pp. 55, 63; D. H. R., p. 43; Stat. Realm, i. 203; Newmin. Ch., pp. 16, 58, 59, 274; Guisbor. Ch. i. 278; Bold. Bk., p. 572; Hexh. Pr. ii. 24, 55.

[4] Winch. Pipe Roll, p. 78.

[5] Hexh. Pr. ii. 143, 144; Feod. Dun., p. 2 n.: 'Et ut molant sine mul-tura de propriis bladis suis quae crescent in terra illa.'

[6] Reg. Worc. Pr., p. xi.

[7] Ram. Cart. i. 464, 473; ii. 29. Cf. D. H. R., p. 111; Bold. Bk., p. 572; Burt. Ch., p. 76; Newmin. Ch., pp. 86, 87; Hexh. Pr. ii. 43; Cock. Ch. ii. 173.

bought his corn he might grind it at the nearest mill. An
order of precedence in grinding is described in the Durham
Feodary,[1] which perhaps explains the *foregrist* of the Domesday of St. Paul.[2]   At Worcester there was in the manor of
Bradewas a mill to which the *sequela* of three vills was
attached.   The 'persona' and heirs of one Alan had multure
next after the Prior, and the lord of *suckel*, or some one to
whom he assigned the right, had free multure also.   The
barley of all following the mill was free of toll, unless the
ale made from it were sold.   If it were sold, the person, free
or forinsec, who followed *de gratia* gave a penny or four
gallons, a villein 2*d.*, that is a penny or four gallons for
multure, and a penny or four gallons for *theoloneum*. All
except the *persona* aided in carrying millstones, the prior
furnishing the cart, the man, and two oxen.[3]

Regulations with regard to the baking oven of the villata
are less common and clear.   At Durham and elsewhere there
was a common *furnus*, and also often a common *forgium*, in
a vill, for which the villata paid an annual sum, and which
it kept in repair.[4]   The rent to the king from ovens in the
demesne is one of the articles of inquiry in certain hundreds
in the Hundred Rolls ; the *furnus* was evidently a regality
not yet always surrendered.[5]

A liability of villeins, regarding which the custumals have
much to say, was the obligation to serve in manorial offices.
The provisions regulating this service are of interest in show-

---

[1] Feod. Dun., pp. 46 n., 122 n.; cf. Reg. Worc. Pr., pp. 32, lxiii.
[2] D. S. P., p. 76 : ' In eodem molendino curia canonicorum habet foregrist sed dat molturam.'
[3] Reg. Worc. Pr., p. 32.
[4] Bish. Hatf. Surv., pp. 4, 18 ; D. H. R., pp. 90, 236 ; Feod. Dun.,
pp. 317, 321, 327 ; Northamp. Ass., p. 365 ; Eng. Hist. Rev. xv. 498 ;
Denton, Eng. in 15th Cent. p. 254 ;   Comp. of Ketteringe, p. 12 : ' Et de
xx*s*. de omnibus villanis ut possint tenere furnum de Ketteringe a Natale
Domini anno r. r. E. xxi usque ad terminum xii annorum proximo sequen-
tium.'
[5] Rot. Hund. i. 25, 26 (Bucks) : 'Et plura sunt ibi furna set nesciunt
nomina tenencium ipsa furna.'   Other tenants pay the king a money
rent for a *furnus*; and i. 402 (Linc.) : 'Dicunt quod episcopus Linc'
aliter usus est libertate quam predecessores sui facere consueverunt eo
quod distrinxit pistores ville ad furniandum ad furnum ipsius episcopi
sibi appropriatum.'

ing the subdivisions and gradations in importance among the
customary tenants, the more important villeins being probably
exempt from the less important offices, and also in occasionally
throwing a little light on the manner of collecting rents, on
cases of exemption from ordinary dues, and on the possibility
of common action on the part of the villeins in avoiding an
unpleasant burden. The total number of manorial officers
mentioned in the records is large, the emphasis falling differently in different localities, according to the nature of the
land ; the *punderus*, for example, or keeper of the pound and
live stock, being very prominent at Durham,[1] the *lignarius*
and woodwards at Abingdon and Glastonbury,[2] the *dichreves*
in the fen country.[3] In the Rochester custumal a *custos ville*
appears in connexion with merchet, who does not seem to
have been very closely identified with the lord.[4]

The liability to serve as reeve or in any other manorial
office was generally considered an evidence of villeinage. In
Brithwolton, Berkshire, for example, it was permissible for
the lord to choose his reeve or other minister from the *virgarii* or from the *cottarii* or from those holding assarts, ' for
all are villeins, and of servile condition.'[5] ' To serve as reeve '
stands in the Hundred Rolls side by side with ' talliagible at
the lord's will ' as a sign of serfdom. In many cases, however,
there was in practice, as has been said, a gradation in respect
of the liability to such offices. Thus, for example, at Sutton
in Warwickshire, men of the bondage with one virgate were
liable to be officers of the king or lord, as was pleasing ; but
men with a half virgate, or a *nocata*, or a cottage, were liable

---

[1] Bish. Hatf. Surv., pp. 13, 95 ; D. H. R., p. 50.
[2] Abing. Acc., pp. 5, 145, 150, *pass.* ; Inqu. 1189, pp. 10, 14, *pass.* ;
Mich. Ambr. Rent., pp. 56, 57, 72, *pass.*
[3] Claud. C. xi, f. 75 : ' Item si dominus voluerit iste erit prepositus ad
castrum vel ad bertone vel ad redditum colligendum vel Dichreve.'
[4] Cust. Roff., p. 2 : ' Si quis autem in predicta villa maritare voluerit
filiam suam alicui de ipsa villa tantumodo ostendet illud custodi ville
et rogabit eum ut veniat ad nupcias et maritabit eam sic. Si quis vero
filiam suam extra villam dare voluerit non licebit ei hoc facere nisi per
licenciam et voluntatem domini sui.'
[5] Batt. Abb. Cust., p. 67 : ' Licebit etiam domino eligere sibi Prepositum et alios ministros vel de virgariis vel de cottariis vel de hiis qui
tenent de assarto pro voluntate sua, quia omnes sunt villani sui et
servilis condicionis.'

only to be beadles or *decenarii*.¹ At Dereham in Norfolk the lord could make a reeve of any molman holding at least twelve acres, or of any *operarius* holding a half virgate at least; he could make a beadle of a molman with six acres, or an *operarius* with six acres, and a forester of a molman with six acres.² Again, three men in a vill were liable to reeveship, the others were liable to be beadles or shepherds.³ At Bury St. Edmunds any of the *pokeavers* might be made either beadle or collector of malt.⁴

Among the duties of the reeve is occasionally mentioned the collecting of the rents. Thus in Ely manors it was usual to have a reeve *ad castrum*, probably at the castle at Ely, which was in the hands of the bishop, a reeve *ad bertona*, a *dichreve*, and a reeve *ad colligendum redditum*, the last office being held in one case *secundum turnum vicinorum*.⁵ Again, at Glastonbury the reeve ranked with the virgater, was free from the services of the virgater except the *donum*, and was to receive all the toll which fell in a vill held at farm by the villata and 2*s.* additional for carrying the *gabulum* or farm to Glastonbury, of which 2*s.* the vill gives 10½*d.* in common.⁶

As a rule certain privileges and exemptions went with the tenure of manorial offices. Freedom from some of the services

---

¹ Dugdale, Antiq. Warw. ii. 911.

² Claud. C. xi, f. 232 : ' Sciendum quod dominus potest facere prepositum suum de quolibet molman duodecim acras terre tenente ad minus, vel de quolibet operario unam virgatam terre vel dimidiam virgatam tenente ad minus si voluerit. Et tunc ille molman qui fuerit prepositus erit quietus de tota annuali redditu suo et de omnibus consuetudinibus.' The beadle may be chosen from molmen with six acres, the forester from the same.

³ Ibid. ff. 252, 270, 304.

⁴ Harl. MSS. 3977, f. 37 : 'Et dominus faciet quemcunque voluerit de pokaveris Bedellum aut collectorem brasei.' Compare ff. 38, 80, and Harl. MSS. 1005, f. 69.

⁵ Claud. C. xi, f. 75 : Wisbech, a censuarius with a half ninemandale : ' Item si dominus voluerit iste erit prepositus ad castrum vel ad bertona vel ad redditum colligendum vel dichreve.' Again, ff. 82, 203, 205, 90 : ' Erit prepositus ad colligendum redditum in eodem hameletto et non extra vel dichreve secundum turnum vicinorum suorum.' For the *ninemandale* see Tiber. B. ii, ff. 144, 147.

⁶ Mich. Ambr. Rent., pp. 56, 57, 67 : 'Et debet habere totum tolnetum, quod accidit in villa et duos solidos pro gabulo portando Glaston' unde x*d.* et *ob.* debent dare de tota villata communicatus, scilicet, dum manerium est ad firmam in manu illorum.'

was common; for example, at Bury the beadle or forester was
free from half the work except the ploughing, and free also
from the gavol ploughing;[1] the *berebrit* at Glastonbury was
free from one man's work,[2] the *heyward* was free from one
man's work and 3s. *gabulum*,[3] the field hayward at Bury was
free from some services but gave *felsten* and carried the farms,[4]
the reeve who collected rents at Ely was free *de messione*.[5]
A molman who was reeve at Derham 'was free from all his
annual rents and from all his customs for the year',[6] but elsewhere a customar was not free.[7] At Bleadon the reeve was
free from *daynae manuales* and pannage.[8] The woodward at
Glastonbury was free from 4s. *gabulum*.[9] Sometimes the
privilege of office consisted in receiving certain perquisites;
for example, the same woodward who was free from *gabulum*
at Glastonbury could take dead wood, and other woodwards
received corn.[10] The shepherd at Glastonbury had one lamb
and one fleece, the herdsman at Bleadon had milk and whey.[11]
At Bury certain officers had the right to receive *glovesilver*
and *lammessilver*.[12] The most common and interesting privilege of office, however, was the tenure of small pieces of land
regularly belonging to the office and called sometimes by its
name. Thus on a Glastonbury manor a certain tenant held
five acres *quia bedellus est*;[13] elsewhere *Budellond* appears,[14]
and there are mentioned certain bits of land which pertain to
the ploughs called *Sulstiche* and *Goddingstiche*, one of which
should go to each *carucarius*.[15] The Glastonbury reeve received one acre of corn, one acre of meadow, one lamb, the
pasture of two oxen, and was free from all services except

---

[1] Harl. MSS. 3977, f. 90.
[2] Mich. Ambr. Rent., pp. 56, 57, a very interesting list of officers and
exemptions.
[3] Ibid. pp. 56, 57.
[4] Harl. MSS. 3977, f. 86.
[5] Claud. C. xi, f. 89.
[6] Ibid. f. 232.
[7] Ibid. f. 205.
[8] Blead. Cust., p. 194.
[9] Mich. Ambr. Rent., loc. cit.
[10] Inqu. 1189, pp. 14, 79.
[11] Mich. Ambr. Rent., pp. 56, 57, 138.
[12] Harl. MSS. 3977, ff. 28, 110.
[13] Inqu. 1189, p. 61.
[14] Mich. Ambr. Rent., p. 35: 'Acra et dimidia prati que vocantur
Budelland.'
[15] Ibid. p. 139: 'Et sunt particule terrarum super venientes que pertinent ad carucas que vocantur Sulstiche et Goddingchestiche unde iste,
si est carucarius, debet habere particulam sicut ceteri carucarii.'

the *donum ad lardarium*.[1] *Reeveland* is mentioned, probably
as another name for the acre of corn which he received,[2] and
refhammes which are explained as two *hammes* of pasture
belonging to the office of reeve.[3] *Reeveland* occurs also at
Bleadon,[4] and again, together with *revemede* and *revesgore*, at
Ramsey, where the reeve was commonly free from *consuetudo*
and ate for part of the year at the lord's table.[5] *Smithland*
occurs in Durham,[6] and also *punderland*, land which is said
to belong to the office of *punderus*, although it was held,
together with the office, by the men of the vill.[7] At Sutton
in Warwickshire the half part of the fee of the woodward, *de
venatione capta*, is mentioned.[8] One is reminded of the constantly recurring statement in the Welsh laws regarding the
officers of the king's household—'he is to have his land free'.[9]

In spite, however, of the appurtenant privileges, the impression given by the documents is that the holding of office
was very unpopular and burdensome, and to be avoided
wherever possible. Occasionally a payment like the *Revekeye*
or *Keyesilver* is made by the villata in common in order that
an office may not be incumbent upon them.[10] In Durham
manors the office of *punderus*, together with the *punderland*,
was commonly held by the tenants *inter se* and paid for with
a money rent, the hens and eggs incumbent on *punderland*
being still rendered.[11]

[1] Mich. Ambr. Rent., pp. 56, 57.
[2] Ibid. p. 34: 'que vocantur Reflond'; cf. p. 54.
[3] Ibid. p. 140: If he be reeve he shall have 'ii hammes prati . . . que
vocantur Refhammes'.
[4] Blead. Cust., p. 194: a ferdel of land called reeveland belonged to
the reeve *ex officio*.
[5] Ram. Cart. i. 283, 295, 307, 318, 320, 326, 338, 340, 399, 473, 496 ;
Rot. Hund. ii. 768.
[6] Bish. Hatf. Surv., p. 142 ; cf. Mich. Ambr. Rent. for lists of officers ;
Rot. Hund. ii. 768: the Smith to have one acre for sharpening the
scithes of customars.
[7] Bish. Hatf. Surv., p. 5: 'Tenentes redd. per annum pro officio pun-
deri ad quod officium pertinent ix acre terre et prati . . . 53s. 4d.'; cf.
pp. 13, 18, 95, 142, and 169: 'Punderus . . . habet, causa officii sui, ii
placeas prati.'
[8] Dugdale, Antiq. Warw. ii. 911: (The customars) 'solebant habere
inter eos dimidiam partem feodi woodwardi de venatione capta'.
[9] Anc. Laws and Instit. i. 17 sqq.
[10] See the Revekeye, or Keyesilver rent, below.
[11] Bish. Hatf. Surv., pp. 5, 100.

CHAPTER V

MISCELLANEOUS RENTS

A NUMBER of rents are mentioned in the custumals and rolls very briefly, and without explanation of the object for which they were paid. Suggestions regarding the meaning of some of them have been hazarded : of others no interpretation has been attempted. Greater philological knowledge and familiarity with local customs would, however, probably explain most of them. For convenience these obscure rents have been arranged alphabetically, and to them have been added a few others whose classification has, for one reason or another, proved difficult.

Achabe was a rent paid in Cambridge on Hock Tuesday.[1] With it may perhaps be compared *Hocselver*, but a relation between the two rents is very doubtful.

Akergeve,[2] a rent or ' giving ', probably based on the acre.

Bedgeld[3] was probably another form of merchet. The form is suggestive also of the commutation of a boon service.

Bickton silver. It is suggested in Hazlitt's Blount's Tenures that this rent was the commutation of the service of emptying the lord's jakes at Bickton.[4]

Biresilver.[5]

Booting corn was a Buckinghamshire corn rent, commuted.[6]

Braybotpeni.[7]

---

[1] Harl. MSS. 3977, f. 93: 'Tenentes et tenementa et redditus in Cantebrig'.' A messuage pays 12*d*. 'et Regi ij*d*. quod dicitur Achabe in die Hoxtiwesda'. Cf. f. 94 : a rent paid 'ad husteng' ville' at Michaelmas, 'et similiter ad alium terminum ad diem qui vocatur hoxtiwesda.'

[2] Harl. MSS. 3977, f. 37: 'De auxilio franci plegii xij*s*. Akergeve iiij*li*. vs. x*d*. ob. cum pleg'.'

[3] Blomefield's Norfolk, ix. 294 ; Hazlitt's Blount's Tenures, p. 114.

[4] Hazlitt's Blount's Tenures, p. 25.

[5] Ibid. glossary.

[6] Ibid. p. 138.

[7] Harl. MSS. 3977, f. 108: (Fornham) 'Et dabit preterea per annum xij*d*. de redditu et pro braybotpeni 1*d*.'

*Browernesilver*¹ was a rent paid at Saint Edmund's for licence to hold a brewery. See New Eng. Dict. *sub voce Brewern*.

Byscot,² an occasional fine in East Anglia for not repairing ditches and causeways. It is probably mentioned in an Ely custumal as the *forisfactura de Belawe*, of which the lord receives half. The rent arose evidently from infringements of rules imposed by the village community—the *by-laws*.

Censar' is a rent found in Devon and Cornwall in documents of the reign of Edward III.³ It may be simply a variation of the form *census*, but seems to have had a more specific meaning. *Census* and *tunnus census* appear in East Anglia (see *Marcselver*). It is barely possible, however, that it might be connected with the *tenserie* of the Chronicle for Stephen's reign, which was especially heavy in the west and East Anglia, and has lingered on as a manorial due.

Census, Tunnus Census, see *Marcselver*.

Clyff silver, a rent mentioned in a late document, without explanation.⁴ Possibly it should be compared with the pasturage on the ' cliffs ' received by the tenant of Battle.⁵

Craweselver, Craueselver, a very common Ely rent, probably a commutation of some service connected with crows. The ' rook boy ', who now receives a small compensation for his service of keeping the rooks from the corn, may be a survival of manorial custom.⁶

¹ Harl. MSS. 1005, f. 68 : (Pakenham) ' xxi*s*. vj*d*. de Browernesilver ' ; f. 69 ; Harl. MSS. 3977, f. 84.
² Hazlitt's Blount's Tenures, p. 369 : Tiber. B. ii, f. 106.
³ Exeter Vac. Roll, 1138/2 : (Paignton) ' Et de xviij*s*. ij*d. ob. qu.* superoneratis per auditores in titulo redditus assise ibidem et redditus censar' et cariag' et restyngwode ad festum Sancti Martini ' ; (Cornwall, Penryn) : ' Et de ij*s*. iij*d*. superoneratis per auditores pro quadam consuetudine vocata censar' et auxilio custumariorum ibidem pro eo quod tenentes et custumarii que consuetudines et auxilia predicta facere solebant mortui sunt.' Also, Eng. Hist. Rev. xv. 310, Laws of Breteuil, in a charter to Bideford burgesses freeing them from all toll, custom, censary, or stallage. They are to choose one burgess to be head officer, to have ' throughout the year toll and censary of the town by land and water, to the year's end, for 10*s*. to be paid '. Ashmol. MSS. 864 (Bl. Bk. Coven.), f. 17 : from several tenants small sums are due, ranging from a penny to sixpence, ' pro censar' et aysiamentis.'
⁴ Mon. Angl. i. 527 : (Berks) ' Redd' vocat' Clyffsilver '.
⁵ Batt. Abb. Cust., p. 51 : quoted above.
⁶ Ely Vac. Roll, 1132/10 : (Dodington, Cambs.) ' Et de vij*s*. v*d*. de

Custumpand, see *Marcselver*.

Dissilver was the commutation of the rent of dishes, or of the service of supplying them for special occasions. It occurs in the description in the Hundred Rolls of the Earl of Cornwall's manor at Glatton, and in a compotus roll of Queen Philippa's manor there.[1] Tenants of Peterborough in villages near Glatton paid *disci*, to the number of five, ten, or forty, in addition to their rents of bread, sheep, cloth, and poultry, *de consuetudine Sancti Petri*.[2] The *custos discorum* appears at Ramsey.[3]

Dortron'ng ;[4] the form is possibly a variant of Bortreming.

Elsilver is probably the English form of *ulnagium*, a toll on sales of cloth by the ell or yard.[5] (Or perhaps *Eel*-silver ?)

Ffelstne, Felsten. These forms occur in rolls of St. Edmund's manor of Pakenham.[6] Possibly it should be connected with *filstingpound*, or with some rent supplementary to the farm.

Feoderfe was perhaps the commutation of the ordinary *foddercorn*, or rent of fodder. It occurs on a Cambridgeshire manor.[7]

Ferthing, Ferthingsilver. This rent occurs in the important Ely manor of Wisbech, but the object for which it was paid is not stated.[8] Compare Whitson farthings.

quodam certo redditu quod vocatur Crawesiluer per annum ad terminum S. Michaelis'; Claud. C. xi, f. 66; Tiber. B. ii, *pass.*

[1] Rot. Hund. ii. 651 : a half virgate ' dat obolum ad dissilver'; Min. Acc. 876/16-21.

[2] Chron. Petrob., p. 168 n.

[3] Ram. Cart. i. 363 : 'Custos discorum percipiet ... dimidiam acram frumenti et dimidiam acram avene'; cf. i. 408.

[4] Harl. MSS. 3977, f. 38 : (Neutone) 'Redditus Mutabiles . . . dortron'ng xij*d.*' See below, 'borchsilver.'

[5] D. H. R., p. 23 : a quarter of a bondage tenement pays 'terrario pro elsilver, ob.' Cf. Mon. Angl. v. 6.

[6] Harl. MSS. 1005, f. 68 : (Pakenham) 'Et lx*s.* de ffelstne'; Harl. MSS. 3977, f. 86 : (Pakenham) 'Et ex consuetudine ut dicitur habere debet stipulam pisarum et fabarum et erit quietus de auxilio quod vocatur felsten quia colligit illud auxilium.' If he be feldhayward, he is free from some services and felstne. Blomefield (Norfolk, ix. 294) may refer to the same rent : 'Felsne is money paid by the tenant to the lord, and was 30*s.* per annum for the common aid.'

[7] Rot. Hund. ii. 492 : (Wilburham Parva) 'Et ij*d. ob.* pro feoderfe'.

[8] Ely Vac. Roll, 1132/10; Claud. C. xi, f. 75 : '1 mes' cens' et half ninemannedole dat de ferthing' ad Annunciationem B. Marie ij*d.* et *ob.*'; f. 80 : a *plena terra* of 34 acres gives 2*d.* at Easter. 'Summa ferthing-silver'; ff. 86, 89, 94.

Foselver[1] was perhaps a commutation of ditch digging.

Foxalpeni is a curious rent which ' emerged ' in Wye, Kent, in the year of the war between King John and his barons.[2] If the rent were not paid, the juga owing it were heavily amerced, at 100s., and declared *gavellate*.[3]

Frisilver is probably only another form of the common *frithsilver*.[4]

Greensilver. At Writtle in Essex a halfpenny was paid to the lord from every house whose door opened towards Greenbury.[5]

Grippure, possibly a pasture rent.[6]

Gryvespound,[7] possibly a rent resembling the witepund.

Haworthsylver.[8]

Hocselver,[9] possibly a rent at Hokeday, analogous to the Whitson farthings, or the *Achabe*.

Hognell Rent.[10]

Horderesyft[11] occurs in Devon as a payment subtracted by a tithing.

Hulvir.[12]

Hyndergeld or *hinderselver*.[13]   It is barely possible that this

---

[1] Harl. MSS. 3977, f. 61 : (Neutone) a tenement of 15 acres ' dabit iij *ob.* de foselver et erit quietus de dimidia operacione '.

[2] Batt. Abb. Cust., p. 125 : ' Anno quo guerra fuit inter Regem Johannem et barones Angliae ad festum S. Thomae Apostoli, emergebat obolus qui dicitur foxalpeni de v. jugis ' (which are enumerated) ; cf. p. 129.

[3] Misc. Bks. Augm. Off., vol. 57, f. 99 ; cf. Pollock and Maitland, Hist. Eng. Law, i. 336 n., ii. 269 n.

[4] Ashmol. MSS. 864, f. 17 : ' pro frisylver iiijs.'

[5] Charnock, Man. Cust. Essex, p. 7.

[6] Ely Vac. Roll, 1132/10 (Wysebech) ' Et de viijs. de redditu vocato bosing' grippure et shepestate.'

[7] Norwich Vac. Roll, 1141/1 : (Thornham) ' Et de vij*li.* xiiijs. viij*d.* de diversis consuetudinibus videlicet presentsilver gryuespound iuncandi triturandi.'

[8] Mon. Angl. iii. 512: (Selby, Yorks.) ' Redd' custum' tenen' pro quadam custuma vocata Haworth sylver.'

[9] Reg. Worc. Pr., p. 153 b : ' Wychium excepto hocselver.'   For *inhoc* see Vill. in Eng., p. 226 n. ; Hone, Manor, p. 148 : for money paid the lord at Hockeday.

[10] Mon. Angl. iii. 527 (Shrewsbury) 'Annual' Redd.' voc' Hognell Rente.'

[11] Rot. Hund. i. 66. The tithing did not reply to the bailiff of the hundred at Michaelmas ' ad tremur', 'et nichilominus subtraxerunt xviij*d*. . . . annu' de Hord' esyft consuetos ' ; cf. i. 92.

[12] Rot. Hund. i. 105 (Northerpingham Hund., Norfolk) a ' service'.

[13] Glouc. Cart. iii. 188.   Three virgates give 12*d*. ' ad hyndergeld ' at Martinmas ; cf. pp. 189 (*bis*), 191, 200.

Gloucester rent may have some connexion with hunting service.

Insute occurs in the Crondal Records, the editor suggesting that the form is for *in secta*.[1]   The suggestion seems not very probable, yet *suitsilver*, money for suit, occurs,[2] and perhaps the phrase *suete de prison* has a similar derivation.[3]

Kemersh rent possibly refers only to a place name.[4]

Keyesilver, see *Revekeye*.

Leppe and *Lasse* was an Essex custom, probably a toll levied according to some ancient measures.   Every cart that came over Greenbury, perhaps an ancient market-place, paid four pence to the lord of the manor, unless the cart belonged to a nobleman.[5]   Compare *Greensilver*.

Loretsilver.[6]

Lythsilver, probably *lightsilver*, money *ad candelam*.[7]

Marcselver.   On the manors belonging to St. Edmund there is often mentioned a rent of a fixed sum of money, sometimes a marc, sometimes a pound, due from the vill, to which the tenants contributed according to their holdings.   It is called *marcselver, redditus census, tunnus census, auxilium statutum, custumpand*,[8] but the object for which it was paid

---

[1] Crondal Records, p. 94 : (Yateleigh) 'Tota villata de Yatelegh dat domino 2*s*. de Insutes'; p. 97: 'Totus hamelettus de Suthwode dat domino 12*d*. de Insute.'   [2] Hazlitt's Blount's Tenures, p. 77.
[3] Eng. Hist. Rev. xxiv. 506, xxv. 307.
[4] Mon. Angl. ii. 486: (Shaftesbury) 'Redd' Ass voc' Kemersh Rent.'
[5] Charnock, Man. Cust. of Essex, p. 8.
[6] Harl. MSS. 3977, f. 83: (Heringwelle) 'Habent de loretsilver xii*d*.'
[7] Abing. Acc., pp. 145, 150, 159.
[8] Harl. MSS. 3977, f. 91 : (Sudreya) 'Auxilium statutum.   Notandum quod quolibet anno accipiendum est ad festum S. Michaelis auxilium statutum i marce. Tunnus census. Notandum quod semper ab ad Vincula S. Petri accipiendus est census ville ad Purificationem'; f. 89: (Bradefeud) 'Item dabit ad marcam vii*d*.'; f. 39: (Werketune) 'De auxiliis abbatis di' marc.'; f. 62: (Pakeham) 'Hoc est auxilium aule di Pak' lx*s*.'; f. 93: (March) '*xd*. census a (*sic*) Purificacionem'; Harl. MSS. 1005, f. 69: (Bradefeud) 'De marcseluer xiij*s*. iiij*d*.'; f. 72: (Sudreya) 'Ad festum S. Etheldrede 1 marc. de auxiliis cum ij*s*. de merch'; f.73: (Nova Berton) 'Omnes sunt gersumarii ad voluntatem domini ad festum S. Michaelis de redd' ville xxi sol. . . . De auxiliis albis dim' marc. . . . Ad festum S. Edmundi de redd. ville xxi*s*. . . . De auxiliis ville xixs. iij*d*.'; Harl. MSS. 3977, f. 100: (Cokefeld) 'Et sciendum est quod omnes custumarii predicti dabunt xvj*s*. ad custumpond' de jure'; f. 101: Those belonging 'ad aulam inferiorem' of Cokefeld pay custumpund xv*s*. iij*d*. *ob*. ; Harl. MSS. 1005, f. 68: 'De custumpany xvj*s*.'

is not stated. It is possible that it may be another form of *witepund*, or *fulstingpound*, and that *pundscot* may be identical with it. It may, on the other hand, refer to the customary tallage of the villeins, or it may be a rent distinct from either.

Master's Rent.[1]

Melderfe.[2]

Mowetsilver.[3]

Netsilver[4] was probably a pasture rent, the form being derived from the Anglo-Saxon *neat*.

Nodway money.[5]

Pincrecheyeld.[6]

Pukerelleschild or *Auxilium Purificationis*, a rent occurring frequently in the Somersetshire Hundred Rolls; the passages usually refer to a subtraction from the king.[7]

Radbodispund was a royal rent subtracted from the king in Norfolk.[8]

Revekeye. This rent is probably explained by the *Keyesilver* of Tynewell, which is paid by twelve tenants of virgates lying at a distance from Tynewell, 'that they may not be chosen for the reeveship.'[9]

Ruschewsylver.[10]

Saddlesilver occurs at Wimbledon. At the first coming of

---

[1] Mon. Angl. vi. 306: (Hants.) 'Redd' voc' Master's Rent.'
[2] Norwich Vac. Roll, 1144/1: (Rollesby) 'Et de vs. xid. ob. de consuetudinibus vocatis Turfdole fermpenes et melderfe.'
[3] Faust. A. 1, f. 56: '1 sulung pays 5d.'
[4] Harl. MSS. 1005, f. 68: 'Redditus mutabiles. Netsilver et scepselver herbagium ad bidentes.'
[5] Mon. Angl. ii. 87: 'Cum quodam . . . redd' voc' Nodway Money.'
[6] Ib. ii. 272: 'Redd' voc' Pincrecheyeld.'
[7] Rot. Hund. ii. 130: 'De Cloptone, de auxilio Purificationis quod vocatur Pukerelleschild ijs.'; p. 136: 'Et quod dicti comites per xv annos non permiserunt auxilium quod dicitur Pur' Beate Marie dari domino Regi scilicet de Rodesloke iiijs.'; pp. 132, 133. Again, ii. 688: (Oxon.) 'et pro tallagio ad purificacionem Beate Marie vijd. ob.' (probably manorial).
[8] Rot. Hund. i. 445: 'Consuetudines' subtracted from the hundred of Fourhove; tenements 'et terra Flamberti in Wiclewd solebant facere consuetudines scilicet ad turnum Vicecomitis et auxilium ejusdem et radbodispund.'
[9] Min. Acc. 850/10: Barton Regis, with geresgive. See Keysilver. Comp. of Ketteringe: 'Et de xxxixs. de xxxix virgatis de consuetudine de Keyesilver in festo S. Andree.' Again, p. 45.
[10] Mon. Angl. i. 443: Barking, Office of Cellaress, 'Sche must pay to every ladye of the covent . . . for their ruschewsylver.' Cf. p. 445.

the archbishop the customary tenants gave a 'gifte, called saddlesilver, accustomed to be five marks'. Such payments at the coming of lords of fees were common. At Hexham a palfrey was bought for the new abbot. At Tynemouth the *welcom Abbatis* was paid.[1]

Scap.[2]

Schepersulfer[3] was probably a payment made to the shepherd.

Schrebgavol.[4]

Schydselver.[5]

Scorfee.[6]

Sesilver, a rent in East Anglia, probably another form of *Sefare*, or commutation of the carriage by water.[7]

Shesilver,[8] perhaps another form of *sesilver*.

Snotteringsilver was a customary rent paid to the Abbot of Colchester.[9] Charnock suggests that the word is derived from *snode*, a morsel, or *snathe*, to lop or prune.

Spenningfe was a common customary rent on the manors of Worcester.[10] Possibly it was some commutation of the service of spinning, surviving on the old *scrudland* of the monks.

---

[1] Hazlitt's Blount's Tenures, p. 372. Cf. Hexh. Pr. ii. 76: and 'Welcom Abbatis,' above. Mr. Gray has kindly given me a reference to another palfrey payment. At the change of every lord is payable a contribution 'by the name of Palfrey mony amounting to the sum of 60s. leviable upon the copiehold lands only.' Misc. B. Land Revenue, 214, f. 206; Customs of Abbeshall in Wigborough [Essex].

[2] Rot. Hund. ii. 608. It may be an estover right, and not a rent.

[3] Abing. Acc. p. 40: 'Item pro schepersulfer ij*d. qu.*'

[4] Rot. Hund. i. 163: (Colchester) 'Item abbas subtraxit . . . xv*d. ob.* annui redditus de schrebgavel quos . . . reddere debet predicto burgo.'

[5] Add. MSS. 6159, f. 176. Chert, Kent, an l (schyldsilver) has been erased.

[6] Davenport, Norf. Manor., p. 47, App. p. xxx: 'Et de x*s.* de scorfe ad Natale Domini de leta de Hadesco.'

[7] Harl. MSS. 1005, ff. 38, 69; Ibid. 3977, f. 61; Tiber B. ii. f. 177,*pass.*

[8] Claud. C. xi, f. 279: (Rathlesdene, Suff.) a plena terra gives 2*d.* shesilver at the feast of St. Andrew. Again, f. 283.

[9] Charnock, Manor. Cust. Essex, p. 8.

[10] Vac. Roll, 1143/18: (Hanbury in Salso Marisco) 'Et de iiis. 1*d. ob.* de quadam certa consuetudine que vocatur spenningfe relaxata'; (Stoke) 'et de vij*s.* vj*d.* de quadam certa consuetudine que vocatur spenningfe arentata ad terminos pasche pentecostes et Natalis Domine.' The word occurs frequently in the roll.

Storefe[1] was possibly another form for *scorfe*, or should be so written.

Sulsilver was probably a commutation of the service of giving the lord ploughshares. It occurs on St. Edmund's manors in both the English and the Latin forms.[2] Elsewhere ploughshares were frequently paid to the lord.[3]

Suttonsilver.[4]

Towirst.[5]

Unthield, Unchield, Hunthield, was a Kentish rent,[6] perhaps commuting old hunting services, and to be compared with the Gloucester *huntenesilver.* It may, on the other hand, have been the same as *Unyeld.*

Unyeld, Onziell, Ungeld, Onyeld, was an East Anglian rent, perhaps the same as the foregoing.[7] In the form *Ongiell* it appears at Great Tey, Essex.[8]

Waurscot, a rent in Lincolnshire for wax for the church. The Ely *waursilver,* or *waresilver,* is probably the same rent.[9] Compare *waxsilver.*

Whitehartsilver.[10]

Whitson farthings.[11] There is nothing to show the object of this Whitsuntide rent.

---

[1] Rot. Hund. ii. 491: (Cambs.) Customary tenants with twenty acres give 'xiii*d.* nomine storefe'.

[2] Harl. MSS. 1005, f. 68: 'et ix*d.* de iij vomeribus'; f. 69; f. 73: 'de sulsilver v*s.*'; Harl. MSS. 3977, f. 39: 'de sulselver iij*d.*'

[3] Faust. A. i, ff. 11, 53, 78; Tiber. B. ii, f. 90: 'Preterea dabit per annum tres denarios quando dominus voluerit ad emendum ploutimber et erit quietus de opere unius ebdomadae.'

[4] Crondal Records, p. 383.

[5] Bish. Hatf. Surv., p. 167: (Stockton) 'Burgus . . . cum . . . tolneto, vocato towirst'.

[6] Harl. MSS. 1006, f. xiv.: (Borlee) 'ad purificationem de vnchiel ij*s.* ij*d. ob. qu.*'; f. xv.: 'de vnthield ad festum Purificationis, iii*s.* v*d. ob.*' Add. MSS. 6159, f. 22: (Borle) paid by molmen and custumarii at Purification, 'de vnthiel ij*s.* ij*d. ob. qu.*. . . . de vnthield per annum iiij*s.* v*d. ob.*'

[7] Harl. MSS. 3977, f. 93: (March) 'et de consuetudine quadam que vocatur onyeld vj*d.* in festo S. Etheldrede'. Five acres 'ad onyeld vj*d.*'; three acres, 4*d.* Compare Powell, Rising in East Anglia, Ipswich Assize, 1385. Hazlitt's Blount's Tenures, pp. 314, 315, quoting a case of 1618: the refusal of customary tenants to pay 40*s.* at Michaelmas of the rent in question. The editor identifies it with *tallagium custumariorum.*

[8] Astle's Great Tey, p. 8.

[9] Hazlitt's Blount's Tenures, p. 380; Tiber. B. ii, ff. 125, 236.

[10] Ibid. p. 367.

[11] Mon. Angl. ii. 45.

Wightfee was possibly another form of *Witepund*[1].

Wiveneweddinge was a service or rent on the Gloucester manor of Barton Regis.[2] It is probable that it was a payment levied on marriage: *wivene weddinge*, wives wedding. Cf. Liebermann, Gesetze der Angelsachsen, i. 442 : *wifmannes beweddung*.

Wodehac was a royal rent paid to the abbot in Ramsey manors, by the ' free hides of Hirstingston hundred'.[3] It may have denoted a rent similar to *boistagium*.

Wodewelleschot[4] was a royal rent occurring in Northgrenehow hundred, Norfolk, probably paid in the beginning by geldable land for the maintenance of the woodwork of fortifications.

Yerdsilver[5] was possibly the equivalent of *ulnagium*.

[1] Mon. Angl. iv. 563 : (*temp*. Hen. VIII, Walton S. Felix, Suffolk) ' Idem respondet . . . de 5*d*. de quadam consuetudine vocata Wightfee '.

[2] Glouc. Cart. iii. 70, 71 : ' debet quoddam wiveneweddinge in vigilia Beati Johannis Baptiste et valet obolum ' ; cf. p. 72. See *pro weddis*, Ram. Cart. i. 59.

[3] Ram. Cart. i. 285.

[4] Rot. Hund. i. 526 : ' Et iiijs. x*d*. *ob*. de quodam annuo redditu qui vocatur Wodewelschot '; cf. 483 : ' Idem tenentes subtrahunt v*s*. viij*d*. *qu*. quos reddere solebant ad com' Norwic' quod vocatur wodewellehot per predictum tempus ' : *pass*. in hundred. See below.

[5] Worcester Vac. Roll, 1143/18 : (Hartlebury) ' Et de xiij*d*. *ob*. de certa consuetudine que vocatur yerdsilver ad festum S. Michaelis '.

CHAPTER VI

ROYAL RENTS: ADMINISTRATIVE

RENTS of a second class incumbent on the customary tenants of the manor were those in origin not customary and not manorial, but political, resulting from public imposts, and paid to the king through his officers or to the lord of the manor as the holder of a franchise. These payments, or the services of which they were sometimes the commutation, made up the national obligation of the land, the financial burden which when paid to the king caused the land to be considered geldable, when paid to the manorial lord for his own uses caused it to be considered non-geldable. Theoretically all land was in its origin geldable and could be made non-geldable only by express grant. The lord, that is to say, had his rights by charter from the king; he might exercise some royal rights over land in certain localities, other royal rights over land in other localities, but in no case, as the lawyers of the crown argued, could he exercise justly any right unless he could show a definite grant of it. All rights were annexed to the crown and liberties pertaining to the dignity of the crown could not be alienated by general words nor did long use justify usurpation. Yet the fact that public justice often assumed a private character and also that the payment both of certain services which by this time had little but a financial value, and also of many or all royal dues had become matters of arrangement between the lord and the king led necessarily to confusion with regard to the incidence of the burden, and gave opportunities for unchecked usurpations and extensions of charter privileges.

The arrangements regarding the collection and destination of royal rents were intricate. The king in some cases was in seisin of payments which in other cases went to manorial lords. The manorial lords collected such dues with or without the presence of the royal bailiffs, as the case might be, and paid the bailiffs for the privilege of retaining them for their own uses, or retained them without payment, or paid them over entirely or in part to the king. Moreover, such royal dues were, by the time of the Hundred Rolls at least, to some extent localized. Payments connected primarily with the view of frankpledge do not, for example, appear in counties where that view was not exercised; hidage appears in some counties and not in others. Some dues, too, were paid occasionally, some annually. In short, the Hundred Rolls and the Quo Warranto Rolls disclose a very tangled network of judicial and financial rights and duties, the understanding of which is not helped very greatly by the study of other material.

If the rents which were royal in origin be considered from the point of view of the manor, and the more general subject of their relation to the central government be left to one side as beyond the particular field of this study, two main questions seem to present themselves; first, which of the manorial payments should be properly included in the class of those which, when paid to the king, made the land geldable, and, secondly, what was the method of assessment of such dues within the manor. It will be convenient to discuss these questions together, in an enumeration of royal rents, beginning with those that were specifically part of the geld of the kingdom and continuing with those that were connected in one way or another with the courts and the administration of justice. A table compiled from the Hundred Rolls placed at the end of this study will indicate roughly the general distribution of royal rents or tests of geldable land, as they may be called, in different counties.

Hidagium. In the thirteenth and fourteenth centuries the old geld or land tax appeared in many localities as hidage. As the name indicates, hidage was based on the hide and was not paid to the king by land *extra hidam*,[1] land which, like the

---

[1] Ram. Cart. i. 334: A virgate once gave hidage, sheriff's aid, and pontage. 'Quae servitia a tempore J. R. tunc temporis firmarii . . . qui eandem virgatam terrae . . . fraudulenter posuit extra hidam, omnia hactenus detinentur'; i. 440: 'Terrae quae sunt extra hidam et quae non dant hydagium.' And, i. 308, 438; ii. 13, *pass.*

old royal manors of Domesday Book owing a farm and no geld, was usually described not in fiscal hides but in areal measures. Land *extra hidam* as far as the king was concerned, sometimes included a whole manor or fee, sometimes only certain lands within the manor, and the profits of it were taken by the lord of the fee justly or unjustly when it was free from the royal hidage. The most common exemption was of land 'elemosinata', in the hands of the church,[1] but honours and parts of lay fees were also often non-geldable.[2] Such exceptions were based, as has been said, on charter or were the result of long usurpation or, occasionally, of more recent aggression on the part of the great lords. Complaints that the lords have subtracted hidage are frequent in certain parts of the Hundred Rolls: it is disappointing, however, to find that in the Quo Warranto Rolls such subtractions are rarely the subject of separate pleadings,[3] and exact statements concerning the nature of the payment are therefore not easy to find.

It is clear, however, that hidage is frequently mentioned among the financial burdens in some counties, and is not mentioned at all in other counties. Thus in the Hundred Rolls we find it recorded commonly and indisputably in the counties of Bedford, Buckingham, and Oxford, more rarely in Cambridgeshire, where it is usually, though not exclusively, found on the lands of the Abbot of Ramsey, in Huntingdonshire, where it occurs on Ramsey lands only, and very occasionally elsewhere. In other counties it may sometimes have been included under vague words like scot and lot, regalities, forinsec service, especially since it is several times mentioned in the custumals of manors in counties in which it is not recorded in the Hundred Rolls. The Domesday of St. Paul's, for example, though at an earlier date than the Hundred Rolls, shows that the manor of Barling in Essex, a county in which the payment is not mentioned in the Hundred Rolls, paid 31*d.* to the bailiff of the hundred 'pro

---

[1] Rot. Hund. i. 16, 17, 31 ; ii. 323, 457, 477, *pass.*
[2] Ibid. i. 2, 27, 32, 41, 53 ; ii. 343, 693, *pass.*
[3] But see P. Q. W., p. 88.

hidagio'.[1] Yet while this is true occasionally, the constant inclusion of hidage in some counties and exclusion of it from others in the Hundred Rolls, and the generally corresponding distribution of it in manorial customaries and extents of the same approximate date, would seem to show that at the time the Hundred Rolls were compiled the rent was not of universal and regular occurrence under the name hidage. Perhaps the explanation of this irregular distribution may lie in the fact that in the counties where it occurs most commonly it seems to have become usually an annual payment, and is therefore included naturally among the regular sources of revenue.[2] In a few cases even in these counties there are references to a more occasional hidage. On the manors of Ramsey in Cambridgeshire and Huntingdonshire, for example, hidage is paid 'quando currit' or 'quando evenerit'.[3] The Ramsey hidage, however, seems to have been exceptional; it was, we learn, from the chartulary, a levy made by the abbot usually on his non-military tenants, not paid to the king, but turned over to the support of the four knights who were due from the abbey, and it took the place among non-military tenants, in many, though not in all, cases, of the scutage on military tenants. The conditions of knight service were somewhat unusual at Ramsey.[4] Again, the Devonshire Hundred Rolls refer to definite specific occasions on which a hidage was levied by the sheriffs from the county,[5] and the Glastonbury hidage seems to have been of this kind.[6] Once a hidage was

---

[1] D. S. P., p. 64; and see also Harl. MSS. 1005, f. 72, and Gough MS. Suff. 3 Bodl. (13 H. vi.) for the occurrence in East Anglia.

[2] See especially Rot. Hund. ii. 812: (Oxon.) 'Quod vero hydagium modo redactum est in annuum redditum et nichilominus amerciantur homines tot'; and ii. 495.

[3] Econ. Cond. Ram. Man., p. 14.

[4] Feudal England, pp. 296–298.

[5] Rot. Hund. i. 63: (Barnstaple) 'Dicunt Rogerus Pridyas dum fuit vicecomes cepit de hominibus dicti burgi xls. pro hidagio faciendo contra libertatem dicti burgi ubi nuncquam hydagium facere solebant et antequam pacem habere possent finem fecerunt cum predicto vicecomite per predictos xls.'; again, i. 72: 'Dicunt quod in ultima itineracione justiciarum sedencium apud Exon' fuit quoddam hydagium de tribus solidis ad quamlibet hydam'.

[6] Inqu. 1189, p. 115: 'Canonici de Bradenestoca tenent unam virgatam et debent acquietare donum vicecomitis et hidagium et nichil modo inde

paid in Bedfordshire at the need of the king.[1] In Cambridge-shire hidage was paid 'as it is placed in the county on hides'.[2]

In the great number of cases in the counties of Bedford-shire, Buckinghamshire, and Oxfordshire especially, hidage was paid by the year, a definite statement being made to that effect in the Hundred Rolls. The usual rate of this annual payment was two shillings on the hide, and even small frac-tions of holdings paid their correct proportion of this amount.[3] The variations are comparatively infrequent.[4] The rate bears, evidently, no uniform relation to the size of the knight's fee, and the payment was not, except in Ramsey, a military or peculiarly feudal payment, for very often one fee paid twice as much as another fee.[5] Hidage was paid usually to the king through the sheriff, by the fee,[6] or the vill,[7] or even the hundred.[8] Whether the sheriff came into the fee to receive the money or had it sent up to his tourn, in cases where suitors from the manor in question still attended the tourn, or to the ordinary hundred court, if that were in his hands, or to the county court, does not appear. Very often, however, the payment was made to the lord of the manor, and either retained by him as, for example, in the case of the Earl of Gloucester,[9] or paid over to the king. Sometimes an adjust-ment was made regarding the amount. Thus in Oxfordshire

---

faciunt . . . et in tempore Edwardi vicecomes solet defendere homines Glastonie ad comitatum. Sericus aliquando recepit tres denarios pro dono vicecomitis et hidagium similiter quod canonici modo detinent'; and Mich. Ambr. Rent, p. 155.

[1] Rot. Hund. ii. 321, 492, 507.
[2] Ibid. ii. 494 : 'et solvit hydagium, pontagium, prout ponitur in comi-tatu per hydam' ; again, 495: 'et debet scutagium, pontagium, et hydagium quando evenerit.'
[3] Ibid. i. 5, 6, 7, 23, 25, 27, 29, 31 ; ii. 321, 323, 324, 325, 326, 330, 332, 339, pass. The rate was less uniform in Oxon., e.g. ii. 44, 782, 812, 843, 847, pass.
[4] Ibid. i. 4, 20 ; ii. 44.
[5] Ibid. i. 4, for example.
[6] Ibid. i. 30, 33, 53 ; ii. 44, pass.
[7] Ibid. i. 20, 31, by certain vills 'de corde comitatus'; ii. 34, 44.
[8] Ibid. i. 3, 21.
[9] Ibid. i. 29: S. holds two hides and a half and receives 'ad opus suum proprium de hidagio quinque solidos set nescitur quo waranto'; and i. 1, 34.

in one instance the king received one-third of 4s. 6d.[1] Sometimes the vill *conjunctim*, in common, paid the hidage.[2]

It is possible, moreover, that an explanation of the occurrence of hidage as an annual payment in certain localities
and not in others may lie in the general tendency which is
evident towards lumping together sources of revenue, royal or
otherwise, towards commuting, that is to say, occasional and
more or less uncertain obligations, into fixed annual sums.
Such a tendency is evident enough in the payment of other
rents,—in the *fulstingpound*, for example,—and is only one
manifestation of the strength and prevalence of the farming
system. If the sheriff paid a stated annual sum or farm for
the county to the king, and the bailiff or private lord paid
a farm for the hundred to the sheriff, and the men of the vill
paid a stated annual sum for any given rent or for all rents to
the lord for the vill, it is clear enough that the farmers of
county, hundred, or vill would have gained a very desirable
certainty regarding the amount of their revenue. In earlier
times it is true that the farm of the county probably did not
include the Danegeld, which was rendered separately by the
sheriff, and the hidage seems to be a survival of the Danegeld;
yet even so it is possible enough that in some counties a
general tendency towards uniformity may have modified earlier
conditions and changed the occasional Danegeld into the fixed
hidage, part of the regular farm.

The understanding of hidage in Oxfordshire is complicated
by an apparent connexion made between it and the payment
which seems to be identified with the *fulstingpound* of other
localities. It would even seem in some cases as if in Oxfordshire this payment of 6d. before judgement and 12d. after judgement made by the tenants that they might be quit of fines in
the hundred or the view, were actually called hidage. While
this may be true, it does not seem probable that such is
necessarily the meaning of hidage elsewhere; it is more likely
that in Oxfordshire, as other passages show clearly enough,

---

[1] Ibid. ii. 741.
[2] Ibid. ii. 835 : 'Et tota villa predicta conjunctim dat domino xs. de
hydagio per annum'; again, p. 838.

the payment for misdemeanours was called hidage because made by those in the hidage of the vill, and not by those who lived on land *extra hidam*.

Cornagium, Hornagium, Noutegeld, Horngeld. The payment called cornage found on the lands of Durham, and commonly in Northumberland, Cumberland, Westmoreland,[1] has been a good deal discussed, and some questions regarding it are still unanswered. Dr. Round has disentangled it from castle guard.[2] Mr. Lapsley, in a long and instructive paper,[3] going over all the printed evidence, believes that it was a seigniorial due, in the beginning given by vills probably for right of pasture, basing his argument for the connexion of cornage and pasture on the name itself, on the fact that cattle are the basis of the assessment, and that it is found especially in certain vills in Boldon Book, which in his interesting division of Boldon vills into certain regular types he calls pasture vills. Mr. Lapsley believes that this seigniorial due, whose origin he considers obscure, but which was incumbent on the unfree, became attached in the course of time to certain tenements, became a real burden, or, as he puts it, immediately 'a part of the forinsec service' of the land, and, as a burden on the land, paid by any tenants free or villein who might come to hold such tenements. Later this due was, he believes, used as the symbol of a certain kind of tenure, probably *drengage*, which was called for convenience *per cornagium*. One point in Mr. Lapsley's explanation seems to present grave difficulties. How can the transformation of a seigniorial due for pasturage into a royal payment be accounted for? If cornage had been originally or at any early stage of its development simply a payment to the lord of the vill, why should, then, its change into a burden on the land instead of on the person of the tenant, change it also into a payment to the king instead of to the feudal lord? The process of change is usually in the other direction:—that is to say, originally royal pay-

---

[1] Cornage is sometimes included in immunity lists of lands elsewhere ; for example, P. Q. W., p. 253, in Edmund Crouchback's fees.

[2] Commune of London, pp. 278–288.

[3] Lapsley, Cornage and Drengage, Am. Hist. Rev. ix. 670 sqq.

ments are absorbed by the manorial lords until their original royal character may be almost lost sight of. Is it not more probable that cornage in its origin was simply a form of the geld which, in the north, in localities where pasture was common and agriculture less common than in the south, happened to be levied on the number of animals possessed by the individual or by the vill instead of on the unit of land? It would then have been called in the north cornage, just as in the south a similar payment based on land might be called hidage, being levied at the rate of 2d. an animal.[1] Its inclusion in the list of burdens on geldable land,[2] with the other royal obligations from which land is freed by charter, becomes natural, and it would have no necessary connexion with pasture beyond the fact that the number of animals held forms a natural basis of assessment for taxes in a pastoral community.[3] Indeed, the number of animals is a common enough basis of assessment for the incidence of a fiscal burden within the manor throughout England. Thus the wardpenny is frequently so assessed,[4] and in some cases even the hidage itself.[5] Cornage was evidently one of the royal payments that fell annually, and not on occasion only. It is accounted for regularly in the Pipe Rolls.[6] In this case, as in the case of hidage in certain southern counties, the geld may have become fixed at a certain annual sum, perhaps under the influence of the farm system, which seems to have preferred a certain to an uncertain rent. It was included in the sheriff's

[1] Feod. Dun., p. 145 n.; Vill. in Eng., p. 295.
[2] Newmin. Ch., pp. 197, 269; Cock. Ch. i. 41 ; Rievaulx Ch., p. 214: North. Ass. Roll, pp. 237, 335 ; Feod. Dun., p. 145 ; Rot. Hund. ii. 18 (ii. 472, a misprint for *homagio* ?).
[3] Probably this would explain the passage, Bold. Bk., p. 571, where it is stated that certain *villani* pay rent and labour services like others of Boldon except cornage, ' que non dant pro defectu pasture ' ; compare Bish. Hatf. Surv., p. 173: (Norton) ' Toti villani nichil solvunt de cornagio ibidem, eo quod non habent pasturam, prout patet in libro de Boldon.' In this survey cornage was paid commonly on St. Cuthbert's day, for example, pp. 18, 21, 45. On p. 143 it appears as horneyeld : ' Praedicti cotagii solvunt quolibet anno inter se pro operibus vocatis Horneyeld 12d.'
[4] See below, wardpenny.
[5] See above.
[6] Compare Red Bk. Excheq., p. 797 : ' Idem Vicecomes lv*l*. xix*s*. iij*d*. de Notegeldo quolibet anno reddendo.'

farm ordinarily, although not invariably. It may, of course, have been an annual payment from the beginning, as were, for example, sheriff's aid and probably the payment of suit and pontage, but in these cases the reason for the appearance of the payment as an annual rent is clear, while cornage looks more like the hidage of Bedfordshire and Buckinghamshire.

This interpretation of cornage may make more clear also the reason for the fact that it is paid commonly, though not invariably, by the vill or villata as a whole, especially as recorded in the Boldon Book.[1] It was pointed out by Professor Maitland that 'tributes to be paid by the vill as a whole in money or in kind are not of recent origin. They are more prominent in the oldest than in other documents';[2] and Professor Maitland uses the cornage of Boldon Book and the payments in the Black Book of Peterborough as illustrations of his statement. It may be that they were more common also in the vills where conditions were pastoral. Whether or no we may believe that seigniorial pressure has in such cases necessarily intervened to call forth communal action, or whether with Professor Vinogradoff we may believe in the possibility of initial responsibility of the vill as a whole for such burdens,[3] it is certainly clear that an obligation for which the vill as a whole was responsible in the twelfth century would be more likely to be a royal than a seigniorial payment. Seigniorial dues were more often and conveniently apportioned individually among the tenants.

Cornage and the *vacca de metride* are usually coupled together in the Boldon Book, payment being made in money for cornage and one cow *de metride*. Some connexion between the two is accepted as possible by Dr. Round,[4] and Mr. Lapsley believes that the *vacca de metride*, or milch cow, was a regular part of the cornage payment, and an indication that it was

---

[1] Bold. Bk., pp. 567, 568, 569, 571, 580 ; 570: 'Queryngdonshire redd. lxxv. sol. de cornagio et iij vaccas de metirede'; ibid.: 'Villani redd. xx sol. de cornagio.' Cf. Rent. & Surv. Roll, i. 730.
[2] D. B. B. p. 147.
[3] Gr. of Man., pp. 318, 319, 360, *et seq*.
[4] Comm. of Lond., p. 287: 'From the above important charters (to St. Bees) it would seem that the two dues went together.'

once made in kind and was now in part commuted. Certainly the payment of the cow fell like the payment of the money-rent on the vill as a whole, for where a part of the vill is answerable for a part of the cornage, the same part of the vill is answerable for a corresponding fraction of the cow also. If the payment of *metrez, metreth,* is the same as the *metride* the connexion is not altogether so clear. A charter of 1149 may point to a distinction.[1] Roger, to whom land is conveyed, ' was to render thereby two pence annually, two shillings for cornage, for " metreth " as much as belongs to the land.' In the later Surveys, moreover, the two payments are separately entered, and are paid at different terms,[2] cornage by bond and free, *metrith* usually by bond alone. On the lands of St. David's, especially in Cardiganshire, sometimes elsewhere, there is an ancient rent of a cow *de commorth* or *commortha,* sometimes a cow and her calf, paid at the Kalends of May in every third year, and occasionally commuted by a yearly sum, the annual payment being valued at 6s. 8d., the third of the pound. The cow was levied almost certainly on the *gwele,* the number paid by the vills corresponding in almost every case with the *gweles* or *lecti* in the vill, even to fractional parts,[3] and was probably a pasture payment, possibly resembling the English *gaerswin.*[4] It is tempting to find some connexion between the cow *de commorth* and the cow *de metride,* but there is no proof. In any case, however, it may well be that

---

[1] Amer. Hist. Rev., *loc. cit.*; cf. Feod. Dun., p. 114 n.

[2] See Bish. Hatf. Surv., where the payment of the cow is common but is not always connected with cornage. The two rents are entered separately, and paid at different feasts, St. Martin's and St. Cuthbert's. Cornage varied in amount, metrith was 3s., or 6s., or 12s., 6s. being the value of a cow: e.g. p. 18: ' Metrith. Omnes bondi et cotagii solvunt inter se pro i vacca de Metrith ad festum S. Martini ibidem quolibet anno, ut dicunt . . . 6s. ;' and pp. 17, 28 (*antiqui bondi*), 31, 128, 171, 183.

[3] Black Book of St. David's (Cymm. Rec. Soc.), p. 200: 8 lecti, ' qui vocantur gwele' give 8 cows ; so also pp. 204, 210, 212, 214, 216, 236, 254, *pass.*; and especially p. 232, where the rate is observed even by small fractions of the gwele. Slight variations occur, pp. 206, 208, 260, 274, which can probably be explained as the result of later confusion ; cf. Mon. Angl. iv. 166, 633, 675.

[4] Ibid., p. 236: ' Et si aliqui dictorum tenencium non resideant super terram domini et vaccam ibidem habuerint nisi inter alios vacce proportionaliter soluerint quod terra in manu domini debet capi nisi alia districtio super terra inveniatur.

the conjunction of *cornage* and *metride* in the lists of obligations on land is purely verbal.

Auxilium vicecomitis. Sheriff's aid was one of the most common burdens on geldable land. It is recorded in the Hundred Rolls for the counties of Cambridge, Derby, Devon, Dorset, Essex, Hertford, Huntingdon, Lincoln, Norfolk, Northampton, Nottingham, Suffolk, Sussex, Warwick, and Wilts. In certain other counties it may be included under some general head ; in Hereford, for example, as perquisites of sheriffs, or prises and farms of beadles.[1] Its non-appearance in other counties, however, especially in Bedford[2] and Buckingham, for which we have the very full double set of reports, can hardly be explained as merely an omission on the part of the scribe. It may be worthy of remark that four of the counties in which sheriff's aid probably does not appear, Bedfordshire, Buckinghamshire, Berkshire, and Oxfordshire, are the counties in which an annual hidage was levied, more or less generally, at the rate of two shillings on the hide. Both payments occur in Cambridgeshire, but the hidage there is occasional and often subtracted by great lords. In Huntingdonshire also, where sheriff's aid is common, hidage appears only on the lands of Ramsey, and goes to the abbot. Although the two payments were quite different in their origin it would look as if the annual hidage of two shillings on the hide might in some cases have been considered as the equivalent of the sheriff's aid.

In view of the large number of references to the sheriff's aid, and the importance of the payment, it is disappointing to find so little explanation of its exact nature. The accepted definition[3] of the aid as money paid to the sheriff to meet his expenses seems to be upheld by occasional passages. The *shirreveswelcome* paid at the tourn in Essex, for example, was probably the same as sheriff's aid,[4] and so also the *donum*

---

[1] Rot. Hund. i. 186.
[2] The peculiar Ramsey hidage occurs in Cranfield, Bedfordshire, but is paid to the abbot. Ram. Cart. i. 276, 277, 439, 451, and above, hidage.
[3] Stubbs, Con. Hist. i. 282 ; Round, Feud. Eng., pp. 500-501 ; Kennet, Par. Antiq. Gloss.
[4] Rot. Hund. i. 157 : 'Dicunt quod vill' de Chaur' solebat venire ad

vicecomitis of Wiltshire and Kent.[1] It may, in the beginning, have been a commutation of the sheriff's right of purveyance, traces of which linger perhaps in the oats paid at the tourn, in the sheaves and poultry sometimes extorted by bailiffs, and in the *palefridus vicecomitis*, the aid for fodder for the sheriff's horse. In Norfolk the rent was sometimes called *shirreve-scot*,[2] in Northamptonshire *shirevesyelde*,[3] and in Suffolk *scherreveselver*.[4] Dr. Round's identification of the *consuetudo*, over which Becket and the king quarrelled at Woodstock, with the sheriff's aid will be remembered.[5] The opposition of the archbishop to the transformation of the aid into a royal payment was, however, evidently of no permanent avail: it is clear from the Hundred Rolls that the kings of later days in large measure had gained Henry's point, and no distinction is made between the destination of the aid to the sheriff and that of any other royal payment.[6] The aid was no longer apparently the sheriff's peculiar property, but the king 'was seised of it and all other gelds'.[7] Its subtraction was a heavy loss to the king.[8] This assimilation of the aid to the other

turnum vicecomitis bis per annum et contribuere ad communem finem xij*d.* et solebat dare ad shirreveswelcome ij*d.* et facere sectam ad hundredum.'

[1] Ibid. ii. 260, 276: 'Dicunt quod dominus Rex percipit per annum ...de dono Vicecomitis'; Inqu. 1189, p. 115: 'et debent acquietare donum vicecomitis et hidagium et nichil modo inde faciunt et in tempore Edwardi vicecomes solet defendere homines Glastonie ad comitatum. Sericus aliquando recepit tres denarios pro dono vicecomitis et hidagium similiter quod canonici modo detinent'; Mich. Ambr. Rent. p. 167: 'Memorandum quod homines petierunt inducias de dono vicecomitis, scilicet, de qualibet virgata iij*d.* et de H. .... ij*s.* vi*d.*' In Kent the rent was very common, e.g. Faust. A. i, ff. 18, 53 (a sulung gives 12*d.*), 43, 65.

[2] Rot. Hund. i. 454, 483: 'quos reddere solebant annuatim ad hundredum ad redditum quod vocatur Schirreveschot'; and ii. 734: (Oxon) 'schirpeni.'

[3] P. Q. W., p. 557.   [4] Ibid. p. 731.

[5] Feud. Eng., p. 498, quoting Grimm's Life of St. Thomas: 'Consuetudo: dabantur de hida bini solidi ministris regis qui vicecomitum loco comitatus servabant, quos voluit rex conscribere fisco et reditibus propriis associare.'

[6] Rot. Hund. ii. 275, paid by sheriff to king; see also p. 276.

[7] Rot. Hund. i. 335 n.: 'Postea convictum est per xij et per vicecomitem quod terra illa est geldabilis et quod dominus Rex est scisitus de auxilio vicecomitis et de omnibus aliis geldis per manum Elye de Rabayn capitalis domini feodi illius ita quod nichil inde deperdit domino Regi'; and i. 329, 331; ii. 448, *pass.*; P. Q. W., pp. 293, 300.

[8] P. Q. W., p. 302.

royal payments was probably easy enough under the system of farming the revenues of the county. It could be included by the sheriff with other sources of his revenue, and to the holder of the knight's fee or the small tenant from whom it was ultimately due, the original distinction would soon be a matter of no importance.[1]

It is clear from a number of passages in the Hundred Rolls that the aid was paid usually, if not always, at the sheriff's tourn. In the roll of the sheriff's tourn in Wiltshire in 1439 it is recorded as paid by the tithing at the tourn.[2] In Clifton hundred in Devonshire the sheriff made one tourn a year and took then from the hundred of Clifton 10s. 2d., 'qui denarii appellantur auxilium vicecomitis.'[3] Again, in Dorsetshire, until the Provisions of Oxford and the subtractions of Richard of Gloucester, the men of the hundred used to come twice a year to the sheriff's tourn and give 8s. to the sheriff's aid.[4] In Essex a vill used to go to the tourn and contribute to the common fine and to the *shirreveswelcome*.[5] In Norfolk tenants used to pay annually at the hundred the rent called *shirreveschot*.[6] The aid cannot be identified with another payment made 'ad turnum vicecomitis' which was sometimes paid by the same man by whom the sheriff's aid was also paid,[7] nor usually with hundred aid.[8] Nor can it be identified with money paid as composition of suit at court, although there are occasionally evidences of some confusion between the two payments, especially in Northamptonshire. The abbot of Crowland endeavoured, unsuccessfully, to prove that a rent paid by him was for quittance of suit, the sheriff main-

---

[1] Compare Rot. Hund. ii. 226.

[2] Wilts. Arch. and Nat. Hist. Mag. xiii, p. 117 (Roll of tourn) : the tithing of Coulesfeld pays 4s. 3d., and presents that all is well, but is fined for not bringing the sheriff's aid as it should have done; compare P. Q. W., p. 183.

[3] Rot. Hund. i. 67.

[4] Ibid. i. 100.   [5] Ibid. i. 157.

[6] Rot. Hund. i. 454, 483 : ' Idem tenentes subtrahunt vs. viijd. qu. quos reddere solebant annuatim ad hundredum ad redditum qui vocatur schirreveschot.'

[7] P. Q. W., pp. 731, 774, *pass.*

[8] But see Rot. Hund. ii. 666: 'et hundr'heyld scilicet auxilium vice-comitis'; and ii. 172, where it is said to 'pertain to the hundred', probably with reference to its payment at the court of the hundred.

taining that the rent in question was paid 'for sheriff's aid, and not for any suit'.[1]

It is difficult to discover the unit of assessment of the sheriff's aid, or any regular and uniform rate at which it was levied. The frequent connexion of the payment with the hundred would suggest that it may originally have been assessed on the hundred and subdivided among the vills. Within the hundred, however, there seems to be no uniformity except perhaps in Lincolnshire, where 20d. is paid usually by the carucate,[2] and in Kent, where it is stated that the rent is taken by hides or by carucates.[3] Sometimes it was made by all classes within the vill together, free, *custumarii, coterelli* ;[4] and it is stated that a man paid *secundum proportionem tenementi sui*.[5] It was paid by the vill direct to the hundred,[6] or by the knight's fee through the hands of the lord of the fee,[7] or by tithings.[8] Like all other burdens on geldable land it was frequently subtracted by lords, either justly or more often unjustly. The Abbot of Ramsey collected it and retained it, by reason of his regality, through all his hided lands,[9] except in Woldhyrst, where the tenants of the Prior of St. Ives collected and handed over to the reeve of the prior the sheriff's aid, *wardpenny*, and *wodehac*, which used to be collected by the abbot's bailiff of the hundred (the abbot held the hundred in which St. Ives lay).[10] The abbot collected his

---

[1] P. Q. W., p. 302 ; compare ibid., p. 239 : The prior of S. Waleric is summoned to say why he does not permit his villeins to make suit at the tourn. He replies, 'quod ipse quietus est pro se et hominibus suis de auxilio vicecomitis, per cartam . . . et quod ea ratione clamat ipse esse quietus pro se et hominibus suis predictis de secta facienda ad turnum predictum ;' also pp. 390, 396, 402, 404, 406, 408, 412, 415, 416 ; and Add. MSS. 35,169 : Auxilium vicecomitis is paid and for it 'clamat predictas terras suas ibidem quietas a secta comitatus hundr' wap' et tithing' murdrum et commune amerciamentum '.

[2] Rot. Hund. i. 255, 280 : 'quelibet carucata terre xxd.'; and pp. 365, 378, 388 ; cf. P. Q. W., pp. 152, 154 : (Derby) 'sive capiatur per hidatas vel carucatas'; again, p. 47, and Rot. Hund. i. 286.

[3] P. Q. W., p. 320.

[4] Rot. Hund. ii. 456, *pass.*   [5] Ibid. ii. 418.

[6] Ibid. ii. 258, 428, 429, 456, 559.

[7] Ibid. ii. 418, 434, 445, 468, 477, 478; P. Q. W., pp. 393, 394, 397.

[8] Rot. Hund. ii. 119.

[9] Ibid. ii. 629 ; cf. pp. 483, 680 ; i. 197.

[10] Ram. Cart. i. 285.

aid from all classes of tenants, the holders of the free hides, the free tenants, the *censuarii*, the virgaters, the cottars. The rate varied from 2*d.* to 6¼*d.* a virgate.[1] The Bishop of Ely kept the aid in parts of Cambridgeshire,[2] the Abbot of Gloucester collected it in Gloucestershire,[3] the Bishop of Lincoln, the Abbot of Peterborough, and the Abbot of Barling collected the ' pennies of the sheriff ' from their ' rustics ' and retained them to their own uses, by what warrant was not known.[4] The Earl of Gloucester was a serious offender in the same respect,[5] and innumerable lords—all to the heavy loss of the king.[6] The account of Lincolnshire in the Hundred Rolls is especially instructive. Sheriff's aid was, in this county, one of the most common and important of the royal payments, being assessed at the rate of 20*d.* on the carucate. In a surprising number of cases land had become non-geldable at the wapentake, it was no longer talliagible,[7] it was demense of the king and perhaps never gelded,[8] it was part of the honour of Richmond,[9] or had been subtracted by some lay lord,[10] but much more often, having once been geldable it was at the time of the Hundred Rolls ' terra elemosinata ad grave dampnum domini regis'.[11] The church, rightly or wrongly, had obtained the royal dues from a great deal of land, and it was necessary to have the witness of the men of the hundred to prove that land

---

[1] See Ram. Cart. *pass.* for rate, especially i. 364, 456.
[2] Rot. Hund. ii. 485.
[3] Glouc. Cart. iii. 97.
[4] Rot. Hund. i. 372 : ' Collegerunt vic' denar' de rusticis suis. Et sic retinuerunt ad opus suum vel non antiquo waranto aut quantum nesciunt.' Cf. i. 243, 244, 251, 280, 301, 335, 368, 373, 445.
[5] Rot. Hund. i. 100: ' Item dicunt quod homines hundredi . . . solebant venire ad turnum vicecomitis et dare ad auxilium vicecomitis et sic semper fecerunt usque ad provisiones Oxon' a quo tempore nichil solverunt de auxilio predicto, subtrahuntur per Ric' quondam com' Glouc.' Cf. p. 191 ; ii. 132, 137, 484, 666.
[6] Ibid. ii. 9, 129 ; i. 193, 197, 457, *pass.*
[7] Rot. Hund. i. 316.
[8] Ibid. i. 260.
[9] Ibid. i. 329.   [10] Ibid. i. 335, 374, *pass.*
[11] Ibid. i. 335 : ' Item prior de Ormsby subtraxit forinsecum servitium in Elkineton jam xx annis elapsis scilicet auxilium vicecomitis quo warento nesciunt ad dampnum Regis xij*d.* de duabus bovatis terrae et sic elemosinatur illa terra que solet esse gueldabilis.' Also i. 260, 277, 278, *pass.*

was still geldable at the wapentake, and owed *auxilium vice-comitis*.[1]

Palefridus Vicecomitis. With the sheriff's aid there is sometimes mentioned ' the aïd called *palefridus vicecomitis* '.[2] This rent is evidently a survival of the old purveyance right of the sheriff to obtain fodder for his horse. It may be compared with the common pasture rents for the horses of *raglots* and other bailiffs mentioned in the Welsh extents,[3] and with the oats due at the tourn,[4] and with the common duty of feeding *satellites*, horses, and dogs, of the lord's hunting parties.[5]

Hundred aid, Hundred scot, Hundredsilver, Hundredgeld. In certain localities another payment is mentioned with the sheriff's aid, the aid of the hundred,[6] or as it should perhaps sometimes be extended, the aid of the *hundredar*.[7] It was probably a payment similar in character to the sheriff's aid, made to the bailiff of the hundred, who is sometimes called the *hundredarius*,[8] for his personal expenses. It is clearly distinguished from money paid in quittance of suit at the hundred court. In Norfolk, for example, certain tenants paid 12*d*., by which they desired to be free of suit, but the king declared that the 12*d*. had always been paid for *hundredscot* and not for quittance of suit,[9] just as in the case of Crowland he declared that a certain rent was for sheriff's aid and not

---

[1] Rot. Hund. i. 335 n.

[2] P. Q. W., p. 147: 'de aux' vic' . . . et de aux' quod vocatur palefridus Vicecomitis '; also pp. 419, 635 ; Rot. Hund. ii. 291 : 'Et hundredum le Repindune valet per annum vij*li*. et palefridus Vicecomitis valet xl*s*.' Again, p. 297 : (Hundred of Appeltre) ' solebat reddere domino R. *cs*. donec W. vetus comes Derb' fecit excambium cum domino Rege Iohanne pro tercio denario firme de Derb' et modo placita et perquisita valent x*li*. per annum et reddit ad palefridum per annum ix*li*. viij*s*. et viij*d*. et pro auxilio vicecomitis xl*s*. per annum.'

[3] Denbigh Survey, *loc. cit.* ; Trib. Sys. in Wales, App. pp. 117 sqq.

[4] Rot. Hund. ii. 31.

[5] Ibid. ii. 60, and above.

[6] Rot. Hund. ii. 605 : (Hunts) 'Item dicunt quod abbas Ram' capit hundredesgeld de omnibus feodis suis infra hundredum'; and pp. 114, 629, 632, 676, 680 ; i. 469, 470, 510, 527, 541.

[7] Ram. Cart. i. 275, 491 n., 364.

[8] See below, and Rot. Hund. i. 41 : ' Non dederunt hundredariis nisi quinque marcas pro isto hundredo et modo xv marcas ' ; also Vill. in Eng., App. p. 441.

[9] P. Q. W., pp. 482, 495.

for suit. In the Hundred Rolls *hundredscot* occurs most commonly in Norfolk as one of the burdens on geldable land, part of the *geldagium* of the hundred, which is paid over to the king's bailiff unless the *geldagium* has been subtracted by lay lords or the church.[1] In Huntingdonshire the hundred aid was collected and kept by the Abbot of Ramsey for his own uses by reason of his regality.[2] In Staffordshire a hundred aid is mentioned occasionally,[3] and in Hereford *hundredfey*, which may, however, have included all sorts of perquisites of the bailiff of the hundred.[4] Outside of the Hundred Rolls it is found sometimes in manorial documents. It is mentioned once or twice as *hundredpeny* on church manors in Somersetshire, where it was collected probably by the church:[5] it occurs in descriptions of Gloucester manors as the *hundredsilver, hundredfe*, which was paid once by the customars in common,[6] and in another case was paid to the king as *hundredsilver*, or as *hundredwite*, by a tenant *pro capite suo*.[7] It may be referred to in the Domesday of St. Paul's, in the description of the year 1181 of Beauchamp in Essex, when it is stated that the manor defended itself for five hides and gave the sheriff 4s. and the reeve of the hundred 5s. by the hand of the *firmarius* of the manor.[8] It is very common also in lists of franchises.

The comparatively rare occurrence of the aid in the thirteenth century may be due to the fact that the hundreds were either in private hands, or if still in the hands of the king were usually farmed by bailiffs of the sheriff. Suit at court was so often commuted that probably the meetings, except those for the sheriff's tourn, were unimportant, and sparsely attended, and the aid once generally paid on such occasions to the presiding officer had become merged in the

---

[1] Rot. Hund. i. 469, 470, 527, 528, 531, 539, 540, 541.
[2] Ibid. ii. 629: 'Dat annuatim xij*d*. ad auxilium Vicecomitis et hundredi quos abbas de Rameseia percipere consuevit per regalitatem quam habet de Rege'; also pp. 605, 632, 666, 676, 680.
[3] Ibid. ii. 114.   [4] Ibid. i. 186.
[5] Bath and Wells Vac. Roll, 1131/3; Winch. Pipe Roll, Taunton.
[6] Glouc. Cart. iii. 158: 'et dabit hundredselver pro capite suo domino Regi'; and iii. 213; ii. 223.
[7] Ibid. iii. 104, 158.   [8] D. S. P., p. 114.

less specific perquisites of bailiffs or of the hundred, which
went to make up the farm. That there was not, however,
a tendency toward the final abandonment of any of the
sources of revenue in the hundred, whether royal or private,
is clearly enough shown in the Hundred Rolls, in the
exorbitant increase in the amount of farms since earlier times,
and the frequent references to the oppression of bailiffs.[1]

Wardsilver, Wardpenny, Streteward, Wakefe,[2] *Waytefe.*
One of the most common duties incumbent on geldable land
was the service of guard, ward, or watching, a service which
by the thirteenth century had often become commuted into
wardsilver, wardpenny, or some other payment for ward.
Various kinds of ward duty must be distinguished from one
another: some were manorial, some were feudal, some were
royal. Probably in origin, however, all kinds of ward were
royal or public services, and part of the maintenance of order
in the kingdom. Fairs and markets, for example, at which
watches were often made, were, in theory at least, always
franchises granted away with their appurtenant profits by the
king, while watching in manors might be considered part of
the duty of watch and ward, provided for in such detail in
the familiar series of regulations of Henry III and Edward I.
Ward duties of a higher nature also affected, indirectly, the
manorial classes. The ward incumbent on the military tenants
was usually castle guard. This duty, originally rendered in
service,[3] had by the thirteenth century, in a great number of
cases, become commuted, so that it was rendered in money in
time of peace, although sometimes still rendered in actual
service in time of war.[4] The service was paid at royal or
private castles, at the castles of the shires,[5] sometimes at the
castle of the hundred,[6] or at castles outside the shire which

---

[1] See below.   [2] Burt. Ch., pp. 93, 94.
[3] Compare the service of furnishing *castelmen* usual on Durham
manors; Bish. Hatf. Surv., pp. 21, 28, 129, 157 ; Bold. Bk., pp. 571, 579,
580, 584, 585, 586.
[4] Rot. Hund. ii. 232, 235, 236, 238 ; i. 27.
[5] Ibid. ii. 527, 549, 360 : The king has the Castle of Cambridge
' in manu sua cum comitatu '.
[6] Ibid. ii. 25, 31, 568, 705; i. 108, 113, 152 ; and ii. 214: a hundred
attached to a castle, see below.

were often the castles of the honour of which the fees were held.[1] The castle of Devizes could be guarded in time of peace, the Hundred Rolls state, by twenty-five marcs a year, and no less; and a long list of Wiltshire fees that owed ward at the castle, or had owed it in the past, is appended to the statement.[2] Fees in Bedfordshire owed ward or *ward-selver* at Rockingham and Beverley; in Buckinghamshire at Dover, Northampton, and Rochester; in Cambridgeshire at Cambridge, Rockingham, Craven, Richmond, and, by special arrangement with the Bishop of Ely, at the island of Ely;[3] in Kent at Dover and Rochester; in Lincolnshire at Rockingham; in Norfolk at Norwich and Dover; in Northamptonshire at Northampton, to whose ward we are told fifteen fees in different counties contributed,[4] and at Rockingham; in Oxfordshire at Dover, Banbury, and Windsor; and in Wiltshire at Devizes, and formerly, probably, at Old Sarum. These were some of the chief castles at which ward was due, according to the Hundred Rolls, and these the counties in which payment for ward is commonly mentioned.[5] The interest of the subject from the point of view of the manorial classes lies in the fact that the commuted service of the castle guard was borne by the customary tenants. The lord of the fee recouped himself for his payment by a collection from his tenants,[6] and, just as in the case of scutage, there was a presumption that the money for the payment would be taken from the military tenants of the lord, from the freeholders and important *censuarii*, rather than

---

[1] Rot. Hund. i. 20, 26, 29, 31, 491, 495; ii. 235, 460, 461, 486, 518, 567, 568, 580, 785.   [2] Ibid. ii. 236.

[3] Ibid. ii. 495; Claud. C. xi. f. 7: ' Et sit quieta de warda militum in castella nostra de Norwyco ita quod milites de honore S. Etheldrede qui solebant facere wardam in dicto castello faciant eam in Ely ad summonicionem Elyensis episcopi. Sit etiam quieta ipsa ecclesia de xxxvs. vd. *ob.* qui dabantur vigiliis ejusdem castelli de liberacione sua unoquoque anno de terra de S. Etheldrede et sit quieta de xls. de warthpeny qui requirabantur de terra sua et hominibus suis.'

[4] Ibid. i. 31; cf. i. 16; ii. 301.

[5] Cott. MSS. Julius F. x. f. 142 b (155 b) gives a list of the castles and towers in Northumberland, royal and private, the names of the castles in Hants, Sussex, Essex, Suffolk, Norfolk, Kent, Somerset, and Devon.

[6] Harl. MSS. 3977, f. 87.

from the villeins proper. Even more often than in the case of scutage, however, the presumption did not hold, and villeins paid their regular quota to the castle guard.[1] The villata sometimes paid the wardsilver in common, or through the lord, becoming responsible for the annual payment of a certain amount;[2] sometimes they paid it according to the number of inhabitants.[3] Very often the rent had got attached to certain tenements in the vill, and not to others.[4] Occasionally the assessment of payment for ward of some kind was made according to the number of animals owned by a man,[5] just as hidage was assessed according to tenement and beasts. Sometimes the ward is recorded in terms of days or weeks or even years,[6] sometimes again it was paid by a sort of rotatory system, a tenant paying men in alternate years.[7] All such arrangements would be the result of local convenience. Often, of course, the wardpenny, like other royal dues, was subtracted from the royal castle and retained by the lord, to the loss of the king.[8] At Forncett in Norfolk, and on Ely manors in the same county, the term *forward* or *forwardsilver*, or *forwach* occurs.[9] It seems to refer to castle guard or some other watching service.

The term *wardsilver* or, more often, *wardpenny*, was probably used also for the commutation of other wards than

---

[1] Rot. Hund. ii. 459, 499, 513, 846 ; Batt. Abb. Cust., p. 32. It is often not possible to tell what kind of ward is indicated by the common wardpenny often due from customary tenants.

[2] Ibid. i. 27, 31, 152 ; ii. 426, 456, 843.

[3] Reg. Worc. Pr., p. 171. The assessment at Ely was on the individual rather than the tenement. Thus the *plena terra*, the *dimidia terra*, and the *cotland* each gave a penny at Stratham, see Claud. C. xi. f. 43, cf. f. 176. Every *tenens de hundredo* gave a penny, see f. 54. The wardpenny belonged to the hundred (ff. 52, 54), but the hundred was in Ely's hands.

[4] D. S. P., pp. 72, 74, 85 ; Add. MSS. 35, 169, and elsewhere.

[5] Ram. Cart. i. 365, 390: 'Sciendum etiam quod quilibet habens in festo S. Martini vivum catallum ad valentiam triginta denariorum dabit in eodem festo ad warpeny unum obolum, sive fuerit virgatarius, sive croftarius'; Rot. Hund. i. 137: ward taken from beasts at pasture where the fee owed none. Again, ii. 453, and D. S. P., p. lxxx ; Vac. Roll, 1143/18 ; Kennet, Par. Antiq., vol. i. 450.

[6] Rot. Hund. i. 474 ; ii. 785.

[7] Ibid. i. 474; ii. 552, 864.

[8] Ibid. i. 49, 52, 53, 484, 526 ; ii. 432, 519, 534 ; P. Q. W., p. 234, *pass.*

[9] Davenport, Norf. Man. App. in the account rolls of 1272, 1376 ; Claud. C. xi. f. 234.

those of castles. Bridges were guarded, or the duty of guarding them commuted for a money rent.[1] Ward was kept also at the gates of towns,[2] 'and along the ways of the hundred,'[3] and in meadows near the Severn.[4] In the Hundred Rolls' accounts of Shropshire *streteward* takes the place of castle guard as the common payment.[5] *Streteward* is coupled regularly with *motfech* as the most important of the burdens on geldable land in the county, and is assessed usually, though not invariably, at the rate of fourpence on the hide.[6] The payment is not called *wardpenny* in this shire, but may well have gone under that name elsewhere. *Streteward* was probably simply part of the familiar duty of watch and ward, applied primarily to watches within villages, but including also the maintenance of order in the roads of townships. The legislation of Henry III and Edward I for the maintenance of order in the vills describes the watches of four or more men, the number varying according to the size of the vill, who are to ensure protection from any form of disturbance, and who have authority to arrest strangers over-night until they can prove the innocence of their intention.[7] A passage quoted by the editor of the Domesday of St. Paul's from the Domesday of 1222 is interesting as showing the incidence of watch and ward on the villagers. 'Whoever has cattle on the lands of the lord to the value of 30*d.* shall give one penny

---

[1] Ely Inqu., D. B. Add., p. 507 ; Rot. Hund. i. 30, and see pontage.

[2] Lib. Alb., p. 646 : ' Quod quilibet bedellus summoneat certos homines in warda sua armatos ad custodiendas Portas, et qui defecerit solvat loco suo substituto xij*d.*'

[3] Inqu. 1189, p. 84.

[4] Reg. Worc. Pr., p. 134 a : ' De vigilia prati de Kyngesham. Post primam falcationem prati de Kyngesham ultra Sabrinam usque dum fenum levetur faciant vigiliam in prato qualibet nocte successive.'

[5] Rot. Hund. ii. 778 (cf. stritpeni).

[6] Ibid. ii. 55, 56, 57, 62, 75, *pass.* ; P. Q. W., p. 93. The rate was higher in some hundreds, e. g. ii. 70 ; cf. ii. 83 : ' Dicunt quod hundredum de Stottesdene est in manu domini Regis et respondit vicecomiti annuatim de xiiij marcis excepto stretwarde quod valet per annum xviij*s.* 1*d.* et motfe xxxv*s.* 1*d.* et exceptis duobus turnis vicecomitis.'

[7] See Select Charters, p. 362, for the provisions of 1233 ; pp. 370–1 for the writ of 1252 ; p. 374 for the writ of 1253 ; and p. 469 for the provisions of the Statute of Winchester ; cf. Reg. Worc. Pr., 171 a ; and Leg. Will. Pr. i. 26 (Schmid, p. 341) : ' De chascuns x hidis del hundred un hume dedenz le feste S. Michel et la S. Martin ad stretwarde' ; Schmid, p. 355.

at the feast of St. Martin, which is called *wardpenny*, except those that are watching *de ward*, who watch at the royal street at night—(twelve names follow)—and they shall receive the *wardstaf* and make the summons of the watch, and shall be quit for the summons from the pennies which are called *wardpennys*.'[1] Another passage in the Domesday of St. Paul's shows the tenants of Chingford, free and villeins, anciently attending unsummoned three *lagehundreds* in the year.[2] At one of these, the Hokeday *lagehundred*, the tenants were bound 'praesentare quandam Wardam in quodam baculo qui vocatur Wardestaf.' When, later, the view of frankpledge was held by the bailiff of the hundred and the bailiff of the manor in the church of Chingford, 10*d*. was paid for *wardpenny*. The picturesque customs relating to the *wardstaff* are described in other accounts of Essex. A willow bough was cut in a certain wood on a certain day, it was wrapped in a 'faire fyne lynnen cloth' and taken by the bailiff (of the hundred) to the place assigned, where the lord and his tenants on whom the service of watch and ward devolved should attend. A rope was stretched across the road with a bell on the end, and near the bell was the staff laid on a pillow and representing the king's majesty. The bailiff called the roll:—
'The said Bailiffe shall severally call the names of all the aforesaid tenants, landowners, who shall present their said ordinarie number of men accordingly. Then shall the said Bailiffe in the king's name straightlie charge and comande them and everie of them to watch and keep the ward in due silence soe that the Kinghe harmless and the countrie scapeless until the sunne arising.' Notches were cut in the staff for the 'full ordinarie number of able men well harnessed with sufficient weapon' that appeared ready to perform the service. The staff was carried through towns and hundreds and then thrown out to sea.[3] There was thus ensured a 'yearly

[1] D. S. P., p. lxxx, quoting I. 28 (Survey of 1279).
[2] Ibid., p. lxxx, quoting I. 65.
[3] Charnock, Man. Cust. Essex, pp. 17 et seq.; for *wardstaf* see Rot. Hund. i. 155, ii. 235; Batt. Abb. Cust., p. 126: 'Baculus debet currere a festo S. Michaelis usque ad Nativitatem, et a Pascha usque ad festum S. Petri ad Vincula ; et sunt xiiij borgi scilicet . . .' (the names follow). For watching fugitives, see Rot. Hund. i. 240.

muster of fencible men' to guard the hundred against murder and robbery, for both of which it was liable to pay a fine. At Glastonbury the villeins guarded the way of the hundred.[1]

Sometimes the service of watching seems to have lost in large measure its royal character and to have become quasi-manorial. Thus the watches at fairs had become a customary service in the many cases where the fair, in origin royal, had become the franchise of a private lord. The Ramsey villeins commonly kept watch at the fair of St. Ives, each in his turn; but this service did not free the villein from the payment of *wardpenny* to the abbot for castle guard or other services of ward. It should be noted, however, that such watching at St. Ives or 'at other times for the guarding of robbers,' was sometimes considered as the equivalent of some purely manorial services to the lord.[2] In such cases the original royal service has become wholly manorialized. The Prior of Boulton in one instance seems to have used some watching service, a 'congregacio hominum que vocatur wach', as the occasion for instituting a fair and holding it without warrant.[3] Other forms of manorial watches are described in the Domesday of St. Paul. At Wicham in Essex the virgater watched one night around the *curia* of the lord at Christmas, a service which is described more fully in a later document quoted by the editor of the Domesday. The customary tenant was bound with other tenants of the same rank to provide that one of them should keep watch at the court from Christmas to Twelfth Day, and have a good fire in the hall, and food. If any damage were done during the watches, he that watched had to make the loss good unless he had raised the hue and cry for the village to go in pursuit. The editor believes that the commutation of this service would have been called *ward-*

---

[1] Inqu. 1189, p. 82: 'Ad custodiam regis obolum' (*bis*); and p. 84: 'custodiam reddunt ad custodiendum vias per hundredum.'
[2] Ram. Cart. i. 301: 'et vigilabit ibidem (at St. Ives) ad turnum suum quotiens dominus voluerit; et si summonitus fuerit die operis sui ad vigilandum, si in crastino illius noctis debeat operari, ab illa operatione erit quietus'; and pp. 290, 325, 337, 345, 354, 385, 390.
[3] P. Q. W., p. 212.

penny also.[1] The *messor* of the village watched the lord's crops at night.[2] Guarding the grange is a common manorial service commuted as the rent *hedernewech*.

It is clear enough that the same tenant might sometimes have to pay *wardpenny* or *wardsilver* to help his lord recoup himself for his castle guard, and might, in addition, have to perform some service connected with watch and ward, or some manorial watches.[3] Such matters would be managed differently in different manors, according to the convenience of the lord or communal custom. The assessment of the *wardpenny* upon the village, as has been said, was either in accordance with a man's tenement, certain tenements being charged with some such forinsec ward service just as they were charged with suit of court, or in accordance with the number of animals possessed by the tenant. Of course, where the profits of geldable land had been subtracted by the lord *wardpenny* was taken by him for his own uses, together with the other royal payments. The Hundred Rolls furnish many instances of the subtraction of it 'to the grave loss of the king', and in the compotus rolls it is accounted for among the regular profits of the lord of the manor.

Pontage. Another common impost, in origin public or royal, was the pontage or duty of maintaining by labour or money contributions the public bridges, a service not to be confused with the *passagium*, or toll for passing over the bridge, or the *briggeward* paid in commutation of the duty of watching it. In the thirteenth century the levy of pontage had become in so many cases a franchise and a means of extortion that it is difficult to discover the original system of assessment; clearly, however, the duty of maintaining the chief bridge of the county, that is to say, the bridge in the chief town, was, in Cambridgeshire and Nottinghamshire in any case, incumbent on the county.[4] In the Quo Warranto

---

[1] D. S. P., note, p. lxxiii, quoting I. 98, and p. 34: 'et vigilabit circa curiam domini una nocte Nath' ad cibum domini'; Harl. MSS. 3977, f. 86 : 'wardbedrips' [probably for waterbedrips?].
[2] Claud. C. xi. f. 117.
[3] Rot. Hund. i. 152, 156; ii. 448; and Ram. Cart., references given above.   [4] P. Q. W., pp. 633, 655.

Rolls the obligation is sometimes placed with some clearness. The pontage is defined in relation to certain tenants-in-chief as the actual *factura* of the bridges, the maintenance of them according to certain fixed dimensions, and not as a money fine,[1] and it is shown that the actual labour was to be performed by the villeins of the lord in question, or on certain ancient demesne manors by his sokemen, the wood for repairs being furnished by the lord. Thus in Hertfordshire bridges had been allowed to become weak, and the king, on a recent visit, had incurred grave danger. A long list of the tenants holding by pontage service is therefore given, with the names of the bridges at which their service was due, and the exact amount of service, either in the making of small bridges or in the number of feet of repair on larger ones, to be performed, and three tenements are especially mentioned on whose holders was incumbent a duty of bridge inspection, the duty of examining all the bridges of the county before a royal visitation to see that they were in repair, and of riding over them before the king.[2] Pasture privileges were sometimes held in return for pontage.[3] In the fen district of Lincolnshire bridge services and the related making of ditches and gutters were of special importance, and the responsibility for them was laid very definitely upon certain abbots and priors and their tenants, who are declared to be responsible according to the acreage of their tenements, 'every acre being equal to every other acre in this region.'[4] The duty of maintaining Rochester bridge was distributed pier by pier. The Bishop of Rochester was responsible for the first pier, for the planting

---

[1] P. Q. W., p. 633 : ' Abbas et omnes monachi sui et omnes res et homines eorum villani quieti sunt et liberi de omnibus quietanciis supradictis except' de pontagio tamen si per hoc verbum pontagium intelligatur factura pontis quia dicunt quod idem abbas et homines suis facere debent pontem Notingham qui dicitur le Tounbrigge una cum tota communitate comitatus Notingham'; see also pp. 284, 745, 748. Cf. Feod. Dun., p. 27 ; Glouc. Cart. iii. 51.

[2] Ibid., pp. 284–6, especially 286: 'Per tale servicium quod ipsi contra adventum domini R. predictum deberent circuire omnia loca ubi predicti pontes debent fieri et videre quod bene et sufficienter fient et equitare ante dominum Regem'; cf. Rot. Hund. i. 118.

[3] Ibid., p. 284: 'pro pastura habenda ad duodecim animalia.'

[4] Ibid., p. 406.

of three 'virgates' or rods, and the finding of three 'sullives', and this duty was performed for him by four of his vills. He was responsible for the third pier also, and the other piers were apportioned to others, the sixth being divided among many tenants of sulungs, juga, and acres.[1]

In general, pontage was due from the geldable hides of the county, and might be levied by the sheriff when occasion demanded. Religious houses were usually exempt, but were sometimes, perhaps as a survival of the old bridge-building service, held for the maintenance of certain bridges.[2] The Templars, for example, were responsible with the community of the county for the *Tounebrigge* of Nottingham,[3] and Ely for the bridge at Alderhithe.[4] Within the exempt fees pontage was levied in many cases by the lord of the fee as he might wish, often as a money payment of regular annual amount. In Ramsey pontage was paid by the ' free hides of Hirstingston hundred ' and by many of the customary tenants, and the collection of it was a regality exercised by the abbot.[5] The corrupt practices and methods of extortion of lords and of sheriffs are frequent causes of complaint in the Hundred Rolls, and some excellent examples of their evil doings are given. The Bishop of Ely, instead of keeping in repair the bridge and causeway of Alderhithe, a royal way, for which, as has been said, he was responsible, left it *dissolutum* for sixteen years, and established a ferry at which he took a toll of a halfpenny from every horseman and a farthing from every foot-passenger, his receipts being so large that he sometimes let the ferry at farm for as much as 20s. a year.[6] Other pontages too were exacted by the bishop. The vill of Chatteris paid him a yearly sum to be exempt from extra-

---

[1] Lambard's Perambulation of Kent, pp. 415, *et seq.*; cf. Stat. Realm, 21 Rich. II. The old bridge had been destroyed by Simon de Montfort, and by severe frosts in the following years.

[2] Rot. Hund. i. 221 : 'Et idem cepit et injuste asportavit xxx*s.* de collectione pontagii Roff' tocius hundredi predicti et communie.'

[3] P. Q. W., p. 655.

[4] Rot. Hund. ii. 411.

[5] Ram. Cart. i. 287, 295, 309, *pass.*

[6] Rot. Hund. ii. 411 : 'Dicunt quod calceta et pons de Alderhethe est regalis via et fuit fracta et dissoluta jam per sexdecim annos elapsos et debet reparari per Episcopum Eliens' et per tenentes suos.'

ordinary imposts,[1] and other Ely vills paid *briggebot*.[2]   Much
worse offenders were the sheriffs of Cambridgeshire.   The
great bridge of Cambridge was weak, and whenever it needed
repair it was the custom for the sheriff to levy a pontage on
the geldable hides of the county.   William le Moygne during
his sheriffdom took a shilling from every geldable hide, and
rendered no account of his expenditure, but repaired only
part of the bridge, pocketing meanwhile 40s. passage money.[3]
Still more extortionate was Robert de Lestire; in his
sheriffdom the bridge was broken by a great flood, and
Robert allowed it to remain untouched for six weeks and
more, making meanwhile a *bargia* or ferry and carrying
passengers over for a toll, 'to the loss of the country ten
pounds.'[4]   On this occasion, or some other like it, the same
unrighteous sheriff made a ferry and took 100s. from it, and
in addition levied 15d. pontage on every geldable hide before
he repaired the bridge.[5]   Again, he took once a pontage of
2s. from every hide where there had never been taken more
than 6d. *ad hidam*, and applied only one-third of the proceeds
to the bridge.[6]   When the county forced him, on another
occasion, to repair the bridge, he used very light stones and
woodwork.[7]   Still again, to bring the tale of his iniquities to
a close, he took from the poor men of Barnwell 40s. when he
ought to have taken only a mark, 'nor did he ever apply that
money to the bridge.'[8]   The sheriff of Lincoln declared that
a sound bridge was weak and levied a pontage.[9]   Other
sheriffs seized the chattels of individuals and refused to return
them until a very high pontage of 16d. had been paid.[10]   Sometimes the towns had taken over the maintenance of the bridge
and held it at farm.[11]

---

    [1] Ram. Cart. i. 437.
    [2] Vac. Roll, 1132/10: (Lyndon) 'et de ijs. de quodam certo redditu
quod vocatur Briggebot.'
    [3] Rot. Hund. ii. 407.   Compare pp. 452, 481.
    [4] Ibid. i. 55.   Compare i. 52; ii. 407, 452, 481.
    [5] Ibid. ii. 407.   [6] Ibid. i. 50, 52, 54.
    [7] Ibid. i. 54.   [8] Ibid. i. 50.
    [9] Ibid. i. 258.   [10] Nott. Rec. i. 82.
    [11] Rot. Hund. i. 406: 'Dicunt etiam quod cum pons London' fuisset
multo tempore in manibus civium civitatis et semper consueverint
de communi assensu facere custodem ad commune proficuum domini

With the pontage is often connected the *pavage, pavagium*, or *paagium*, which is defined in the Liber Albus as the tax levied on horses or vehicles 'for keeping the middle of the street in repair',[1] and appears in the Hundred Rolls, especially in Lincolnshire, as money taken to sustain the paving of the bridge or causeway.[2] It was levied upon boats, foot-passengers, horses, and carts, and was in these cases a toll rather than a regular impost. Occasionally, however, certain tenements were definitely responsible for the *paagia*, probably as part of their duty of maintenance of bridges.[3] With this or murage the old *stangeld* may perhaps be identified.[4]

Muragium. Of murage, or the money paid for wall-work, there is less frequent evidence than of pontage. In the Hundred Rolls it occurs usually in the descriptions of Lincolnshire as a common article of inquiry in the wapentakes and as a common burden in the borough. It was granted to the citizens of Lincoln by Henry III, and the mayors collected it for their own uses, through receivers who carried peculation very far. An honest collector who rendered a faithful account is mentioned as an exception.[5] The money which should have been spent 'ad emendacionem murorum civitatis'[6] was usually kept for the private uses of the receiver, who on one occasion refused to render any account of his expenditures, beyond stating the amount of his balance and declaring that the rest had been spent on the walls; 'where, however, that money was expended,' the jurors say, 'we do not know, since it does not appear in the walls or in any other works of the lord king.'[7] Occasionally the term murage seems to refer to the actual stone used in the wall-work, which was sometimes taken unjustly and used for private buildings.[8] Two receivers

Regis et sue civitatis et omnium transeuncium nunc est dictus pons in manibus domine Regine . . . est in magno periculo cadendi.'
[1] Munim. Gildh. vol. 2, pt. 2, pp. 818, 819.
[2] Rot. Hund. i. 249, 259, 293, 298, 308, 314, 321, 322, 333, 385, 402, *pass.* ; P. Q. W., p. 392.
[3] Ibid. i. 249.   [4] P. Q. W., p. 550.
[5] Rot. Hund. i. 322.
[6] Ibid. i. 108, 259, 276, 298, 301, 304, 314, 315, 322, 338, 355, 398, 399 ; ii. 517.   [7] Ibid. i. 315.
[8] Ibid. i. 322 : 'fecit cariare apud Sanctum Botulphum meliorem

took rock to the value of 100s. from a quarry at Lincoln which belonged to the murage and kept it, and one of them carried to St. Botulph the same excellent stone and made himself a house valued at £20, and with murage and *boistagium* bought arable land.

Boistagium. A rent called *boistagium* occasionally appears, once in connexion with murage,[1] and seems to be explicable as a payment made for wood to be used in public works. One of the franchises often claimed by religious houses, and especially by the Hospitallers, was freedom from requisitions of wood for royal buildings or fortifications.[2] Similar payments were *truncage*,[3] and possibly *bustsilver*[4] and *wodwelschot*, the last a curious rent lingering in the hundred of Northgrenehow in Norfolk, and clearly royal,[5] and the Ramsey *wodehac*, due from free hides of Hirstingston hundred.[6] A *tolnetum buste navium* is mentioned as a royal due at Windsor.[7]

The line between payments like these, for the maintenance of public works and fortifications, and tolls taken on various occasions is sometimes very difficult to draw. The history of tolls forms a subject by itself, or is part of the study of customs revenue or of trade and towns rather than of cus-

petram scissatam de quareria Linc' et liberam et ibi fecerit quandam domum de dicto muragio ad valenciam xx*li*.'; cf. p. 315.

[1] Rot. Hund. i. 322 : 'de pecunia muragii et boistagii Linc'.'

[2] P. Q. W., p. 503 : land freed from ' operibus castellorum parcorum et poncium clausuris et omni careio et summagio et navigio et domum regalium edificacione et omnimoda operacione. Et quod ne bosci eorum ad predicta opera vel ad aliqua alia ullo modo capiantur et quod bladum eorum vel hominum suorum vel aliquid de rebus suis vel hominum suorum ad castella munienda non capiantur.' Cf. pp. 464, 538, 654.

[3] Red Bk. Excheq. ii. ccxlvii, referring to the carrying of timber for the fortification of Bamburgh Castle.

[4] Reville, Le Soulèvement des Travailleurs d'Angleterre, App., p. 260 ; ' de quadam custuma vocata poundale et bustsilver', taken at markets, from merchandise sold.

[5] Rot. Hund. i. 526 : ' Et de iiij*s*. x*d. ob.* de quodam annuo redditu qui vocatur wodewelschot' ; again, 483 : 'subtrahunt v*s*. vij*d. qu.* quos reddere solebant ad com' Norwic' quod vocatur wodewellshot' ; *passim* in the description of the hundred.

[6] Ram. Cart. i. 297 : 'Forinsecum servitium cum wodehac' ; again, iii. 324 : 'Item solutae vicecomiti Huntindoniae pro Wdehac x marcae' ; and i. 284, 288, 296, 297, 308, *pass.*

[7] Rot. Hund. i. 18 : ' Tota villata de Eton solebat dare tolnetum buste navium et omnia regale tangencia.'

tomary rents. *Prisage, stremtol, watertol, aquage, ankerage, kaiage, keletol, quarterage, rivage, wharfage, butlerage, lestage, mensurage, pesage, tonnage, tronage, ulnage* have little to do in most cases with ordinary manorial life. Yet the records do not distinguish clearly between regular and occasional sources of revenue, the difference between public and private dues was often lost, and there was, moreover, a constant tendency to put uncertain and occasional obligations *ad certum*, at a fixed annual sum, an arrangement preferred by the lord and apparently acquiesced in by the villata. It might become the 'custom of the manor' for almost any occasional due or toll to be paid *ad certum*. The tolls most frequently so converted, to which, in any case, whether as fixed or occasional rents, the villeins were most often subject, were the tolls for passage of one kind or another, and the tolls connected with buying or selling in the ordinary village market.

The most important tolls taken for passage were the following:—

Cheminagium. Chiminage was the toll exacted for passage through the forest. To the warden of the forest belonged certain perquisites of office, collected for him by the foresters, among which were fines for lawing dogs, dead and dry wood, collected without an iron instrument, bark and crops of oak, windfall, *cablish*, pleas of little thorns called *bestnaweger*, of those, namely, that 'cannot be perforated with an auger', nuts, hens, oats, retropannage, and chiminage.[1] Chiminage was collected from those not living in the forest who passed through it with carts or horses, either for the purpose of carrying goods and merchandise,[2] in which cases the toll was properly a *transversum*, or for the purpose of collecting from it certain kinds of wood.[3] The amount of chiminage due to the foresters is clearly stated in Henry III's charter: it was 2*d.* a cart for the first half-year, and 2*d.* for the second half-year, and a

---

[1] Rot. Hund. i. 22, 24, 26 ; ii. 40 ; Sel. Pleas. For., p. 122.
[2] Rot. Hund. ii. 848 ; Burt. Ch., p. 151.
[3] Sel. Pleas. For., p. 8 ; Rot. Hund. ii. 267 : 'De qualibet carecta differente buscam brueram et turbas de Nova foresta . . . unum denarium ' ; and ii. 233, 248, 249.

halfpenny from a horse for the first half-year and another halfpenny for the second. Usually, however, the foresters took far in excess of this amount; from a poor man with wood on his back, for example, 6*d.* ; from a rich man as much as can be got; from a cart 2*s.*, 3*s.*, 4*s.* ; from a horse with a load 12*d.*, 16*d.*, 18*d.* ; 'to raise the fine which they have made with the chief forester.'[1] The Hundred Rolls have many references to the unjust tolls levied in the name of chiminage. Thus in Wiltshire the Earl of Gloucester had afforested a large district (*totam patriam*), probably inclusive of several hundreds, and had put in office foresters who were taking chiminage.[2] Royal foresters were constantly exercising their power unjustly, and long lists of grievances were presented at the eyre.[3] Chiminage was occasionally paid at a regular annual rate by an individual or a villata, and in such cases may be rightly included among customary rents. Thus in Oxfordshire all in the vill of Hensington gave the chief forester 2*s.* for which they had free chiminage in the forest, for collecting *virgae* for their ploughs, three times a year, and for collecting old brushwood through the rest of the year.[4] All the villata of Parva Trewe gave the same forester 6*d.* for chiminage.[5] Occasionally a customary tenant made individual fine for his chiminage.[6] The English form of chiminage was probably *weypeny*,[7] and in Durham a similar payment made by a vill was called *forestagium.*[8]

Thurctol. *Thurctol, thurghtol,* variously spelled, was paid

---

[1] Sel. Pleas. For., pp. 8, 125-8.
[2] Rot. Hund. ii. 233, 245, 248, 249, 267 ; i. 47, 152.
[3] Sel. Pleas. For., pp. 125-8.
[4] Rot. Hund. i. 24, 25, 26, 28, 64, 76, 152, ii. 874 ; ii. 866 : 'et villatae de Derneford et de Wichel dant forestario de Wichewod de certo per annum xij*d.* ad habendum liberum cheminagium eundo ad forestam et redeundo de foresta et viij*d.* pro ward' ballivo hundredi ' ; and Batt. Abb. Cust., p. 92.
[5] Ibid. ii. 875.
[6] Ibid. i. 28 : a customary tenant gives 'per hyemem pro chiminagio 2*s.* et per estatem 4*s.*'; and i. 24, 25.
[7] Ibid. ii. 214 : 'Forestarii . . . recipiunt ubique weypeny.'
[8] Feod. Dun., pp. lxxii, lxxxvi, 233 : No one is to take in the forest wood or vert except by permission or view of the bishop's bailiff, 'nisi mortuum boscum, pro quo villatae vicinae dant forestagium, sive capiant sive non,

when merchandise passed through a vill or through the demesne of a lord where there was no common way. Thus the Bishop of Ely took 2*d.* from every cart passing through his demesne, from every horseload 1*d.*, and from every footload a farthing.[1] *Thurctol* was not justly taken in 'the common road where every one goes freely'.[2] If manors lay on two sides of a 'civitas', and a plough were driven across, *thurctol* was paid.[3]

Passagium. *Passagium* was the general toll taken commonly from boats passing under bridges or into and out of ports, and from foot-passengers and carts passing over bridges or ferries. The passage by water was very often obstructed or in some way made the occasion of unjust levies. Thus the passage over the Ouse, once free, became subject to toll;[4] boats going into Huntingdon were impeded by a *stagnum,* where *passagium* was taken;[5] and in Devonshire, especially, many extortions were practised.[6]

Occasionally the *passagium* may have been paid as an annual rent, and may refer to passage through a manor.[7] It sometimes occurs in the Latin forms, *transversum*[8] and *transitum viae,*[9] and in the form *travers.*[10] *Viagium* may be the same toll.[11] *Pedagium* levied on foot-passengers occurs in

quemdam certum redditum, quidam gallinas, ut audivit pro virgis et aliis aisiamentis ad carucas'; and pp. 236, 237, 240 ; cf. also Red Bk. Excheq. ii. 657, 682.

[1] P. Q. W., p. 584; compare pp. 154, 212, 302, 392, 401, 415, 552, 557, *pass.*

[2] Ibid., p. 546.

[3] Rot. Hund. i. 126: 'Et si aliquis maneria habeat ex utraque parte civitatis et ducat suam carucam per mediam civitatem ballivi capiunt teoloneum quod vocatur thurctol'; and i. 120, 121.

[4] Ibid. i. 105 ; cf. ii. 7, 106, 411, 517.

[5] Ibid. i. 198.   [6] Ibid. i. 76, 77, 81.

[7] Feod. Dun., p. 83; Rot. Hund. ii. 702; Burt. Ch., p. 119.

[8] P. Q. W., p. 418 : the *transversum* belongs to the manor.

[9] Eng. Hist. Rev. xv, 499; Winch. Pipe Roll, p. 80.

[10] P. Q. W., p. 730: 'Et episcopus (of Norwich) venit et quoad predictum Travers dicit quod predecessores sui et ipse capere consueverunt quoddam Travers de mercatoribus extraneis transeuntibus quendam pontem in eadem cum mercandisis suis ... ad sustentacionem predicti pontis ita quod nullus de patria aliquid ibi dat et dicit quod si predictum Travers auferetur predictus pons decideret.'

[11] Rot. Hund. ii. 705 : 'Tota villata ... dat domino xij*d.* pro viagio'; cf. Reg. Worc. Pr., p. 78 b.

lists of immunities.[1]   *Haleday toll*, perhaps a toll levied on
a holiday, from those passing along the highway is once
mentioned.[2]

Other tolls which were sometimes turned into fixed rents,
and were in any case closely connected with the customary
tenants, were those due in the ordinary rural markets, and at
the buying or selling of merchandise or cattle. There were
many tolls of this kind, some of which have been discussed
already. Goods brought into a town by buyers or sellers
were subject to a toll at the gate called *Huctol et Dortol*;[3]
goods brought by strange merchants were subject to *scavage,
sceawyn, ostensio*.[4] The most common toll at the market was
the *stallagium* or toll paid for 'stondynge in strites in feyre
tyme', for having stalls in markets or fairs,[5] the English
equivalent of which was probably the Durham *bothsilver*.[6]
The receipts from stallage were among the large perquisites
of markets.[7] Occasionally the villein helped in the construc-
tion of booths or stalls as part of his regular work.[8]

Pacagium is mentioned in connexion with stallage.[9] *Pikagium* occurs, occasionally, as the duty charged on fairs and
markets for licence to break the ground or pitch stalls.[10]
Many tolls for buying and selling, for weighing and measuring,
must often be included in the general *teoloneum nundinarum*.[11]

---

[1] Riev. Cart., p. 365 n. 2 ; Munim. Gild., vol. 2, pt. 2, p. 665 and gloss.
[2] Rot. Hund. i. 461 : 'Episcopus Norwic' facit purpresturas super
dominum Regem eo quod sine waranto capit toloneum quod vocatur
Haleday tol et pro eo usualiter distringit in via regia.'
[3] Ibid. i. 127 : 'quia ceperunt teoloneum de rebus venditis et emptis
extra forum venale . . . ad ostia vendencium et emencium et vocant illud
teoloneum Dortol et Huctol. Et si vendentes vel ementes in aliquo
illis contradixerint illos amerciant et alia faciunt contra usum antiquum.'
[4] Munim. Gild. vol. 3, 58, 230 ; Red Bk. Excheq. iii. 1033 ; compare
Commune of London, p. 255.
[5] Higden, Polychronicon, ii. 96 ; Nott. Rec. i. 62 ; Lib. de Hyd.,
p. 44 ; Rot. Hund. i. 408, 431.
[6] Bish. Hatf. Surv., p. 100.
[7] Rot. Hund. i. 16, 132 ; ii. 214, 286 ; Feod. Dun., pp. 236, 238, 243 ;
Glouc. Cart. iii. 179.
[8] Bish. Hatf. Surv., p. 190: 'In nundinis S. Cuthberti singuli ii
villani (faciunt) i botham' ; Hone, Manor, pp. 237, 239.
[9] Feod. Dun., pp. 236, 238.
[10] Nott. Rec. ii. 351 ; Kennet, Par. Antiq. i. 156.
[11] For large receipts from this source see Min. Acc. 1128/4, 1131/3,
1132/5, 1141/1, 1143/18, 1144/1.

The instances of special unjust tolls on merchandise and cattle entered in the Hundred Rolls and elsewhere are far too numerous to be given.[1] Travellers were often at the mercy of plundering officers of royal towns and villages, and of extortionate men like the four messors in Lincolnshire who acted for their lords.[2]

Impositions of another kind, very burdensome to the customary tenants, resulted from the undue use of the opportunity of collecting various rents which went with the office of royal or private bailiff. Oppressive measures were especially common in raising farms. Hundreds, whether royal or private, were often put at undue farms, and the burden of raising the sums required, in money or in kind, fell in large measure in the last instance upon the villagers. Examples of unjust exactions are given in the Hundred Rolls of almost every county. Alexander Hameldene, the extortionate sheriff of Bedfordshire, systematically raised the farms;[3] in Buckinghamshire the sheriff held the hundreds at higher farm than he ought, and his bailiffs oppressed the people by collecting sheaves and the like;[4] in Yorkshire[5] and Essex[6] the same custom prevailed. In Gloucestershire a hundred was much oppressed by a multitude of bailiffs; where once there were only five, later the bailiff appointed a sub-bailiff, and the sub-bailiff appointed other bailiffs.[7] In Suffolk, St. Edmund had eight and a half hundreds, and he let them all in most unsaintly fashion at much too high a farm, to the injury of the whole liberty.[8] In Cornwall a hundred, once royal and farmed at £8, became private and was farmed at £40, by the extortion and malice of the bailiffs,[9] and in Kent a lord made a hundred pay 20s. to the Exchequer which he himself should

---

[1] Rot. Hund. i. 90, 118, 122, 123, 124, 126, 127, 185, 280, 345, 377, 397, 441, 473, 533, 535, 538; Norw. Leet, 17, 21, 35, 38, 59; Burt. Ch., p. 71.
[2] Ibid. i. 258.   [3] Ibid. i. 4.
[4] Ibid. i. 40, 41.
[5] Ibid. i. 110, 111, 115, 118, 127, 128.
[6] Ibid. i. 136, 139, 143, 150, 153, 158, 159.   [7] Ibid. i. 172.
[8] Ibid. ii. 143, 155, 182: 'Dicunt quod Abbas de Sancto Edmundo tradidit istud hundredum diversis ballivis ad altam firmam per quod populus patrie multum gravatur. Ita quod ubi non reddidit nisi iiij^{or}*li.* modo reddit viij*li.*'   [9] Ibid. i. 56.

have paid.[1] The cry against the bailiffs, royal or private, is insistent enough, and is evidently raised by the men of the vills. The farm, as in the time of Domesday Book, became a burden *quod non potest pati.* Its exact weight upon the vills of the hundred is, however, difficult to measure, and it is difficult also to tell how much of its unjust excess was due to the systematic increase in the rents of which it was composed, how much to occasional exactions from individuals. Certainly out of the profits of the hundred, in some way, year after year, the sum required had to be raised, and when the regular sources of profit proved insufficient, additional ones had to be supplied.

There is special insistence in the Hundred Rolls on the grievance of the collection of rents in kind for the farm, a grievance so common that it suggests for the undue exactions of extortionate bailiffs some basis of ancient privilege of office, some old purveyance rights. The officers of the king should receive their *fastung* like the *festingmenn* of the Saxon Charters, and the *raglots* and *ringilds* and *coidars* of the Welsh law. Food rents had once formed an important part of the *firma comitatus*, although by the thirteenth century they had usually long been commuted. Requisitions of food are mentioned especially in the rolls for Buckinghamshire,[2] Devonshire,[3] Hereford,[4] Shropshire,[5] and Lincolnshire.[6] They were made by sheriffs and their bailiffs,[7] and, commonly, by foresters and constables. In Nottinghamshire the number of *servientes*, and consequently the demands for hay and corn, had been largely increased, to the great distress of the county.[8]

---

[1] Rot. Hund. i. 227; cf. i. 51, 100; ii. 7, 20, 38, 469, *pass.*

[2] Ibid. i. 40: ' Omnes vicecomites tradunt hundreda sua ad altas firmas . . . et hac de causa ballivi gravant populum multis modis eo quod colligunt garbas in autumpno fenum in estate bladum trituratum in quadragesima denarios et alia.'

[3] Ibid. i. 84.   [4] Ibid. i. 186.

[5] Ibid. ii. 108: ' sed . . . extorquunt garbos et blada similiter ipse (firmarius) et ballivi sui ad gravamen patrie.'

[6] P. Q. W., pp. 390, 421.

[7] Rot. Hund. ii. 31, 307, 848; i. 25, 225, 456; cf. i. 138: where ' deberent panem vinum et servisiam secundum consuetudinem regni ballivi de hundredo et de honore de Reilee amerciant eos ad eorum voluntatem et capiunt de eis emend' in denariis.'

[8] Rot. Hund. ii. 307 : Where there used to be in a certain wapentake

In parts of Buckinghamshire foresters took money rents from certain manors, undue chiminage, hens, oats, retropannage, and dead wood.[1] In Oxfordshire they took poultry ' at the will of the giver '.[2] In one case a private forester took a day's entertainment.[3] Constables of castles were even more extortionate. To a castle might appertain manors,[4] woods,[5] hundreds[6]—to the castle and county of Northampton pertained, once, the shire of Rutland;[7] it was also in receipt of labour services, and of rents of various kinds, in addition to castle guard. To the castle of Marleberg, for example, the hundred supplied men for ploughing, haying, reaping, and carting services.[8] The castle was the prison[9], and it had a court like the tourn,[10] presided over by the constable. Private castles, or royal castles in private hands, claimed privileges like those exercised by castles still royal. The constable had thus great opportunities for extortionate demands which, according to the Hundred Rolls, he was not slow to use.[11] The provision contained in charters of certain

only six ' servientes pedites ibi sunt modo duo bedelli equitantes cum duobus suis garcionibus in le Nordelay et duo bedelli pedites in le Sudclay et duo sunt in Haytfield unde unus equitans et alius ad pedem per quod patria multum aggravatur et maxime ex hoc quod colligunt fenum in fenacione et garbas in autumpno et avenam.'

[1] Rot. Hund. i. 24, 25, 26, 33 : 'forestarii pedes aliquando colligunt avene garbas gallinas sua non ex consuetudine sed ex gratia'; and ii. 40, 249, 710 ; P. Q. W., p. 83.

[2] Ibid. ii. 40 : ' colligunt gallinas contra Natale scilicet aliquando xl aliquando plures aliquando pauciores quia nullus dat nisi ad voluntatem suam.'

[3] Ibid. ii. 337 : 'et pascet forestarium dicti Prioris ad Natale Domini per i diem.'

[4] Ibid. ii. 234, 287.   [5] Ibid. i. 52.

[6] Ibid. ii. 234 ; cf. i. 227.   [7] Ibid. ii. 1.

[8] Ibid. ii. 234 : ' Jur' presentant quod hundredum istud est liberum hundredum domini Regis et pertinens ad Castrum de Marleberg'. . . . Dicunt quod xliij solidatas et iiij denarios de redditu assiso de predicto hundredo pertinent ad castrum de Merleberg. Et similiter predictum hundredum invenit de consuetudine predicto castro per annum xv carucas ad arandum apud La Bertone ad frumentum et xv ad avenam et l homines ad sarclandum et xvij homines ad prata falcanda et xvij carectas ad fena ducenda et l homines ad blada metenda et xvij carectas ad blada carianda per unum diem.'

[9] Ibid. i. 538.   [10] Ibid. i. 113, 352 ; ii. 234, 301.

[11] Rot. Hund. ii. 225 ; i. 76, 113, 473, 538 ; see also Winch. Pipe Roll, p. 73 : ' In braseo in hospitio die Natalis pro hundredo de consuetudine i quarterium in prebenda constabularii, ibidem in adventu suo i quarterium '; compare Madox, Baronia, p. 19.

churches, and of the Hospitallers, that the corn of the Master
or abbot shall not be taken for the castle, is usually united
with the provision that private wood shall not be taken for
royal buildings.[1] Sheriffs and *castellani* are forbidden to
' vex the monks, in droves of oxen, or in any other thing, as
they have been accustomed to do, but to buy all such beasts
in markets as do others coming from afar '.[2] The constable
had, probably, a fee of his own attached to his office, and
personal purveyance rights.[3]

One common method by which foresters, bailiffs of sheriffs,
and bailiffs of private lords put money into their own purses
was the holding of scotales, or enforced beer drinkings.[4] We
can distinguish manorial scotales, on the model probably of
those held by king's officers, scotales of the sheriff and his
bailiffs, from which freedom was granted by charter,[5] foresters'
scotales, holy ales, church ales, leet ales, filsun ales, lamb ales,
clerk ales, bread ales, midsummer ales, gystales, field ales,
tenants' ales, bydales, Whitsun ales, Easter ales, bridales, and
wetherhales.[6]

The manorial scotales were held on the manor by the reeve
at certain seasons of the year, perhaps to celebrate the accom-
plishment of certain parts of the routine of agriculture.   On
a manor of St. Paul's the demesne land had to furnish 7*d*.,
and the hearth of every tenant of the vill a penny, to a scotale,

---

[1] P. Q. W., pp. 464, 503, 538, 654 ; cf. pp. 383, 742 ; and Rot. Hund.
i. 80 ; ii. 15, 106, 237.   [2] P. Q. W., p. 643.

[3] Rot. Hund. ii. 278 : ' Item comes Herefordie tenet unam carucatam
terre in Cuweleston' de domino Rege in capite pertinens (*sic*) ad con-
stabular'.'

[4] For scotales in general see Du Cange, and Spelman, and Stat.
Realm, i. 120, 234, 321 ; Hampson, Med. Aev. Kal. i. 287, 288 ; Norton,
Const. City of London, pp. 386, 387 ; D. S. P., p. cvii ; Mich. Ambr.
Rent., p. 143 ; Hibbert, Ashton under Lyne, p. 18 ; Hone, Manor, pp. 94,
119, 229 ; Hist. Fund. Batt., p. 20.

[5] P. Q. W., p. 281 : ' De chacer ad establ' de scothale Regis et auxiliis
seu donis vicecomitis et ballivorum.'

[6] See Hampson's lists, Med. Aev. Kal., pp. 281, 282, 287, and Ram. Cart.
i. 312, 493 (the wetherhale) ; Hampson quotes (p. 287) 26 H. VIII. cap. 6,
which prohibits unlicensed persons from collecting commorth, Bydale,
or tenant's ale.   Commorth (cf. 4 H. IV. cap. 27) is defined as contributions formerly collected on marriages or when young priests first sang
masses (but see Bl. Bk. S. Davids, and above under *metride*), bydale
as the invitation to drink ale after the manner of a housewarming, and
tenants' ale as the feast provided by the tenants.

called elsewhere the scotale of the reeve.[1] On Winchester manors the bailiff is constantly accounting for the wine and cider expended in the scotales.[2] Fuller accounts of the manorial scotales occur in Michael Ambresbury's Rental of Glastonbury. To have a scotale is declared to be the lord's right and duty, and the people are bound to attend. The young men and the married come on Saturday to drink at the Cunninghale ; on Sunday and Monday husbands and wives come and bring a penny, and young men on Sunday bring a halfpenny. On Monday night the young men may drink without a fee if they are below the settle. The *plena scotalla* should last three days, and the free and customary tenants are distinguished from one another by the places assigned them. A villein drank three such scotales, one before Michaelmas, to which he went with his wife and gave 3*d.*, and two after Michaelmas, at which he gave 2½*d.* Special provisions were made regarding *extranei* and those in the service of others.[3] The great marling feasts, called gystales in Lancashire, held in the spring after the manuring with marl, yielded to the lord as much as 20*s.*[4] Hampson's tenants' ale is clearly a manorial scotale of this kind,[5] and so also is the

---

[1] D. S. P., Introd., p. cviii, quoting I. 65 : ' De dominico ad scotallam vij*d.* et de quolibet astro tenentium ejusdem villae 1*d.* ad scotallam ' ; again, p. 144 : ' Veniebant homines ejusdem tenementi ad scotallam prepositi.'

[2] Winch. Pipe Rolls, p. 20 : ' Reddit compotum . . . de xxiij*s.* pro 1 tonello dimidio vini ad scotallam' ; again, pp. 41, 52, 55 (scotale of cider), 64 (scotale domini episcopi), 68, 69 ; also, compare Blead. Cust. pp. 182, 210 : ' Manducare debet coram domino in primo die adventus sui.' In this case the tenant was amerced if he failed to eat.

[3] Mich. Ambr. Rent., p. 143 : ' Homines . . . dicunt quod dominus potest facere tres scotallas per annum in Longo Ponte et possunt omnes sponsi et juvenes venire die Sabbati post prandium et potare sicut ad Cunninghale, et habebunt ter ad potandum, et die Dominica sponsus et sponsa venient cum denario suo, et die Lune similiter. Juvenes vero venient die Dominica cum obolo et die Lune possunt venire et potare libere sine argento, ita quod non sint inventi super scamnum. . . . Hoc tantum possunt nativi domini et liberi sui, sed extraneus qui servit alicui in manerio vel maneat non potest sic facere ' ; also, p. 108, and Inqu. 1189, p. 112 : ' Et debet bibere scotellam domini sicut scotellam vicini ' ; also, pp. 123, 125, 129.

[4] Hibbert, Ashton under Lyne, p. 18.

[5] Med. Aev. Kal., p. 287 : ' a feast provided by contributions from the tenants of a manor.'

scotale of Kent, the 'shot or contribution of ale to entertain the lord, or his bailiff or beadle, holding a " Parrock " to take an account of the pannage '.[1]

Another manorial scotale of a different character is that which was given to the villagers by the lord. Of this scotale the Ramsey *scythale* is a good example. It was the custom in a number of manors on the day on which some special meadow was mown for the mowers to receive 8*d*. or 12*d*. from the abbot's purse for a drinking bout.[2] Mowers usually received some special compensation for work in the demesne meadows ; very often it took the form of hay, as much as could be lifted on the scythe without breaking ; occasionally a ram or sheep was given. The *wetherale* of Girton, the *lambale* mentioned by Hampson, was probably the feasting on the occasion of the presentation.[3]

The bailiff's receipts from the hundred were sometimes supplemented by money from scotales. In a Winchester manor there was a drinking bout of the hundred,[4] which probably furnishes an example of the hundred ale or leet ale mentioned by Hampson. The field ale was another name for this same custom—'a kind of drinking anciently used in the field by bailiffs of the hundreds, for which until prohibited they collected money from the inhabitants (Coke, 4 Inst. 307), and which seems to be the custom so often mentioned in Latin deeds and exemplifications of manorial customs under the name *putura* or *potura* '.[5] To such a scotale the *Liber Custumarum* refers as the *felisonunshale* or scotale that small bailiffs extort from the suitors of the hundred.[6] The sheriff of London

---

[1] Robinson, Gavelkind, p. 220.

[2] Sel. Pl. Man. Courts, p. 103 ; Ram. Cart. iii. 61 ; i. 398 : ' Die vero quo falcabunt Haycroft, tota villata habebit bursa abbatis octo denarios ad Sythale. Et si ea die orta fuerit inter ipsos aliqua contentio dominus Abbas inde non occasionabit eos, nec implacitabit, sed quicquid ibi transgressum fuerit inter ipsos emendabitur.' Also, i. 49, 286, 301, 311, 367 ; ii. 18, 45 ; Reg. Worc. Pr., pp. 14 b, 34 a, 43 a, 65 b, 83 b.

[3] Ram. Cart. i. 493.

[4] Winch. Pipe Roll, p. 72: ' In expensis hospitii pro hundredo convivando de consuetudine die Natalis 1 *qu*. In braseo ad idem, de eadem consuetudine 1 *qu*.' Also p. 73, and *Gloss*.   [5] Med. Aev. Kal., p. 287.

[6] Lib. Cust. i. 351 : ' De parvis ballivis quibuscunque facientibus cervisiam quae vocatur *Felesonunehale* quandoque *Scotale*, ut extorqueant pecuniam a sequentibus Hundredorum et eorum subditis ' ; see *Gloss*.

once had a scotale, which was forbidden later with all other scotales, except those of such men as might wish to build with stone, so that the city might be secure.[1]

The forest charters show that one of the most oppressive scotales was that levied by foresters. ' Although the charter says that no forester or beadle shall make scotale or collect sheaves or oats or other corn, or lambs or little pigs, or shall make any other collection, yet the foresters come with horses at harvest time and collect every kind of corn in sheaves within the bounds of the forest, and outside near the forest, and then they make their ale from that collection, and those who do not come there to drink and do not give money at their will are sorely punished at their pleas for dead wood, although the king has no demesne ; nor does any one dare to brew when the foresters brew, nor to sell ale so long as the foresters have any kind of ale to sell ; and this every forester does year by year to the great grievance of the country, and besides this they collect lambs and little pigs, wool, and flax, from every house where there is wool a fleece, and in fence month from every house a penny, or for each pig a farthing. And when they brew, they fell trees for their fuel in the woods of the good people. . . . After harvest the riding foresters come and collect corn by the bushel, sometimes two bushels, sometimes three bushels, sometimes four bushels, according to the people's means ; and in the same way they make their ale, as do the walking foresters, to the great grievance of the country.'[2]

---

[1] Red Bk. Excheq. ii. ccxlix ; Liber Albus, i. 249 : ' Quod omnes sint quieti de Brudtol et de Childwyte et de Jeresgive et de scotale ita quod vicecomites nostri Lond' vel aliquis ballivus scotales non faciant.'

[2] Sel. Pl. For., p. 126 ; compare Rot. Hund. ii. 249, 253 ; Reg. Worc. Pr., p. 145 b ; P. Q. W., p. 218 : ' Et forestarii illi cum veniant ad domum alicujus mane ad petendum puturam . . . quilibet eorum capit a domino domus illius sex denarios pro putura illius diei et tunc vadunt ad aliam domum et sic ad terciam et ad quartam etc. eodem die et capit de quolibet domino domorum illarum singuli eorum vj denarios pro putura ita quod capiunt pro uno die pro putura quantum capere debent per sex vel septem dies.'

CHAPTER VII

ROYAL RENTS: JUDICIAL

BESIDES serving as convenient occasions for the receipt of payments connected with the geld, the communal courts had a financial value of their own. They were in and for themselves a source of profit, and it was from this point of view, rather than as instruments for the maintenance of order and justice, that they were chiefly regarded by the king's officers and the lords of franchises.[1] When the court was still in the hands of the king financial profit accrued to the crown, when the court was transferred to a private lord, or its competence cut down by the abstraction of suitors or functions, loss to the *patria*, that is to say, to the crown, resulted, and the land which had been so removed from royal jurisdiction, and from the rents and dues connected therewith, was no longer *terra sectabilis, terra geldabilis, terra de corde,* or *corpore comitatus.*[2] Although county and hundred still served as the basis for the assessment of certain fines and rents—the common amercement of the county, for example, for false judgements given in its courts, and the *murdrum* fine which fell on the hundred— yet much of their older judicial importance had passed, old rents due to them had become manorialized, and, as page after page of the Hundred Rolls and Quo Warranto Rolls show, suits once owed had been subtracted.[3] 'Justice cannot be done in the county unless suitors be there';[4] but the

[1] See on this point, P. Q. W., p. 560: 'Unde cum predictus abbas ea clamat virtute predictorum verborum in predicta carta Regis Knout infertorum que pocius sonant in cognicione causarum habenda quam in hujusmodi aliquo proficuo percipiendo.'

[2] Rot. Hund. i. 31 ; P. Q.W., pp. 118, 305 ; and compare, ibid., p. 169 : 'quod hundredum est quoddam corpus pertinens et annexum coronae domini Regis.'

[3] See, for example, Rot. Hund. i. 4, 9, 16, 37, 50, 51, 53, 78, 84, 91, 97, 101, 180, 190, 196 ; ii. 7, 8, 9, 10, 13, 205, 432, 570, 732 ; for subtractions from the tourn, i. 51, 53, 87, 97, 157, 434 ; ii. 432, 448, 508; P.Q. W., p. 733. The examples are endless.

[4] Sel. Pl. Man. Courts, p. xv ; P. Q. W., p. 414 : 'Maxime cum justicia non poterit fieri in comitatu nisi fuerint ibi sectatores.'

loss of suit was accepted with some measure of acquiescence. More question arose with regard to the withdrawal of suits from the two great meetings of the hundred court, which, since the Assize of Clarendon, had served for the holding of the sheriff's tourn.[1] The financial value of the tourn was great; it was the occasion of the payment of many rents, and the crown was as reluctant to yield the claim to it as were the great lords to surrender their frequent usurpations. The holding of the tourn usually carried with it the right of holding the three-weekly hundred courts, but the reverse is not necessarily true, the right to hold the ordinary courts did not imply in every case the right to hold the tourn,[2] and persons whose suits had been subtracted from the ordinary meetings were still obliged, at the instance of the sheriff, to render suit at the tourn or give the money equivalent. ' The tourn is not a liberty annexed to a manor or a hundred,' the lawyers said, ' but belongs specially to the crown and dignity of the lord king,' and can be alienated only by direct grant.[3]

In multitudes of cases, however, the franchise of the hundred was made to include the tourn of the hundred, or else the right to inquire concerning the articles of the tourn was exercised by the great lords within their manors, whether those manors lay in a royal hundred or in a hundred held by another lord. In Berkshire,[4] Derbyshire,[5] Devonshire,[6] and Kent[7] many hundreds were private, ' ubi nihil acrescere potest domino Regi.'[8] In Hertfordshire, on the other hand, out of seven and a half hundreds, the king had six, the Bishop of London half a hundred, and the Abbot of St. Alban's one.[9] In Buckinghamshire there were in all eighteen and a half

---

[1] Sel. Pl. Man. Courts, Introd., especially pp. i–xxxviii.
[2] Rot. Hund. ii. 227, 745, 828; i. 206—the tourn is excepted from the farm of courts; P. Q. W., pp. 165, 253, 395.
[3] Ibid., p. 171: ' Dicit ... quod turnus vicecomitis non est libertas annexa manerio neque hundredo set specialiter pertinet ad coronam et dignitatem domini Regis;' p. 289: ' predictus visus est quedam specialis libertas non pertinens ad shyras et hundredos'; again, pp. 160, 290.
[4] Ibid., pp. 81 sqq.
[5] Ibid., pp. 152–4.
[6] Ibid., pp. 164–5.
[7] Ibid., pp. 319, 321, 329, 332, 334, 338; Rot. Hund. i. 200, 218, 223.
[8] P. Q. W., p. 167.
[9] Rot. Hund. i. 188, 191; P. Q. W., p. 290.

hundreds, all royal, although many liberties had been subtracted from their courts.[1] The claim to the hundred was
based usually on a charter freeing the land in question from
suits at shires and hundreds. Sometimes, especially in Berkshire, Devonshire, and Kent,[2] it was based on the fact that
the hundred was said to be appendent to a given manor
which was held by the lord exercising the franchise, but such
survivals of ancient arrangements were not usually allowed
to pass without criticism by the king's lawyers, who declared
that a charter granting a manor was not enough to include
the hundred also, since the hundred was larger than the
manor, 'hundreda extendunt se ulterius quam predictum
manerium.'[3] In still other cases the hundred was claimed on
the ground that the lord was *hundredarius*, that he held, in
other words, the *bedeleria* or bailiwick of the hundred as
appendent to his fee, together with the right to receive all
'pennies which the sheriff or royal *hundredarii*, or their
bailiffs used to receive',[4] but this claim too was rejected by
the lawyers on the ground that the office of *hundredarius* was
'quasi quedam justiciaria, spectans mere ad coronam et non
ad aliquid tenementum',[5] and also that the king had the
power of appointing 'bedelles' as he would.[6] Elsewhere the
hundred was held at fee-farm of the king by the lord, the
profit in such cases arising from an undue increase in the
receipts.[7] A hundred in Staffordshire, for example, was held
at fee-farm from the king for 6 marcs and 6s. 8d., but when

[1] Rot. Hund. i. 21.
[2] P. Q. W., p. 81 : ' Seisiti fuerunt de predicto hundredo tanquam per-
tinente ad manerium predictum quod quidem hundredum est in eodem
manerio et non excedit metas predicti manerii ' ; and p. 343 : the abbot of
Faversham claims ' habere in manerio suo de Faversham libertates sub-
scriptas per cartam Regis Stephani videlicet hundredum de Faversham
cum omnibus libertatibus et liberis consuetudinibus simul cum omnibus
sectatoribus ' ; also pp. 321, 334, 342. An excellent example is Wye, to
which 22½ hundreds were once attached, later seven. Five others
were summoned, but Battle got nothing because they had their own
ditches ; Batt. Abb. Cust., pp. 126, 306.
[3] P. Q. W., p. 82.
[4] Ibid., pp. 252, 264, 298 ; Rot. Hund. ii. 27 ; see Vill. in Eng.,
App. xi, p. 441, for hundredors as suitors at the hundred, and Claud. C. xi,
ff. 49, 54, 61, *pass.* ; Tiberius B. ii, ff. 100, 105, 107.
[5] P. Q. W., p. 255.   [6] Ibid., p. 174.
[7] Ibid., pp. 298, 306, 319, 365.

the king recovered seisin of it it was assessed at $33\frac{1}{2}$ marcs a year additional.[1] The division of hundreds between the king and lords, or among different lords, was sometimes intricate.[2]

The classification of the rents and dues that formed the profits of jurisdiction is difficult for several reasons. The constant subdivisions and subinfeudations of franchises and their money proceeds are confusing ; the terminology varies in different localities ; and last, but perhaps not least, there is a lack of clear definition of the purpose of some of the rents, a vagueness of nomenclature which may indicate that uncertainty as to their meaning and origin prevailed even in the thirteenth century. The most important sources of information are the Hundred Rolls and Quo Warranto Rolls, and there is valuable supplementary material in manorial custumals and court rolls. Bailiffs' accounts are less important for this than for other groups of rents, because, as a rule, they do not differentiate the perquisites of courts, except by putting chevage often under a separate heading. In general, the rents and dues which made up the profits of jurisdiction seem to fall into the following classes : commutations of the duty of attending the various courts; rents which probably contributed in some way to the maintenance of the courts ; the fines of individuals or groups of individuals placed *ad certum*, and fines or amercements imposed upon the hundred or county as a whole. This division has been followed in the main in the following discussion, although for convenience the payments connected with the view of frankpledge have been grouped together.

Payments 'pro sectis.' The basis of the distribution of suit of court or its money equivalent among the vills of the hundred, and among the villagers of each vill, is obscure, the records dealing with specific cases in which it was not rendered, and not with the general principles determining its incidence. An interesting description is given in an Ely custumal of the

[1] P. Q. W., pp. 167, 170, 574, 694, 695, 698 ; Rot. Hund. i. 201.
[2] P. Q. W., pp. 54, 257, 360, *pass.* ; Rot. Hund. i. 179, 200, 218, 227, *pass.*; compare Harl. MSS. 1005, f. 70 : ' Nota quod si prepositus hundredi capiat gresumam de aliquo libero Dominus habebit medietatem.'

distribution of suits of vills within a private hundred and a half in Norfolk, a distribution which may well represent old arrangements. The hundred and a half of Midford belonged to Ely, and under the vill Shipdham is given a list of the vills owing suit at the hundred, and the amounts of sheriff's aid and *forwach* due there from some of them, and the money for renewing the pledges from all. Seventeen vills owed seventy-nine suits and a half suit, and of these Shipdham owed seven. The vill of Tynebrigge was *infra sedem*, but owed no suit.[1] The basis of the assessment of suits and rents is not apparent, but clearly Ely's profit was large.

Within the vills different customs regarding the rendering of the suit prevailed. Sometimes all freeholders made suit or paid the money equivalent;[2] in other cases the attempt to make suit binding on all met with opposition.[3] In still other cases the suit had become attached to certain tenements in the vill—'hundredlands' they were called in Kent, when they made suit at the hundred—whose tenants acquitted the lord of the manor or the rest of the vill.[4] In Hetherste, an Ely manor in Suffolk, one suit was owed at Saint Edmund's hundred of Badberghe, but this suit was divided among three free tenants who were responsible for the fine if the suit were not rendered.[5] In Brandon, Suffolk, one suit was owed similarly by eight *parcenarii*.[6] A rotatory system prevailed at Bury also,[7] and in Warwickshire a peculiar arrangement

---

[1] Claud. C. xi, ff. 233, 234.

[2] Rot. Hund. i. 173 ; ii. 461 ; P. Q. W., pp. 183, 292, 299, 783.

[3] Rot. Hund. ii. 27 (Nottingham) : 'Dicunt enim quod non solebant esse nisi xii antiqui sectatores et modo coguntur omnes libere tenentes de wapp' facere sectam vel finem pro secta sua.' Cf. i. 101, 352.

[4] P. Q. W., p. 349 : 'qui tenent hundreslaund solebant sequi hundredum . . . de tribus septimanis in tres septimanas.' Also pp. 348, 350, and compare the Ely *hundredarii*.

[5] Claud. C. xi, f. 270: 'Et ista et duo alii pares sui simul facient unam sectam ad quodlibet hundredum per annum; et si forsan villata inciderit per illorum defaltam tunc idem tres misericordiam acquietabunt.' Cf. f. 209.

[6] Ibid., f. 308: 'secundum turnum septem parcenariorum suorum.' Cf. f. 312.

[7] Harl. MSS. 3977, f. 98: 'Tunc debent quatuor homines ire ad primum comitatum scilicet ad festum S. Michaelis et ad primum hundredum et sic acquietare villam. Et ad aliud comitatum ibunt alii quatuor.'

was made by which three *rudmanni* owed suit at the hundred
every three weeks for all the vills of the hundred but Erdintone, where the free made suit in person or made fine for it
with 19*d*.[1] The number of suits from customary tenants
within the vill was either determined by the number of
tithings or acquitted by the reeve and four men, or, in the
south, by the *decennarius* and four men.[2]

The commutation of suit of court for money paid to the
sheriff or lord of the manor was obviously a convenience.
Sheriffs and lords were glad to put the obligations due to
them on a financial basis, and fractions of suit due to the
splitting up of tenements could thus be adjusted. The
rate of commutation is not easily determined. Sometimes it
was 12*d*. but the amount varied.[3] In the Ely custumals
there seems to be some indication of the commutation of suit
at the shire for a regular rent called *syrapeni*, or *shirepenny*,
to which the tenants paid according to some system of regular
apportionment.[4] In Stratham, Wychford hundred, Cambridgeshire, in which *syrapeni* was paid, and in other manors in the
same hundred, a rent called *sixtihepany* or *sixtepeny* is frequently mentioned, paid by free tenants and *hundredarii*.[5]
The custumal of 1222 explains that ' each hide gives *de sixtepeni* 12*d*., and owes one suit within every fifteen days at the
hundred '.[6] The rent was paid at the hundred or to the
bailiff of the hundred. It may have been the commutation
of some fractional part of a suit at the hundred by an arrange-

---

[1] P. Q. W., p. 780: 'Et juratores . . . dicunt . . . quod tres rudmanni
de Wycton alternatim faciunt sectam ad hundredum domini Regis. . .'
[2] Sel. Pl. Man. Cts., *loc. cit.*, especially pp. xxix, xxxiii; Rot. Hund. i.
66, 101, 141, 154; ii. 469; P. Q. W., pp. 6, 164, 169, 259, 289, 292, *pass*.
[3] Rot. Hund. i. 26, 78, 82, 505, *pass.*; P. Q. W., p. 178.
[4] Claud. C. xi, f. 43: 'et dat partem suam de syrapeni secundum portionem
scilicet 4*d*. ad festum S. Michaelis et ad Annunciationem Beate Marie.'
[5] Ibid., ff. 43, 49, 54, 61. Cf. f. 52 : ' Et sciendum quod isti denarii de
wardpani et sixthipani pertinent ad hundredum.' Cf. Eng. Hist. Rev.
ix. 418.
[6] Tiber. B. ii, f. 98 : ' De hundredariis (holding 24 acres) . . . et dat
sixtepen' quantum ad eum pertinet quia sciendum quod quelibet hida dat
de sixtepen' duodecim denarios et debet unum (*sic*) sectam infra quoslibet
quindecim dies et debet precar' arure . . . et dabit gersom'.' Cf. ff. 105,
107, where the statement is repeated and the tenant said to be ' tenens de
hundredo '.

ment not clear to us, but at the time of the Survey it was
paid in addition to the suit. Suit at the tourn was occasionally valued at 4s. for two suits,[1] but there is no certainty in
regard to the amount. Normally the tourn was held twice
a year, but it was the not infrequent practice of sheriffs and
private lords to increase the number of meetings of the tourn
in order to add to the profit.[2] Occasionally only one meeting
a year instead of two is recorded.[3]

Auxilium ad turnum, or *de turno*. The most important
payments connected with the tourn were those that resulted
in one way or another from the holding of the view of frankpledge there, and the attendant franchise of the assize of bread
and ale. In addition to these there seems to have been due
one payment of a more general kind, the object of which is
not clear. This is the payment *de turno*, or *ad turnum*, called
the *auxilium debitum ad turnum*,[4] and again, the *extorsio* levied
in the hundred called *turnus vicecomitis*.[5] Many times a payment like this made to the sheriff at his tourn is recorded;
for example, the sheriff of Suffolk took *ad turnatum suum*
40s. where his predecessor took only 20s.,[6] in Somerset many
men were not permitted to go to the tourn, nor to give
money, probably two shillings, *ad turnum*,[7] in Kent the men
of William de Caniso used to give money at the hundred

---

[1] Rot. Hund. i. 102; P. Q. W., pp. 692, 801.
[2] Rot. Hund. i. 63 : 'Dicunt etiam quod idem Rogerus dum fuit vicecomes turnum suum pluries per annum ubi semel tenere debuit per
annum et amerciabit homines ad voluntatem suam et injuste.' Also i. 38,
81, 166, 173. Cf. also i. 143, 145, 170, 182; ii. 174, *pass.* for the tourn as
a means of oppression. For private lords holding the tourn like the
sheriff, see Rot. Hund. i. 113 : 'Dicunt quod ballivi predicti castri semper
postquam illud fuit extra manus domini Regis H. tenuerunt turnos suos
loco vic' aliquando ter aliquando quater in anno et habent quatuor
bedellos ubi non solent esse nisi duo.' And i. 53, 111, 132; P. Q. W.,
pp. 6, 253, 308; Claud. C. xi, ff. 182, 254.
[3] Rot. Hund. i. 67, 78, 81.
[4] Ibid. i. 527.
[5] Ibid. i. 223: 'Et est in eodem hundredo levata quedam extorsio
vocata turnus vicecomitis scilicet xlvs. iiijd. et valet preterea perquisite
ejusdem hundredi per annum xxvs. salva omni justicia.' Cf. i. 232.
[6] Ibid. ii. 180.
[7] Ibid. ii. 136. Cf. Mich. Ambr. Rent., p. 203 : 'Tota villata dabit ad
turnum vicecomitis ijs. per annum, scilicet, ad Natale xijd. et ad
Hockeday xijd.'

court at the feast of St. Martin, and other money at the tourn of the sheriff, and used also to make suit every three weeks at the hundred and at the two *laghedays* for the sheriff's tourn.[1] At Kettering the bailiff accounts for 6s. 8d. for suit, 6s. 8d. for the view of frankpledge, and 18s. 9½d. *de turno vicecomitis*, and the last rent is assessed at the rate of 5½d. on a virgate.[2] Passages like this seem to show that the money paid at the tourn was not in any way a commutation for suit, nor, since the suitors still attended a royal court, in any way part of a payment made by a private lord for the right to hold a court. Other passages seem to differentiate it from the sheriff's aid,[3] with which perhaps one would be at first inclined to identify it, and from the *hundredscot*,[4] since the same person makes two payments of sheriff's aid and *ad turnum*, which are clearly distinguished in name and amount, and in like manner of *hundredscot* and *ad turnum*. Tithing-peny and money *ad turnum* are also distinguished from one another.[5] It seems possible that it was the custom for each vill or homage to make a payment to the king or his officer as compensation for holding the tourn, the payment forming one of the *perquisitae curiarum*, and being in nature not unlike the hundredscot, or the sheriff's aid, or perhaps the payment *pro pulchre placitando*. It may have been of not very definite amount or settled occurrence, and have lent itself readily, therefore, to unjust increase. It was paid

---

[1] P. Q. W., p. 345. Cf. p. 350: 'Et idem homines proporcionem suam solebant solvere ad turnum vicecomitis et in omnibus esse gildabiles domino Regi.' Rot. Hund. ii. 292: 'Dicunt quod vicecomes non facit turnum suum in dicto hundredo quia capit de dicto hundredo pro turnis suis xls.' And ii. 31, 728, 730, 731 (Oxon); 230, 237, 245 (Wilts); 291, 292 (Derby); i. 84 (Devon).

[2] Compot. Ketteringe (1292), p. 25: 'videlicet de quadam virgata vd. ob.' Cf. p. 45: 'Item petit sibi allocare de consuetudine unius virgate de terra tradite ad firmam . . . vd. ob. de turno vicecomitis et ijd. pro secta.'

[3] Rot. Hund. i. 445: 'et subtraxit ijd. de turno vicecomitis et ijd. de shireveschot.' Also i. 526; ii. 245; and, very clearly, P. Q. W., p. 731: 'tenent tenementum . . . de quo residuum tenetur domino Rege videlicet xd. ob. ad scherreveselver et ixd. ad turnum vic'.'

[4] Rot. Hund. i. 527: 'Item subtrahunt xijd. de hundredeshot et ijd. de turno vicecomitis.' And p. 531: 'de turno vic' et de geldagio hundredi.'

[5] Ibid. ii. 237: 'quod hundredum istud est in manu Regis et Vice-comes percipit inde per annum xls. ad duos turnos suos et pro auxilio xjs. et xd. de thetinpeny.'

usually as a lump sum by the vill or homage, and its incidence on the individual villager is not usually specified.

Letefe. A rent probably similar to the payment *ad turnum* or to the *hundredscot* was the Norfolk *letefe*, taken by the bailiff, according to the Hundred Rolls, *de antiqua consuetudine*, on the day of the leet.[1]

Motfech. The Shropshire *motfee* was probably the *letefe* under another name.[2] It is a question whether it was due at all the meetings of the hundred, or at the meetings for the tourn only. It was paid always at the rate of 4*d.* from one geldable hide.

Payments connected with the View of Frankpledge. In most counties the most important and profitable function of the tourn, and the function most often subtracted, was the holding of the view of frankpledge. The rents connected with the view fall into three general groups—first, the payments made in some cases by the lords for the right to exercise the view; secondly, the chevage, which was, in general, the composition for attendance at the view, though sometimes paid by those present; and, thirdly, fines and amercements arising in the view, some of which were paid occasionally, and do not fall properly, therefore, within this study, others of which seem to have been commuted, curiously, into fixed rents.

Payments for the right to hold the view, *pro visu.* The possible relations between the lord and the sheriff regarding the exercise of the view of frankpledge were many. Probably in the majority of cases the private view was not exercised without some definite recognition (usually in the form of a money payment made to the sheriff) of its original character as a regality. Sometimes, however, the view was exercised in the hundred court in private hands, or in the manorial courts of great lords within the hundred, in com-

---

[1] Rot. Hund. i. 495 : ' vjs. iiijd. quos dominus Rex Henricus pater Regis qui nunc est habere consuevit et debuit ad istud hundredum per annum de quodam servicio quod vocatur Letefe.' Also, i. 442, 474, 505, 516, 541, *pass.* P. Q. W., pp. 10, 475, 487.

[2] Rot. Hund. ii. 55 : '(1 hide) dat motfey iiijd. stretward iiijd. et sectam facit ad hundredum de tribus septimanis ad tres septimanas.' Also, pp. 58, 62, *pass.* The *botfech* of p. 63 is probably an error for *motfech.*

plete independence of the sheriff or his bailiff. The sheriff was not admitted to the view, and no compensation was made to him for the curtailment of the competence of his tourn.[1] The Hospitallers and Templars were often free from interference,[2] as were also some of the honours of the kingdom whose fees, we are told in the Hundred Rolls, paid nothing to the king, and some of the greater lords.[3] The Earl of Gloucester furnishes an excellent example of a great lord, who in certain counties, not always with any just warrant, held very numerous views very freely.[4] Where the claim to hold the view in such cases was based upon a charter freeing the donee from attendance at shires and hundreds and royal views, the king sometimes strove to maintain that freedom from the royal view was not equivalent to the right to hold a view, but that the view was in itself a royal franchise, not to be alienated except by express grant.[5]

Occasional instances occur of the recognition of the sheriff's right to be present at the view in private hands, where no compensation for the trouble of attending is made to him, either by direct grant of money or by a share in the proceeds of the court. The Abbot of Ramsey is the best example of cases of this kind. He summoned to his views in Cambridgeshire and Huntingdonshire the royal bailiff 'ad videndum quod visus franciplegii rationabiliter fiat in curia'. If, however, the royal bailiff did not come, and the mere love of seeing justice rendered would rarely bring him in cases where no profit was to be had, the abbot held the view without him.[6] Again, the

---

[1] P. Q. W., p. 308: (The Abbot of Peterborough) 'clamat habere . . . visum de omnibus commorantibus in predictis villis et tenet visum suum bis per annum et sine presencia servientis Regis. Et nichil dat Regi pro visu habendo.' Also, p. 253, and Rot. Hund. i. 113, 132.

[2] Rot. Hund. i. 49 ; Sel. Pl. Man. Cts., p. xxvi.

[3] Rot. Hund. i. 32 ; ii. 230, 323, 868, *pass.* ; P. Q. W., p. 104, *pass.*

[4] Rot. Hund. i. 2, 23, 32, 41 ; ii. 332, 562, 740 ; P. Q. W., pp. 253, 348.

[5] P. Q. W., p. 242 : 'Et W . . . qui sequitur pro domino Rege dicit quod predicte libertates de visu et weif suntm ere ad Coronam domini Regis spectantes contra quam Coronam nulla longi temporis praescripcio locum tenere debet . . .'

[6] P. Q. W., p. 104 : 'Quod predictus dominus J. Rex concessit predictis Abbati et monachis visum de franco plegio. . . . Ita tamen quod ballivus Regis per sum' ejusdem Abbatis veniat ad curiam ipsius abbatis ad videndum quod visus franciplegii rationabiliter fiat in eadem curia. Et

M 2

sheriff of Oxford came once a year to Spelsbury, if he wished, to hold the view, but he took nothing away, nor did he eat, nor was he entertained there, except by courtesy.[1] In the Quo Warranto proceedings for Huntingdonshire the king's lawyers, to meet conditions like these, take the extreme ground that the view can never be rightly exercised without the king's bailiff.[2]

Much more common are cases where the sheriff received a compensation from lords exercising the view in their manors or hundreds, in the form either of a definite sum of money, or of a share of the profits of the court. Very important people sometimes entered into such arrangements with the sheriff. A long dispute is recorded regarding the barony of Bedford, for example, in which it appears that the barony held its views by the payment of 40s., and in which the further question arises whether two views within the barony, which were held of the barony by certain individuals by the annual payment of 12d., could be distrained to make up a deficit in the 40s.[3] The Abbot of Waltham summoned the royal bailiff for his views in Cambridgeshire, as did the Abbot of Ramsey, but paid 2s. a year to the king whether the bailiff appeared or not.[4] In many cases where money was paid for the view,[5] it was the custom for the bailiff of the king to sit with the lord's bailiff at the court,[6] and to receive either a fixed sum,[7] or a share of the amercements,[8] or both. The Earl of Gloucester had an arrangement for certain Oxfordshire manors, whereby the bailiff of the king was to receive one half the amercements of the tourn, and his own bailiff the other half.[9] Sometimes it is stated expressly that the sheriff is to attend the court,

si predictus ballivus ad racionabilem sum' predicti Abbatis in curia ipsius Abbatis non venerit quod predictus Abbas nichilominus faciat visum.' Compare pp. 234, 249, 302, 303 ; Rot. Hund. ii. 458, 472, 514, 523.
[1] P. Q. W., p. 723.
[2] Ibid., p. 292: '. . . quia nullus visus teneri debet nisi in presencia servientis Regis.' Again, p. 294.
[3] Ibid., p. 58.　　　　　　　　　　[4] Ibid., p. 106.
[5] Among many such cases the following may be noted : Rot. Hund. i. 4, 5, 7, 20, 31, 53, 172, 173, 182, 188, 191 ; ii. 321, 323, 325, 326, 330, 339, 548, 553, 554, 556, 559, 562, 563; P. Q. W., pp. 91, 93, 295, 297.
[6] Rot. Hund. ii. 740, 842, 859, pass.; P. Q. W., p. 236.
[7] Rot. Hund. ii. 44, 323.　　　　[8] Ibid. i. 278, 287, 296.
[9] Ibid. ii. 736. Cf. ii. 272.

and receive a sum of money, but is to take no share of the amercements.[1] Very occasionally the lord received the fixed sum, and the sheriff the amercements.[2] Sometimes still other arrangements were made; the bailiff, for example, received an allowance of food.[3] Occasionally the lord held a private view after his men had attended the tourn,[4] or unduly increased the number of views.[5] Divisions of the profits of the view between private lords occurred, but were sometimes questioned by the king's lawyers, since they were in the nature of subinfeudations of franchises which were not recognized by the crown.[6] In cases where the lord held his view freely, without payment, he sometimes still rendered suit, or its equivalent, at the sheriff's tourn in the hundred. Thus in Bedfordshire 2s. a year was paid to the king for the right to hold the view, but all the *franciplegii* within the view went once to the hundred court and there presented all the articles of the view, and gave the 2s. to the sheriff with their own hands.[7] The admission before the king's lawyers of the obligation to attend the tourn in addition to holding the private view was, however, dangerous, because the king's lawyers did not hesitate to declare that such an admission was a recognition of the king's seisin of the view,[8] although

---

[1] Rot. Hund. ii. 478: 'Ballivus nichil asportabit de amerciamentis.' Also ii. 481, 733.

[2] Ibid. ii. 718.   [3] P. Q. W., p. 581; cf. p. 254.

[4] Ibid., p. 783: 'sed dicunt quod postquam ballivus domini Regis fecerit turnum suum et tenuerit visum idem Ricardus per injuriam tenet de tenentibus suis aliam curiam de visu franci plegii.'

[5] Ibid., p. 312: 'Quod ipsi usi sunt tenendi visum franciplegii ad curias suas de Westerham de tribus septimanis in tres septimanas . . . Inhibitum est eidem Abbati per justic' ne ulterius abutatur libertate illa et quod teneat visum predictum de cetero bis per annum tantum,' &c.

[6] Ibid., p. 262: Liberties are claimed by the grant of Edmund Crouchback, but the king's lawyer replies that Edmund is 'privata persona non habens potestatem aliquem feoffandi de libertate visus franci plegii . . . nec de aliquibus aliis regiis libertatibus.' Cf. p. 297; also Rot. Hund. i. 51; ii. 464.

[7] P. Q. W., p. 68: 'Et dicit alterius quod ipse reddit domino Regi per annum duos solidos pro predicta visu tenenda in forma predicta. Ita quod omnes franciplegii infra visum suum predictum quolibet anno ad hundredum Regis . . . conveniunt et omnes alios articulos ad visum spectantes ibidem presentant et denarios predictos ballivo Regis per manus suas persolvunt.' Also pp. 50, 170, 179.

[8] Ibid., p. 248: All presentments arising *infra villam* are made at the Abbot of Gloucester's view, all arising *extra villam* at the tourn. It is

they thus went far towards reversing, conveniently, the argument used elsewhere, that the tourn or view was a separate privilege not necessarily connected with the hundred.[1]

The impression gained from the perusal of the Hundred Rolls and Quo Warranto proceedings is that of constantly attempted encroachments on the part of private lords, met, not always by any means unsuccessfully, by efforts on the part of the sheriff to prevent such encroachment. Loss, inevitable in one place, was sometimes met by unjust extortion in another, the sheriff also, like a private lord, extorting unjust dues from his shire, and retaining money for himself. A passage like one in the Hundred Rolls in which certain lords wish to give back a half hundred to the king because they cannot bear the expense of pleading is unusual.[2]

The money necessary for the payment to the king must have been derived by the lords from their villages, probably from the perquisites of the courts held there. It is a general payment, and difficult to trace among the villages, unless the payment *pro visu*, frequently mentioned as paid by individuals, may be considered as always made for this purpose. In Staffordshire there seems to be evidence of a somewhat regular system of the levying of one shilling on the geldable hide.[3]

The second class of payments made to the lord at the view includes the common *chevage, capitagium, headpenny* or *havedscot*; the *tithingpenny*, or money, in the Latin form, paid *de decenna*; *frithsilver, fricsilver*, or *fripenni*; the *borghesealdorpeni* of Kent, and probably the *bornsilver* or *borchsilver* of Essex. These payments were connected in some general way with the appearance at the view of men within the tithings and the renewing of pledges, but the exact connotation of the terms probably varied somewhat in different localities and at different times.

The composition of the court held for the view, and its

argued for the king: 'quod ex quo predictus abbas cognoscit quatuor et prepositus veniunt ad turnum vicecomitis satis concedit seisinam domini Regis.' Also pp. 259, 296, 299; Rot. Hund. ii. 740.
[1] See above, p. 155.
[2] Rot. Hund. ii. 74.   [3] Rot. Hund. ii. 44, 114, 323, *pass.*

procedure, has been discussed by Professor Maitland,[1] and it
is not necessary to repeat his conclusions regarding the double
system of presentment within the court by the representatives
of the vill to the body of twelve or more freeholders, and the
two systems of representation, or appearance at the view, by
the capital pledges of the tithing, or by the reeve and four
men of the vill, or sometimes where in the south the tithing
was territorial by the *decennarius* and four men, or by the
reeve and four men, and the capital pledges concurrently.
The question that is important in a study of the financial
aspects of the view is, rather, for what purpose was chevage
paid, and by whom, and what relation do certain other payments made at the view bear to chevage? Chevage was given,
in the first instance, by the capital pledges for the other men
in the tithing, that they might not all come, 'pro illis qui sunt
in decenna ne omnes veniant'.[2] The rate at which it was
paid was usually, as the English form *headpenny* indicates,
a penny a head;[3] but sometimes the idea of the householder
was introduced, and a distinction made between the *husbond*,
the married man with a hearth and a family, and the unmarried man. The one paid usually a penny, the other
a halfpenny; but at Peterborough a man paid a penny and
a woman a halfpenny,[4] and on the manors of St. Paul's a man
with a wife or a home paid as much as 2*d.* because he took
wood and water, whereas an unmarried man paid only a penny.[5]
Boys of 'full age', over twelve, or eighteen, paid their chevage,
or attended the court,[6] and the duty fell in some form upon

[1] Sel. Pl. Man. Cts., Introd., p. xxxviii.
[2] Ibid., p. xxx: 'The duty of appearing seems to have been very
generally commuted for a small money payment, head money, *capitagium*, *chevagium*, a sum paid by the frank pledges *ne vocentur per
capita.*' And, quoting Roll Augment. Off. P. 34, No. 46, m. 4 d: 'Capitales plegii et eorum decene nichil dant ad capitagium; ideo vocandi
sunt omnes per capita.' See Ram. Cart. i. 491; Rot. Hund. ii. 656; and
Sel. Pl. in Man. Cts., p. 91, for the excellent case of John de Elton and his
tenants.
[3] Ram. Cart. i. 309, 323, 335, 345; ii. 47.
[4] Chron. Petrob., p. 163.
[5] D. S. P., pp. 81, 144, 154*, and 83: 'Et si habent uxores ij*d*. de
havedsot quia capiunt super dominium boscum et aquam et habent
exitum et si non habent uxorem vel uxor virum dabit unum denarium.'
[6] Rot. Hund. ii. 631; Reg. Worc. Pr., p. 15 b.; Min. Acc. 742/17-19;
P. Q. W., p. 50, *pass.*

all the members of the vill. Large freeholders levied it from their under-tenants, and unless they retained it for themselves, paid it over to the lord. Ordinary *custumarii, husebondi,* virgaters, cottars, crofters, all paid it.[1] In one curious case mentioned in the Peterborough records it was not paid by the *servi,* probably because they were in the mainpast of others,[2] and an occasional exception was made in the case of those who, as an Ely custumal puts it, were in the service of their fathers or mothers, for whose good conduct the householder was responsible.[3] Once it had apparently become attached to a tenement; the person that held a certain *pightel* paid it.[4]

Although chevage was thus in its simplest form a personal payment, rendered to secure exemption from the view, its original character became apparently sometimes transformed, or at least obscured. It appears in some cases as a fixed annual rent, *certus redditus,* paid by the vill, *tota villata,* no allowance being made for necessary variations from year to year.[5] In this sense, perhaps, it was sometimes called *cert money.*[6] The lord was desirous of reducing it, like other variable rents, to a certain basis, and hence it was placed *ad certum* or even sold, *venditum,* to the villagers,[7] as the phrase goes, at a fixed amount. Moreover, the money payment being secured by custom, the actual presence of those paying it was required at the view, ' the tenants of land shall come per-

---

[1] For example, Rot. Hund. ii. 630, 849, 858; D. S. P., pp. 83, 145; Chron. Petrob., pp. 163, 164; Ram. Cart. i. 309 sqq., 323, 329, 369.

[2] Chron. Petrob., p. 163.

[3] Claud. C. xi, f. 247: 'Et sciendum quod unusquisque anilepiman et anilepiwyman qui lucratus fuit in autumpno duodecim denarios vel amplius dabit domino episcopo unum denarium per annum de chevagio ad festum sancti Michaelis preter illos qui fuerunt in servicio patrum vel matrum suorum.' Tiber. B. ii, f. 207.

[4] Ram. Cart. i. 284: 'Et quicunque sit ille residens semper ad visum franci plegii veniet, chevagium sicut alii ceteri pro se facturus.' Cf. Claud. C. xi, f. 85.

[5] Rot. Hund. ii. 44, 45, 136, 138, 146, 336, 723 et seq., 838, 843, 849, 858, 871; i. 146, 181, 182. Ely Vac. Roll, 1132/10: (Derham) 'Et de ijs. viijd. de chevagio posito ad certum.' Rot. Hund. ii. 849: 'Tenentes de dicto feodo vjd. pro havedpeny certo hundr' de Wotton.' See especially, Court Rolls, Ramsey, 179/10, where the amount was usually a marc or a fraction of a marc.

[6] Crondal Records, 377, 383; Hone, Manor, 147, 156, 157, 158.

[7] Worcester Vac. Roll, 1143/18; Ely Vac. Roll, 1132/10.

sonally, and nevertheless they shall pay their pennies,' and if they do not come they are heavily amerced.[1] Thus a certain villata gave every year on the day of the view 10s. through the capital pledges that it be not 'occasioned', and for the absent that they should not be amerced, while it was sworn that they were keeping the peace; but now, the record states, the 10s. are enrolled, *inrotulati*, and paid like a rent, *inrentati quasi redditus*, and the seneschal nevertheless *currit ad occasiones*, and amerces the capital pledges heavily for those that are absent and desires that all be present on the day of the view, or, on pain of amercement, at the next court, wherever they be, whether in service, or elsewhere, even if they be beyond the sea.[2] Sometimes there seem to be indications of a theory that the chevage or *de certo* rent was a commutation for presence at the three-weekly meetings of the halmote, but that attendance at the great view was still required.[3] Not only was the presence of all at the view of frankpledge required under pain of amercement; it was also apparently the custom for those that came to pay in addition probably to the chevage or *certus redditus*, and to the amercements of those absent paid by the chief pledges, a penny 'for the renewing of pledges'. In the Quo Warranto Rolls it is stated that a view is to be held and payments made in the following manner : At Hokeday all resident in the given lordship shall come together, and inquiry is to be made concerning those that are in tithing and also concerning those that have not appeared, by name. From

---

[1] Rot. Hund. i. 6 : 'Item dicunt quod visus franci plegii tenetur ... et tunc tenentes terre venient personaliter et nichilominus solvunt denarios et absentes qui non habent terram mittunt argentum et sunt quieti.' And i. 8, 15, 259, 456; ii. 631 ; P. Q. W., p. 349 : 'ad duas laghedays per annum per unumquodque capud plene etatis.'

[2] Ibid. i. 8 : 'Dicunt ... quod villata ... solebat quolibet anno die visus dare xs. per capitul' sine occasione ostendendo et pro absentibus ne gravarentur dum testificaretur quod essent boni modo inrotulati dicti x solidi et inrentati quasi redditus nec tenent locum ville quia J.... . seneschallus ... nichilominus currit ad occasiones et decennarios pro absentibus graviter amerciat et vult quod omnes sint presentes die visus vel quod veniant ad proximam curiam ubicunque fuerunt in servicio vel alibi etiam si essent ultra mare vel ammerciabuntur.'

[3] Rot. Hund. ii. 849; P. Q. W., pp. 341, 344, 349 ; Ram. Cart. i. 369 : 'Et per predictum hevedpeny quieti debent esse a secta omnium halimotorum per annum praeterquam duorum.'

each person present a penny is then to be taken, and the absent are to be amerced.[1]

'The pennies taken from those present' were sometimes called *chevage*,[2] but perhaps more accurately and commonly, the money for renewing the pledges, *tithingpenny*, in its various forms, or *frithpenny* or *frithsilver*, the money for keeping the peace, or perhaps recognition money, money paid *de recognitione custumariorum*.[3] It is, however, often very difficult to tell from the rolls and custumals whether forms like *tithingpenny* and *frithsilver* apply to the original *chevage*, or *certus redditus*, paid by the capital pledges, or to the payment made by those that attended for renewing pledges. Sometimes, too, there seems to be an identification of the *de certo* payment with the money paid *pro visu*,[4] and in other cases the pennies of those present are regarded as *pro pulchre placitando*.[5] It is possible there may have been some looseness of nomenclature, and the meaning of the rent may have varied with the locality and the date. In general the forms *chevage, capitagium, headpenny, headsilver* (*hefdsulver*), *denarii capitales* occur very commonly in Huntingdonshire, Norfolk, Gloucestershire, Berkshire, and in the Burton manors in the north.[6] The form *tithingpeni, tygenpeni, theginpeni, tynpeni, thetinpeni*, and the like, the penny paid *de decenna*, occurs especially in documents relating to manors in Bedford-

---

[1] P. Q. W., p. 50: 'Quolibet anno super le hockeday omnes infra dominium suum residentes ibidem conveniant et per eosdem inquiratur quales et quanti (*sic*) residencium predictorum qui in decenna ponendi sunt et non ponuntur. Et eciam de nominibus eorum qui eodem die non comparuerint ibidem. Ita quod de quolibet comparente unus denarius capiatur et quod absentes amercientur et similiter si quis etatis duodecim annorum extra decennam inveniatur quod tunc ille sub- cujus manupastu fuerit amercietur pro eodem.' Repeated ibid., and compare pp. 58, 68, 69, and Rot. Hund. i. 259: 'Et ad illum visum fraunplegg' non solebant amerciari nisi absentes et quatuor annis elapsis levaverunt novam consuetudinem ita quod capiunt quolibet anno tres marcas de sectatoribus illius franci plegii injuste pro pulcre placitare.'
[2] For example, Rot. Hund. ii. 631.
[3] See especially, Worcester Vacancy Roll, 1143/18.
[4] Rot. Hund. ii. 837, 847, 859, 875; P. Q. W., p. 50.
[5] Rot. Hund. i. 136, 259.
[6] For example, P. Q. W., pp. 250, 293; Rot. Hund. i. 77, 83, 95, 96, 196, 524; ii. 629, 639, 656, 666, 726, 835, 843, 858, 860, 875, 876; Burt. Ch., p. 57; Norwich Vac. Roll, 1141/1; Min. Acc. 742/17–19.

shire, Gloucestershire, Wiltshire, Southampton.[1] *Frithpenny*, *fricsilver, fripeni*, is found especially in Buckinghamshire and in the manors of Lichfield and Burton, being the money for keeping the *frith*, or peace, 'pro conservanda pace.'[2] Still other forms of the rents are derived from the word *borgh*, or *borgha*, the equivalent of tithing. Thus the Kentish tithing is called a *borgha*, its capital pledge the *borghesealdor*, and the chevage payment the *borghesealdorpeni*.[3] The Kentish material throws some light on the working of the *borgha* and the functions of the *borghesealdor*—he was elected by the *borgh*,[4] he had the custody of prisoners suspected of theft, and with his *borgh* he presented offenders at the hundred.[5] He followed the three-weekly hundred occasionally with several men of his *borgha*, but the law-days he followed with all the tenants over twelve or fifteen years.[6] The Cambridgeshire and Essex *bornsilver, bornpene, borsilver*, is defined in a Bury St. Edmunds custumal as the penny for suit paid to the court at which 'they renew their pledges'.[7] The *bortreming* or

---

[1] For example, P. Q. W., pp. 27, 28, 72, 257 ; Rot. Hund. ii. 221, 236, 237, 245, 260, 273, 278, 669, 842.

[2] Rot. Hund. i. 41, *pass.* in the county ; Brewood, Lichfield Manor, p. 14 ; Burt. Ch., p. 94. For Fricsilver see Rot. Hund. ii. 838 ; Fripeni, D. B. Add., 539. The 'frith' corresponds to 'by-law'. The Durham Halmote Rolls contain many references to the maintenance of the frith, or freth ; for example, p. 16 : 'Preceptum est omnibus quod servent frithes sub poena 2*s* '; p. 17 : ' Preceptum est omnibus villae quod servent frithes in blado pratis pasturis et semitis et quod nullus eorum sit contrarius aut rebellis vicinis suis ' ; p. 123 : 'Et injunctum est omnibus tenentibus villae quod quilibet eorum veniant (*sic*) pro freth', birlaws, et aliis comodis et proficuis dictae villae ponendis, ad praemunicionem dictorum praepositorum.' Also pp. 13, 50, 101, 102.

[3] Rot. Hund. i. 202, 203, 210, 215, *pass.* : ' Solebant habere boregesaldr' de eisdem tenentibus dicti abbatis ad respectum et fac' in eodem hundredo quod pertinuit.' Batt. Abb. Cust., p. 136 ; P. Q. W., p. 325. The payment should not be confused with bordalpeny, boothsilver (Du C. and Liber Cust. ii. 660), nor with any borough payment.

[4] Rot. Hund. i. 212 : J. distrained ' ut esset borgesaldre sine electione borge sue '.

[5] Ibid. i. 215, 232. Batt. Abb. Cust., p. 136 : 'Borghesaldrus cum tota borgha sua ducit ipsum latronem ad hundredum de Wye, et ibi judicium suum per judicem dicti hundredi sustinebit.'

[6] P. Q. W., pp. 341, 344, 350.

[7] Rot. Hund. i. 53, 160 ; ii. 408, 411 ; Harl. MSS. 3977, f. 13 : 'Borchsilver. Statutum est ideo ut homines celerarii venirent ad domum thelonei et ibi renovarent plegios suos et scriberentur in rotula. Et ibi darent pro secto denarium quod dicitur Borchsilver et celerarius habebit dimidiam partem.' Cf. ff. 37, 62.

bortremium of Suffolk seems to be another word for *frank-pledge*,[1] and perhaps the *boreupeny* also may be connected with it.[2] In immunity lists *borghalpeny* is mentioned in Derbyshire, Essex, and Bedfordshire,[3] and *bornewing* in Yorkshire, and elsewhere.[4]

Notwithstanding the uncertainty regarding the exact meaning of the various terms used to denote the rents paid at the view, a general process of development seems to be evident, the setting of rents, in the beginning generally occasional in nature, *ad certum*, and the later enforcement of the original service for which the rents were an equivalent, together with the requirement of new rents connected with that service. An analogous process may be observed in the development of boon services. But the payment of chevage involves another question also, the question of the stability of the manorial population. Where are the men of the tithing who do not come to the view, and why is their attendance compounded for by chevage, or by amercements? It seems probable that allowance must be made for two general classes of persons paying the original chevage or commutation of appearance at the view, those within the manor who did not go to the view because their attendance was inconvenient and unnecessary, and those, for one reason or another, outside the manor. It seems probable that the first class must be allowed for as well as the second, and that, therefore, for this reason, as well as because of the difficulty of knowing the exact connotation of the word, the appearance of chevage cannot be taken as necessarily indicating residence outside the manor. Besides the resident householders who paid their chevage and were represented by the capital pledges at the view, there is often indicated in manorial documents a large number of men, usually not landholders but holding a subordinate position to the customary tenants and free tenants, whose households in a sense they form. Having no land they do not often appear

[1] Harl. MSS. 3977, ff. 16, 61 ; Rot. Hund. ii. 147, 186, 197.
[2] P. Q. W., p. 727.
[3] Ibid., pp. 33, 132, 149, 238.
[4] Ibid., pp. 211, 540, 653 ; Mon. Angl. ii. 812.

as a separate class in the custumals, whose divisions are usually based on landholding. They must, however, with the cottars and crofters and lesser men, especially of the older enfeoffments, have formed an important part of the working force of the manor. The Glastonbury records[1] and Ely chartulary of 1277[2] give especially clear evidence of this class of men, the *undersetles*, the *anilepimen* and *anilepiwymen* who may 'remain' on the land of the bishop, or on the land of some customary tenant ('alicujus custumariorum'), who may or may not have a house in the vill, or who may or may not be in the service or mainpast of some one, perhaps of their fathers or mothers. While it is clear that these men must often have been resident on the manor in which were their chief pledges, it is equally clear that it is among them that the greatest amount of movement to and from the manor must be expected. They were the freest, least attached part of the population, the floating population, from among whom hired labourers would be gradually appearing. Of the same general character were also probably the different 'grades' of *selfods*, appearing at Durham[3] and at Tynemouth, Yorkshire.[4] The *halliwimen*, or reapers at the harvest in

---

[1] Mich. Ambr. Rent., p. 108: 'Et si habet famulum vel famulam et undersetles quilibet dabit *ob.* et potabit per i diem.'

[2] Claud. C. xi, f. 60: 'Unusquisque anlepiman et anlepiwyman manens super terram episcopi debet metere unum sellionem in autumpno sine cibo et consuetudine que vocatur luuebene et similiter unusquisque coterellus manens super terram episcopi vel super terram alicujus custumariorum suorum metet unum sellionem eodem modo.' Also f. 312: 'Et sciendum quod unusquisque undersetle vel anilepiman vel anilepiwyman domum vel bordam tenens de quocunque illam teneat inueniet unum hominem ad quamlibet trium precariarum autumpni ad cibum domini. Item sciendum quod unusquisque anlepiman non habens aliquem mansionem in villa sive sit in servicio sive non, inveniet unum hominem.' And ff. 29, 42, 80, 85, 191.

[3] Bish. Hatf. Surv., p. 174: Servientes at Norton. 'Et quilibet serviens cujuslibet predictorum bondorum etatis xvj annorum et ultra, solvit Domino, quolibet anno, pro precariis in autumpno, ad festum Michaelis 12*d.* tantum Selfodez. Et quilibet selfode, cujuscumque gradus, manens in villa solvit Domino per annum ad idem festum S. Michaelis 3*d.*' Cf. pp. 168, 232 (shelfodes), and D. H. R., p. 128: 'Injunctum est . . . praeposito et forestario quod ipsi arrestari faciant omnes hujusmodi tenentes et servitores ac operarios villae ita quod non exeant villam ad metendum nisi cum domino et tenentibus suis sub poena 20*s.*'

[4] Mon. Angl. iii. 315: 'Omnes illi qui terras tenent et tofta . . . omnes selfodes.'

Nottinghamshire,[1] the Bury *pokeavers*,[2] the Ely *pocarii* and *cumeling*,[3] the *gressemen* of York,[4] and the curious *landlesemen* of Ely, who hold tenements.[5] The Ely chartulary shows especially clearly the movement in this class of population: it states that cottars, *undersetles*, and *anilepimen*, the workers at the harvest boons, for example, are 'innumerabiles . . . quia quandoque acrescunt et quandoque decrescunt,'[6] and it shows that from most of these *anilepimen* chevage was due.[7] A penalty of 20s. was incurred at Durham by leaving the village in order to reap for others than the lord and his tenants.[8] The attempt to keep the chevage of the migrating portion of this class of men within the manor must have been attended with difficulties. The records give evidence, however, of the obligation of men who 'remain outside the houses of their fathers' to pay their chevage with their old tithing,[9] and they indicate the actual receipt of such chevage in what must be a fair proportion of cases.[10] The absent members of the tithing would also, of course, but probably less frequently, have included men of better status, often resident in other manors or in towns.[11] The expert artisans of the account rolls, the carpenters, threshers, winnowers, who are paid 'ad suos adventus', form an interesting and highly respectable section of this fluctuating population.

A difficulty arose concerning the chevage and other

---

[1] Hazlitt's Blount's Tenures, p. 320.
[2] Harl. MSS. 1005, f. 69; Harl. MSS. 3977, ff. 37, 38.
[3] Tiber. B. ii, ff. 117, 238.
[4] Vac. Roll, 1144/1 : 'de operibus bondorum, gressemen' et cotariorum.' Cf. Rent and Surv. Roll, 730.
[5] Claud. C. xi, f. 194; Tiber. B. ii, f. 167 (20 acres).
[6] Claud. C. xi, ff. 89, 93, 94.
[7] Ibid., f. 247 : ' Et sciendum quod unusquisque anilepiman et anilepi-wyman qui lucratus fuerit in autumpno duodecim denarios vel amplius dabit domino episcopo unum denarium per annum de chevagio ad festum S. Michaelis preter illos qui fuerunt in servicio patrum vel matrum.' Cf. ff. 23, 26 ; Tiber. B. ii, f. 207.
[8] D. H. R., p. 128 ; passage quoted above.
[9] Chron. Petrob., p. 163 : ' Homines qui serviunt extra domos patrum suorum dat pro capite suo unusquisque 1d.' Claud. C. xi, ff. 167, 184.
[10] Abing. Acc., p. 150 ; Min. Acc. 742/19, 945/2, and *passim* in ministers accounts.
[11] Ingoldsmell Court Rolls, p. 195 : Bondmen pay 3d. yearly for chevage, but have lately acquired land in the manor, and therefore the steward declares them free of the charge. Ely, Extent. Maner.

perquisites of the view coming from another class of men commonly mentioned in the Quo Warranto proceedings. These are the scattered tenants of certain lords, who reside singly or in very small groups in diverse vills, but who do not exactly reside on the fee of another lord, since their tenements are part of the fee of their own lords. The pleadings concerning the view over such men is interesting. It was maintained by the king's lawyers, for one thing, that vill and view of frankpledge went together, that in order to have a view in a vill the lord should hold the whole vill—manor and vill, in other words, should be co-terminous, and a view for fractions of a tithing or for one or two tithings in a vill was illegal.[1] Men in the vill should make presentments with their neighbours of the vill, and not with the *extranei* of other vills. Such a theory seems to point to the belief, in the minds of the lawyers of Edward's reign at least, that frankpledge was in origin an arrangement for the administration of the vill rather than of the manor, the original presentment at the hundred being made by the vill and not by the manor.[2] The actual contraventions of this theory were, however, very numerous, although perhaps in some cases fairly recent at the time of the pleadings. The worst, and most instructive, offenders, were the Templars, who had acquired in many vills very small numbers of tenants. In Bedfordshire, for example, 'in aliqua villa non habet (the Master), nisi duo tenentes in aliqua tres vel quatuor.'[3] In Bollestrode in Buckinghamshire 'non habet villam integram sed tantummodo collectam et Bollestrode non est villa sed tantummodo quoddam manerium';[4] and again the Hospitallers held no vill, but only in some

---

[1] P. Q. W., p. 294 : ' Et Simon venit et dicit quod habet in predicta villa duodecim tenentes tm̄ de quibus clamat habere visum . . . bis per annum et sine presencia servientis Regis. Et nichil dat . . . Et G. qui sequitur pro Rege dicit quod non potest gaudere predicto visu desicut non est dominus ville nec habet villam integram ' ; also pp. 295, 673.

[2] Ibid., p. 681 : A special statement made by defendant that suit is due not from vills but from men and tenants : ' Preterea dicit quod secte fieri non possunt per villatas set per homines et tenentes suos.'

[3] Ibid., p. 673 : ' Et preterea dicit quod predictus Prior habet tenentes suos in diversis villis qui presentaciones ad Coronam Regis spectantes facere deberent cum vicinis suis propinquioribus et vicini eorum cum ipsis et non cum extraneis de aliis villis ' ; cf. pp. 85, 98, 244, 293, 294, 392.

[4] Ibid., p. 89.

places a half vill, in others a quarter vill, in still others only
four or five tenants, 'nec est juri consonum quod visus fiat
de hujusmodi collecta.'[1]

The practical objections to such customs are clear. It was
not worth while to hold a view in the vill in question for so
small a number of tenants, while it was inconvenient for them
to attend views held at a distance. The lord, moreover, had
no *judicialia*, tumbrel or pillory, in the vill where he had few
tenants. The result was, necessarily, that the tenants' chevage
was paid, instead of attendance, and that in many cases their
offences were punished by fines instead of corporal punishment. Their position in matters of justice must thus have
been somewhat anomalous, and their chevage was often lost
entirely.[2] Such men, the king claimed, should properly attend
the tourn. An instructive case in point is recorded in the
custumals of Battle. Certain men belonging to the manor of
Brithwolton in Berkshire dwell in Covenholt in Hampshire.
They do not perform services because they have augmented
their money rents, but the ordinary tests of villein status
apply to them. One of them, however, pays no rent himself,
but it is said that the other tenants divide the payment of the
two shillings he would owe normally among themselves, in
order that he may defend them against evilly disposed natives
(*patriotas*) of the county.[3] The chevage of men in the tithings
of weak lords, or loosely attached to a view, like the men of
Brithwolton, or remote from their lords, was naturally enough
a tempting bait. It was the well-known custom of the Hospitallers in Devonshire, for example, to 'attract men' into
their tithings by promising them a share in the freedom from
toll in the kingdom which was their privilege. They put
their crosses on the new tenant's doorway, and then pocketed
the chevage and other profits arising in the view.[4] The

---

[1] P. Q. W., p. 90.   [2] Ibid., p. 255.   [3] Batt. Abb. Cust., p. 71.
[4] Rot. Hund. i. 77, 83, 95, 96 ; P. Q. W., p. 251 : '... quare levavit signum
hospital' in quadam domo in Wynchecumbe quam Thom' Nightigale et
Elena uxor ejus tenent . . . Et super hoc venit predictus Thomas et
requisitus quare permisit predictum Priorem predictum signum in domo
sua levare dicit quod non permisit hoc gratis levari set quia nitebatur
predictum signum prosternere implacitabant ipsum coram conservatore
suo et ibidem extorquebant ab eo x*s*.'

Templars took the penny *de advocaria* from men in Sussex who were not properly their tenants, but on whose shops and houses they had put their sign.[1]

The third great source from which profit came to the sheriff or lord who held the view, the fines and amercements arising therein, does not at first sight seem to fall within this study, since such payments would naturally be made on the occasion of the offence by the individual offender, and would not therefore be customary, regular obligations resting upon the members of the manor. Many fines were necessarily occasional, it is true; but with regard to some of the minor offences which were presented at the view of frankpledge a very curious custom prevailed in some localities. Occasional fines for such offences as trespass, breach of manorial custom in regard to agriculture, and the like, or breach of the assizes of bread and ale, were changed, in some cases, into customary fines, the burden of the responsibility being shifted in large measure from the individual offender to the vill as a whole, and the lord becoming assured of at least a certain amount each year from fines imposed by his court. By a fixed annual payment, paid according to some definite system of assessment by all or certain members of the villata, the men of the vill were allowed to insure themselves either against corporal punishment for minor offences, or against ever having the fines for certain specified misdemeanours exceed a certain amount. The custom is difficult to understand clearly, especially since it seems to have been confusingly connected or identified sometimes with other payments of an apparently different character. The clearest cases of its occurrence are on certain of the manors of Ramsey Abbey in Bedfordshire, Cambridgeshire, Huntingdonshire, and probably in one case in Hertfordshire, where the rent is called *fulstingpound, filstinpund*.[2] In the extent of Cranfield, Bedfordshire,[3] we are told

---

[1] Rot. Hund. i. 96: ' Item dicunt quod Hospitallarii assumunt diversos homines per chevagium.'

[2] The forms *filsinale, felisonunhale, felsten*, and *filsingerthe* should be compared with *fulsting pound*, or *filstinpund*.

[3] Ram. Cart. i. 441: ' Villata dat ad viginti solidos, qui dantur, quod cum aliquis cadat in misericordia domini, det ante iudicium sex denarios,

that the villata gave ' to the 20s.' which were paid in order that, when anyone fell *in misericordia domini* he should give 6*d.* *ante judicium*, and 12*d. post si expectet judicium*, unless the offence were theft, or any great transgression. Not all contributed to the 20s., however, as the extent goes on to say, and not all made fines for offences in one and the same way. Tenants of hided and unhided land, virgaters, and cottars, are recorded as contributors to the 20s. In another extent of the same manor[1] it is stated that all the villata except the free give at the feast of St. Andrew 20s., which is called *filstinpound*, and by this payment they are free from all fines and penalties, before judgement for 6*d.* and after judgement for 12*d.*, except from the fines for shedding blood, cutting oaks, and theft. In Shitlingdon, Bedfordshire,[2] there is a slight difference in the form of the statement. A virgater pays 4*d.*, a half virgater 2*d.*, and a crofter in proportion, yearly, at the feast of St. Andrew, in order that, being accused of some transgression in his agricultural services, such as ploughing or reaping, he should be amerced 6*d.* before judgement, 12*d.* after it. If his offence be more serious, shedding blood, rape, or taking of oak wood, he makes the best terms he can with his lord. In this manor it seems probable that a 20s. to accord with the *filstinpound* has been divided, originally, among the members of the vill according to their tenements. In Barton,

---

et post, si expectet judicium, duodecim denarios, nisi sit pro furto, vel aliqua maxima transgressione. Sciendum quod non omnes dant ad viginti solidos, et ideo non omnes sunt facturi finem de misericordia uno et eodem modo.' And (ibid.) a half-virgate *extra hidam* pays ' ad viginti solidos qui appellantur fustingpound.' See also pp. 439, 442.

[1] Ram. Cart. ii. 22 : ' Tota villata praeter liberos, dat in festo Sancti Andreae viginti solidos, qui vocatur filstinpound ; et per hoc quieti debent esse de omnibus misericordiis, ante judicium pro sex denariis, et post judicium pro duodecim denariis, nisi pro effusione sanguinis, vel pro excisione quercus pro furto.'

[2] Ibid. i. 464 : ' Ad festum S. Andreae dat quatuor denarios ut super transgressionibus operum convictus, ut arurae, messis, et aliorum hujusmodi, ante judicium amercietur sex denarios, post judicium duodecim denarios. Cum autem super sanguinis effusione, raptu puellarum, et captione querc', que apertionem de restingwymbes possit sustinere, fuerit convictus ratione delicti, prout melius possit, gratiam petit domini.' Cf. pp. 466, 467, 468, 470, and especially 473 : ' Si vero convictus fuerit, quod debito modo ad molendinum domini sectam non fecerit, ante judicium dabit sex denarios ; et si judicium sustinuerit, dabit duodecim denarios.'

another Bedfordshire manor,[1] all the villata but the free paid
30s. *ad fulstingpounde* on the feast of All Saints. In Burwell,
Cambridgeshire, the payment appears by name as *fulstingpound*, with the rate at which it was paid, 24 acres with croft,
16¼*d*.,[2] 20 acres with toft, 14½*d*.,[3] one virgate 21¾*d*.,[4] 8 acres
5½*d*., 12 acres 7½*d*.[5] In Elton, in Huntingdonshire, the *filstyngpound* of 13*d*. a virgate is mentioned,[6] and in Therfield in
Hertfordshire[7] a half-virgate gave 6*d*. to 'the pennies which
are called the twenty shillings'. The occurrence of the payment, clearly defined like this, is fairly frequent outside the
lands of Ramsey, but it is nowhere else called *fulstingpound*.
That it is the same payment elsewhere, however, seems un-
questionable. There are good instances in Bedfordshire,[8] for
example, of the 6*d*. before and 12*d*. after judgement, and
a great many instances in Oxfordshire, where the payment
was especially common. In the hundred of Chadlington, for
example,[9] which was held at farm by the Earl of Gloucester
for £4 hidage, 30s. 2*d*. tourn payment, and 10s. for a certain
view, and in which the sheriff held two tourns and took one
half the profits, and the earl the other half, the latter holding
the view of frankpledge in all the manors also except two,
into which he had ingress once a year with the sheriff, and
three where he had no ingress—in this hundred, which is
labelled *forinsecum*, a custom suggesting a payment like
fulstingpound occurs unmistakably.[10] In Saltford, and in
Certedon, all in the hidage when amerced gave 6*d*. before
judgement, 12*d*. after, *pro misericordiis* at the hundred;[11] in
Podelicot the tenants paid 14s. 'de hidagio ut sint quieti de
misericordia in hundredo ante judicium 6*d*. post judicium
12*d*.;'[12] and in Teinton,[13] Chadlington Wahull,[14] and foreign

---

[1] Ram. Cart. i. 486 : 'Tota villata praeter liberos dat in festo Omnium
Sanctorum triginta solidos ad fulstingpounde.'
[2] Ibid. ii. 28.   [3] Ibid. ii. 30.   [4] Ibid. ii. 30.
[5] Ibid. ii. 33.   [6] Rot. Hund. ii. 657.   [7] Ram. Cart. i. 46.
[8] Rot. Hund. i. 5.   [9] Ibid. ii. 736.
[10] Ibid. iii. 723, 736.   [11] Ibid. ii. 730.
[12] Ibid. ii. 731.   [13] Ibid. ii. 743.
[14] Ibid. ii. 738 : 'si aliquis fuerit amerciatus in hundredo qui fuerit in
hidagio et vadiet ante judicium quod det pro sua misericordia ante
judicium vi*d*. et post judicium xii*d*.'

Enneston the same custom prevailed, although the amount paid *de hidagio* varied.[1] It will be noticed that the payment in this hundred is called hidage, and is assessed on those in the hidage. The same terminology appears elsewhere in Oxfordshire. In Ewelme hundred in Bensington each virgate gave 2*s.* hidage, and therefore the tenants of these virgates should have been quit for 6*d.* before judgement and 12*d.* after judgement, yet now 'they are amerced at the will of the bailiff and nevertheless give the said hidage'.[2] In Leuknor hundred an additional identification occurs in the manor of Padehale; all give hidage 'pro pulchre placitari videlicet' 6*d.* before, 12*d.* after judgement, and the same is true throughout the hundred.[3] In Banbury hundred it is said that the bailiffs of the Bishop of Lincoln, the lord of the hundred, 'take a certain portion of the pennies from every villata of the hundred at the view of frankpledge for *pulchre placitando*, and nevertheless they cause the *villate* to be amerced at their will.'[4] The payment called on Ramsey manors *fulsting-pound* is then identified in Oxfordshire with hidage and *beuplet*, or *belplayder*. Since hidage and *beuplet* are clearly distinguished in Bedfordshire,[5] where the yearly hidage of two shillings on the hide occurs commonly, it seems probable that hidage may be a local name in Oxfordshire, given because all in the hidage, all holding land geldable to the king unless the geld has been transferred to a private lord, were accustomed to make the amercement payment. It is curious, however, that the rate of hidage, which is commonly mentioned in the county, and in many cases without explanatory details to connect it with the payment for low

---

[1] Rot. Hund. ii. 740: 'Dabunt xxii*s.* de hidagio ... et xxii*s.*.... ita quod si aliquis qui fuerit in hidagio fuerit amerciatus sive amerciandus dabit vi*d.* ante judicium et post judicium xii*d.* videlicet in hundredo de Chadelenton' aut in visu francorum plegiorum.'

[2] Ibid. ii. 31 : 'Dicunt quod quelibet virgata terre de eodem manerio (Bensington) dat duos solidos annuatim de hidagio et sic deberent tenentes earundem esse quieti ante judicium pro sex denariis et post judicium pro duodecim denariis et modo amerciati sunt ad voluntatem ballivi et nichilominus dant dictum hidagium.'

[3] Ibid. ii. 783.   [4] Ibid. ii. 32.

[5] Ibid. i. 4: 'Datur pro hidagio x*s.* domino Regi pro secta et warda v*s.* pro visu iij*s.* pro beuplet' ij*s.*' Cf. p. 6.

amercements, should be usually 6*d.* a virgate, that is to say, 2*s.* on the hide.[1] A payment for a special purpose by all in the hidage of the manor may have become confused with the ordinary hidage, or occasional land-tax turned into a yearly customary payment, of Bedfordshire and Buckinghamshire. The converse, that the hidage of Bedfordshire and Buckinghamshire, and elsewhere, is the *fulstingpound* payment, is not probable, especially since tenants of Ramsey pay both hidage and *fulstingpound*. The other identification, with the payment for having one's cause pleaded well, is even less easy to explain. *Beuplet, belplayder, pro pulchre placitando,* is very common. It seems to have been in reality a personal payment to a sheriff or bailiff of a lord for performing his office, not unlike sheriff's aid, if the ordinary interpretation of that payment be the true one, or the payment to the coroner. It is found, not necessarily identified with *fulstingpound,* in Berkshire,[2] Buckinghamshire,[3] and Cambridgeshire,[4] where it is stated that the amercement for this purpose is taken on the day of the view, and is against the statute of the king; in Derbyshire,[5] as a new imposition raised by the seneschal of the king; in Essex,[6] where the money was given to the bailiff of the hundred, and where, at a vill in Wexeden hundred,[7] the sheriff took at each tourn 12*d.* 'pro pulchre plac'', and yet took amercements too; in Huntingdonshire,[8] where it was taken unjustly by bailiffs of a lord, and in Kent,[9] Lincolnshire,[10] Nottinghamshire,[11] Northamptonshire,[12] Sussex,[13] and Wiltshire.[14] Most clearly of all it occurs in Bedfordshire and

---

[1] Rot. Hund. ii. 812, 853, 860.   [2] Ibid. i. 17, *pass.*

[3] Ibid. ii. 485 : 'Item die visus franciplegii sunt amerciati pro pulchre placitando et hoc contra statuta domini Regis.'

[4] Ibid. i. 37: 'Item de beupleder ejusdem hundredi xix*s.* . . . et de ceteris perquisitis ejusdem hundredi.'

[5] Rot. Hund. i. 58 : 'Levavit quemdam finem . . . bis in anno pro pulcre placitando quod ante dictum tempus fieri non solet.'

[6] Ibid. i. 136.   [7] Ibid. i. 139.

[8] Ibid. i. 198.   [9] Ibid. i. 202.   [10] Ibid. i. 259.

[11] Ibid. ii. 301: 'Est 1 wapentak' et valet modo per annum de perquisitis vi*m.* pro pulchre plac' xxvi*s.* iii*d.* et de auxilio vicecomitis xxxviii*s.* vi*d.*'   [12] Ibid. ii. 12.   [13] Ibid. ii. 203.

[14] Ibid. ii. 272 : 'Preterea idem vicecomes capit decem marcas de thethingis pro pulcre plac' coram eo per duos dies quarum Abbas Malm' habet quinque marcas.'

Buckinghamshire, where the very oppressive sheriff, Alexander Hameldene, whose other sins of extortions were very numerous, made a practice of taking it, whereas before him it was not taken.[1] In almost all these cases the *beuplet* payment is regarded as a distinct injustice, usually of recent origin, its unrighteousness lying, it would seem, in the fact that amercements are taken also, as if it were held that in some way the payment of *beuplet*, like the payment of *fulstingpound*, should free men from some or all amercements. Possibly, we may suppose that unrighteous bailiffs, sheriffs, or private lords are forcing an additional payment from their bailiwicks, perhaps in some cases where by previous arrangement it was already the custom for men to pay a small regular sum for their offences, 6*d.* before judgement, 12*d.* afterwards, either as the result of purchase on their part or of convenience on the part of their lords.

A very important question suggests itself regarding the *fulstingpound* payment in any case, and perhaps regarding *beuplet* also, if a connexion between the two can be established. What is the connexion between the *fulstingpound* or similar payment for amercements, and the twelve-penny amercement shown by Miss Bateson to be, with the 12*d.* burgage rent, the most distinctive privilege offered by the 'laws of Breteuil'?[2] The twelve-penny amercement, valuable because fixing within reasonable, though by no means merely nominal, limits the fines which were likely enough to be made unjustly oppressive by the lords, Miss Bateson found in certain boroughs whose connexion with Breteuil she has traced; especially in Hereford and Rhuddlan, and in certain others where the connexion is not stated. These boroughs are generally in the west of England, or in Wales and Ireland, some of the derived cases extending as far as Cheshire, Staffordshire, and Devon. Outside the boroughs, into the country districts, she does not follow the payment. The phrasing of the amercement clause, as cited by Miss Bateson, is usually a little different from that

---

[1] Rot. Hund. i. 38: 'Item dicunt quod Alex' de Hameldene vic' Bok' primo levavit injuste unam injuriam que vocatur beupleder.' Cf. 4, 5, 6, 37, 45.   [2] Eng. Hist. Rev. xv, xvi.

of the *fulstingpound* clauses ; it limits the fine to 12*d*. without mentioning the payment before and after judgement, except in one instance, that of Macclesfield, where 12*d*. is to be given before judgement, and after judgement a reasonable *misericordia* according to the character of the offence, unless the forfeiture pertain *ad gladum nostrum*. This passage reads very like the passages relating to the Ramsey *fulstingpound*, and the Oxfordshire hidage, and in any case the principle at the base of the rents seems to be the same. The direct connexion with Breteuil in the wide country districts in which so similar a payment seems to have been customary, would be difficult to establish, and it would look, perhaps, as if the fixed, rather low, rate of amercement for offences were far from being distinctive in later times exclusively of towns modelled after Breteuil.

One other point possibly explanatory of this group of payments should be mentioned. It is common to find in the Placita de Quo Waranto, in certain counties, especially in Bedfordshire, Buckinghamshire, Derbyshire, Herefordshire, Huntingdonshire, Lancashire, Nottinghamshire, Northumberland and Northamptonshire,[1] that the lords of franchises lose their views or are obliged to compound for them, because they have taken fines for breaches of the assize of bread, or ale, or both, which are presented at the view, instead of punishing offenders in the regular way by corporal punishment, defined in the Statutes of the Realm. The brewers, for the third offence, should have gone to the tumbrels, the bakers to the pillory.[2] Either the lords have in such cases no *judicialia*, a state of affairs probable in vills in which the number of their tithings or individual tenants was very small, or, more often, having *judicialia* they do not use them, but contrary to the law of the land prefer a money remuneration for offences.[3] They even allow them to fall to the

---

[1] P. Q. W., pp. 5, 6, 22, 23, 27, 29, 30, 32, 65, 85, 87, 89, 90, 133, 135, 144, 154, 155, 156, 210, 217, 268, 270, 294, *pass.*; Rot. Hund. i. 4, 6.

[2] P. Q. W., pp. 268, 372, 374, 378, 505, 523, 530, *pass.*

[3] Ibid., p. 505 : 'non habet tumbrellum quod est proprium judiciale ab inicio institutum . . . et non per amerciamentum quod est singulare proficuum et contra justiciam et communem legem.'

ground.¹ There is, however, always a financial limit recorded in the *Placita* beyond which the lords do not exact fines for breaches of the assize, and it happens that in cases where the two payments can be compared, this financial limit agrees with the amount paid by the vill for *fulstingpound* or its equivalent. Thus especially in Cranfield and Shitlingdon, the villata pays 20s. *fulstingpound*, and also the Abbot of Ramsey punishes all misdemeanours in the assize up to 20s. worth, by fine instead of pillory.² It may be that the Abbot of Ramsey took from his vill a sum of money equal in amount to the sum of the fines normally received, and in consideration of that sum of money, which he was thus assured of obtaining whether his tenants committed any offence or not, let them off with very moderate fines for offences actually committed. The emphasis on fines for breaches of the assize in the Quo Warranto proceedings and the omission of other possible offences mentioned in the Ramsey Cartulary, such as negligence in agricultural matters, would be explained by the fact that the latter offences were purely manorial, and the royal officers were not interested in the lord's arrangements regarding them, whereas the maintenance of the assize of bread and ale was in theory a regality, separate from, although usually exercised at, the view of frankpledge.³

Witefe, Whytepund, Wytepenny, Witepont, Wytepeni, Wytepanes. A rent which may have been of the same nature as the *fulstingpound* is found on Ely manors in the counties of Cambridgeshire, Huntingdonshire, Essex, and Suffolk.⁴ This is the customary rent paid to the bishop, which appears in some compound form of *wite*, like *witefe, witepund*, or *witepenny*.

¹ P. Q. W., p. 546.
² Ibid., p. 65 (Shitlingdon): 'Et quod idem Abbas et predecessores sui seisiti fuerunt de praedictis visubus libera warennam (sic) infangthef weyf et stray et tam libertatibus illis quam quietanciis predictis usi sunt in omnibus prout debuerunt hoc tantum excepto quod idem Abbas nunc levavit fines et amerciamenta de transgressionibus contra assisam panis et cervisie usque ad summam viginti solidorum in casibus quibus per judicium pillorii et tumbrelli puniri meruerunt.' Also pp. 499, 501, 508, 515, 517, *pass.*
³ Ibid., p. 270, and pp. 196, 210, 219, 725.
⁴ Vac. Roll. 1132/10, *pass.*; Claud. C. xi, ff. 30, 43, 49, 53, 96, 111, 127, *pass.*; Tiber. B. ii. *pass.*; Rot. Hund. ii. 538, 543, 605; Eng. Hist. Rev. ix. 418.

The rate of payment varied very much from manor to manor, twelve acres, for example, paying in one vill $4\frac{5}{6}d.$, in another $12d.$, one virgate paying in different localities $6d.$ or $4d.$, or $8d.$ or $8\frac{1}{4}d.$[1] Sometimes there is evidence of a system of grouping of tenants, in order to make up definite portions of the rent; for example, at Ely twelve-acre holdings paid $4d.$ and one-third of a halfpenny, so that three tenants of twelve acres each paid together $14d.$ approximately,[2] and in Somersham, Huntingdonshire, a cottar gave $2\frac{1}{2}d.$ and $\frac{1}{3}d.$ so that three cottars together gave $8\frac{1}{2}d.$[3] The minute fractions noted in other manors probably indicate a similar grouping.[4] The rate of assessment was evidently a matter of individual adjustment between each vill and the lord, regard being had, probably, to some final sum desired, like the *fulstingpound*, a sum which varied in amount in different places, however, and was often more than $20s.$[5] Ely's freedom from amercement is recorded in the Quo Warranto Rolls,[6] and in the earlier custumal the sheriff of Essex turns over to the bishop $115s. 8d.$ 'de misericordiis hominum villarum et decennariorum',[7] and a list of the bishop's fines follows.

Pundscot, Custumpand, Marcselver, Tunnus Census. On Ely manors in Norfolk the rent *pundscot* occurs, paid by all the

---

[1] Claud. C. xi, f. 30: twelve acres de wara 'dat de Wytepund episcopi xii*d.*' Again, ff. 49, 96, 263. Rot. Hund. *loc. cit.*; Eng. Hist. Rev. *loc. cit.*

[2] Claud. C. xi, f. 30: a plena terra of 18 acres de wara paid $7d.$, a dimidia terra of 12 acres paid $4d.$ $\frac{1}{2}d.$ $\frac{1}{3}$ of $\frac{1}{2}d.$: 'Ita scilicet quod tres hujusmodi tenentes dant quatuor decem denarios.' A six-acre holding paid $2\frac{1}{2}d.$; a cotland of one acre $1d.$ The sum from the vill was $43s. 5\frac{1}{2}d.$ The same arrangement exactly is seen in the earlier extent, Tiber. B. ii, ff. 86 *seq.*

[3] Claud. C. xi, f. 105. [4] Ibid., f. 263, for example.

[5] Ibid., ff. 30, 198, 199, 203, 263; Vac. Roll. 1132/10.

[6] P. Q. W., p. 280: 'Et si idem episcopus et homines de feodis suis coram justiciariis itinerantibus in misericordiam inciderint vel finem fecerint pro misericordia sint quieti de illa misericordia. Et si finem fecerint nichil dent ad finem illam.'

[7] Tiber. B. ii, f. 249: 'Vicecomes Essex' reddidit compotum de cxv*s.* viij*d.* de misericordiis hominum villarum et decennar' quorum nomina et causa annotantur in rotulo de Itinere Roberti de Lexintone et sociorum suorum cum hoc signo Ely preposito in margine ejusdem rotuli. In thesauro nichil. Et Episcopo Elyensi c. xv*s.* viij*d.* per libertatem cartarum Reg.' et quietus est.' The fines include: pro falso appello, falso clamore, transgressione, contemptu; quia non est presens, quia retraxit se, &c.

villata except the free, the *husebondi* contributing equally.[1]
In Suffolk a *poundsilver* is recorded in the extent of Hadleigh.[2]
On St. Edmund's manors the rents *Census, Tunnus Census,
Custumpand, Marcselver*, occur.[3] These rents may be the
witepund in other forms ; they may, on the other hand, refer
to the customary tallage or aid. The names seem to indicate
at least that like the *fulstingpound* they refer to rents assessed
at a fixed round sum, a pound or a marc, on the vill to which
the tenants contributed their appropriate shares.[4]

Common amercements and fines. Another kind of dues which
may properly be included among the profits of jurisdiction
were fines or amercements laid upon the county, hundred, or
wapentake as a whole, which were levied usually on the
occasion of some special offence or failure of justice, but in
some cases assessed at a definite annual sum, placed *ad
certum*.

Amercements or *misericordiae* of this kind were due from
county and hundred ; from the county when the court made
a false judgement, or when the county was amerced for some
reason in the eyre of the justices, from the hundred when the
murdrum had to be exacted, and when it became responsible
for other offences, for the failure to produce robbers, for
example.[5] Occasionally a common amercement connected
with the eyre of the forest is mentioned.[6]

Freedom of the franchise from the *misericordiae* and
amercements of the county and hundred, especially from the
murdrum, was usually coupled with freedom from suit of
court,[7] but occasionally lands free from suit were still geldable
for the common amercement. The *murdrum* was often levied

[1] Claud. C. xi, ff. 198, 199 ; Tiber. B. ii, ff. 163, 172.
[2] Suff. Instit. Archaeol. iii. 229 sqq.
[3] See above under miscellaneous rents.
[4] See Hazlitt's Blount's Tenures, p. 439, for *poundland,* and the Scotch
shillingland.
[5] Rot. Hund. i. 528 : ' Item Abbas ... et predecessores sui solebant
contribuere ad commune amerciamentum et ad murdrum quando accidit
cum hominibus hundredi et dare quartam partem.' Also pp. 244, 248,
371, 388 ; P. Q. W., pp. 375, 407, 415, 777, 779, 780, 783 ; Mich. Ambr.
Rent., p. 135 ; Red Bk. Exch. ii. 651, 655, 657.
[6] P. Q. W., pp. 384, 407, 641.
[7] Ibid., pp. 791, 792, *pass.*, 797.

by lords of franchises. In manorial records the common fine of the hundred seems to be sometimes regarded as a certain source of annual revenue, paid by the vills, but the information is not very clear.[1] A late *custuma* called *wapentake fine* is mentioned which seems to indicate a fixed rent.[2]

[1] Worc. Vac. Roll, 1143/18 ; Reg. Worc. Pr., pp. xxxvi, 5, 157 ; York Vac. Roll, 1144/1 ; P. Q. W., pp. 195, 196, 212, 217, 248, 261 ; Mich. Ambr. Rent., p. 93 : 'Item dominus habebit annuatim de consuetudine hundredi de Beato Martino vj*s*. v*d*., et de consuetudine hundredi de Hokedai vj*s*. v*d*.' Perhaps *hundredscot* is meant.

[2] Mon. Angl. iv. 551, 552.

CHAPTER VIII

CHURCH RENTS

CHURCH rents, being of general occurrence and not peculiar to manorial society, do not fall within the field of this study except in so far as they were influenced by the manor and assimilated to customary obligations. The influence of the manor upon them was due in large measure to the fact that the lord of the manor was often the monastery to which the parish church might belong, and which thus gained a power of interference in purely parochial and ecclesiastical arrangements, and turned part of the revenue from the church to private uses. Church rents may be divided into the following classes :—first, rents paid primarily to the parish church or to the monastery which has stepped into its place, including especially *tithes*, *ploughalms*, *soulscot*, and *lightscot*; secondly, *churchscot*, which in later times had become altogether manorialized ; thirdly, rents paid to the provincial church or to Rome direct, especially *synodaticum* and *Peter's Pence*.

Tithes. The important controversies regarding the early history of tithes need not be considered in a brief discussion of the place of tithes in the manor. Briefly stated, the safest conclusion seems to be that in origin the endowment of parish churches resulted from arbitrary dedication to them by laymen of a certain proportion of their revenues.[1] The existence of tithes, of the consecration to the church of the tenth of one's possessions, dates from the earliest times, but the payment was voluntary until 787, when legatine councils made it imperative but did not prescribe a particular destination. Edgar's law[2] first made the payment of tithes to the 'Old Minster', the head church of the district, incumbent, except in cases where a thegn had a church with a burying-ground

---

[1] Selden, History of Tithes ; Stubbs, Con. Hist. i. 248 ; Hunt, in Hist. Eng. Church, i. 160, 161, 224, 239, 290, 359 ; Roundell Palmer, Ancient Facts and Fictions, p. 292, *pass.*   [2] Edg. ii.

attached to it on his private estates and should wish to dedicate to it a third of his tithes. If his church had no burying-ground, the thegn paid the priest, and all tithes went to the Old Minster. These provisions were repeated in later laws.

Though paid normally to the parish church, tithes were yet often appropriated in part or wholly by a monastery or religious house, and for long this appropriation was acquiesced in with little protest. In the thirteenth century, however, the assignment of tithes to churches was clearly recognized, and in theory monasteries or religious houses claiming them must produce documentary evidence of their right.[1] The monks were constantly struggling to gain papal exemption from the burden of tithes for their demesne land; the parochial clergy, depending upon the tithes for support, were as constantly struggling against it; and the Pope vacillated between the two, desiring the friendship of both. In 1215 the Lateran Council declared that monks and religious houses, except Hospitallers, Templars, and Cistercians, must pay tithe to the village church, but even after this decree the monks frequently gained their point, and had their demesne declared exempt, either as the result of direct grant or of customary use. Professor Savine has shown how important a part of the spiritual revenues of monasteries at the time of the Dissolution was thus derived from the tithes of the monastic demesne.[2] In cases where the parish church was in the hands of the monastery the appropriation of tithes to the monastery was common and easy.

In the Anglo-Saxon Laws tithes appear as the tenth part of the young cattle, paid at Pentecost, and the tenth part of the fruits of the earth paid at All Souls or the autumn equinox,[3] 'the tithe of yong cattell to be paid at Whitsontide and of fruits of the earth at All Hallows.'[4] By the thirteenth century these had been stretched to include, as titheable products, corn crops,

[1] Capes, in Hist. Eng. Ch. iii. 261 ; Stubbs, Con. Hist. i. 248 sqq.
[2] Oxford Studies, vol. i. 107–13. Trevelyan, England in the Age of Wyclif, p. 125 (1st ed.).
[3] Ethelred, v. 11 ; Cnut. i. 8.   [4] Selden, Tithes, p. 222.

hay, fruit, honey, butter, cheese, wool, chickens, doves, lambs, calves, fish from the water, venison from the forest, gains of the miller and merchant, the professional man's earnings.[1] Frequent disputes occurred between church and lay courts in the thirteenth and fourteenth centuries regarding tithes, especially regarding the tithes of wood, *sylva caedua*.[2]

The descriptions of tithes in the custumals vary very much in fulness. The lord's bailiffs were little concerned with the payments made to parish churches; but when the tithes had been appropriated by the monastery or a division was made between the vicar and the monastery some statement of the character of this obligation is given, and of the division of the burden between tenants' land and lands in demesne. Worcester and Ramsey furnish excellent examples of the incidence of tithes on church manors. At Worcester the villeins paid the greater and the lesser tithes, which are described in detail;[3] they threshed and carried the tithes of grain.[4] In some manors the parish church received all the tithes of the demesne except the *decimae nutrimentorum et novalium*, which were paid yearly to the Prior and convent *de pensione*.[5] Cases of commuted tithes occur.[6] The Ramsey Cartulary also, in the description of most manors, states the division and destinations of the tithes.[7]

Plough alms. *Ploualmes*, the ancient *sulhaelmessan* or *elemosina carucarum*, was a common obligation due to the church in Saxon times. Fifteen days after Easter a penny was paid by every plough which had been yoked between Easter and Pentecost. Ethelred's statement of the law is clear :—' And that there be given from every plough a penny or penny's worth, and every one that has a family shall see to

[1] Capes, Eng. Ch. iii. 268.

[2] Pollock and Maitland, Eng. Law, i. 106, quoting Matt. Paris, C. M. iv. 614 ; Bracton, ff. 402 b, 403 ; Circumspecte Agatis Stat. Realm, i. 101, c. 3 ; Articuli Cleri, i. 171, c. i. ; Stubbs, Con. Hist. ii. 627. Compare ibid. iii. 352, for the tithe of personality.

[3] Reg. Worc. Pr., p. 44 a.

[4] Ibid., pp. 32 b, 43 a.

[5] Ibid., pp. 53 a, 55, 64 b, 67 b, *pass*.

[6] Ibid., pp. lxxvi, 59 b, 60 a, 64 b.

[7] Ram. Cart. i. 279 sqq. ; D. S. P., pp. 64, 150; Abing. Acc., pp. 85, 88, 102, and *pass*. in manorial extents.

it that each *hirmannus* of his shall give it, or, if he have it not, his lord shall give it for him.'[1]

In later times *ploughalms* was a rare payment. It occurs on the Ramsey manor of Saint Ives as a penny paid the vicar from every plough yoked between Easter and Pentecost, and from every plough yoked in the hamlets of Waldhirst and Woodhurst at the same time as a loaf of bread, half of which went to the vicar and half to the poor.[2] At Wistowe a similar provision appears, except that the payment of bread called *soloualmes* was made at the rate of six loaves from a virgate, two at All Souls, two at Innocents, and two on the morrow of Pentecost.[3] Elsewhere payments assessed on the plough were for the maintenance of church lights, and took on a different form. At Peterborough a heavy food rent like the farm was paid *ad caritatem S. Petri*. In Undele, for example, one cow worth 30*d.* and three hundred loaves were given for this purpose,[4] and at Wermintone the *pleni et semi villani* paid ten rams, four hundred loaves, forty dishes, one hundred and thirty-four hens and two hundred and sixty eggs.[5] The cloth paid in connexion with this rent suggests the *scrud* rent, the rent *ad vestimentum*, in ancient times due from *scrudland*. At Abingdon a heavy poultry rent was due at the 'misericordiae' made at Martinmas and Christmas.[6] The large donations of eleemosynary bread mentioned in the charters will be recalled, and also the *almesfeoh* of the Laws and *Rectitudines*. *Sulsilver*, a rent in Saint Edmund's manor

---

[1] Ethel. vii. 1, 2; E. and G. 6, 3; Athel. 1, 4; Edm. 1, 2; Ede. ii. 2, 3; Aethel. v. 11, vi. 16, vii. 1, viii. 12; Cnut. i. 8.

[2] Ram. Cart. i. 282: 'De qualibet caruca juncta inter Pascha et Pentecosten unum denarium qui dicitur ploualmes, recipit apud Sanctum Ivonem, et pro singulis capitibus junctis eodem tempore in carucis apud Waldehyrst et Wodehyrst unum panem cujus collectionis medietas remanet vicario, et alia medietas pro voluntate parochianorum erogatur pauperibus.' Cf. pp. 294, 331, 341.

[3] Ibid. i. 353: 'De qualibet etiam caruca juncta infra festum Sancti Michaelis et Natale percipit vicarius unum denarium. Et de qualibet virgata terre habebit vicarius sex panes, qui dicuntur soloualmes.'

[4] Chron. Petrob., p. 158.

[5] Ibid., p. 161. Cf. pp. 159, 160, 162, 163, 165.

[6] Abing. Acc. ii. 317: 'Item de Bertune reddent ad misericordiam quae fit circa festum S. Martini x et viii gallinas et ad aliam misericordiam quae fit post Natale Domini x et viii.'

of Werketon, which sometimes has the form *culsilver* paid at
Pentecost and was uncertain in amount, may possibly be
a form of *ploughalms*, but seems more probably the commutation of a rent of ploughshares to the lord.[1] *Ploughsilver* is
mentioned at Durham, but without explanation.[2]

Light scot, another *rectitudo* of the church in Anglo-Saxon
times, was paid usually at Candlemas,[3] but according to Cnut
three times in the year, first at Easter, again at All Saints,
and again at Candlemas, at the rate of a halfpenny's worth
of wax from every hide.[4] In later times this rent was common,
occurring usually in the form of *ad luminare Beatae Mariae*
or *ad candelam*. It was due at Candlemas and was used for
lighting the church. It was paid in the Ramsey manors of
Abbot's Ripton and Broughton at the rate of a penny from
a married cottar, and a halfpenny from an unmarried cottar.[5]
In Wistowe every house with a hearth paid a halfpenny at
Easter to light the church.[6] At Brancester the *persona*
received a penny from every plough of the *curia* for Easter
wax.[7] At Glintone, a manor belonging to Peterborough,
a penny was paid by every plough for Easter wax,[8] and on
St. Paul's manors and elsewhere similar rents were fairly
common.[9] In the north in the manors of Durham the rent
appears as *ad luminare*,[10] and also as *candelwekesilver*.[11]
Waurshot or *waresilver* seems to have been a similar rent.[12]

Soulscot was in origin the Anglo-Saxon mortuary due, paid
at the open grave, if a man were buried in his own parish,
and if he were buried elsewhere still paid to the minster to
which he had properly belonged.[13] Of mortuary dues the

---

[1] See *sulsilver*, above.   [2] Hazlitt's Blount's Tenures, p. 132.
[3] E. and G. 6, 2 ; Ethelr. viii. 12.
[4] Cnut. i. 12 ; Ethelr. v. 11, vi. 19.   [5] Ram. Cart. i. 321, 331, 341.
[6] Ibid. i. 294, 353.   [7] Ibid. i. 413.
[8] Chron. Petrob., p. 163 : 'Et de quaque caruca ejusdem villae *id.* cere
ad lumina ecclesiae de Burch.'
[9] D. S. P., pp. 161, 162, 163 ; Rot. Hund. ii. 842.
[10] Feod. Dun., pp. 35, 43.
[11] D. H. R., p. 243 : 'Tenentes . . . pro candlewekesilver ibidem per
annum 2*s.*' Feod. Dun., p. 314.
[12] Hazlitt's Blount's Tenures, p. 380; and see *waursilver* above.
[13] Aethel. i. 4 ; Edgar, ii. 5 ; Ethelr. v. 12, vi. 20, 21, viii. 13 ; Cnut. i. 13 ;
Earle, Land Charters, p. 265 ; Seebohm, Tribal Custom in A. S. Law,
p. 461 n.

custumals usually tell very little. *Soulesilver*, if this be the same as the *soulscot* payment, amounted to a large sum in the receipts of Durham,[1] and occurs again at Abingdon.[2] The vicar's right to a second best beast after the lord has chosen the best for heriot was fairly common.[3]

Occasionally other rents to the church or monastery are mentioned, which are rather general in character. Thus the *alteragium* or *altelagium* were fees of one kind or another made at the altar for services and the maintenance of vestments.[4] The *consuetudo prebende* was paid commonly at Martinmas by villeins at Tischerton, a Peterborough manor, at the rate of 2*d.* from a full villein, a penny from a half villein.[5] At St. Paul's a rent called *dizenae* was collected, 'possibly the denus denarius . . . the seven pence per week or penny per day, in some way a tenth penny or tithe which was paid to the almoner of the cathedral, and denas may be a form of dizenas, quasi diesenas . . . all that we know certainly of the dizenae is that they were money payments made in each of the fifty-two weeks of the year by each manor in turn.'[6]

Church scot was a rent of another kind, paid to the lord of the manor. The provisions regarding it in Domesday Book have been most fully discussed by Professor Vinogradoff, who finds in the incidence of the rent on the hides of Worcestershire and Berkshire an evidence of premanorial conditions, where it was paid by the normal householder with a hide, and was a rent for church purposes, parallel to the king's gafol.[7] On the questions regarding its earlier history, especially the attempt of Anglo-Saxon kings and the church to turn a special church rent into a rent of general incidence,[8] later conditions throw very little light, except in the one particular

---

[1] Feod. Dun., p. 211.   [2] Abing. Acc., p. 5.
[3] See above.
[4] Glouc. Cart. ii. 224; Worcester Vac. Roll, 1143/18, *pass.*
[5] Chron. Petrob., p. 164.
[6] D. S. P., pp. cxxvii. 154.
[7] Eng. Soc. Elev. Cent., pp. 419, 441, 454, and see also Mr. Round's note in Eng. Hist. Rev. v. 101.
[8] Kemble, Saxons, ii. 490; Schmid, Gesetze, p. 545; Domes. Book and Beyond, p. 321.

that the *churchscot* of the later manorial documents seems to
have been limited to the counties that were generally within
the limits of the West Saxon kingdom. There are no clear
cases of it in East Anglia, or in the north or northern midlands. It occurred commonly, on the other hand, in the
twelfth and thirteenth centuries, on the lands of St. Augustine,
Worcester, Gloucester, Glastonbury, Abingdon, Winchester,
Battle, and elsewhere in the counties of Oxfordshire, Gloucestershire, Berkshire, Somersetshire, Hampshire, and Wiltshire,
and perhaps in Surrey. In many manors belonging to various
lords in these counties it was a heavy burden on the customary tenants, paid in the form of grain, poultry, or money.
Very occasionally there is a regulation regarding *churchscot*
that may point back to the *cyresceatweorc*, once mentioned
in Anglo-Saxon times,[1] and perhaps forming a fourth variety
of early labour service, in addition to *gavolerth, graserth*, and
benerth. As would be expected from its prominence in
Domesday Book, *churchscot* survived at Worcester and formed
one of the articles of inquiry for the Register of the Priory in
the middle of the thirteenth century.[2] The rent was paid in
hens and in grain, and was not one of the 'new customs' by
which some tenants had been enfeoffed, but was always part
of the old enfeoffment. Thus, at Stoke one-sixth of a *cron* of
corn paid according to the older customs is not mentioned
among the new customs.[3] In the vacancy rolls of Worcester
Martinmas hens are frequently mentioned.[4] The *churchscot* rent
in Buckinghamshire, Domesday states, was not paid after the
Conquest.[5] On Gloucester manors *churshaec* was paid commonly in the form of grain or poultry,[6] and in Glastonbury
churchscot formed a usual part of the customary obligation,
being rendered, however, usually only when services were
rendered in labour, and not when they were put *ad censum*
in any year.[7] It was paid often at the rate of four hens or

[1] Kemble C. D., 1086.
[2] Reg. Worc. Pr., p. 25[a] : cf. pp. lvii, 43[b], 52[a], 79, 83.
[3] Ibid., p. 102.   [4] Vac. Roll, 1143/18.
[5] D. B. i. 143[b] ; Eng. Soc. Elev. Cent., p. 441.
[6] Glouc. Cart. iii. 37, 40, 43 ; i. 158.
[7] Inqu. 1189, pp. 28, 110, 117, 124.

a bushel of grain from a virgate, a distinction being made sometimes in the amount owed by the married or unmarried tenant, and it was paid by all classes of customary tenants, by cottars and *undersetles*, as well as virgaters.[1] Once it is called 'churchscot of the priest'.[2] At Abingdon it appears as grain or poultry.[3] The Winchester *churchscot*, a very heavy rent, is described clearly in the Pipe Rolls of that church. It was paid in grain, in hens, which are distinguished from the hens *de consuetudine*, or in money, and is regularly accounted for by the bailiff.[4] At Sutton account is rendered of 23*d*. *cheriset* in addition to 20 quarters and 2 bushels of corn, and 100 hens. These are sent to the deacon;[5] elsewhere the food rent is received by the constable and his family,[6] or is given to the huntsmen.[7] 'The men who give *cheriset*' are specially distinguished as a class by themselves among the tenants.[8] Crondal records give further evidence of this heavy payment in Hampshire.[9] *Churchscot* is common also on the manors of Battle, where in Brightwaltham, Berkshire, it appears in the account rolls as *arentatus in certo*, and was paid in grain, poultry, or money.[10] Elsewhere, possibly, Battle records connect it with labour; the villeins gather *stipula* on the demesne, and on account of this give *churchscot*,[11] or plough, or give *churchscot* as the lord chooses.[12] The Bleadon custumal shows that sometimes it was called *hensyeve* when paid in hens, and at Christchurch, Hampshire, it was called *Martinrent*.[13] The Hundred Rolls record it commonly in the counties enumerated, especially in Oxfordshire, where, as at Battle, it is once stated that it was paid in return for permis-

---

[1] Mich. Ambr. Rent., pp. 8, 9, 12, 59.   [2] Ibid., p. 115.
[3] Abing. Acc. ii. 53, 301, 305, 306, 309.
[4] Winch. Pipe Roll, pp. 3, 8, 9, 10, 11, 12, 15, 23, *pass*.
[5] Ibid., pp. 41–43 ; cf. pp. 10, 25, 30.
[6] Ibid., pp. 71, 73.
[7] Ibid., p. 57.   [8] Ibid., p. 20.
[9] Crondal Records, pp. 57, 60, 78, 84, 86, 92, 95, 105.
[10] Min. Acc. 742/17, 18, 19. Also Batt. Abb. Cust., pp. 60, 77, 78, 80, 85.
[11] Batt. Abb. Cust., p. 89; Misc. Bks. Augm. Off., vol. 57, ff. 43, 51, 57.
[12] Ibid., p. 74. The tenants plough, sow, and harrow grasacre, and for this are free from churchscot ; cf. p. 58.
[13] Blead. Cust., pp. 182–210, especially 196, 201.

sion to gather stubble on the demesne after Martinmas.[1] It is
usual in Oxfordshire to find it paid to the lord of a lay manor
as a villein rent, and similar cases occur occasionally elsewhere. It is sometimes found in account rolls regularly included among *minute consuetudines*, or under the *exitus
manerii*.[2]

Churchscot probably appears sometimes in the form of a rent
of seed given to the church called *church seed*. On account of
the many possible variations in the spelling of *churchscot* the two
forms are sometimes difficult to distinguish from one another,
and probably in any case both refer to the same payment,
churchseed, that is to say, forming a part of the *churchscot*.[3]
Thus in Cnut's letter from Rome provision is made as
follows: 'Et in festivitate S. Martini primitiae seminum ad
ecclesiam sub cujus parrochia quisque deget quae Anglice
cyricsceat nominatur.'[4]   In the Red Book of the Exchequer,
in the *Expositiones*. the following definitions occur:—*Chirchesed
Chircheomer vel Chircheambre.* ' Une certaine mesure de ble
batu qe chescun homme donoit au temps des Bretons et des
Englois al eglise le jor Seint Martyn.'[5] The form appears in
later times very rarely. In the Domesday of St. Paul's,
however, it is written in the margin of the account of Bernes
in Surrey as a gloss on *mantecorn*, and an interesting note is
added by the editor in which the rent is connected with a
very ancient Celtic custom taken over by the church.[6]

Another class of payments went beyond the parish church
and the monastery or lay lord of the franchise, to the church
at large, and had little connexion, as a rule, with customary
rents. The most important representatives of this class
were the *Synodaticum* and *Peter's Pence*. Occasional re-

---

[1] Rot. Hund. ii. 712, 757, 758, 763, 775, 776, 779, 780, 782, 785, 786,
818, 874.
[2] Min. Acc. 850/10 ; Kennet, Par. Antiq., p. 262 ; D. S. P., p. cxxiv.
[3] Rot. Hund. ii. 712, 757, 776, 779, 782.
[4] Thorpe's Gloss. to Vol. I., with references.
[5] Red. Bk. Excheq. iii. 1039: the passage continues ' Mais puis la
venue des Normans, si le pristent a lor oeps plusors seignurs et le donerent
solonc la veu ley Moisi *nomine primitiarum* sicome vous trouverez en les
lettres le roi Cnut qil envoia a Rome, et est dit Cherchesed ; quasi semen
ecclesiae.'
[6] D. S. P., p. 105. Cf. pp. 154* and cxxiv.

ferences occur also to payments to archdeacons for various
purposes.

Payments to Synods.   'By canon law . . . a bishop holding
a synod was entitled to receive 2*s.* from every person
cited to it, the payment being termed *synodaticum*, the
object being to tempt the bishop to hold synods. . . .
Probably synods of bishops were held twice a year even
after William I.'[1]   The payment is thus defined by the
editor of the Domesday of St. Paul's in explanation of the
common occurrence of the *synodaticum* on St. Paul's manors.
On each manor a yearly rent is mentioned, paid at Michaelmas, for this purpose, amounting to something over a shilling,
collected like the Peter's Pence, and once retained by the
firmarius for his own purposes.[2]   As in the case of other
rents, the lord, paying an annual sum himself, may have
recouped himself with a larger sum exacted from his customary tenants and paid under the name of the original rent
or some other.   The Hexham documents include a quit claim
of 4*s.* of synodal rent from an archdeacon of the West Riding.[3]
The payment occurs in the Gloucester Cartulary ;[4] Durham,
in a probably spurious charter, is exempted from it.[5]   'Aids'
of archdeacons and bishops are sometimes mentioned also,[6]
and at Ramsey there were various payments made to the
archdeacons appointed to collect the papal dues.[7]   A curious
collection of a different character was the *Confraria, Fraria,
Collectae,* voluntary contributions collected by the Knights
Hospitallers from 'diverse churches' of the neighbourhood,
originally in virtue of some papal bull.[8]

Peter's Pence.   The controversy regarding the origin and
early history of the *Romescot* or *Peter's Penny* has little
bearing on the incidence of the payment on the manorial
population.   The disappointing meagreness of the information
regarding it in the later documents probably results from the

---

[1] D. S. P., p. cxv.
[2] Ibid., pp. 140 et seq.
[3] Hex. Pr. ii. 86.
[4] Glouc. Cart. ii. 125.
[5] Feod. Dun., p. lxxvii
[6] Feod. Dun., p. lxxxvii.
[7] Ram. Cart. ii. 152.
[8] Knights Hospitallers, xxx. 4, 7.

extra-manorial character of the due. The researches of Favre
and Jensen have proved that the actual amount of money
sent to Rome annually from this source was approximately
300 marcs, whether that fixed sum may have been the survival of an old customary assessment, or the result of a
twelfth-century convention between the pope and bishops,
and that papal attempts to secure more than this amount
were unsuccessful.[1] From the information given in the
custumals it seems probable that a much larger sum than this
was collected each year, or at least in years in which the
payment was made to Rome. Custumals often state that
every one with goods to the value of 30d., the later Saxon or
early Norman alteration of the original assessment on each
householder, contributed a penny to St. Peter.[2] Sometimes
if a villein were married he paid a penny, if unmarried, only
a halfpenny. The custom at Ramsey is clearly stated :
Whoever, being married, has on Christmas Eve *averia*, plough
beasts, to the value of 30d. at least, shall give at *Ad Vincula*
a penny, which penny is called the *denarius Sancti Petri*, and
a man without a wife and a widow shall give a halfpenny.
For chattels, moreover, the said penny shall not be given.[3]
The restriction of liability to those with *averia* is rare. At
Battle the more common assessment on chattels, movables,
to the value of 30d., occurs on one manor ;[4] on another it is
stated that *omnes tenentes* pay the due.[5] The provisions
regarding marriage are found also at Glastonbury and
elsewhere.[6] Sometimes the form of statement in the records
suggests that the tax was levied on the villata as a fixed sum,
the distribution of which would be a matter of local custom
and arrangement, and the total amount not necessarily, therefore, an indication of the capacity of the vill. Thus in the

---

[1] Favre, Mélanges Rossi. Jensen in Trans. Roy. Hist. Soc., vol. xv
and xix, especially documents printed in Appendix.
[2] For example, Edw. Conf. Leg. 10; Leg. Will. Pr. i. 17.
[3] Ram. Cart. i. 331. Cf. i. 282, 321, *pass.*
[4] Batt. Abb. Cust., p. 90.
[5] Ibid., p. 89. Cf. Rot. Hund. ii. 723, 764.
[6] Mich. Ambr. Rent., pp. 72, 81, 149 ; Batt. Abb. Cust., p. 12 ; D. S. P.,
p. cxvii, quoting the Inquest of 1279.

Register of Worcester long lists are given of the amounts from various manors, amounts ranging from 5d. to 3s. 5d.,[1] and in the Gloucester Cartulary the total amount due from Littleton is given as 20d. a year as if the sum were not subject to change.[2] Custumals give occasionally the total sum due from a vill.[3] Whatever may have been the variations in local custom, it would seem probable that the amount collected within the manors would have brought a sum far in excess of the 300 marcs paid to the pope, and on the appropriation of the surplus we get sometimes a little light. Thus Innocent in a letter inquires concerning the unjust appropriation of the due by prelates, and commands an inquiry to be made in the matter.[4] More specific information may be had from the Domesday of St. Paul's regarding the method of collection in the manor and the possibilities of misappropriation. In Cadendon and Kenesworth it was collected by the rural dean.[5] In several manors the collection was made by the *sacerdos*.[6] At Tidwolditon it was collected and paid by the clerk,[7] and in still other cases it was collected by the *firmarius* and paid by him to the dean,[8] but in Sutton and Norton the *firmarius* collected it and retained it.[9] The money collected was paid usually by the dean to the archdeacon. Still clearer evidence of the retaining of Peter's Penny is furnished by the account rolls of Winchester. The bishop was responsible for the payment of a given amount to the pope's representative, but collected evidently the total sum himself of which his manors were capable, and, handing over only the correct proportion of the total English assessment which was due from his diocese, regularly included the *residuum* in the *exitus* of his manors.[10] Thus in the account of Wittene the bailiff 'reddit compotum de 3s. 6d. de residuis denariorum Sancti Petri', and at Wicumbe the words 'hoc anno' are added. In

---

[1] Reg. Worc. Pr., pp. 25ᵃ, 98ᵃ.   [2] Glouc. Cart. iii. 37.
[3] Abing. Acc., pp. 6, 39; Cust. Roff., pp. 7, 8.
[4] Jensen, Trans. Roy. Hist. Soc. xv.; and Rymer's Foedera, i. 176, 182.
[5] D. S. P., p. 147.   Cf. pp. cxvii, 148 (*bis*).
[6] Ibid., pp. 149, 150, 151.   [7] Ibid., p. 148.
[8] Ibid., p. 151.   [9] Ibid., pp. 150, 151.
[10] Winch. Pipe Rolls, pp. 16, 20, 32, 64. For excellent examples of such disparity, see Vac. Rolls, 1131/3 and 1128/4.

the Black Book of St. Augustine's the Romescot is included regularly in the list of customary dues without a statement of its destination.[1] The Bishop of Worcester granted Peter's Penny by a charter to the monks of Worcester.[2] Jensen has shown the various methods used in the collection of rent. Before Becket's time the Archbishop of Canterbury was responsible for the collection ; from the time of Becket to 1284, a bishop was commissioned by the pope, while at the end of the thirteenth century a special collector took charge of Peter's Penny and other payments, and had under him, and responsible to him, a number of sub-collectors for different districts. England was divided for this purpose into districts, in accordance with the two archbishoprics, the bishoprics, and archidiaconates, and the sum due from each district was fixed.[3] The exact method by which manorial collections reached the collectors, and the power of the collectors to interfere in manorial arrangements, does not appear. In the earlier period the king might be called upon to require his justices to enforce the payment,[4] and the sheriffs may have been given some authority in the matter.[5]

Other names for Peter's Penny were *Romescot*, *hearthpenny*, *smokepenny*, *swarfmoney*, and *fire harth*. The identification of *Romescot* with Peter's Penny is probably unvarying, but the exact meaning of *hearthpenny* is not always so clear. In the laws the two names, *hearthpenny* and *Peter's Penny*, refer to the same payment ; thus Edgar states that every *hearthpenny* shall be paid at St. Peter's and the usual *Peter's Penny* penalty is attached to failure to pay it.[6] In the *Rectitudines*, on the other hand, and in the Battle custumals, a difficulty arises from the appearance of *hearthpenny* side by side with *Romescot*.[7] Possibly the payment was made twice a year at

[1] Faust. A. i, ff. 10, 17, 60 *pass.*   [2] Reg. Worc. Pr., p. 98[b].
[3] Trans. Roy. Hist. Soc., *loc. cit.* Cf. Ram. Cart. i. 109, ii. 152.
[4] Trans. Roy. Hist. Soc., n. s. xix, p. 224. Letter of Foliot to the king quoted : ' write to your justices about it and order that it shall be done.' See Hist. Eng. Law, i, p. 539, n. 2.
[5] Trans. Roy. Hist. Soc., n. s. xix. 228.
[6] Edgar, ii. 4.
[7] Schmid, Anh. iii. 3, and note. Batt. Abb. Cust., pp. 4, 5, 7, 8, 10 : ' Pro Romescot et hertyeld ' 2*d.*, 1*d.*, or 4*d.* ; p. 43, hertheld at the feast

Battle and the payment at the feast of St. Thomas was called *hearthyield*, while that at *ad Vincula* was called *Romescot*, or else the name *hearthpenny* at Battle is applied to a payment resembling *churchscot* or some other church due. At Glastonbury, on the other hand, the two names, *Peter's Penny* and *hurtpeni*, seem to have been used interchangeably.[1] Probably *hearthpenny* was a more general name applicable to any tax levied primarily on householders, but usually identified with the Peter's Penny.

Smokepenny or *Smokesilver* is curiously defined in a late document : 'To the summer for Peterpence or smoke farthings sometyme due to the Antecriste of roome x*d*.'[2] *Swarfmoney*[3] and *fire harth*[4] appear to be other late names for the same payment.

The study of church rents shows that they, like the royal rents, although in less measure, yielded to the co-ordinating forces of the manor and were assimilated in part to customary rents proper. When the lord of the manor had become the immediate, if not the ultimate, recipient of such extra-manorial dues, the further step, the placing of them *ad certum* for a fixed annual sum, was not difficult to take.

of St. Thomas Apostle, Romescot at the feast of St. Peter ad Vincula ; pp. 5, 8, 9, 113, Romescot without herthyeld. Misc. Bks. Augm. Off., vol. 57, ff. 15, 33.
　[1] Inqu. 1189, pp. 22, 36, 82, 84, 86 ; Mich. Ambr. Rent., pp. 12, 72, 81, 120, 121, 197.
　[2] Hazlitt's Blount's Tenures, p. 441, quoting Archaeol. xxxv, p. 430, in a document of 1575.
　[3] Ibid., p. 202.　　　　　　　　　　　[4] Ibid., p. 380.

RENTS PAID FROM GELDABLE LAND AS THEY APPEAR IN THE HUNDRED ROLLS

County.	Hidage.	Aux' Vic'.	Ward.	Pontage.	Murage.	Hundred Aid.	For Suit.	For View.	Turnus Vic'.	Beuplet.	Common Fine.	Miscellaneous.
Beds.	common		common				common	common				low amercement
Berks.	common	common					common	common		occasional		
Bucks.	common		common	common			common	common (frithpenny)	common	common		
Cambs.	occasional; to Ramsey	common	common				common	common (bornselver)		common		
Cornwall			common									
Derby		common					common	common	common	occasional	common	
Devon	quando currit	common					common	(chevage)				
Dorset		occasional					common	common	common			
Essex		common	common				common	common (bornselver)		common		shirreveswelcome
Gloucester							common	common				
Hereford		Perquisites of sheriffs.				hundred fees	common	common				
Herts.		common					common	common	common			
Hunts.	to Ramsey	common	common			to Ramsey	common	common (hevedpenny)	common	common	common	
Kent			common	common			common	(borghes-ealdrespeni)	common			

County	1	2	3	4	5	6	7	8	9	10	11
Leicester		common	commo		common	common	common			common	
Lincoln		common	common		common	common	common			common	murdrum
Norfolk		common (shirreve-scot)	common		common (hundred-scot)	common (letefe)					wodwelschot radbodispund
Northants.		common	common		common	common	common	common			
Northumb.						common	common	no turnus vic' in county	common		cornage pannage
Notts.		common		common	common	common					
Oxon.	common	(schirpeni once)	common	common	common	common	common (hevedpenny) (friesilver)	common	common		low amercement
Rutland					common	(motfe)				common	
Salop	very occasional	(aux' prepos')	(strete-ward)			common	common	common			pukerelleschild
Somerset		common			common	common	common				
Southampton											
Stafford		common				common	common				
Suffolk		common	common			common	common (bortremium)				
Sussex		common				common			occasional		
Warwick		common	occasional			common	common			common	
Wilts.		common	occasional			common (tithingpeny)	common	common		common	
Worcester								occasional	common occasional		
Yorks.						common					wapentake fines

DOCUMENTS FROM WHICH THE LIST OF RENTS HAS BEEN CHIEFLY COMPILED

Abingdon Abbey: Obedientiars' accounts (Camden Society).

St. Augustine's, Canterbury: Cott. MSS., Faust. A. i.

Bath and Wells, See of: Vacancy Roll, P.R.O., Min. Acc. 1131/3, (30 Edw. I).

Battle Abbey: Custumals of (Camden Society).
　Misc. Bks., Augm. Off. vol. 57 (custumal).
　Brightwalton, Berks., Min. Acc. 742/16–19 (22–34 Edw. III).
　Wyr, Kent, Min. Acc. 899/1 (8–9 Edw. III); 899/11 (30–31 Edw. III).

Burton Abbey: Abstract of the Burton Chartulary (Wm. Salt Archaeol. Soc.).

Bury St. Edmunds: Abbey of St. Edmund, Harl. MSS. 3977 (custumal); Harl. MSS. 1005 (custumal); Harl. MSS. 743 (custumal).

Cambridgeshire Manor: F. W. Maitland, E. H. R. ix. 417.

Canterbury, Christ Church: Add. MSS. 6159 (custumal).
　Harl. MSS. 1006 (custumal).
　Vacancy Roll, 1128/1 (54–55 Hen. III); 1128/4 (6–7 Edw. II).

Chichester, See of: Vacancy Roll, 1131/11 (33 Edw. I).

Cockersand Abbey, Chartulary of (Chetham Society).

Coventry and Lichfield, See of: Vacancy Roll, 1132/5 (15 Edw. II).

Durham, See of: Boldon Book (D. B. iv. Add. and Surtees Society).
　Bishop Hatfield's Survey (Surtees Society).
　Feodarium Prioratus Dunelmensis (Surtees Society).
　Halmota Prioratus Dunelmensis (Surtees Society).
　Vacancy Roll, 1144/17 (4 Edw. II); 1144/18 (7 Edw. III).

Ely, See of: Inquisitio Eliensis (D. B. iv. Add.).
　Cott. MSS. Tiber. B ii (custumal); Claud. C. xi (custumal).
　Extenta Maneriorum, Ely Muniment Room.
　Poss. Elien. in Norfolk, *temp*. Edw. III, Add. Ch. 37763.
　Vacancy Roll, 1132/10 (26–28 Edw. I); 1132/13 (9–10 Edw. II).

Essex, Manorial Customs of, Charnock,
　Customs of 1298, Essex Archaeol. Trans. N. S. 109.
　Misc. B. Land Revenue, 214, f. 206.
　Customs at Great Tey, Essex, Astle, Archaeol. vol. xii.

Exeter, See of: Vacancy Roll, 1138/2 (43–44 Edw. III).

Glastonbury, Abbey of: Inquest of 1189 (Liber Henrici de Soliaco (Roxburghe Club).
　Rentalia et Custumaria Michaelis de Ambresbury (Somerset Record Society).

Gloucester, Abbey of: Historia et Cartularium Monasterii S. Petri Gloucestriae (Rolls Series).
　Barton Regis, Min. Acc. 850/8–80 (*temp*. Hen. V.).

Guisborough, Priory of: Cartularium Prioratus de Gyseburne (Surtees Society).

Hampshire: Crondal Records, ed. Baigent (Hampshire Record Society).
Hertfordshire: Compotus Roll of Anstie, in Cunningham, Growth of English Industry and Commerce.
Hexham, Priory of: Chroniclers, &c. (Surtees Society).
Huntingdonshire: Glatton, Min. Acc. 876/14 (7–8 Edw. II).

Lancashire: Ashton under Lyne (Chetham Society).
Customs of Manor in North of England, Hibbert.
Lichfield: see Coventry.
Lichfield Manor, Brewood.
Lincolnshire: Terrier of Fleet, Add. MSS. 35169.
Ingoldmells Court Rolls (Associated Archit. Societies).
London: Munimenta Gildhallae (Rolls Series).
See of: Vacancy Roll, 1140/20 (16–17 H. VI).

Newminster, Abbey of: Chartularium Abbathiae de Novo Monasterio (Surtees Society).
Norfolk: Walsingham, Min. Acc. 945/2 (*temp*. Hen. V, or later).
Norfolk Manor, Davenport, Compotus rolls of Forncett.
Northamptonshire: Compotus of Ketteringe, Wise.
Norwich, See of: Vacancy Roll, 1141/1 (18–20 Edw. II).
Nottingham Records, Stevenson.
Cuxham, Bailiff's Account, Rogers' Agriculture and Prices.

Oxfordshire: Parochial Antiquities, Kennet.

St. Paul's Cathedral, Domesday of St. Paul's (Camden Society).
Peterborough, Abbey of: Chronicon Petroburgense (Camden Society).

Ramsey, Abbey of: Cartularium Monasterii de Rameseia (Rolls Series).
Economic Conditions on Ramsey Manors, Neilson, Compotus rolls of Wistowe, Hunts.
Court Rolls, 179/10.
Rievaulx, Abbey of: Cartularium Abbathiae de Rievalle (Surtees Society).
Rochester, See of: Custumale Roffense ed. Thorpe.
Registrum Roffense ed. Thorpe.

Suffolk: Suffolk Instit. Archaeol. iii, p. 229; Extent of Hadleigh.
MSS. Gough, Suff., 3 (Bodl.)
Misc. B. Treas. of Rec. 163, f. 111.

Warwickshire: Antiquities of Warwickshire, Dugdale, ii. 911.
Wiltshire: Sheriff's Tourn in Wilts., 1439, Archaeol. and Nat. Hist. Mag. 13, p. 111.
Winchester, See of: Liber Winton (D. B. iv. Add.).
Winchester Pipe Rolls.
Vacancy Rolls, 1142/25 (44–45 Hen. III).
Troyle; Add. Ch. 17457.
Bleadon Custumal, ed. Smirke, Roy. Archaeol. Instit., Mem. Wilts. and Salis., pp. 182–210.
Worcester, See of: Registrum Prioratus B. Mariae Wigorniensis (Camden Society).
Vacancy Roll, 1143/18 (30–31 Edw. I).

York, See of: Vacancy Roll, 1141/1 (32–34 Edw. I); 1144/5 (*temp*. Edw. II ?).

Wales : Record of Carnarvon (Record Commission).
Black Book of St. David's (Cymmrodorion Record Society).
Denbigh, Survey of, 1334.
Denbigh Lordship, Min. Acc. 1182/4 (34 Edw. III).
Tribal System in Wales, Seebohm, Documents in Appendix.

Rotuli Hundredorum.
Placita de Quo Waranto.
Dugdale, Monasticon Anglicanum.
Hazlitt's Blount's Tenures of Land and Customs of Manors.
Select Pleas in Manorial Courts (Selden Society).
Select Pleas of the Forest (Selden Society).

INDEX

Rents paid in food or money are italicized.   References to the notes are not, as a rule, given.

Abbot's Ripton, 192.
Abingdon, 23, 34, 39, 51, 72, 76, 78, 80, 101, 191, 193, 194, 195.
Achabe, 105, 108.
Addington, 59, 65.
Adulvesnasa, 23.
Aid, see Auxilium.
Aid of archdeacons and bishops, 197.
Aid on installation, 93.
Aid of St. Michael, 91, 93.
Akergeve, 105.
Alderhithe, 139.
Aldremanlond, 10.
Alemol, 37.
Ale of St. Mary, 36.
Alepenny, 35, 97.
Ale rents, 22, 35 sqq.
Aletol, 97.
Allec, Ad, 34.
Almesfeoh, 191.
Almessecorn, 29.
Altelagium, 193.
Alteragium, 193.
Amercement, 154, 164, 165, 169, 172, 177 sqq., 180, 181, 182, 186.
Ancient demesne, 96, 138.
Anilepiman, 10, 76, 173, 174.
Anilepiwymen, 173.
Ankerage, 143.
Antiqua tenura, 21, 23, 24, 44. See Assize.
Apuldreham, 77.
Aquage, 143.
Aree, 40.
Arietem Ad, 82.
Ashton under Lyne, 30.
Assart, 10, 12, 23, 24, 47.
Assize or enfeoffment, old and new, 22, 33, 92, 93, 97, 173, 194. See Antiqua tenura.
Assize of bread and ale, 160, 177, 183.
Auxilium Abbatis, 92.

Auxilium custumariorum, 90 sqq. See Tallagium.
Auxilium nativorum, 95. See Tallagium.
Auxilium Prioris, 93.
Auxilium Purificationis, 110.
Auxilium Regis, 95.
Auxilium statutum, 109.
Auxilium ad turnum, 160. See Turnus vicecomitis.
Auxilium vicecomitis, 92, 124, 127, 129. See Sheriff's aid.
Avera, 67.
Averacres, 64.
Averagium, 61, 63, 66. See Carting.
Averakersilver, 66.
Avererth, 64.
Averes, 64.
Avereth, 64.
Averlonds, 8, 12, 64, 65.
Avermalt, 29, 64,
Avermalth, 29.
Averpennies, 63, 64.
Aversilver, 61, 62.

Badberghe hundred, 158.
Banbury hundred, 132, 180.
Barking, 23, 42, 45.
Barling, 116, 128.
Barnwell, 140.
Barton, 178.
Barton Regis, see King's Barton.
Bath and Wells, 78.
Battle, 34, 37, 38, 39, 64, 66, 73, 77, 78, 106, 176, 194, 195, 198, 200, 201.
Beauchamp, 45, 130.
Bedeleria, 156.
Bedewedinge, 60.
Bedfordshire, 69, 72, 116, 118, 122, 124, 132, 147, 165, 170, 172, 175, 177, 179, 180, 181, 183.
Bedgeld, 105.

Bedlands, 18.
Bedripsilver, 59.
Bees, 42.
Belawe, 106.
Belplayder, 181. See *Beuplet*.
Ben, 43. See Boons.
Bene, 60. See Boons.
Benerth, 194.
Benesed, 25, 60.
Bensington, 180.
Berebrit, 103.
Berkshire, 47, 124, 155, 156, 170, 181, 193, 194.
Bernes, 196.
Bestnaweger, 143.
Beuplet, 180, 181, 182. See *Belplayder* and *Pulchre placitari*.
Beverley, 132.
Bickton, 105.
Bicktonsilver, 105.
Bindinglond, 8.
Biresilver, 105.
Bleadon, 33, 55, 70, 103, 104, 195.
Boistagium, 113, 142.
Bollestrode, 175.
Bolton, 136.
Boons, 23, 43, 48, 49, 55, 59, 60, 70, 105, 172. See Ben and Bene.
Booting corn, 105.
Borchsilver, 166.
Boreupeny, 172.
Borgh, borgha, 171.
Borghalpeny, 172.
Borghesealdor, 171.
Borghesealdorpeni, 166, 171.
Bornewing, 172.
Bornpene, 171.
Bornsilver, 166, 170.
Borsilver, 171.
Bortreming, 107, 171.
Bortremium, 172.
Bosing, 76, 77.
Bosingsilver, 76, 77.
Bossilver, 76, 77.
Botes, 84.
Bothsilver, 146.
Braciandum, Ad, 36. See *Maltsilver*.
Bradewas, 100.
Brakemol, 40.
Brancester, 192.
Brandon, 158.
Brawby, 99.
Braybotpeni, 105.
Bread ales, 150.
Bread rents, 22, 24, 191.
Brechegavel, 47, 84.
Breches, 84.
Bredsilver, 40.
Bredwite, 40.
Bremegavol, 44.

Breteuil, 182, 183.
Breweresteresgeld, 35.
Brewingsilver, 35.
Bridales, 150.
Bridges, 134, 137, 138.
Briggebot, 140.
Briggeward, 137.
Brigham, 76.
Brightwaltham, see Brithwolton.
Brithwolton, 78, 101, 176, 195.
Broughton, 192.
Browernesilver, 106.
Buckinghamshire, 87, 105, 116, 122, 124, 132, 147, 148, 149, 155, 171, 181, 182, 183, 194.
Budellond, 103.
Bulleatores, 40.
Bullockpenny, 76.
Bullocksilver, 76.
Burgabulum, 85 *n*.
Burton, 31, 34, 73, 97, 98, 170, 171.
Burwell, 45, 179.
Bury St. Edmunds, 10, 27, 45, 55, 59, 62, 66, 70, 74, 76, 82, 91, 102, 103, 158, 171, 174. See St. Edmund's.
Busagium, 76, 77, 81.
Bustsilver, 142.
Butlerage, 143.
Bydales, 150.
Byscot, 106.

Cablish, 143.
Cadendon, 45, 199.
Cain fowls, 15, 30.
Cambridge, 62, 105, 132, 140.
Cambridgeshire, 50, 57, 66, 74, 77, 82, 93, 105, 107, 116, 117, 118, 124, 128, 132, 137, 140, 163, 164, 171, 177, 181, 184.
Can, 15.
Canage, 30.
Candelam, Ad, 42, 109, 192. See *Ad luminare*.
Candelcorn, 27.
Candelwekesilver, 192.
Caniso, William de, 160.
Canterbury, 53, 58, 66, 81, 200.
Capitagium, see *Chevage*.
Carriage, see Carting.
Cartbote, 84.
Carting rents and services, 27, 34, 39, 49, 60 sqq., 65, 66, 77, 103, 111, 143, 149.
Castellani, 150. See Constables.
Castle, 131, 149, 150.
Castle guard, 120, 131.
Censar', 106.
Census, 42, 46, 49, 95, 106, 186.
Certedon, 179.

Cert money, 168.
Certus redditus, 54, 168, 170. Rents de certo, 169 ; in certo, 195 ; ad certum, 7, 63, 143, 168, 172, 186, 201.
Chadlington Wahull, 179.
Chatteris, 139.
Cheeselonds, 8.
Cheminagium, 143 sqq. See Chiminage.
Chepsester, 39.
Cheriset, 195. See Churchscot.
Chesgavel, 44.
Cheshire, 79, 182.
Chevage, 157, 162, 166 sqq. See Capitagium and Headpenny.
Childwite, 86, 90.
Chiminage, 149. See Cheminagium.
Chingford, 135.
Chircheambre, 196.
Chircheomer, 196.
Chirchesed, 196.
Christ Church, 27, 28, 32, 42 ; Hants, 195.
Christmas present, 30. See Lok.
Church ales, 150.
Church rents, 6, 188 sqq.
Churchscot, 22, 23, 32, 44, 188, 193 sqq., 195. See ciricsceott, and Cheriset.
Churchseed, 196.
Churshaec, 194. See Churchscot.
Ciric sceott, 73. See Churchscot and cyricsceat.
Cistercians, 189.
Clera, 46.
Clerk ales, 150.
Clifton hundred, 126.
Cloth rent, 191.
Clyffsilver, 106.
Coidars, 148.
Colchester, 62, 111.
Collectae, 197.
Collingham, 95.
Collyngsilver, 53.
Commorth, Commortha, 123, 150 n.
Commutation, 7, 15, 32, 33, 42, 46, 47, 48 sqq., 59, 157, pass.
Confraria, 197.
Consuetudines firmae, 19, 70.
Consuetudines minute, 6, 196.
Consuetudines non taxatae, 87.
Consuetudo, 104, 125,
Consuetudo prebende, 193.
Consuetudo S. Petri, 107.
Consuetudo Wodiarorum, 53.
Constable, 39, 148, 149, 150, 195. See Castellani.
Conveth, 15.
Conveyes, conyeyes, 33.
Cornagium, 41, 120 sqq.

Cornbote, 25, 26, 28.
Cornegavell, 44.
Cornlode, 65.
Cornwall, 106, 147.
Cotsetlescorn, 23.
Coupenny, 76.
Courtegere, 65.
Court haver, 29.
Court otes, 29.
Covenholt, 176.
Coventry, 53.
Cranfield, 45, 177, 184.
Craueselver, 106.
Craven, 132.
Craweselver, 106.
Crondal, 58, 109, 195.
Crowland, 126, 129.
Culsilver, 77, 192.
Cumberland, 120.
Cumeling, 174.
Cunninghale, 151.
Cupeny, 76. See Cusilver.
Cusilver, 76, 77. See Cupeny.
Customary aid, see Tallage.
Custos discorum, 107.
Custos ville, 90, 100.
Custuma, 187.
Custumpand, 91, 107, 109, 185, 186.
Cyricsceat, 196. See Churchscot.
Cyricsceat weorc, 194.

Danegeld, 119.
Danger, 74, 75.
Dartmoor, 76.
Daverpennies, 64. See Averpennies.
Daynae manuales, 103.
Decenna, see Tithing.
Decenna, De, 166, 170. See Tithingpenny.
Decennarius, 102, 159, 167.
Deiwercas, 8.
Demesne, 10, 11, 12, 18, 19, 60, 71, 95, 128, 152, 190, 196.
Denarius S. Petri, 198. See Peter's Pence.
Dengmarsh, 54.
Denus denarius, 193.
Derbyshire, 124, 155, 172, 181, 183.
Dereham, 102, 103.
Devizes, 132.
Devonshire, 106, 108, 117, 124, 126, 145, 148, 155, 156, 176, 182.
Dichreve, 101, 102.
Disci, 107. See Dishes.
Dishes, Rent of, 191. See Dissilver.
Dissilver, 107.
Dissolution of Monasteries, 189.
Dizenae, 193.
Dodcorn, 29.
Dominium of lord, 87.

Donum, 32, 95, 102.
Donum ad lardarium, 104.
Donum vicecomitis, 124.
Dorsetshire, 124, 126.
Dortol, see *Huctol*.
Dortr'nng, 107.
Douereth, 20.
Dover, 132.
Dovraeth, 15, 20.
Drayton, 23.
Drifft' pullanorum, 79.
Drofmannus, 79.
Drove, 79.
Droveland, 79.
Dunham, 57.
Durham, 19, 28, 29, 37, 38, 41, 53, 54,
    60, 63, 64, 65, 78, 89, 96, 100, 101,
    104, 120, 144, 146, 173, 174, 192,
    193, 197.

East Anglia, 43, 44, 47, 56, 84, 106,
    111, 112, 194.
Easter ales, 150.
Edernewech, 50.   See *Hedernewech*.
Eels, 35.
Elemosina carucarum, 190.
Elsilver, 107.
Elton, 36, 41, 179.
Ely, 8, 10, 12, 25, 26, 34, 36, 41, 43,
    45, 48, 50, 51, 52, 53, 55, 57, 58, 60,
    62, 63, 73, 76, 77, 81, 82, 89, 96, 97,
    102, 103, 106, 107, 112, 128, 132,
    133, 139, 140, 145, 157, 159, 168,
    173, 174, 184, 185.
Enfeoffment, see Assize.
Enneston, 180.
Erdintone, 159.
Escapium, 79.
Esctone, 95.
Essex, 8, 46, 55, 62, 109, 124, 126,
    135, 147, 166, 171, 172, 181, 184,
    185.
Estovers, 30, 83.
Ewelme hundred, 180.
Eyre of forest, 143, 186.
Eysilver, 23.
Exennium, 30, 32, 53.
Exennium Archiepiscopi, 32.
Exennium S. Andree, 28, 32.
Exeter, 95.
Exitus *manerii*, 196.
Extranei, 175.

Fairs, 131, 136.
Falconers' rent, 19.
Faldage, 71, 80 sqq., 87, 98.
Faldgabul, 80.
Faldicium, 81.

Faldrove, 76, 79.
Farm system, 7, 16, 18, 22, 41, 42, 64,
    100, 102, 119, 121, 124, 131, 147,
    148, 156, 179, 191.
Farm of the county, 16, 119, 126, 148.
Farm of hundred, 119, 147, 148.
Farm of St. Edmund, 17.
Farm of St. Etheldreda, 17.
Farm of vill, 119.
Farms, monastic, 16.
Fastung, 148
Feeding horses and dogs, 2, 19, 20, 129.
    See Hunting.
Felisonunshale, 152.   See Filsunales.
Felsten, 103, 107.
Feltwell, 76.
Feoderfe, 107.
Feorm, see farm.
Fermfultum, 17.
Fermiping, 18.
Fermpenes, 18.
Ferry, 139, 140.
Ferthing, 107.
Ferthingsilver, 107.
Festingmenn, 148.
Ffelstne, 107.
Fieldale, 150, 152.
Field hayward, 103.
Filsinerthes, 59.
Filsingerthes, 43.
Filsing services, 70.
Filstingpound, see *Fulstingpound*.
Filstinpund, see *Fulstingpound*.
Filstyngpound, see *Fulstingpouna*.
Filsunales, 150.   See Felisonunshale.
Fine for ingress, 89.
Fines or amercements, 157, 162, 177.
    See Amercements.
Fines ad certum, 157.
Firebote, 84.
Fireharth, 200, 201.
Firma comitatus, see Farm of county.
Firmarius, 23, 62, 130, 197, 199.
Firme Glastonie, 17.
Fisfe, 92.
Fishfee, 33.
Fishpene, 34.
Fishsilver, 34.
Flaxsilver, 41.
Fleet, 31, 39, 40, 96.
Fleggavel, 44.
Flexlonde, 42.
Foddercorn, 23, 25, 26, 27, 107.
Foodrents, 15 sqq., 148 *pass*.
Folding, see *Faldage*.
Foregrist, 100.
Forestagium, 144.
Foresters, 20, 53, 102, 143, 144, 148,
    149, 150, 153.
Forgabulum, 44.

Forgium, 100.
Forinsec burdens, 11, 37, 116, 120, 179.
Forisfactura de Belawe, 106.
Forncett, 133.
Forthdrove, 56, 79.
Forthdrovesilver, 79.
Forwach, 133, 158.
Forward, 133.
Forwardsilver, 133.
Foselver, 108.
Fosterlands, 18.
Fotaver, 66.
Foxalpeni, 108.
Franciplegii, 165.
Frankpledge, see View of.
Fraria, 197.
Frissilver, 166, 171. See *Frithpenny*.
Fripeny, 171. See *Frithpenny*.
Frisilver, 108.
Frith, 171.
Frithpenny, Frithsilver, 108, 166, 170, 171.
Fulstingpound, 52, 91, 107, 110, 119, 179, 186.
Fultume, 18.
Furnagium, 35.

Gabulo, De, 95.
Gabulum, 32, 47, 49, 95, 103.
Gabulum, Ad, 46.
Gabulum assisum, 46.
Gadercorn, 28.
Gaerswin, Gaerswyn, 68, 75, 82, 123.
Gafol, 42, 46, 193. See *Gabulum*.
Gafolerth, 55. See Gavolerth.
Galunsilver, 38.
Garsanese, 74.
Gavelacres, 44.
Gavelbere, 44.
Gavelcorn, 44.
Gaveles, 44.
Gavelgeld, 44.
Gavelkind, 28. See Gavolkind.
Gavellate, 47.
Gavelmanni, 64. See Gavolmanni.
Gavelote, 44.
Gavelsest, 44.
Gavelsester, 39.
Gaveltimber, 44.
Gavelwerkes, 59.
Gavolbord, 44.
Gavolerth, 43, 194.
Gavolkind, 42. See Gavelkind.
Gavolland, 42, 43, 47.
Gavolmanni, Gavolmen, 8, 42, 44. See Gavelmanni.
Gavolmerke, 44.
Gavol ploughing, 103. See Gavolerth.
Gavolrafter, 44.

Gavolrep, 43.
Gavolsed, gavolseed, 23, 44, 60.
Gavol services, 70.
Gavolswine, 69.
Geldable land, 114 sqq., 116. See Terra Geldabilis.
Geldagium, 130.
Gellicorn, 29.
Geresgive, 31.
Gershenese, 68.
Gersuma, 86.
Gevesilver, 31.
Ghestum, 33.
Girton, 80, 152.
Glastonbury, 32, 33, 37, 39, 45, 46, 47, 48, 52, 53, 54, 58, 70, 75, 81, 82, 97, 101, 102, 103, 117, 136, 151, 173, 194, 198.
Glatton, 74, 107.
Glintone, 192.
Gloucester, 21, 34, 46, 47, 48, 54, 72, 87, 91, 97, 109, 112, 113, 128, 130, 194, 197, 199.
Gloucester, Earl of, 118, 126, 128, 144, 163, 164, 179.
Gloucestershire, 51, 59, 74, 79, 147, 170, 171, 194.
Goddingstiche, 103.
Goveles, 44, 70.
Govelwerkes, 43.
Grain rents, 21 sqq., 143, 149, 194.
Grantesdon, 63.
Graserth, 9, 55, 59, 68, 69, 70, 194.
Grasherthe, 71.
Grashurde, 70.
Gravesend, 64.
Great Tey, 112.
Greenbury, 108, 109.
Greensilver, 108, 109.
Gresenese, 69.
Greserthes, 43.
Gressemen, 174.
Grestakes, 74.
Grippure, 108.
Gryvespound, 108.
Guildford, 21.
Gwele, 123.
Gwesta, 15, 33.
Gystales, 150, 151.

Hadleigh, 186.
Haleday toll, 146.
Halew, 84.
Halliwimen, 173.
Hameldene, Alexander, 147, 182.
Hammes, 104.
Hampshire, 58, 194, 195.
Hams, 80.
Hanbury, 17.

Hangerlond, 84.
Hangerlondsilver, 84.
Harengsilver, Haringsilver, 34.
Hartest, 34.
Hatfield, 18.
Havedscot, 166. See *Chevage*.
Hāwgafol, 45, 84.
Hawkston, 63.
Haworthsylver, 108.
Headpenny, 166, 170. See *Chevage*.
Hearthpenny, 200, 201.
Hearthyield, 201.
Hecham, 26.
Hedercorn, 27.
Hedernewech, 50, 137. See *Ederne-*
wech.
Hedgebote, 57, 83.
Hefdsulver, 170. See *Chevage*.
Heggingsilver, 56, 83.
Heggingwoodsilver, 26.
Hemingford Abbots, 84.
Hensinton, 144.
Hensyeve, 195.
Herbage, 68, 71, 75 sqq., 82.
Herdershift, 82.
Hereford, 182.
Herefordshire, 74, 124, 148, 183.
Heregeat, 86.
Heringlode, 33.
Heringsilver, 33.
Heriot, 86 sqq., 96.
Hertfordshire, 90, 124, 138, 155, 177.
Hertlebury, 55.
Hethernewech, 50. See *Hedernewech*.
Hetherste, 158.
Heuschire, 84.
Heusire, 84, 85.
Hexham, 28, 37, 99, 111, 197.
Heybote, 57, 83.
Heyningsilver, 56.
Heyningwode, 83.
Heynwode, 57.
Heynwodeselver, 26, 51, 56, 57, 83.
Hidage, 115 sqq., 121, 122, 133, 179, 180, 181, 183.
Hidam, Extra, 115, 120.
Hidarii, 23.
Highgabull, 85.
Hilderselver, 57.
Hill lands, 9.
Hinderselver, 108.
Hirdelpenny, 57.
Hired carters, 60.
Hirmannus, 191.
Hirsill, 78.
Hirstingston hundred, Free hides of, 113, 139, 142.
Hock Tuesday, 105.
Hocselver, 105, 108.
Hogae, 40.

Hognell rent, 108.
Holy ales, 150.
Honilonds, 8.
Honeysilver, 41.
Hoplands, 8.
Hoppgavel, 44.
Horderesyft, 108.
Horloch, 95.
Hornagium, 120.
Horngeld, 120.
Horsavers, 66.
Horseacre, 66.
Horsgabulum, 44, 66.
Hospitallers, 142, 150, 163, 175, 176, 189, 197.
Housebote, 53, 65, 83.
Househire, 85.
Huctol et Dortol, 146.
Hulvir, 108.
Hundred, 27, 118, 127, 129, 144, 147, 155, 166, 181, *pass*.
Hundred Aid, 126, 129 sqq.
Hundred ale, 152.
Hundredarii, 129, 156, 159.
Hundredfe, 130.
Hundredfey, 130.
Hundredgeld, 129.
Hundredlands, 158.
Hundredpeny, 130.
Hundredscot, 129, 130, 161, 162.
Hundredsilver, 129, 130.
Hundredwite, 130.
Hunninggabulum, 44.
Hunteneselver, 20, 112.
Hunthield, 112.
Hunting, 16, 19, 20, 109, 112, 129, 195.
Huntingdon, 85, 145.
Huntingdonshire, 69, 84, 87, 116, 117, 124, 130, 163, 164, 170, 177, 181, 183, 184.
Hurtpeni, 201.
Husebondi, 28, 168, 186.
Husegabell, 85.
Hussilver, 85.
Hydarii, 24.
Hyndergeld, 20, 108.

Innedge, 80.
Innynge, 80.
Insute, 109.
Inwards, 67.
Ipswich, 62.
Ireland, 182.

Judicialia, 35, 176, 183.
Juga servilia vel averagia, 64.

Kaiage, 143.
Keletol, 143.
Kemersh rent, 109.
Kenesworth, 23, 199.
Kent, 8, 34, 38, 42, 44, 45, 47, 52, 55, 57, 64, 66, 69, 74, 79, 81, 84, 89, 112, 125, 127, 132, 147, 152, 155, 156, 158, 160, 166, 181.
Kettering, 82, 161.
Keyesilver, 104, 109, 110.
Kilgh' Hebogothion, 19.
King's Barton, 31, 51, 59, 60, 71, 79, 113.
Kyn' multure, 99.

Lacsulfer, 78.
Lactagium, 78.
Ladas, 63.
Lades, 66.
Lagehundreds, 135.
Lagerthes, 59.
Laghedays, 161.
Lak, 29, 30. See *Loc*.
Lambale, 150, 152.
Lamb peni, 81.
Lamgabulum, 81.
Lamgafol, 42, 44.
Lammessilver, 103.
Lamselver, 42, 81.
Lanam, Ad, 41.
Lancashire, 78, 151, 183.
Lancectagium, 10.
Landavese, 45, 46.
Landcheap, 46.
Landchere, 45.
Landgabulum, 95.
Landgafol, 45, 46, 84.
Landgavel, 41.
Landlesemen, 174.
Landmale, 46.
Landselver, 45.
Langerode, 62.
Langhsester, 39.
Langol, 46.
Lardarium, Ad, 32, 58. See *Larder-silver*.
Lardersilver, Lardresilver, 32, 58.
Law of riding, 73.
Leafyield, 74.
Leavesilver, 74.
Lecti, 123.
Leet ales, 150, 152.
Leirwite, 86, 87, 90.
Leppe and Lasse, 109.
Lesselver, 78.
Lestage, 143.
Lestire, Robert de, 140.
Letefe, 162.
Leuknor hundred, 180.

Leverington, 77.
Lewes, 32, 69.
Lichfield, 72, 171. See Coventry.
Lincoln, 142, 180.
Lincolnshire, 87, 112, 124, 127, 128, 132, 138, 140, 141, 147, 148, 181.
Lightscot, 188, 192.
Lightsilver, 109.
Lignagium, 53.
Lignarius, 101.
Linum, 42.
Littlebury, 55.
Littleport, 63.
Littleton, 54, 199.
Loc, lok, 30, 31, 32, 41.
Lodesilver, 63.
Lodland, 8.
Loksilver, 31, 32.
Londgavel, 45.
London, 60, 62, 63, 64, 66, 152, 155.
Londonelode, 63.
Londonepeny, 63.
Lookmete, 31.
Loretsilver, 109.
Luminare, Ad, 42, 192. See *Ad Candelam*.
Lyngmole, 54.
Lyngpeny, 54.
Lythsilver, 109.

Macclesfield, 183.
Mal, 42, 43. See Mol.
Maldon, 97.
Malling, 45.
Maltgavel, 38, 44.
Maltlands, 8.
Maltpenny, maltpennies, 37, 38.
Maltpenys, 29.
Maltscot, 38.
Maltsilver, 97. See *Ad Braciandum*.
Maltyngsilver, 35.
Mancorn, 196.
Manesef, 56.
Manorial offices, 10, 87, 98, 101, 103.
Manure, 54.
Marcselver, 91, 106, 107, 109, 185, 186.
Market tolls, 146.
Marleberg Castle, 149.
Marling feasts, 151.
Martinrent, 195.
Master's rent, 110.
Meadow rents, 55.
Medgavol, 47.
Medsilver, 84.
Medsipe, 56.
Medwesilver, 56, 84.
Melderfe, 110.
Melgabulum, 44.
Mensurage, 143.

Merchet, 33, 73, 87, 89 sqq., 93, 96, 101, 105.
Mescingam, Ad, 23, 41.
Messing silver, 23.
Messor, 28, 50, 87, 137, 147.
Mesyngpeny, 41.
Metecorn, 27.
Metegafol, 24, 41.
Metreth, 123.
Metrez, 123.
Metride, 41, 42, 122, 124.
Metsung, 23.
Michilmeth, 31.
Midford, hundred and half hundred, 158.
Midsummer ales, 150.
Mill, 87, 98.
Mill pond, 58, 99.
Mill stones, 65, 99.
Miscellaneous rents, 105 sqq.
Misericordiae, 191.
Mitesilver, 38.
Mol, 47, 50. See *Mal.*
Moleland, 96.
Molland, 40.
Molmen, 9, 10, 26, 28, 51, 96, 102, 103.
Molta, 99.
Moltura, 99.
Monkgeld, 93.
Monks' tallage, 93.
Morgabulum, 47.
Motfech, 134, 162.
Mothow, Le, 40.
Mowetsilver, 110.
Moygne, William le, 140.
Multure, 98, 99.
Murage, 141 sqq.
Murdrum, 154, 186.

Nastok, 45.
Netsilver, 110.
Newton, 63.
Newyeresgive, 31.
Nocata, 101.
Nodway money, 110.
Norfolk, 9, 50, 51, 55, 57, 76, 78, 81, 82, 83, 85, 87, 90, 110, 124, 125, 126, 130, 132, 142, 158, 162, 170, 185.
Northampton, 132.
Northamptonshire, 124, 125, 126, 132, 149, 181, 183.
Northfleet, 64.
Northgrenehow hundred, 113, 142.
Northumberland, 73, 74, 89, 120.
Northwold, 63.
Norton, 23, 199.
Norwich, 18, 27, 50, 82, 96, 132.
Nottingham, 139.
Nottinghamshire, 124, 137, 148, 174, 181, 183.

Noutegeld, 120.
Nutsilver, 54.

Offare, 89.
Onfare, 89.
Ongiell, 112.
Onyeld, 112.
Onziell, 112.
Opera vendita, 49.
Ostensio, 146.
Ouse river, 145.
Outlads, 64.
Outwards, 67.
Oven, 98, 100.
Overgongmid'das, 40.
Oxfoldgable, 80.
Oxfordshire, 69, 72, 76, 87, 116, 118, 119, 124, 132, 149, 164, 180, 183, 194, 196.
Oxpeni, 76, 77.

Paagium, 141.
Pacagium, 146.
Padehale, 180.
Pakenham, 107.
Palefridus vicecomitis, 125, 129.
Palfrey, 111.
Pannage, 52, 68, 69, 71 sqq., 98, 103, 152.
Parkselver, 58.
Parrock, 152.
Parva Trewe, 144.
Passage, 137, 143, 145.
Passagium. See Passage.
Pasture, 7, 32, 38, 42, 56, 68 sqq., 106, 120, 138.
Pavage, pavagium, 141.
Paxford, 93.
Pedagium, 145.
Penilond, 92.
Pennies of the sheriff, 128.
Penny de advocaria, 177.
Penygavelland, 44.
Perquisitae curiarum, 161.
Perquisites of sheriffs, 124.
Pesage, 143.
Peterborough, 24, 34, 36, 76, 95, 107, 128, 167, 168, 191, 192, 193.
Peter's Pence, 188, 196, 197 sqq.
Phishesilver, 34. See *Fishsilver.*
Pidington, 39, 71.
Pightel, 168.
Pihtesle, 95.
Pikagium, 146.
Pincrecheyeld, 110.
Pisces emendos, Ad, 33, 34. See *Fish-silver.*
Placitando pro pulchre, 161, 170, 180, 181. See *Beuplet.*

Placitari pro pulchre, 180.
Ploualmes, 190.
Ploughalms, 188, 190, 192.
Ploughbote, 84.
Ploughing rents, 55.
Ploughshare rents, 112.
Ploughsilver, 192.
Pocarii, 10, 174.
Pokearii, 10. See Pocarii.
Pokeavers, 66, 102, 174. See Pocarii.
Pontage, 122, 137 sqq.
Poperode, 62.
Potura, 152.
Poultry rents, 21 sqq., 143, 149, 191, 194, 195.
Poundpani, 58.
Poundsilver, 58, 186.
Present, Le, 32.
Presentum, 32.
Pridgavel, 44.
Prisage, 143.
Prises of beadles, 124.
Prison, 149. See Suete de Prison.
Privileges of office, 102 sqq.
Profits of jurisdiction, 157 sqq.
Progresses, 15.
Provisions of Oxford, 126.
Pro visu payments, 162, 166, 170. See View.
Pukerelleschild, 92, 110.
Pulham, 55.
Punderland, 104.
Punderus, 101, 104.
Pundpani, 58.
Pundscot, 110, 185.
Purveyance rents, 7, 15, 125, 129, 148.
Putura, 152.

Quarterage, 143.

Radbodispund, 110.
Rades, 66.
Raglots, 129, 148.
Ramsey, 12, 17, 25, 34, 36, 38, 39, 41, 42, 51, 52, 56, 58, 60, 61, 62, 69, 71, 73, 77, 80, 82, 84, 93, 97, 99, 104, 107, 113, 116, 117, 127, 130, 136, 139, 142, 152, 163, 164, 177, 179, 180, 181, 183, 184, 190, 191, 192, 197, 198.
Rattlesdene, 45.
Recognition rent, 33, 170.
Redditus assise, 6–7, 40, 46.
Redditus census, 109.
Redditus mutabiles, 7, 55.
Reek hens, 30.
Reeve ad bertona, 102.
Reeve ad castrum, 102.

Reeve ad colligendum redditum, 102.
Reeveland, 104. See Reveland.
Refhammes, 104.
Relief, 86.
Renewing of pledges, 166, 170, 171.
Rent eggs, 28.
Rent hens, 28.
Repegos, 56.
Repselver, 55.
Resting geld, 78.
Restingwode, 56.
Retropannage, 73, 143, 149.
Revekeye, 104, 109, 110.
Reveland, 10. See Reeveland.
Revemede, 104.
Revesgore, 104.
Rhuddlan, 182.
Richmond, 128, 132.
Riding foresters, 153.
Riding men, 73.
Ringilds, 148.
Ripple, 93.
Ritnesse, De, 43.
Rivage, 143.
Rochester, 28, 32, 56, 64, 95, 101, 132, 138.
Rockingham, 132.
Rodgavel, 44.
Rollesby, 18, 54.
Romescot, 197, 200, 201. See *Peter's Penny*.
Rook boy, 106.
Roserye, 58.
Royal Buildings, 142, 150.
Royal rents, 6, 7, 8, 113, 114 sqq.
Rudford, 54.
Rudmanni, 159.
Ruschewsylver, 110.
'Rustic work,' 19.
Rutland, 149.

Saddlesilver, 110, 111.
St. Albans, 62, 155.
St. Andrew's, Rochester, 17, 42. See Kent.
St. Augustine's, 27, 194, 200. See Kent.
St. Botulph, 142.
St. Edmund's, 31, 34, 63, 69, 77, 106, 107, 109, 112, 147, 158, 186, 191. See Bury.
Saintgelicon, 29.
St. Ives, 80, 127, 136, 191.
St. Neots, 52.
St. Oswald, 73.
St. Paul's, 12, 17, 34, 36, 38, 39, 41, 42, 45, 51, 55, 58, 62, 66, 73, 76, 94, 95, 100, 116, 130, 134, 150, 167, 192, 193, 196, 199.
Sale of grain, 65.

Salt, 65.
Saltford, 179.
Salt lands, 8.
Salt marshes, 40.
Salt rents, 39, 40.
Saltsilver, 40.
Sandgavel, 44.
Sandun, 36.
Sarlond, 55.
Sarpenni, 55. See *Sharpenny*.
Sarum, Old, 132.
Scap, 111.
Scat, 28, 29.
Scatavena, 29.
Scatbraseum, 29.
Scatehaver, 29.
Scatfarina, 29.
Scatfrumentum, 29.
Scatmalt, 29, 38.
Scatpenys, 28.
Scavage, 146.
Sceawyn, 146.
Scharpani, 55. See *Sharpenny*.
Schepersulfer, 111.
Schepsilver, 82.
Schirefore, 62.
Schrebgavol, 111.
Schydselver, 111.
Scorfe, 112.
Scorfee, 111.
Scot, 95.
Scotales, 32, 38, 150 sqq.
Scot and lot, 116.
Scrud, 191.
Scrudland, 18, 111, 191.
Scutage, 87 *note*, 95, 132, 133.
Scythale, 152.
Pro sectis rents, 157 sqq. See Suits.
Sedbede, 27.
Seed rents, 23, 25, 44, 60.
Seesilver, sesilver, 52, 62, 111.
Sefare, 52, 62, 111.
Seggesilver, 57.
Segsilver, 57.
Selfods, 173.
Semen villanorum, 23.
Separacione agnorum, Rent de, 82.
Seracras, 8, 55.
Serlonds, 8, 12. See Sharland.
Sesilver, see *Seesilver*.
Severn, river, 134.
Shack, 83.
Sharland, 54. See Serlonds.
Sharnselver, 54.
Sharpenny, 8, 54. See *Sarpenni, Scharpani*
Sharsilver, 55.
Sheep, 22, 56.
Shelford, 58.
Shepestake, 74, 82.

Shepsilver, 62.
Sheriff, 139, 140, 147, 148, 150, 164, 165, 166, 181, 182, *pass*.
Sheriff's aid, 122, 158. See *Auxilium Vicecomitis*.
Sheriff's farm, 121.
Sheriff's tourn, 118, 124, 125, 126, 129, 130, 149, 155, 160, 161, 163, 165, 176, 181. See *Ad turnum*.
Shernsilver, 54.
Sherntrede, 55.
Sherreveselver, 125.
Shesilver, 111.
Shipdham, 158.
Shirepenny, 159.
Shirevesyelde, 125.
Shirrevescot, shirreveschot, 125, 126.
Shirreveswelcome, 124, 126.
Shitlingdon, 36, 61, 99, 178, 184.
Shot, 152.
Shropshire, 73, 134, 148, 162.
Sithpeni, 56.
Sixtepeni, 159.
Sixtepeny, 159.
Sixtihepany, 159.
Smithland, 104.
Smokepenny, 200, 201.
Smokesilver, 201,
Snotteringsilver, 111.
Soca faldae, 80. See *Faldage*.
Soloualmes, 191.
Somerlode, 51.
Somersetshire, 74, 110, 130, 160, 194.
Somersham, 53, 63, 185.
Soulesilver, 193.
Soulscot, 188, 192, 193.
Southampton, 80, 171.
Southfleet, 64.
Spelsbury, 164.
Spenningfe, 111.
Splotgabulum, 78.
Stabilitio venationis, 19.
Staffordshire, 74, 130, 156, 166, 182.
Stallagium, 146.
Stangeld, 141.
Rents on Status, 86 sqq.
Stedegabol, 85.
Stoke, 17, 194.
Storefe, 112.
Stratham, 63, 159.
Stremtol, 143.
Streteward, 131, 134.
Stuch, 87, 97, 98.
Stud, 97.
Studewerk, 9.
Suete de prison, 109.
Suffolk, 37, 42, 45, 50, 57, 63, 77, 83, 87, 90, 124, 125, 147, 160, 172, 184, 186.
Suitlands, 12.

Suits, 122, 126, 129, 152, 154, 156, 157 sqq., 186.
Suitsilver, 109.
Sulhaelmessan, 190.
Sullmen, 82.
Sulsilver, 112, 191.
Sulstiche, 103.
Sumerewodesilver, 51.
Summagium, 61.
Summerhousesilver, 52.
Surrey, 68, 94, 194.
Sussex, 44, 68, 124, 177, 181.
Sutton, Middlesex, 95, 199.
Sutton, Warwickshire, 20, 88, 101, 104, 195.
Sutton silver, 112.
Swaffham, 25, 58.
Swainmote, 72.
Swarfmoney, 200, 201.
Swinescead, 73.
Sylva caedua, 190.
Synodaticum, 188, 196, 197.
Synods, 197.
Syrapeni, 159.

Tace, 73.
Tak' porcorum, 74.
Tallage, 68, 74, 86, 90 sqq., 93, 96, 110, 186. See *Auxilium*.
Tangavel, 44.
Teinton, 179.
Templars, 32, 139, 163, 175, 177, 189.
Tenants' ales, 150, 151.
Tengavel, 44.
Tenserie, 106.
Teoloneum nundinarum, 146.
Terra de corde comitatus, 154.
Terra de corpore comitatus, 154.
Terra eleemosinata, 116, 128.
Terra geldabilis, 11, 154. See Geldable land.
Terra hydata, 11.
Terra sectabilis, 154.
Thac, 70, 73, 74, 97.
Thac et thol, 92.
Thacsilver, 74.
Thanet, 44.
Thankacres, 43.
Thankeacres, 60.
Theginpeni, 170. See *Tithingpenny*.
Thelford, 63.
Theoloneum, 97. See *Toll*.
Therfield, 36, 179.
Thetinpeni, 170. See *Tithingpenny*.
Thisteltake, thistletake, 79, 82.
Thol, 73, 87, 92, 97. See *Toll*.
Thorney, 25, 34, 51.
Thorpe, 54.
Thurctol, 144, 145.
Thurghtol, 144.

Tidwolditon, 199.
Tischerton, 193.
Tithes, 188 sqq.
Tithing, 108, 126, 127, 159, 171, 172, 174, 176, 183.
Tithingpeni, 170.
Tithingpenny, Tithingpeny, 161, 166, 170. See *De Decenna*.
Tolcester, 39.
Tolkorn, 27.
Toll, 73, 97, 102, 109, 142 sqq.
Tolleray, 97.
Tolls on sale, 96 sqq., 143.
Tolltray, 97.
Tolnetum buste navium, 142.
Tolpot, 36, 39.
Tolteray, 97.
Tonnage, 143.
Tonnutum, 68, 87, 97.
Torefeld, 54.
Tounebrigge, 139.
Tourn, see Sherriff's tourn.
Towirst, 112.
Transitum viae, 145.
Transversum, 143, 145.
Traverse, 145.
Tronage, 143.
Truncage, 142.
Tunc pound, 15.
Tunmannemers, 81.
Tunnus Census, 91, 106, 109, 185, 186.
Turfdole, 54.
Turfeld, 54.
Turnum vicecomitis, Ad, 126. See Turnus vicecomitis and Sheriff's Tourn.
Turnus vicecomitis, 160. See *Auxilium ad turnum*.
Tygenpeni, 170. See *Tithingpenny*.
Tyne, 39.
Tynebrigge, 158.
Tynemouth, 33, 111, 173.
Tynewell, 110.
Tynpeni, 170. See *Tithingpenny*.

Ulnage, ulnagium, 107, 113, 143.
Unchield, 112.
Undele, 191.
Undersetles, 10, 173, 174, 195.
Undersetli, 26, 49.
Ungeld, 112.
Unthield, 20, 112.
Unyeld, 112.

Veal money, 77.
Vedfee, 86.
Veremecorn, 23.
Vestimentum, Ad, 191.
Vestitu monachorum, De, 18.

Viagium, 145.
Victu monachorum, De, 18.
View of frankpledge, 106, 115, 135, 137, 160, 161, 162, 163, 165, 167, 169, 174, 177, 179, 184.
Vinevard, 59. See Wynyardsilver.
Vokepanni, 17.

Wach, 136.
Wakefe, 131.
Walda, 78.
Waldhirst, 191.
Wales, 83, 182.
Waleton, 95.
Wallesilver, 41.
Wallondes, 8.
Wall work, 141.
Walsingham Parva, 51, 54.
Waltham, 46, 164.
Wapentake fine, 187.
Wara, De, 45.
Ward, 131 sqq.
Wardacres, 12.
Wardpenny, 68, 121, 127, 131 sqq.
Wardsilver, 131 sqq.
Wardstaf, 135.
Ware, De, 12.
Waresilver, 112, 192.
Warland, 12.
Warwickshire, 124, 158.
Washeyngpene, 56.
Washingley, 31.
Watelsilver, 57.
Watertol, 143.
Waulassum, 20.
Waurocot, 112.
Waurshot, 192.
Waursilver, 112.
Wax, 112, 192.
Waxsilver, 42, 112.
Waynselver, 63.
'Ways of the hundred,' 134.
Waytefe, 131.
Waytinga, 31.
Wdetale, 52.
Weald, 69.
Weddis, 60.
Wedselver, 55.
Weeding, 60, 113.
Week work, 9, 48, 49 sqq., 59, 61.
Weirs, 59.
Welcom Abbatis, 33, 111.
Wellerelonedes, 40.
Wells, 85. See Bath.
Welsh laws, 104.
Welsh rents, 15, 19, 30.
Wenbote, 84.
Wendi, 65.
Wenlonds, 65.
Werkeithes, 9.

Werketon, 192.
Werklond, 96.
Werkmen, 8.
Wermintone, 191.
Werthale, 56.
Westmoreland, 120.
West Riding, 197.
Wetherale, 152.
Wetherhales, 150.
Wethersilver, 42, 82.
Wexeden hundred, 181.
Weypeny, 144.
Wharfage, 143.
Whitehartsilver, 112.
Whitley, 33.
Whitson farthings, 107, 108, 112.
Whitsunales, 150.
Whytepund, 184.
Wickam, 136.
Wicumbe, 199.
Wightfee, 113.
Willesilver, 41.
Wiltshire, 44, 73, 77, 124, 125, 126, 132, 144, 171, 181, 194.
Wimbledon, 110.
Winchester, 39, 46, 75, 80, 82, 95, 151, 152, 194, 195, 199.
Windsor, 132, 142.
Wine Services, 43, 70.
Winewerkes, 43, 59.
Winterhage, 70.
Winyardsilver, 58.
Wisbech, 77, 82, 107.
Wistowe, 34, 84, 191, 192.
Witefe, 184.
Witepont, 184.
Witepund, 91, 110, 113, 186.
Wittene, 199.
Wiveneweddinge, 60, 113.
Wodecast, 56.
Wodefare, 51, 52.
Wodegonge, 25.
Wodehac, 53, 113, 127, 142.
Wodelade, Woodlade, 63, 64.
Wodeladepenny, 51.
Wodelode, 53, 61, 65.
Wodericht, 26, 30, 52, 53.
Wodevoel, 27.
Wodewelleschot, 53, 113, 142.
Wodladepenys, 64.
Woldhyrst, 127.
Wood rents, 51 sqq.
Woodhen, 22, 25, 26, 53.
Woodhew, 51.
Woodhire, 51, 53.
Woodhurst, 191.
Woodlodepenny, 53.
Woodpenny, 51.
Woodsilver, 51, 53, 63.
Woodstock, 125.

Woodward, 101, 103, 104.
Woodwege, 52.
Woodwerksilver, 51, 52.
Woodweye, 51.
Woodwork, 113. See *Boistagium*.
Wool, 41.
Worcester, 17, 22, 23, 31, 33, 37, 39, 42, 47, 48, 51, 54, 58, 73, 82, 92, 97, 99, 100, 111, 190, 194, 199, 200.
Worcestershire, 193.
Workland, 40.
Worksilver, 50.
Wratting, 26.
Writtle, 108.

Wroughsheryng, 55.
Wye, 27, 64, 83, 108.
Wynsilver, 58.
Wytepanes, 184.
Wytepeni, 184.
Wytepenny, 184.

Yaresilver, 59.
Yerdsilver, 113.
Yolwayting, 31.
York, 29, 38, 44, 54, 74, 85.
Yorkshire, 66, 147, 172.
Yulwayting, 31.